Security+ Prep Guide

Security+ Prep Guide

Ronald L. Krutz and Russell Dean Vines

Wiley Publishing, Inc.

Security+ Prep Guide

Published by
Wiley Publishing, Inc.
10475 Crosspoint Boulevard
Indianapolis, IN 46256
www.wiley.com

Copyright © 2003 by Wiley Publishing, Inc., Indianapolis, Indiana

Published simultaneously in Canada

Library of Congress Control Number: 2003101000

ISBN: 0-7645-2599-9

Manufactured in the United States of America

10 9 8 7 6 5 4 3 2 1

1B/QX/QS/QT/IN

No part of this publication may be reproduced, stored in a retrieval system or transmitted in any form or by any means, electronic, mechanical, photocopying, recording, scanning or otherwise, except as permitted under Sections 107 or 108 of the 1976 United States Copyright Act, without either the prior written permission of the Publisher, or authorization through payment of the appropriate per-copy fee to the Copyright Clearance Center, 222 Rosewood Drive, Danvers, MA 01923, (978) 750-8400, fax (978) 750-4470. Requests to the Publisher for permission should be addressed to the Legal Department, Wiley Publishing, Inc., 10475 Crosspoint Blvd., Indianapolis, IN 46256, (317) 572-3447, fax (317) 572-4447, E-Mail: permcoordinator@wiley.com.

> **LIMIT OF LIABILITY/DISCLAIMER OF WARRANTY: WHILE THE PUBLISHER AND AUTHOR HAVE USED THEIR BEST EFFORTS IN PREPARING THIS BOOK, THEY MAKE NO REPRESENTATIONS OR WARRANTIES WITH RESPECT TO THE ACCURACY OR COMPLETENESS OF THE CONTENTS OF THIS BOOK AND SPECIFICALLY DISCLAIM ANY IMPLIED WARRANTIES OF MERCHANTABILITY OR FITNESS FOR A PARTICULAR PURPOSE. NO WARRANTY MAY BE CREATED OR EXTENDED BY SALES REPRESENTATIVES OR WRITTEN SALES MATERIALS. THE ADVICE AND STRATEGIES CONTAINED HEREIN MAY NOT BE SUITABLE FOR YOUR SITUATION. YOU SHOULD CONSULT WITH A PROFESSIONAL WHERE APPROPRIATE. NEITHER THE PUBLISHER NOR AUTHOR SHALL BE LIABLE FOR ANY LOSS OF PROFIT OR ANY OTHER COMMERCIAL DAMAGES, INCLUDING BUT NOT LIMITED TO SPECIAL, INCIDENTAL, CONSEQUENTIAL, OR OTHER DAMAGES.**

For general information on our other products and services or to obtain technical support, please contact our Customer Care Department within the U.S. at (800) 762-2974, outside the U.S. at (317) 572-3993 or fax (317) 572-4002.

Wiley also publishes its books in a variety of electronic formats. Some content that appears in print may not be available in electronic books.

Trademarks: Wiley, the Wiley Publishing logo and related trade dress are trademarks or registered trademarks of Wiley Publishing, Inc., in the United States and other countries, and may not be used without written permission. All other trademarks are the property of their respective owners. Wiley Publishing, Inc., is not associated with any product or vendor mentioned in this book.

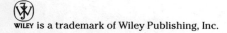
WILEY is a trademark of Wiley Publishing, Inc.

About the Authors

Ronald L. Krutz, Ph.D., P.E., CISSP. Dr. Krutz is Director of Privacy for Corbett Technologies, Inc. He also directs the Capability Maturity Model (CMM) engagements for Corbett Technologies and led the development of Corbett's HIPAA-CMM assessment methodology. He has more that 40 years of experience in distributed computing systems, computer architectures, real-time systems, information assurance methodologies, and information security training. He has been an Information Security Consultant at REALTECH Systems Corporation, an Associate Director of the Carnegie Mellon Research Institute (CMRI) and a Professor in the Carnegie Mellon University Department of Electrical and Computer Engineering. Dr. Krutz founded the CMRI Cybersecurity Center and was founder and Director of the CMRI Computer, Automation and Robotics Group. He is a former lead instructor for the ISC2 Common Body of Knowledge review seminars.

Dr. Krutz conducted sponsored-applied research and development in the areas of computer security, artificial intelligence, networking, modeling and simulation, robotics, and real-time computer applications. He is the author of three textbooks in the areas of microcomputer system design, computer interfacing, and computer architecture. He co-authored the *CISSP Prep Guide,* the *Advanced CISSP Prep Guide,* and the *CISSP Prep Guide, Gold Edition*. Dr. Krutz also holds seven patents in the area of digital systems. He is a Certified Information Systems Security Professional (CISSP), a Registered Professional Engineer, and a Distinguished Special Lecturer in the Center for Forensic Computer Investigation at the University of New Haven. Dr. Krutz is also a consulting editor for the information security series published by Wiley Publishing, Inc.

Dr. Krutz holds B.S., M.S., and Ph.D. degrees in Electrical and Computer Engineering.

Russell Dean Vines, CISSP, Security+, CCNA, MCSE, MCNE. President and founder of The RDV Group Inc., a New York City–based security consulting services firm, Mr. Vines has been active in the prevention, detection, and remediation of security vulnerabilities for international corporations, including government, finance, and new media organizations, for many years. He is the author of *Wireless Security Essentials* and the co-author of the *CISSP Prep Guide,* the *Advanced CISSP Prep Guide,* and the *CISSP Prep Guide, Gold Edition.* He is also a consulting editor for the information security series published by Wiley Publishing, Inc.

Mr. Vines has been active in computer engineering since the start of the personal computer revolution. He holds high-level certifications in Cisco, 3Com, Ascend, Microsoft, and Novell technologies and is trained in the National Security Agency's ISSO Information Assessment Methodology. He has headed computer security departments and managed worldwide information systems networks for prominent technology, entertainment, and nonprofit corporations based in New York. He formerly directed the Security Consulting Services Group for Realtech Systems Corporation, designed, implemented, and managed international information networks for CBS/Fox Video, Inc., and was director of MIS for the Children's Aid Society in New York City.

Mr. Vines' early professional years were illuminated not by the flicker of a computer monitor but by the bright lights of Nevada casino show rooms. After receiving a *Down Beat* magazine scholarship to Boston's Berklee College of Music, he performed as a sideman for a variety of well-known entertainers, including George Benson, John Denver, Sammy Davis Jr., and Dean Martin. Mr. Vines has composed and arranged hundreds of pieces of jazz and contemporary music, which were performed and recorded by his own big band and other musical groups. He also founded and managed a scholastic music publishing company and worked as an artist-in-residence for the National Endowment for the Arts (NEA) in communities throughout the West. He still performs and teaches music in the New York City area and is a member of the American Federation of Musicians Local #802.

Credits

Acquisitions Editor
Katie Feltman

Project Editor
Marcia Ellett

Copy Editor
Gabrielle Chosney

Editorial Manager
Mary Beth Wakefield

Vice President & Executive Group Publisher
Richard Swadley

Vice President and Executive Publisher
Bob Ipsen

Executive Editorial Director
Mary Bednarek

Project Coordinator
Nancee Reeves

Graphics and Production Specialists
Joyce Haughey, Heather Pope,
Erin Zeltner

Quality Control Technicians
Laura Albert, David Faust,
Andy Hollandbeck, Susan Moritz,
Carl Pierce

Permissions Editor
Carmen Krikorian

Media Development Specialist
Kit Malone

Proofreading and Indexing
TECHBOOKS Production Services

Thanks to God and Family for a Healthy Happy Life. Who could ask for more?

RLK

To Elzy Kolb, thank you.

RDV

Acknowledgments

I want to thank my wife, Hilda, for encouragement and support during this project. I also want to express my appreciation to Carol Long and Katie Feltman of Wiley Publishing, Inc., for their support and guidance.

RLK

I would like to acknowledge the help and support of my wife, Elzy Kolb, for her invaluable assistance throughout the book process, and the great assistance of the editors at Wiley, in particular Carol Long, Katie Feltman, and Marcia Ellett.

RDV

Contents at a Glance

Acknowledgments xi
Introduction xxi

Chapter 1: General Security Concepts 1
Chapter 2: Communication Security 49
Chapter 3: Infrastructure Security 117
Chapter 4: Basics of Cryptography 177
Chapter 5: Operational/Organizational Security 215

Appendix A: Answers to Sample Questions 275
Appendix B: Glossary of Terms and Acronyms 323
Appendix C: Common Internet Vulnerabilities 381
Appendix D: NMap Log 405
Appendix E: What's on the CD-ROM? 437

Index 441

Contents

Acknowledgments xi

Introduction xxi

Chapter 1: General Security Concepts 1
- Access Control 2
    - Owner 2
    - Custodian 3
    - End User 3
    - Access Control Considerations 3
    - Mandatory Access Control 4
    - Discretionary Access Control 5
    - Role-Based Access Control 5
    - Access Control Models 6
    - Authentication 8
- Non-Essential Services and Protocols 18
- Attacks 19
    - Denial-of-Service/Distributed Denial-of-Service 19
    - Back Door 20
    - Spoofing 20
    - Man-in-the-Middle 21
    - Replay 21
    - TCP/Hijacking 22
    - Fragmentation Attacks 22
    - Weak Keys 22
    - Mathematical Attacks 23
    - Social Engineering 23
    - Dumpster Diving 23
    - Birthday Attacks 24
    - Password Guessing 24
    - Software Exploitation 26
- Malicious Code 27
    - Viruses 27
    - Trojan Horses 29
    - Logic Bombs 30
    - Worms 30

Malicious Code Prevention 30
    Virus Scanners 30
    Virus Prevention 31
    Virus Detection 31
System Scanning 31
    Vulnerability Scanning 32
    Port Scanning 33
    Vulnerable Ports 40
    Issues with Vulnerability Scanning 40

Chapter 2: Communication Security 49

Remote Access 49
    Virtual Private Networking 49
    RADIUS and TACACS 58
E-mail 61
    E-mail Protocols 61
    Spam and Hoaxes 62
    S/MIME 62
    PGP 62
Web 62
    SSL/TLS 63
    HTTP/S 65
    S-HTTP 65
    Instant Messaging 65
    Vulnerabilities 70
Directory/CA Recognition 76
    Recognition of the CA 76
    Recognition of Certificates 77
    SSL/TLS 77
    LDAP 77
File Transfer Protocols 79
    SFTP 80
    SSH/SSH-2 80
    TFTP 81
Wireless Security 81
    802.11 Standards 81
    802.1x 84
    Wireless Application Protocol 85
    Wireless Transport Layer Security Protocol 88
    Wired Equivalent Privacy 89
    Wireless Vulnerabilities 95

Chapter 3: Infrastructure Security 117

Protocol Models 117
- Open Systems Interconnect Model 117
- Transmission Control Protocol/Internet Protocol Model 119
- TCP/IP Protocols 120

Network Devices 123
- Firewall Types 123
- Firewall Architectures 125
- Hubs and Repeaters 128
- Bridges 128
- Switches 130
- Routers 131
- Wireless Devices 133

Media Types 143
- Cable 143
- Removable and Magnetic Media 146

Infrastructure Topologies 152
- Local Area Networks 152
- Wide Area Networks 153
- Internet 153
- Intranet 153
- Extranet 154
- VLANs 154
- Network Address Translation 155
- VPN Tunneling 156

Intrusion Detection and Response 158
- Types of ID Systems 158
- IDS Approaches 160
- Honey Pots 161
- Intrusion Response 162
- IDS and a Layered Security Approach 163
- IDS and Switches 163
- IDS Performance 164

Hardening 165
- Workstation Hardening 165
- Server Hardening 165
- DHCP 169
- DHCP and BOOTP 169

Chapter 4: Basics of Cryptography 177
- Algorithms 178
  - Exclusive Or 179
  - Hash Functions 179
  - Symmetric Algorithms 181
  - Modern Symmetric Key Encryption Algorithms 184
  - Asymmetric Algorithms 190
- Escrowed Encryption 204
- Hybrid Systems 204
- Cryptographic Attacks 205
- Steganography 207

Chapter 5: Operational/Organizational Security 215
- Physical Security 215
  - Physical Access Control 216
  - Electrical Power 220
  - Fire Detection and Suppression 221
- Disaster Recovery 225
  - Disaster Recovery Planning 226
  - Backups 230
  - Backup Media Protection 231
- Business Continuity Planning 232
  - High Availability and Fault Tolerance 233
  - RAID 235
- Policies and Procedures 236
  - Acceptable Use 237
  - Due Care 238
  - Privacy 238
  - Separation of Duties 241
  - Need-to-Know 242
  - Password Management 242
  - Service Level Agreements 243
  - Disposal/Destruction 244
  - Human Resources Policy 244
  - Code of Ethics 245
  - Incident Response Policy 247
- Privilege Management 249
  - Users, Groups, and Roles 249
  - Single Sign-On 250
  - Centralized versus Decentralized 250
  - Auditing 251
  - Mandatory Access Control 252
  - Discretionary Access Control 253
  - Role-Based Access Control 253

>   Computer Forensics 253
>   Chain of Evidence 254
>   Evidence Life Cycle 254
>   Types of Evidence 256
>   Law Enforcement and the 4th Amendment 256
>   Liability 257
>   Risk Identification 258
>   Risk Assessment 259
>   Asset Identification 260
>   Threat Identification 262
>   Vulnerability Definition 262
>   Security Awareness and Education 263
>   Awareness 264
>   Education and Training 265
>   Documentation 265
>   Documentation Change Control 265
>   Records Retention and Storage 266

Appendix A: Answers to Sample Questions 275

Appendix B: Glossary of Terms and Acronyms 323

Appendix C: Common Internet Vulnerabilities 381

Appendix D: NMap Log 405

Appendix E: What's on the CD-ROM? 437

Index 441

Introduction

The *Security+ Prep Guide* incorporates the authors' extensive background and experience in information security certification instruction and examination into a work designed to prepare the candidate for the Security+ certification examination. Using clear language and detailed explanations, the *Prep Guide* covers all the Security+ domains and their components in significant depth.

The text material is complemented by challenging sample questions that measure the candidate's knowledge of the subject matter. Answers to the sample questions are provided in an appendix so that the reader can evaluate his or her progress. The answers include detailed explanations of both correct and incorrect answers. A companion CD enables the candidate to take simulated exams and review the material covered by questions on the CD.

The *Security+ Prep Guide* is a comprehensive reference and one-stop source for Security+ exam preparation. It is meant to impart, reinforce, and test the knowledge critical to taking and passing the exam.

Background of the Security+ Certification Examination

The CompTIA Security+ certification exam was developed by experts from academia, industry, government, and related organizations. The founding organizations of CompTIA Security+ include the Argonne National Laboratory, U.S. Customs, Entrust, the Federal Bureau of Investigation, IBM/Tivoli Software, Information Systems Audit and Control Association (ISACA), the Information Systems Security Association (ISSA), Microsoft, Motorola, the National Institute for Standards Technology (NIST), Novell, RSA Security, Sun Microsystems, Sybex, the U.S. Secret Service, and Verisign.

The CompTIA Security+ certification exam is aimed at professionals with at least two years of networking experience, with an understanding of TCP/IP. The candidate should have a good grasp of the concepts and information tested in the

CompTIA A+ and Network+ certification examinations. Specifically, the candidate should have a working knowledge of the following domain areas:

- General security concepts
- Communications security
- Infrastructure security
- Basics of cryptography
- Operational/organizational security.

A Security+ beta examination covering the five domains was administered in September 2002, and the first exam was given in December 2002.

Additional information concerning the Security+ certification examination can be found at www.comptia.org/certification/security/general_info.asp.

Exam Contents

The five general domains of the CompTIA exam are subdivided into the following, specific subunits:

- General Security Concepts
  - Access Control
  - Authentication
  - Non-Essential Services & Protocols
  - Attacks
  - Malicious Code
  - Social Engineering
  - Auditing

- Communications Security
  - Remote Access
  - E-Mail
  - Web
  - Directory
  - File Transfer
  - Wireless

- Infrastructure Security
  - Devices
  - Media

- Security Topologies
- Intrusion Detection
- Security Baselines

✦ Basics of Cryptography
- Algorithms
- Concepts of Using Cryptography
- PKI
- Standards & Protocols
- Key Management/Certificate Lifecycle

✦ Operational/Organizational Security
- Physical Security
- Disaster Recovery
- Business Continuity
- Privilege Management
- Forensics
- Risk Identification
- Education
- Documentation

Conduct of the Exam

At this time, the Security+ examination is given only in English. The exam consists of 100 questions, and candidates have 90 minutes to complete them. The domain areas covered by the exam and the amount of coverage they receive (in percentages) are listed in the following table:

Domain	Percent of Exam
1.0 General Security Concepts	30%
2.0 Communications Security	20%
3.0 Infrastructure Security	20%
4.0 Basics of Cryptography	15%
5.0 Operational/Organizational Security	15%
Total	100%

The Security+ examination consists of both multiple-choice and multiple-response questions. For the multiple-choice questions, the candidate selects one option out of four or more options that best answers the question or completes the statement. In the multiple-response questions, the candidate selects more than one option out of four or more options that best answer the question or completes the statement.

The exam code is SY0-101. Security+ is offered at Prometric and Vue centers worldwide for an introductory price of $199 non-member and $149 member.

Approach and Hints

The authors recommend that you take the following approach to prepare for the Security+ certification exam:

- ✦ Absorb the key concepts presented for each of the domains
- ✦ Answer the sample questions at the end of each chapter
- ✦ Reinforce the learning process by studying the correct answers and explanations in the appendix
- ✦ Using the Bosun CD, take multiple practice examinations that can be generated by the Bosun test engine
- ✦ Note the answers and explanations provided by the Bosun test engine while taking the practice examinations

As with any multiple-choice examination, certain techniques can be used to increase the chance of selecting the correct answer. For example, in a question with four multiple-choice answers, a well-prepared candidate can usually identify two of the answers as incorrect. Then, the candidate must choose from the better of the two remaining answers. This process narrows the field of solutions and supports a candidate who has thoroughly studied for the examination.

One mistake that many exam-takers make is not reading the question carefully and deliberately. If he simply skims over the question, the candidate may miss a key word or phrase that would allow him to correctly answer the question. Also, in many instances, exam questions provide the answers or clues to other questions.

Obviously, nothing can replace experience, hard work, and careful preparation when it comes to taking the Security+ certification examination. These efforts, coupled with the structured guidance and information provided in the *Security+ Prep Guide,* will help the candidate achieve the Security+ certification.

General Security Concepts

Information system security covers a broad range of disciplines. To add structure to the field, these disciplines can be subdivided into categories that exhibit common characteristics. These categories comprise general security concepts that provide the foundation for addressing additional, more specific information security technologies. In the context of the Security+ certification, these general concepts are as follows:

- ✦ Access control
- ✦ Non-essential services and protocols
- ✦ Attacks
- ✦ Malicious code
- ✦ System scanning

In the information security (INFOSEC) community, information systems security is defined in terms of protecting the confidentiality, integrity, and availability (C-I-A) of information.

Confidentiality assures that information is not disclosed to unauthorized persons or processes.

Integrity is addressed through the following three goals:

- ✦ Prevention of information modification by unauthorized users
- ✦ Prevention of the unauthorized or unintentional modification of information by authorized users
- ✦ Preservation of the internal and external consistency

Internal consistency ensures that internal data is consistent. For example, assume that an internal database holds the number of units of a particular item in each department of an organization. The sum of the number of units in each department should equal the total number of units that the database has recorded internally for the whole organization. *External consistency* ensures that the data stored in the database is consistent with the real world. In other words, the number of items recorded in the database for each department would equal the number of items that physically exist in that department.

Availability assures that a system's authorized users have timely and uninterrupted access to the information in the system.

Additional important information security factors are authentication and non-repudiation. *Authentication* is the reconciliation of evidence that attests to a user's identity. It establishes the identity of the users and verifies that they are who they say they are. *Non-repudiation* prevents the sender of a message from denying that they sent the message.

Access Control

A principal concern in the practice of information security is controlling what *subjects* (persons or programs) can access which *objects* (files, programs, databases, and so on). In addition, the privileges that a subject has to an object must be defined. For example, Bob may be permitted to read File A, but he may not have the privilege to write to it.

Individuals are given different defined roles in information classification schemes and it is important to understand these roles. The roles are summarized in the following information classification roles.

Owner

An information owner may be an executive or manager of an organization. This person is responsible for the information that must be protected. An owner is different from a custodian. The owner has the final corporate responsibility for data protection and, under the concept of due care, the owner may be liable for negligence for failing to protect sensitive information. However, the day-to-day function of data protection is assigned to a custodian. Some of the responsibilities of an owner include the following:

- ◆ Making the original determination as to what level of classification the information requires, based upon the business needs for the protection of the data
- ◆ Periodically reviewing the classification assignments and making alterations as business needs change
- ◆ Delegating the data protection duties to the custodian

Custodian

As stated previously, the owner delegates the responsibility for data protection to the information custodian. IT systems personnel commonly execute this role. The duties of a custodian include the following:

- ✦ Running regular backups and routinely testing the validity of the backup data
- ✦ Performing data restoration from the backups when necessary
- ✦ Maintaining those retained records in accordance with the established information classification policy
- ✦ In some instances, administering the classification scheme

End User

An end user is an individual who routinely uses the protected information as part of their job. Users may also be thought of as consumers who require daily access to the information to execute their tasks. Users must follow the operating procedures that are defined in an organization's security policy, and they must adhere to the published guidelines for its use. In addition, users must practice "due care" to secure sensitive information according to the information security and use policies. Users must use company computing resources only for company purposes, not for personal use.

Access Control Considerations

In planning and implementing access control systems, the following three items must be considered:

- ✦ **Threat**—An event or activity that may cause harm to the information systems or networks
- ✦ **Vulnerability**—A weakness or lack of a safeguard that may be exploited by a threat to cause harm to information systems or networks
- ✦ **Risk**—The potential for harm or loss to an information system or network; the probability that a threat will materialize

To reduce the risk and the potential for loss, *controls* are used. Controls fall into the categories of preventive, detective, and corrective. *Preventive* controls attempt to inhibit harmful occurrences; *detective* controls are used to find situations that may cause harm to the information system; and *corrective* controls restore the information system to the state that existed prior to an attack.

Preventive, detective, and corrective controls can be implemented using administrative techniques, technical (logical) means, and physical devices. Examples of *administrative* controls are security awareness training, establishment of policies and procedures, personnel background checks, and increased supervision. *Technical* controls include smart cards, encryption, and access control lists (ACLs). *Physical* controls include measures such as securing laptops to desks, locking file cabinets, employing guards, locking doors, and protecting cable runs.

The objective of controls is to provide accountability for individuals who are accessing sensitive information. *Accountability* is another facet of access control that is based on the premise that individuals accessing and using an information system are responsible for their actions. Any activities conducted on an information system by an individual should be traceable to that individual. Accountability is accomplished by requiring the subject requesting access to provide identity and authentication information. For example, a subject may need to present an identity (ID) to log on to a computer and then provide a password as the authentication means to verify his or her identity.

To address the needs of different users and organizations, access control modes are used. These modes are called mandatory access control (MAC), discretionary access control (DAC), and role-based access control (RBAC). They define the access privileges that subjects have to objects.

Mandatory Access Control

In *mandatory access control*, a subject's access to an object is dependent upon labels. In a military context, a subject has a *clearance* and an object has a *classification*. (In a non-military environment, the word *sensitivity* is typically used, rather than *classification*.) The subject's clearance can be compared to the object's classification to determine if the subject can access the object. For example, the military labels documents as unclassified, confidential, secret, and top secret. Similarly, an individual can receive a clearance of confidential, secret, or top secret and can access documents classified at or below his/her specified clearance level. An individual with a clearance of *secret* can access secret documents, confidential documents, and unclassified documents, with a restriction. This restriction is that the individual must have a need-to-know relative to the classified documents involved. In other words, the subject must need the information in order to complete his or her assigned task. Even if the individual is cleared for a classification level, he should not access the information except on a need-to-know basis.

Rule-based access control is a type of mandatory access control, in which access is determined by rules (such as the correspondence of clearance labels to classification labels) and not by the identity of the subjects and objects alone.

A method of implementing mandatory access control is through the use of the *Trusted Computing Base (TCB)* concept. The TCB is the total combination of protection mechanisms within a computer system, including the hardware, software, and firmware that are trusted to enforce a security policy. The *security perimeter* is the boundary that separates the TCB from the remainder of the system. A *trusted path* must also exist so that a user can access the TCB without being compromised by other processes or users. A *trusted computer system* is one that employs the necessary hardware and software assurance measures to enable its use in processing multiple levels of classified or sensitive information. This system meets the specified requirements for reliability and security.

A related concept, the *reference monitor*, is a system component that enforces access controls on an object. It is an abstract machine that mediates all access of subjects to objects. The *security kernel* is defined as the hardware, firmware, and software elements of a trusted computing base that implement the reference monitor concept. The security kernel must accomplish the following:

- Mediate all accesses
- Be protected from modification
- Be verified as correct

Discretionary Access Control

In *discretionary access control (DAC)*, the subject, within limitations, has the authority to specify what objects can be accessed. One method of implementing DAC is to use *access control lists (ACLs)*. With an ACL, subjects and objects are listed along with the privileges that the subjects are assigned with respect to the objects. Access control lists are applicable when the designated authority needs the discretion to specify the resources that certain subjects are permitted to access. ACLs are easy to visualize and understand, but they become unwieldy when large numbers of subjects, objects, and privileges are involved and when frequent changes are necessary.

When a user, within certain limitations, has the right to alter the access control to certain objects, the term *user-directed* discretionary access control is appropriate. *Identity-based* access control is a type of discretionary access control based on the individual's identity.

Role-Based Access Control

In *role-based access control*, a central authority determines what subjects can have access to which objects based on the organizational security policy. The access controls are assigned according to the individual's role or title in the organization. This approach is especially useful in an organization that experiences frequent personnel changes. Role-based access controls do not need to be changed whenever a new person takes over a role or title in the organization.

Task-based access control is similar to role-based access control, but the controls are based on the subject's responsibilities and duties.

A third type of control, similar to that of RBAC, is *lattice-based access control*. This type of control is based on the lattice model, in which element pairs have a least upper bound of values and a greatest lower bound of values. Relative to access control, the pair of elements is the subject and object, and, accordingly, the subject has the greatest lower bound and the least upper bound of access rights to an object.

Role-based, task-based, and lattice-based access controls are sometimes grouped under the heading of *non-discretionary access controls*.

Access Control Models

Certain models have been developed to formalize access control rules and concepts, such as the Bell-LaPadula confidentiality model and the Biba and Clark-Wilson integrity models.

The Bell-LaPadula Model

The *Bell-LaPadula model* was developed to formalize the U.S. Department of Defense (DoD) multilevel security policy. The model formalizes mandatory access control based on labels and the employment of classifications and clearances. It also permits a discretionary access control mode under special circumstances. The Bell-LaPadula model deals only with the confidentiality of classified material. It does not address integrity or availability.

The Bell-LaPadula model defines three multilevel properties. The first two properties implement mandatory access control, and the third permits discretionary access control.

- **The Simple Security Property (SS Property)** — This property states that reading of information by a subject at a lower sensitivity level from an object at a higher sensitivity level is not permitted (no read up).
- **The * (Star) Security Property** — The Star property states that writing of information by a subject at a higher level of sensitivity to an object at a lower level of sensitivity is not permitted (no write down).
- **The Discretionary Security Property** — This property uses an access matrix to specify discretionary access control.

In some instances, a property called the *Strong * property* is cited. This property states that reading or writing is permitted at a particular level of sensitivity, but not to either higher or lower levels of sensitivity.

The discretionary portion of the Bell-LaPadula model is based on the access matrix. The system security policy defines who is authorized to have certain privileges to the system resources. *Authorization* is concerned with how access rights are defined and how they are evaluated. Some discretionary approaches are based on context-dependent and content-dependent access control. *Content-dependent* control makes access decisions based on the data contained in the object, whereas *context-dependent access control* is based on the environment or context of the data, applying determinants such as previous access history, time of day, and location.

The Biba Integrity Model

Integrity is usually characterized by the following three goals:

- The data is protected from modification by unauthorized users.
- The data is protected from unauthorized modification by authorized users.
- The data is internally and externally consistent — the data held in a database must balance internally and must correspond to the external, real-world situation.

To address the first integrity goal, the Biba model was developed in 1977 as an integrity analog to the Bell-LaPadula confidentiality model.

The Biba model classifies objects into different levels of integrity, similar to the Bell-LaPadula model's classification of different sensitivity levels. The model specifies the following three integrity axioms:

- **The Simple Integrity Axiom** — This axiom states that a subject at one level of integrity is not permitted to observe (read) an object of a lower integrity (no read down).
- **The * (Star) Integrity Axiom** — The Star axiom states that an object at one level of integrity is not permitted to modify (write to) an object of a higher level of integrity (no write up).
- **Axiom Three** — This axiom states that a subject at one level of integrity cannot invoke a subject at a higher level of integrity.

The Clark-Wilson Integrity Model

The approach of the Clark-Wilson model (1987) was to develop a framework for use in the real-world, commercial environment. This model addresses the three integrity goals and defines the following terms:

- **Constrained data item (CDI)** — A data item whose integrity is to be preserved
- **Integrity verification procedure (IVP)** — Confirms that all CDIs are in valid states of integrity
- **Transformation procedure (TP)** — Manipulates the CDIs through a well-formed transaction, which transforms a CDI from one valid integrity state to another valid integrity state
- **Unconstrained data item (UDI)** — Data items outside the control area of the modeled environment, such as input information

The Clark-Wilson model requires integrity labels to determine the integrity level of a data item and to verify that this integrity was maintained after an application of a TP. This model incorporates mechanisms to enforce internal and external consistency, a separation of duty, and a mandatory integrity policy.

Authentication

As previously defined, authentication is the process of verifying that a person is who they claim to be. Passwords are commonly used as authentication mechanisms. A user professing an identity to the system establishes accountability for actions on the system.

The following sections describe a number of different authentication mechanisms that illustrate important authentication concepts.

Kerberos

Kerberos implements a trusted, third-party authentication protocol that can also provide *single sign-on (SSO)* capability. Single sign-on refers to a method of eliminating the need for users to log on multiple times to access different resources in a networked environment. Without SSO, the user must remember numerous passwords and IDs. Consequently, the passwords and IDs may be weak and posted in visible areas, becoming more vulnerable to attacks. In SSO, the user provides one ID and password per work session and is automatically logged on to all the required applications. For security, the SSO passwords should not be stored or transmitted in the clear. Single sign-on applications can run either on the user's workstation or on authentication servers. The advantages of SSO include ease of administration when users leave an organization or change roles, the ability to use stronger passwords because there are fewer passwords to remember, and faster access to the required resources. The major disadvantage of many SSO implementations is that once a user obtains access to the system through the initial log-on, the user can freely roam the network resources without restriction.

Kerberos Background and Assumptions

Kerberos was developed under Project Athena at MIT and named for the three-headed dog that guards the entrance to the underworld in Greek mythology.

Kerberos uses symmetric key cryptography to authenticate clients to other entities on a network from which the client requires services. Some basic assumptions that assist in understanding the rationale behind Kerberos are as follows:

- There are numerous networked clients, servers, and network resources available.
- The client location and computers are not necessarily secure.
- The network cabling cannot be assumed to be secure.
- Messages are not secure from interception.

A few specific locations and servers can be secured to serve as trusted authentication mechanisms for every client and service on the network. (These centralized servers implement the Kerberos trusted *Key Distribution Center [KDC]*, *Kerberos Ticket Granting Service [TGS]*, and *Kerberos Authentication Service [AS]*.)

In a Kerberos implementation, all network clients and servers have a secret key. These secret keys are known and used by the KDC to perform authentication and to provide for symmetric key encryption of messages sent on the network. Kerberos authenticates a client to a requested service on a server through special messages called *tickets* and by issuing temporary symmetric session keys. The symmetric session keys are valid for a specified period of time and are used for communications between the client and KDC, the server and KDC, and the client and server.

Kerberos Vulnerabilities

Kerberos addresses confidentiality and integrity of information. It does not directly address availability and attacks such as frequency analysis. Also, because all the secret keys are held and authentication is performed on Kerberos TGS and authentication servers, these servers are vulnerable to both physical attacks and attacks from malicious code. Replay can be accomplished on Kerberos if the compromised tickets are used within the allotted time window. Because the client password is used in the initiation of the Kerberos request for service protocol, password guessing can be used to impersonate a client.

The keys used in the Kerberos exchange are also vulnerable. The client's secret key is stored temporarily on the client workstation and is susceptible to compromise, as are the session keys that are stored on the client's computer and on the servers.

Kerberos Symbols

Kerberos will be explained using the terminology and symbols provided in Table 1.1.

Table 1.1
Kerberos Items and Symbols

Item	Symbol
Client	C
Client secret key	K_c
Client network address	A
Server	S
Client/TGS session key	$K_{c,tgs}$
TGS secret key	K_{tgs}
Server secret key	K_s

Continued

Table 1.1 *(continued)*	
Item	**Symbol**
Client/server session key	$K_{c,s}$
Client/TGS ticket	$T_{c,tgs}$
Client-to-server ticket	$T_{c,s}$
Client-to-server authenticator	$A_{c,s}$
Starting and ending time ticket is valid	V
Timestamp	T
M encrypted in secret key of x	$[M]K_x$
Ticket Granting Ticket	TGT
Optional, additional session key	Key

Client-TGS Server Initial Exchange

To initiate a request for service from a server, s, the user enters an ID and password on the client workstation. The client temporarily generates the client's secret key, K_c, from the password using a one-way hash function. The client sends a request for authentication to the TGS server using the client's ID in the clear. Note that no password or secret key is sent. If the client is in the authentication server database, the TGS server returns a client/TGS session key, $K_{c,tgs}$, encrypted in the secret key of the client, and a Ticket Granting Ticket (TGT) encrypted in the secret key of the TGS server. Neither the client nor any other entity except the TGS server can read the contents of the TGT since K_{tgs} is known only to the TGS server. The TGT is comprised of the following:

- The client ID
- The client network address
- The starting and ending time the ticket is valid
- The client/TGS session key

Symbolically, these initial messages from the TGS server to the client are represented as

$$[K_{c,tgs}]K_c$$
$$TGT [c, a, v, K_{c,tgs}] K_{tgs}$$

The client decrypts the message containing the session key, $K_{c,tgs}$, with its secret key, K_c, and uses this session key to communicate with the TGS server. The client then erases its stored secret key to avoid compromising the secret key.

Client to TGS Server Request for Service

When requesting access to a specific service on the network from the TGS server, the client sends two messages to the TGS server. For one message, the client submits the previously obtained TGT that is encrypted in the secret key of the TGS server and an identification of the server, s, from which service is requested. The other message is an authenticator encrypted in the assigned session key, $K_{c,\,tgs}$. The authenticator contains the client ID, a timestamp, and an optional additional session key. These two messages are:

$$TGT = s, [c, a, v, K_{c,\,tgs}] K_{tgs}$$
$$Authenticator = [c, t, key] K_{c,\,tgs}$$

TGS Server to Client Issuing of Ticket for Service

After receiving a valid TGT and authenticator from the client requesting a service, the TGS server issues a ticket, $T_{c,\,s}$, to the client encrypted in the server's secret key, K_s, and a client/server session key, $K_{c,\,s}$, encrypted in the client/TGS session key. These two messages are:

$$Ticket\ T_{c,\,s} = s, [c, a, v, K_{c,\,s}] K_s$$
$$[K_{c,\,s}] K_{c,\,tgs}$$

Client-to-Server Authentication Exchange and Providing of Service

To receive service from the server, s, the client sends the ticket, $T_{c,\,s}$, and an authenticator to the server. The server decrypts the message with its secret key, K_s, and checks the contents. The contents contain the client's address, the valid time window, v, and the client/server session key, $K_{c,\,s}$, which will now be used for communication between the client and server. The server also checks the authenticator and, if that timestamp is valid, provides the requested service to the client. The client messages to the server are:

$$Ticket\ T_{c,\,s} = s, [c, a, v, K_{c,\,s}] K_s$$
$$Authenticator = [c, t, key] K_{c,\,s}$$

The Challenge Handshake Authentication Protocol

The *Challenge Handshake Authentication Protocol (CHAP)* is an authentication protocol used to verify the identity of a user logging onto an information system from a remote location. CHAP uses a non-replayable challenge-response protocol that verifies the identity of the node attempting to initiate the remote session.

A challenge-response protocol operates in the following manner:

1. A challenge number is presented to the remote user on the log-on screen by the authentication server at the central location.
2. The remote user enters this challenge number into his/her password generator, along with a PIN number.

3. The password generator, using a secret key, K, encrypts the digits entered by the remote user and presents the user with the result, R, which is another series of digits.
4. The remote user enters R as his or her log-on password.
5. Because the authentication server knows the secret key, K, and the remote user's PIN number, it can calculate the required result and compare it with the value, R, entered by the remote user.
6. If the two numbers match, the user is authenticated.

CHAP is commonly used by remote access servers and xDSL, ISDN, and cable modems.

CHAP is an improvement over an earlier remote authentication protocol called the *Password Authentication Protocol (PAP)*. PAP uses a static password for authentication. PAP is considered a weak protocol because the password is subject to replay and the user ID and password are not encrypted during the log-on session.

Callback

Another approach for remotely accessing an information system is *Callback*. In Callback, a remote user dials in to the authentication server, provides an ID and password, and hangs up. The authentication server looks up the caller's ID in a database of authorized users and obtains a phone number at a fixed location. Note that the remote user must be calling from that location. The authentication server then calls the phone number. The user answers and is given access to the system. In some Callback implementations, the user must enter another password upon receiving a Callback. The disadvantage of this system is that the user must be at a fixed location whose phone number is known to the authentication server. Crackers, who can arrange to have the call automatically forwarded to their number, enabling access to the system, pose a threat to Callback.

Certificates

Recall that in public key cryptography, an individual (we'll call him "Bob") has two keys: a public key and a private key. Bob's public key is used by anyone who wishes to send him an encrypted message. If, for example, Alice wants to send Bob an encrypted message, she encrypts the message with Bob's public key. Because Bob's private key is the only key that can decrypt the message, the message is secure from eavesdropping by another person, named "Eve." You may start to wonder how Alice gets Bob's public key in the first place. Alice can obtain Bob's public key from a public central database, or *key ring*, from her own private database, or from Bob himself.

Eve can start an attack against Bob and Alice by substituting her public key for Bob's in the public key ring. Alice uses Eve's public key to encrypt the message she is sending to Bob, thinking that she is using Bob's public key. Instead, Alice receives the message, opens it with her public key, and reads it. Alice can then re-encrypt the message with Bob's correct public key and send it to him. Alice and Bob will never know that their message has been intercepted and read.

One solution to this problem is a public key certificate. In essence, the certificate is an individual's public key that is digitally signed by a trusted entity. This entity could be a certification authority (CA) or an individual that vouches for the public key.

Certificates are held in repositories called *directories*. A directory also holds certificate revocation lists (CRLs) of expired or revoked certificates. Attributes of a Public Key Infrastructure (PKI) Directory are defined in standard X.500, and the structure of a public key certificate is defined in the X.509 protocol.

Public key certificates are discussed in more detail in Chapter 4.

User Name/Password

As previously discussed, one common form of authentication is the use of a user name (or ID) and a password. The user name or ID identifies the user to the workstation or authentication server. Then, a corresponding password is entered to authenticate the ID and verify that the user is the person he or she professes to be.

Individuals typically choose names, initials, or nicknames for their user name or ID. However, a more random choice would be better. Job titles should not be used as passwords, lest extra information be available to crackers.

Passwords can be compromised and must therefore be protected. Choices for passwords should not be intuitive or related to the user's name, occupation, pets, birthday, and so on. The password should be a random sequence of numbers, letters, and symbols at least eight characters in length.

Passwords should be changed at intervals proportionate to the value of the information to be protected. Typical time frames range from one month to six months. A *static password* is the same for each log-on in the interval before it is changed. The more times the same password is used, the more likely it is to be compromised.

Ideally, a password should be used only once. This *one-time password* provides maximum security because a new password is required for each log-on. Such a password is also termed a *dynamic password*.

A *passphrase* is a sequence of characters that is usually longer than the allotted number of characters for a password. It can be a sentence or phrase that the user is able to remember. This passphrase is converted into a virtual password by the system by using transformations such as a one-way hash function.

Tokens

Tokens in the form of credit card–sized memory cards or smart cards, or those resembling small calculators, are used to supply static and dynamic passwords.

An ATM card is a memory card that stores your personal information. Smart cards provide even more capability by incorporating additional processing power on the card. The four main types of tokens are:

- **Static password** — With this type of token, the user authenticates himself or herself to the token and then the token authenticates the user to the authentication server or workstation.

- **Synchronous dynamic password** — A synchronous dynamic password token generates a new unique password value at fixed time intervals. This password is time-synchronized with the authentication server and must be presented to the authentication server along with a PIN (known to the authentication server) within a fixed time window to be accepted. For example, each new password could be generated by encrypting the time of day with a secret key that is known to the token and to the authentication server.

- **Asynchronous dynamic password** — This token generates the new password asynchronously, so entry of the password into the authentication server does not have to fit into a fixed time interval for authentication. The new password is entered into the authentication server, along with the user's PIN.

- **Challenge-response** — The challenge-response token is based on the user's ability to supply a valid response to a challenge number presented by the authentication server or workstation. Specifically, the authentication server generates a random challenge string and the user enters the string into the token, along with the user's PIN. The token takes the challenge string and user's PIN and generates a response string of characters. This response string is usually the result of an encryption process. The user enters the response string into the authentication server, which verifies that it is the valid response based on the user's PIN and the key used in the encryption process. The challenge-response approach is also used in remote access protocols, such as CHAP.

In all these token-based schemes, a front-end authentication device or a back-end authentication server, which services multiple workstations or the host, can perform the authentication.

Multi-Factor Authentication

Multi-factor authentication requires more than one authentication method and, thus, provides increased access protection to an information system. For example, in addition to a password, the authentication entity may require a fingerprint. In general, authentication is based on the following three factor types:

- **Type 1** — Something you know (PIN, password)
- **Type 2** — Something you have (ATM card, smart card)
- **Type 3** — Something you are (fingerprint, retina scan)

Two-factor authentication requires two of the three factors to be used in the authentication process. For example, withdrawing funds from an ATM machine requires two-factor authentication in the form of the ATM card (something you have) and your PIN number (something you know). In today's environment, biometrics is receiving increasing interest and application as a second or third authentication factor. Biometrics is an automated means of identifying or authenticating the identity of a living person based on physiological or behavioral characteristics.

Mutual Authentication

Mutual authentication refers to a situation where two individuals wish to authenticate each other. One approach is to use public key cryptography and passwords that are assigned to each individual and known by the other. For example, if Bob takes the password "PWB" and Alice the password "PWA," Bob can use public key cryptography to encrypt "PWB" with Alice's public key and send it to her. Alice decrypts Bob's message with her private key and reads Bob's password. Because Alice knows that Bob's password is "PWB," she is assured that Bob sent the message. Similarly, for Alice to authenticate herself to Bob, she encrypts "PWA" with Bob's public key and sends it to him. Bob decrypts Alice's message with his private key and reads Alice's password. Because he knows that her password is "PWA," he is assured that Alice sent the message.

The catch is that this scenario is subject to *man-in-the-middle attacks*. This type of attack may be mounted by Eve, for example, who has initially substituted her public key for that of Bob and Alice's. She accomplishes this substitution either by intercepting their initial exchange of public keys or by changing Bob and Alice's public keys to hers on a non-certified public database. To initiate the mutual authentication, Bob encrypts "PWB" with Alice's public key (which is actually Eve's) and sends it to Alice. Eve intercepts Bob's encrypted message and decrypts it with her private key. Eve then re-encrypts the message with Alice's "real" public key and sends it on to Alice. Alice decrypts Bob's message with her private key and reads Bob's password, "PWB." Because she knows that Bob's password is "PWB," she is assured that Bob sent the message. Similarly, for Alice to authenticate herself to Bob, Alice encrypts "PWA" with Bob's public key (actually Eve's) and sends it to Bob. Eve intercepts Alice's encrypted message and decrypts it with her private key. Eve then re-encrypts the message with Bob's "real" public key and sends it on to Bob. Bob decrypts Alice's message with his private key and reads Alice's password, "PWA." Because he knows that Alice's password is "PWA," he is assured that Alice sent the message. Eve is now in a position to read the communications between Bob and Alice.

One way to defeat this man-in-the-middle attack is to have Bob send Alice only one-half of the message he has encrypted with her public key. Even if Eve has substituted her public key for Alice's public key, she cannot decrypt the message when she intercepts it because only one-half of the message is present. However, to execute the man-in-the-middle attack, Eve must send some type of message to Alice, encrypted in Alice's "real" public key. Thus, Eve must make up a message that may be coherent to Alice when it is eventually decrypted and send one-half of it to Alice. When Eve intercepts the second half of Bob's message to Alice, Eve can decrypt the whole message, but it is too late to reconcile her earlier made-up message to Alice with the whole actual message. This methodology is known as the *interlock protocol* (R.L. Rivest and A. Shamir, "How to Expose an Eavesdropper," *Communications of the ICM*, v.27, n.4, April 1984).

Biometrics

Biometric technologies are gaining popularity as one of the factors in multi-factor authentication. *Biometrics* is defined as an automated means of identifying or authenticating the identity of a living person based on physiological or behavioral characteristics. Biometrics is a Type 3 authentication mechanism—something you are.

Biometric technologies can be used for identification or authentication. Biometrics is used for identification in physical access control and for authentication in technical (logical) access. In biometrics, *identification* is a "one-to-many" search of an individual's characteristics from a database of stored images. *Authentication* in biometrics is a "one-to-one" search to verify a claim to an identity made by a person. The three main performance measures in biometrics are as follows:

- ***False Rejection Rate (FRR), or Type I Error***—The percentage of valid subjects that are falsely rejected

- ***False Acceptance Rate (FAR), or Type II Error***—The percentage of invalid subjects that are falsely accepted

- ***Crossover Error Rate (CER)***—The percent in which the False Rejection Rate equals the False Acceptance Rate

In most cases, the sensitivity of the biometric detection system can be increased or decreased during an inspection process. If the system's sensitivity is increased, such as in an airport metal detector, the system becomes increasingly selective and has a higher FRR. Conversely, if the sensitivity is decreased, the FAR will increase. To obtain a valid measure of the system performance, the CER is used. These concepts are illustrated in Figure 1.1.

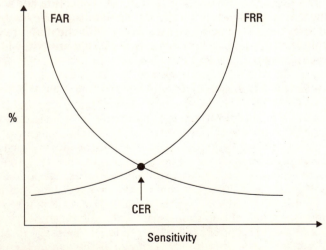

Figure 1.1 Crossover error rate

Other important factors that must be evaluated in biometric systems are enrollment time, throughput rate, and acceptability. *Enrollment time* is the time it takes to initially "register" with a system by providing samples of the biometric characteristic to be evaluated. An acceptable enrollment time is around two minutes.

The *throughput rate* is the rate at which individuals, once enrolled, can be processed and identified or authenticated by a system. Acceptable throughput rates are in the range of 10 subjects per minute.

Acceptability refers to considerations of privacy, invasiveness, and psychological and physical comfort when using the system. For example, one concern with retina scanning systems may be the exchange of body fluids on the eyepiece. Another concern would be the retinal pattern that could reveal changes in a person's health, such as the advent of diabetes or high blood pressure.

Acquiring different data elements reflecting a biometric characteristic can greatly affect the storage requirements and operational speed of a biometric identification or authentication system. For example, in *fingerprint* systems, the actual fingerprint is stored and requires approximately 250KB per finger for a high-quality image. This level of information is required for one-to-many searches in forensics applications on very large databases. In *finger-scan* technology, a full fingerprint is not stored—the features extracted from this fingerprint are stored using a small template that requires approximately 500 to 1000 bytes of storage. The original fingerprint cannot be reconstructed from this template. Finger-scan technology is used for one-to-one verification using smaller databases. Updates of the enrollment information may be required because some biometric characteristics, such as voice and signature, can change with time.

A collection of biometric images stored in an image database is called a *corpus*. Potential sources of error are the corruption of images during collection and mislabeling or other transcription problems associated with the database. The image collection process and storage must be performed carefully, with constant checking. These images are collected during the enrollment process and are critical to the correct operation of the biometric device.

The following are typical biometric characteristics that are used to uniquely identify or authenticate an individual:

- Fingerprints
- Retina scans
- Iris scans
- Facial scans
- Palm scans
- Hand geometry
- Voice
- Handwritten signature dynamics

Non-Essential Services and Protocols

Numerous ports, services, processes, and programs in an information system that are not necessary for day-to-day requirements of the user community may be active. Many of these entities are vulnerable to attacks and should be disabled. For example, many TCP and UDP ports fall into this category. The ports of interest are the "well-known" first 1,024 ports that are used for system services.

For more information on TCP and UDP ports, refer to Chapter 3.

For example, Port 7 provides an Echo service that responds to TCP or UDP connection requests. Disabling this service mitigates against Denial-of-Service (DoS) attacks. Table 1.2 provides examples of other ports that should be disabled unless they are absolutely required.

Table 1.2
Examples of Ports and Services to be Disabled

Port #/Name	Service	Information That May Be Accessible to Crackers
11/SYSTAT	System status	Process status
15/NETSTAT	Network status	Protocols, address, network connections
19/CHARGEN	Character stream generator	Generates characters and can be used to pass data to echo service
21/FTP	File transfer	Daemon information, platform being used, guest account
23/TELNET	Terminal emulation	Resources available, passwords
25/SMTP	Sending e-mail	Discovery data (information gathered to facilitate and attack)
53/DOMAIN	Domain Name Service (DNS) — translates domain names into IP addresses	Discover data, DNS server information
67/BOOTP	Provides diskless workstations with information about their IP address	Configuration information about Bootp daemon note list
69/TFTP	"Light" version of FTP	Readable files, password files
79/FINGER	Provides information about a user	Discovery data

Port #/Name	Service	Information That May Be Accessible to Crackers
80/HTTP	World Wide Web protocol	Web page information
109 & 110/POP	Post Office Protocol that obtains e-mail from mail server	Mail spool files, log-on information, discovery data
111/PORTMAP	Redirection—converts remote procedure call (RPC) program numbers into port numbers	Registered port and program information
135/LOC-SERV	RPC service for Windows NT	Client network information service domain names, passwords
137/NBNAME	NetBIOS name service	Name broadcast queries
161/SNMP	Collects network information	Current users, active processes, and network connections
512/EXEC	Execution of remote processes	Keystrokes and window displays
540/UUCP	Mail delivery management	Commands to be executed on other systems

Another example of a vulnerability caused by failure to disable means of unauthorized entry into an information system is the *maintenance hook*. A maintenance hook is a hardware or software mechanism that is designed to accommodate system maintenance by bypassing the system's security controls. Granted, this capability is necessary under certain circumstances, but left "open," it invites intrusions and the compromising of sensitive information. Maintenance hooks are sometimes called *trap doors*.

Attacks

Attacks against computers, networks, and cryptographic systems are motivated by various reasons. Some attacks are aimed at disrupting service, others focus on illegally acquiring sensitive information, and still others attempt to deceive or defraud. In general, such attacks target the C-I-A components of information security. This section explores the most common types of attacks.

Denial-of-Service/Distributed Denial-of-Service

A Denial-of-Service (DoS) attack consumes an information system's resources to the point where it cannot handle authorized transactions. A distributed DoS (DDoS) attack on a computing resource is launched from a number of other host machines.

Attack software is usually installed on a large number of host computers, unbeknownst to their owners, and then activated simultaneously to launch communications to the target machine of such magnitude that it overwhelms the target machine.

Specific examples of DoS attacks include the following:

- **Buffer overflow** — A process receives much more data than expected. If the process has no programmed routine to deal with the excessive amount of data, it acts in an unexpected way that the intruder can exploit. A Ping of Death exploits the Internet Control Message Protocol (ICMP) by sending an illegal ECHO packet of >65K octets of data, which can cause an overflow of system variables and lead to a system crash.
- **SYN attack** — In this attack, an attacker exploits the use of the buffer space during a Transmission Control Protocol (TCP) session initialization handshake. The attacker floods the target system's small "in-process" queue with connection requests, but it does not respond when a target system replies to those requests. This causes the target system to "time out" while waiting for the proper response, which makes the system crash or become unusable.
- **Teardrop attack** — The length and fragmentation offset fields in sequential Internet Protocol (IP) packets are modified. The target system becomes confused and crashes after it receives contradictory instructions on how the fragments are offset on these packets.
- **Smurf attack** — This attack involves IP spoofing and ICMP to saturate a target network with traffic, thereby launching a DoS attack. It consists of three elements: the source site, the bounce site, and the target site. The attacker (the source site) sends a spoofed ping packet to the broadcast address of a large network (the bounce site). This modified packet contains the target site's address, which causes the bounce site to broadcast the misinformation to all the devices on its local network. All of these devices now respond with a reply to the target system, which is then saturated with those replies.

Back Door

A back door attack takes place using dial-up modems or asynchronous external connections. The strategy is to bypass control mechanisms and gain access to a network through a back door such as a modem.

Spoofing

IP spoofing is used by an intruder to convince a system that it is communicating with a known, trusted entity to provide the intruder with access to the system. IP spoofing involves altering a packet at the TCP level, which is used to attack Internet-connected systems that provide various TCP/IP services. The attacker sends a packet with an IP source address of a known, trusted host instead of its own IP source address to a target host. The target host may accept the packet and act upon it.

Man-in-the-Middle

The man-in-the-middle attack involves an attacker, A, substituting his or her public key for that of another person's, P. Anyone who desires to send an encrypted message to P using P's public key will unknowingly use A's public key. A can thus read the message intended for P. He can send the message on to P, encrypted in P's real public key, and P will never be the wiser. A could modify the message before resending it to P. (See the discussion under "Mutual Authentication" in this chapter.) Figure 1.2 shows the common placement of the attacker in a man-in-the-middle attack.

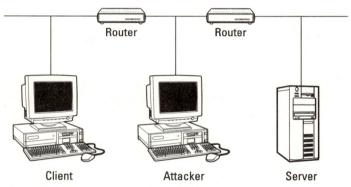

Figure 1.2 A man-in-the-middle attack

Replay

The replay attack occurs when an attacker intercepts and saves old messages and then tries to send them at a later time, impersonating one of the participants. One method of making this attack more difficult to accomplish is by using a random number or string called a **nonce.** For example, if Bob wants to communicate with Alice, he sends a nonce along with the first message to Alice. When Alice replies, she sends the nonce back to Bob, who verifies that it is the one he sent with the first message. Anyone trying to use these same messages later will not be using the newer nonce. Another approach to countering the replay attack is to have Bob add a timestamp to his message. This **timestamp** indicates the time that the message was sent. If the message is used later, the timestamp will show that an old message is being used.

TCP/Hijacking

As an example of this type of attack, an attacker hijacks a session between a trusted client and network server. The attacking computer substitutes its IP address for that of the trusted client and the server continues the dialog, believing it is communicating with the trusted client. The steps in this attack are as follows:

1. Trusted client connects to network server.
2. Attack computer gains control of trusted client.
3. Attack computer disconnects trusted client from network server.
4. Attack computer replaces the IP address of trusted client with its own IP address and spoofs the client's sequence numbers.
5. Attack computer continues dialog with network server (network server believes it is still communicating with trusted client).

Fragmentation Attacks

The following are two examples of fragmentation attacks:

- A *tiny fragment attack* occurs when the intruder sends a very small fragment that forces some of the TCP header field into a second fragment. If the target's filtering device does not enforce minimum fragment size, this illegal packet can be passed on through the target's network.
- An *overlapping fragment attack* is another variation on a datagram's zero-offset modification. Subsequent packets overwrite the initial packet's destination address information, and the second packet is passed by the target's filtering device. This can happen if the target's filtering device does not enforce a minimum fragment offset for fragments with non-zero offsets.

Weak Keys

For many cryptographic algorithms, some keys are weaker than others (that is, not as secure as other keys). Strong keys are generated using truly random number generators. For specific algorithms, keys can be tested for their strength. For example, the data encryption standard, DES, has only 16 weak keys out of its 2^{56} possible keys. Because weak keys for an algorithm can be identified, they should not be used.

When an algorithm has keys that are all of equal strength, it is said to have a *linear, or flat key space*. Conversely, if an algorithm has keys that are all not of equal strength, it has a *nonlinear key space*.

The same use of randomness applies to passwords in that the more random the choice of letters and characters in a password, the more secure it is. However, the more random the sequence of letters and characters in a password, the harder it is to remember.

Mathematical Attacks

Mathematical attacks refer to the use of mathematics to break passwords or cryptographic algorithms, as opposed to other approaches, such as the trial-and-error method of guessing all possible character combinations that might make up a password or cryptographic key.

A good example of a mathematical attack is the use of factoring algorithms to break the RSA public key cryptography algorithm. Recall that the hard problem in RSA is determining the prime factors of a large number. Numbers on the order of 129 digits have been factored using factoring algorithms and thousands of computers on the Internet. One of the better factoring algorithms is the number field sieve (NFS).

Social Engineering

This attack uses social skills to obtain information, such as passwords or PIN numbers, to be used against information systems. For example, an attacker may impersonate someone in an organization and make phone calls to employees of that organization, requesting passwords for use in maintenance operations. The following are additional examples of social engineering attacks:

- E-mails to employees from a cracker requesting their passwords to validate the organizational database after a network intrusion has occurred.
- E-mails to employees from a cracker requesting their passwords because work has to be performed over the weekend on the system.
- E-mails or phone calls from a cracker impersonating an official who is conducting an investigation for the organization and requires passwords for the investigation.
- Improper release of medical information to individuals posing as doctors and requesting data from patients' records.
- A computer repair technician convincing a user that the hard disk on his or her PC is irreparably damaged and installing a new hard disk for the user; the technician then takes the hard disk, extracts the information, and sells the information to a competitor or foreign government.

The best defense against social engineering attacks is an information security policy that educates users about these types of attacks.

Dumpster Diving

Dumpster diving involves the acquisition of information that is discarded by an individual or organization. In many cases, information found in trash can be very valuable to a cracker. Discarded information may include technical manuals, password lists, telephone numbers, and organization charts. One requirement for information to be treated as a trade secret is that the information must be protected and not revealed to any unauthorized individuals. If a document containing an organization's trade secret information is thus inadvertently discarded and found in the trash by another person, that person can use the information because it was not adequately protected.

Birthday Attacks

Birthday attacks are made against hash algorithms that are used to verify the integrity of a message and for digital signatures. A message that is processed by a hash function produces an output message digest (MD) of fixed length, independent of the length of the input message. The MD uniquely characterizes the message. For a strong hash algorithm, H, and message, M:

1. It should be computationally infeasible to find two messages that produce a common message digest; that is, $H(M1) \neq H(M2)$.
2. If a message and its corresponding message digest exist, it should be computationally infeasible to find another message that generates that specific message digest.
3. It should be computationally infeasible to find a message that corresponds to a given message digest.
4. The message digest should be calculated using all of the data in the original message.

The birthday attack refers to the probability of finding two random messages that generate the same MD when processed by a hash function. This exercise is analogous to asking how many people must be in a room to have a greater than 50 percent chance that at least two of them will have the same birthday. The answer is 23.

Cross-Reference

For more information on birthday attacks, refer to Chapter 4.

Password Guessing

Because passwords are the most commonly used mechanism to authenticate users to an information system, obtaining passwords is a common and effective attack approach. A person's password can be obtained in the following ways:

✦ By physically looking around the person's desk for notes containing the password
✦ Bu "sniffing" the connection to the network to acquire unencrypted passwords
✦ Through social engineering
✦ By gaining access to a password database
✦ By outright guessing

The last approach can be done in a random or systematic manner.

Brute Force

Brute force password guessing means taking a random approach that simply involves trying different passwords and hoping that one works. Some logic can be applied by trying passwords related to the person's name, job title, hobbies, and other similar items.

Dictionary Attack

A dictionary attack is one in which a dictionary of common passwords is used in an attempt to gain access to a user's computer and network. One approach is to copy an encrypted file that contains the passwords and, applying the same encryption to a dictionary of commonly used passwords, compare the results.

Password guessing attacks can be automated. For example, the most common software utility for password cracking is L0pht Crack, by @stake. Figure 1.3 shows the result of an LC4 scan on a test Windows NT server using an automated dictionary attack. Of course, this test server was built with only five accounts using very weak passwords, but notice that it took less than one second to get the passwords.

Figure 1.4 shows the same attack retrieving the Lan Manager Hash encryptions.

Figure 1.3 L0pht Crack dictionary attack on NT

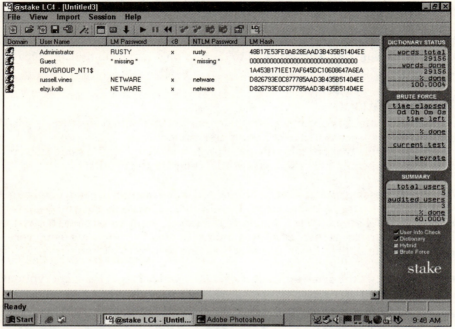

Figure 1.4 L0pht Crack attack to obtain NT LM hashes

One interesting feature of this software is that the security administrator can run the password audit with the option of not displaying the passwords. This enables one to identify users who have weak passwords without actually revealing the password.

Software Exploitation

Vulnerabilities in software can be exploited to gain unauthorized access to information systems' resources and data. Some examples of software exploitation include the following:

- **Novell Web Server** — An attacker can cause a DoS buffer overflow by sending a large GET request to the remote administration port. This causes the data being sent to overflow the storage buffer and reside in memory as executable code.
- **AIX Operating System** — Passwords can be exposed by diagnostic commands.
- **IRIX Operating System** — A buffer overflow vulnerability enables root access by an attacker.
- **Windows 9x** — A vulnerability enables an attacker to locate system and screensaver passwords, providing the attacker with the means to gain unauthorized log-on access.

✦ **Windows NT** — Privilege exploitation software used by an attacker can gain administrative access to the operating system.

Many software-related vulnerabilities can be avoided by applying good software engineering techniques during the software development process and anticipating possible attacks. For example, proper parameter checking can be incorporated into software to prevent buffer overflow attacks.

Additional software-related issues are described as follows:

✦ **Anti-virus management** — If personnel can load or execute any software on a system, the system is more vulnerable to viruses, unexpected software interactions, and the subversion of security controls.

✦ **Software testing** — A rigid and formal software testing process is required to determine compatibility with custom applications or to identify other unforeseen interactions. This procedure should also apply to software upgrades.

✦ **Software utilities** — Systems utilities can compromise the integrity of operating systems and logical access controls. Their use must be controlled by security policy.

✦ **Safe software storage** — A combination of logical and physical access controls should be implemented to ensure that the software and copies of backups have not been modified without proper authorization.

Malicious Code

Malicious code is the name used for any program that adds, deletes, or modifies legitimate software for the purpose of intentionally causing disruption, harm, or to circumvent or subvert the existing system's function. Examples of malicious code include viruses, worms, Trojan horses, and logic bombs. Newer malicious code is based on mobile Active X and Java applets.

Viruses

Viruses attach to a host program and propagate when an infected program is executed.

A virus infects the operating system in two ways: by completely replacing one or more of the operating system's programs or by attaching itself to existing operating system programs and altering functionality. Once a virus changes OS functionality, it can control many OS processes that are running.

To avoid detection, the virus usually creates several hidden files within the OS source code or in "unusable" sectors. Because infections in the OS are difficult to detect, they have deadly consequences on systems relying on the OS for basic functions.

The Virus Lifecycle

There are two main phases in the lifecycle of a virus: *replication* and *activation*. In the first phase, replication, viruses typically remain hidden and do not interfere with normal system functions. During this time, viruses actively seek out new hosts to infect by attaching themselves to other software programs or by infiltrating the OS.

During the second phase, activation, the beginning of gradual or sudden destruction of the system occurs. Typically, the decision to activate is based on a mathematical formula with criteria such as date, time, and number of infected files. The possible damage at this stage could include destroyed data, software or hardware conflicts, space consumption, and abnormal behavior.

Macro Viruses

Macro viruses are the most prevalent computer viruses in the wild, accounting for the vast majority of virus encounters. A macro virus can easily infect many types of applications, such as Microsoft Excel and Word.

To infect the system, macro viruses attach themselves to the application's initialization sequence. When the application is executed, the virus' instructions execute before control is given to the application. Then the virus replicates itself, infecting more and more of the system.

These macro viruses move from system to system through e-mail file sharing, demonstrations, data sharing, and disk sharing. Today's widespread sharing of macro-enabled files, primarily through e-mail attachments, is rapidly increasing the macro virus threat.

Common macro viruses include the following:

- Executable files infecting the boot sector: Jerusalem, Cascade, and Form
- Word macros: Concept
- E-mail-enabled Word macros: Melissa
- E-mail-enabled Visual Basic scripts: I Love You

Polymorphic Viruses

Polymorphic viruses are difficult to detect because they hide themselves from antivirus software by altering their appearance after each infection. Some polymorphic viruses can assume over two billion different identities.

There are three main components of a polymorphic virus: a scrambled virus body, a decryption routine, and a mutation engine. The process of a polymorphic infection is as follows:

1. The decryption routine first gains control of the computer, then decrypts both the virus body and the mutation engine.

2. The decryption routine transfers control of the computer to the virus, which locates a new program to infect.
3. The virus makes a copy of itself and the mutation engine in RAM.
4. The virus invokes the mutation engine, which randomly generates a new decryption routine capable of decrypting the virus, yet bearing little or no resemblance to any prior decryption routine.
5. The virus encrypts the new copy of the virus body and mutation engine.
6. The virus appends the new decryption routine, along with the newly encrypted virus and mutation engine, onto a new program.

As a result of this process, the virus body is not only encrypted, but the virus decryption routine also varies from infection to infection. No two infections look alike, confusing the virus scanner searching for the sequence of bytes that identifies a specific decryption routine.

Stealth Viruses

Stealth viruses attempt to hide their presence from both the OS and the antivirus software by doing the following:

- Hiding the change in the file's date and time
- Hiding the increase in the infected file's size
- Encrypting themselves

They are similar to polymorphic viruses in that they are very hard to detect.

Trojan Horses

Trojan horses hide malicious code inside a useful appearing host program. Once these programs are executed, the virus, worm, or other type of malicious code hidden in the Trojan horse program is released to attack the workstation, server, or network, or to allow unauthorized access to those devices. Trojans are common tools used to create backdoors into the network for later exploitation by crackers.

Trojan horses can be carried via Internet traffic, such as FTP downloads or downloadable applets from Web sites, or distributed through e-mail.

Common Trojan horses and ports include the following:

- **Trinoo**—ports 1524, 27444, 27665, 31335
- **BackOrifice**—port 31337
- **NetBus**—port 12345
- **SubSeven**—ports 1080, 1234, 2773

Some Trojans are programmed to open specific ports to allow access for exploitation. If a Trojan is installed on a system, it often opens a high-numbered port. Then the open Trojan port can be scanned and located, enabling an attacker to compromise the system. Malicious scanning is discussed later in this chapter.

Logic Bombs

Logic bombs are malicious code added to an existing application to be executed at a later date. Every time the infected application is run, the logic bomb checks the date to see if it is time to run the bomb. If not, control is passed back to the main application and the logic bomb waits. If the date condition is correct, the rest of the logic bomb's code is executed and it can attack the system.

In addition to using the date, there are numerous ways to trigger logic bombs:

- ✦ Counter triggers
- ✦ Replication triggers that activate after a set number of virus reproductions
- ✦ Disk space triggers
- ✦ Video mode triggers that activate when video is in a set mode or changes from set modes

Worms

Instead of attaching themselves to a single host program and then replicating like viruses, worms attack a network by moving from device to device. Worms are constructed to infiltrate legitimate data processing programs and alter or destroy the data.

Malicious Code Prevention

Malicious code prevention mostly focuses on scanning, prevention, and detection products.

Virus Scanners

Most virus scanners use pattern-matching algorithms that can scan for many different signatures at the same time. These algorithms include scanning capabilities that detect known and unknown worms and Trojan horses.

Most antivirus scanning products search hard disks for viruses, detect and remove any that are found, and include an auto-update feature that enables the program to download profiles of new viruses so that it possesses the profiles necessary for scanning.

Virus Prevention

Virus infection prevention products are used to prevent malicious code from initially infecting the system and to stop the replication process. They either reside in memory and monitor system activity, or filter incoming executable programs and specific file types. When an illegal virus accesses a program or boot sector, the system is halted and the user is prompted to remove the particular type of malicious code.

Virus Detection

Virus detection products are designed to detect a malicious code infection after the infection has occurred. Two types of virus detection products are commonly implemented: *short-term infection detection* and *long-term infection detection*. Short-term infection detection products detect an infection very soon after the infection has occurred. Short-term infection detection products can be implemented through vaccination programs or the snapshot technique.

Long-term infection detection products identify specific malicious code on a system that has already been infected for some time. The two different techniques used by long-term infection detection products are spectral analysis and heuristic analysis. *Spectral analysis* searches for patterns in the code trails that malicious code leaves. *Heuristic analysis* analyzes malicious code to figure out its capability.

System Scanning

No computer system connected to a public network is immune to malicious or indiscriminate scanning. System scanning is a process used to collect information about a device or network to facilitate an attack on the system. It is used by attackers to discover what ports are open, what services are running, and identify system software. Scanning enables an attacker to more easily detect and exploit known vulnerabilities within a target machine.

Instead of being an end in its own right, scanning is often one element of a network attack plan, consisting of the following:

+ **Network reconnaissance** — Through scanning, an intruder can obtain valuable information about the target network, including:
    - Domain names and IP blocks
    - Intrusion detection systems
    - Running services
    - Platforms and protocols

- Firewalls and perimeter devices
- General network infrastructure

✦ **Gaining system access** — Gaining access to a system can be achieved in the following ways:
- Session highjacking
- Password cracking
- Sniffing
- Direct physical access to an uncontrolled machine
- Exploiting default accounts
- Social engineering

✦ **Removing evidence of the attack** — Doing the following can eliminate traces of an attack:
- Editing and clearing security logs
- Compromising the Syslog server
- Replacing system files by using rootkit tools
- Creating legitimate accounts
- Leaving backdoor Trojan viruses, such as SubSeven or NetBus

Scanning should also be used by security administrators to determine any evidence of compromise and to identify vulnerabilities. Since scanning activity is often a prelude to a system attack, detecting malicious scans should be accompanied by monitoring and analyzing the logs and implementing blocking of unused and exposed ports.

Vulnerability Scanning

Vulnerability scanning should be implemented by the security professional to help identify weaknesses in a system. It should be conducted on a regular basis to identify compromised or vulnerable systems. The scans directed at a target system can either be internal, originating from within the system, or external, originating from outside the target system.

Conducting scans inside the enterprise on a regular basis is one way to identify and track several types of potential problems, such as unused ports that respond to network requests. Also, uncontrolled or unauthorized software may be located using these scanning techniques.

A common vulnerability scanning methodology can employ several steps, including an IP device discovery scan, workstation vulnerability scan, and server vulnerability scan.

Discovery Scanning

The intent of a discovery scan is to collect enough information about each network device to identify what type of device it is (workstation, server, router, firewall, and so on), its operating system, and whether it is running any externally vulnerable services, such as Web services, FTP, or e-mail. The discovery scan contains two elements: inventory and classification. The inventory scan provides information about the target system's operating system and its available ports. The classification process identifies applications running on the target system, which aids in determining the device's function.

Workstation Scanning

A full workstation vulnerability scan of the standard corporate desktop configuration should be implemented regularly. This scan helps ensure that the standard software configuration is current with the latest security patches and software, and helps locate uncontrolled or unauthorized software.

Server Scanning

A full server vulnerability scan determines if the server OS has been configured to the corporate standards and helps to ensure that applications are kept current with the latest security patches and software. All services must be inspected for elements that could compromise security, such as default accounts and weak passwords. Unauthorized programs such as Trojans can also be identified.

Port Scanning

Port scanning describes the process of sending a data packet to a port to gather information about the state of the port. This is also called a *probe*. Port scanning makes it possible to find what TCP and UDP ports are in use. For example, if ports 25, 80, and 110 are open, the device is running the SMTP, HTTP, and POP3 services.

A cracker can use port-scanning software to determine which hosts are active and which are inactive (down) to avoid wasting time on inactive hosts. A port scan can gather data about a single host or hosts within a subnet (256 adjacent network addresses).

A scan might first be implemented using the ping utility. After determining which hosts and associated ports are active, the cracker can initiate different types of probes on the active ports.

Examples of probes include the following:

- ✦ Gathering information from the Domain Name System (DNS)
- ✦ Determining the network services that are available, such as e-mail, FTP, and remote logon
- ✦ Determining the type and release of the operating system

TCP/UDP Scanning Types

Many types of TCP/UDP scanning techniques exist. Some are simple and easily detectable by firewalls and intrusion detection systems; some are more complicated and hard to detect.

Stealth Scans

Certain types of scans are called "stealth" scans because they try to evade or minimize their chances of detection. Several of the scans outlined below, such as the TCP SYN or TCP FIN scans, can be described as stealth scans.

Another example of a stealth scan is implemented by fragmenting the IP datagram within the TCP header. This bypasses some packet filtering firewalls because they don't get a complete TCP header to match the filter rules.

Spoofed Scans

While the term *spoofing* comes up often in any security discussion, it can also be applied here to conceal the true identity of an attacker. Spoofing allows an attacker to probe the target's ports without revealing the attacker's own IP address. The FTP proxy bounce attack described below is an example of a spoofed scan that compromises a third-party FTP server.

The HPing network analysis tool hides the source of its scans by using another host through which to probe the target site. Also, NMap provides spoofing capability by enabling the operator to enter an optional "source" address of the scanning packet.

A list of some TCP-based scanning techniques follows.

- **TCP connect()** — Connect() is the most basic scanning technique. It is also the fastest. Connect() is able to scan ports quickly by simply attempting to connect to each port in succession. The biggest disadvantage for attackers is that it is the easiest scanning technique to detect and can be stopped at the firewall.

- **TCP SYN (half-open) scanning** — TCP SYN scanning is often referred to as "half-open" scanning because, unlike TCP connect(), a full TCP connection is never opened. The half-open scan process follows these steps:
    1. The scan sends a SYN packet to a target port.
    2. If a SYN/ACK is received the port is listening.
    3. The scanner then breaks the connection by sending an RST (reset) packet.
    4. If an RST is received the port is closed.

    A half-open scan is harder to trace because fewer sites log incomplete TCP connections, but some packet filtering firewalls look for SYNs to restricted ports.

+ **TCP SYN/ACK scanning** — TCP SYN/ACK is another way to determine if ports are open or closed. The TCP SYN/ACK scan works by doing the following:

    1. The scanner initially sends a SYN/ACK.
    2. If the port is closed, it assumes the SYN/ACK packet was a mistake and sends a RST.
    3. If the port is open, the SYN/ACK packet is ignored and the port will drop the packet.

    TCP SYN/ACK is considered a stealth scan because it isn't likely to be logged by the host being scanned, but many intrusion detection systems may catch it.

+ **TCP FIN scanning** — TCP FIN is a stealth scan that works like the TCP SYN/ACK scan.

    1. The scanner sends a FIN packet to a port.
    2. A closed port replies with a RST.
    3. An open port ignores the FIN packet.

    One issue with this type of scanning is that TCP FIN can only be used to find listening ports on non-Windows machines or identify Windows machines, because Windows ports send a RST regardless of the state of the port.

+ **TCP FTP proxy (bounce attack) scanning** — TCP FTP proxy (bounce attack) scanning is a very "stealthy" scanning technique. It takes advantage of a weakness in proxy FTP connections. It works like this:

    1. The scanner connects to an FTP server and requests that the server initiate a data transfer process to a third system.
    2. The scanner uses the PORT FTP command to declare that the data transfer process is listening on the target box at a certain port number.
    3. It then uses the LIST FTP command to try to list the current directory. The result is sent over the server data transfer process channel.
    4. If the transfer is successful, the target host is listening on the specified port.
    5. If the transfer is unsuccessful, a "425 Can't build data connection: Connection refused" message is sent.

    Some FTP servers disable the proxy feature to prevent TCP FTP proxy scanning.

+ **IP fragments** — Fragmenting IP packets is a variation on the other TCP scanning techniques. Instead of sending a single probe packet, the packet is broken into two or more packets and reassembled at the destination, bypassing the packet filters.

+ **ICMP scanning (ping-sweep)** — Because ICMP doesn't use ports, a ping-sweep is technically not a port scanning technique. However, it should still be mentioned. Using ICMP Echo requests, the scanner can perform what is known as a *ping-sweep*. Scanned hosts will respond with an ICMP Echo reply, indicating that they are alive. No response can mean the target is down or nonexistent.

Determining the OS Type

Determining the type of OS is also an objective of scanning, as it determines the type of attack to be launched.

Sometimes, a target's operating system details can be found simply by examining its TELNET banners or from its File Transfer Protocol (FTP) servers, after connecting to these services.

TCP/IP stack fingerprinting is another technique to identify the particular version of an operating system. Since OS and device vendors implement TCP/IP differently, these differences can help in determining the OS.

Some of these differences include the following:

- Time To Live (TTL)
- Initial Window Size
- Don't Fragment (DF) bit
- Type of Service (TOS)

Table 1.3 shows some common Time To Live values. Remember that the TTL decrements each time the packet passes through a router. This means that the TTL of a router six hops away is 249 (255-6).

Table 1.3
Time To Live (TTL) Values

Time To Live	Operating System or Device Type
255	Many network devices, UNIX and Macintosh systems
128	Many Windows systems
60	Hewlett-Packard Jet Direct printers
32	Some versions of Windows 95B/98

Another type of OS identification technique is TCP initial sequence number sampling. After responding to a connection request, information about the operating system can be inferred from the pattern of the sequence numbers.

Scanning Tools

Although crackers and intruders use many of these tools, they also help the security administrator detect and stop malicious scans. Used with intrusion detection systems, these tools can provide some level of protection by identifying vulnerable systems and can provide data about the level of activity directed against a machine or network. Since scanning is a continuous activity (that is, since all networked systems are being scanned all the time), it's very important that the security professional know what can be compromised. Common scanning tools include the following:

- **Computer Oracle and Password System (COPS)** — Examines a system for a number of known weaknesses and alerts the administrator.
- **HPing** — A network analysis tool that sends packets with non-traditional IP stack parameters. It enables the scanner to gather information from the response packets generated.
- **Legion** — Will scan for and identify shared folders on scanned systems, allowing the scanner to map drives directly.
- **Nessus** — A free security-auditing tool for Linux, BSD, and a few other platforms. It requires a back-end server that must run on a UNIX-like platform.
- **NMap** — A very common port-scanning package. More information on NMap follows this section.
- **Remote Access Perimeter Scanner (RAPS)** — Part of the corporate edition of PCAnywhere by Symantec. RAPS detects most commercial remote control and backdoor packages such as NetBus, and can help lock down PCAnywhere.
- **Security Administrator's Integrated Network Tool (SAINT)** — Examines network services such as finger, NFS, NIS, FTP and TFTP, rexd, statd, and others to report on potential security flaws.
- **System Administrator Tool for Analyzing Networks (SATAN)** — One of the oldest network security analyzers. SATAN scans network systems for well-known and often exploited vulnerabilities.
- **Tcpview** — Allows identification of which application opened a port on Windows platforms.

NMap

NMap scans for most ports from 1–1024 and a number of other ports in the registered and undefined ranges. This helps identify software like PCAnywhere, SubSeven, and BackOrifice. Now that a Windows interface has been written, it no longer has to be run only on a UNIX system.

NMap allows scanning of both TCP and UDP ports, with root privilege required for UDP. Although NMap doesn't have signature or password cracking capabilities, like L0pht Crack, it will estimate how hard it is to highjack an open session.

The following figures demonstrate various output from different types of NMap scans on our test bed network. Figure 1.5 shows the results of an NMap ping-sweep scan, which does a quick IP discovery. Figure 1.6 shows the output of an NMap SYN stealth scan. Figure 1.7 shows the results of an NMap RCP scan.

Figure 1.8 gives the output from a Windows port scan. This scan can be directed to a text file, as it can be very long. The results of this scan are reproduced in Appendix D.

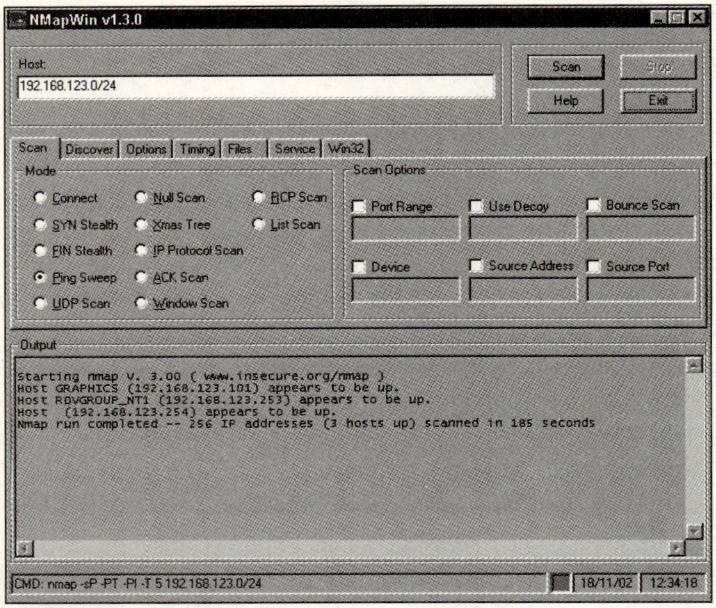

Figure 1.5 NMap ping-sweep scan

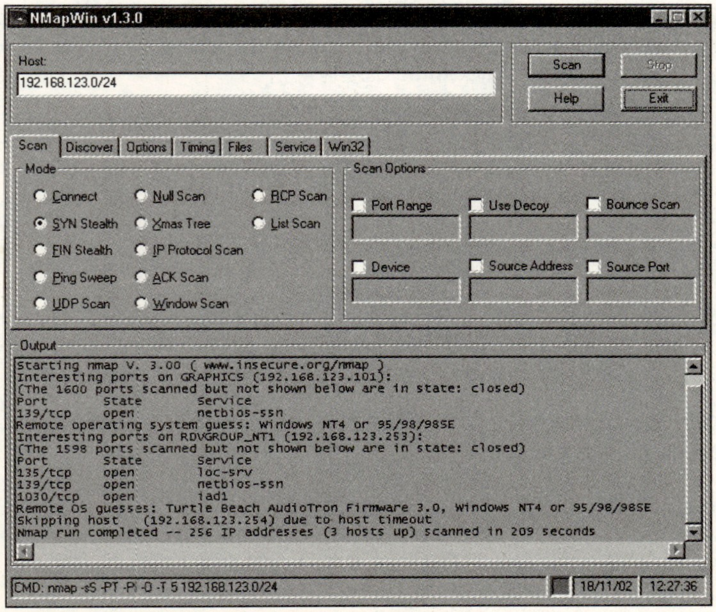

Figure 1.6 NMap SYN stealth scan

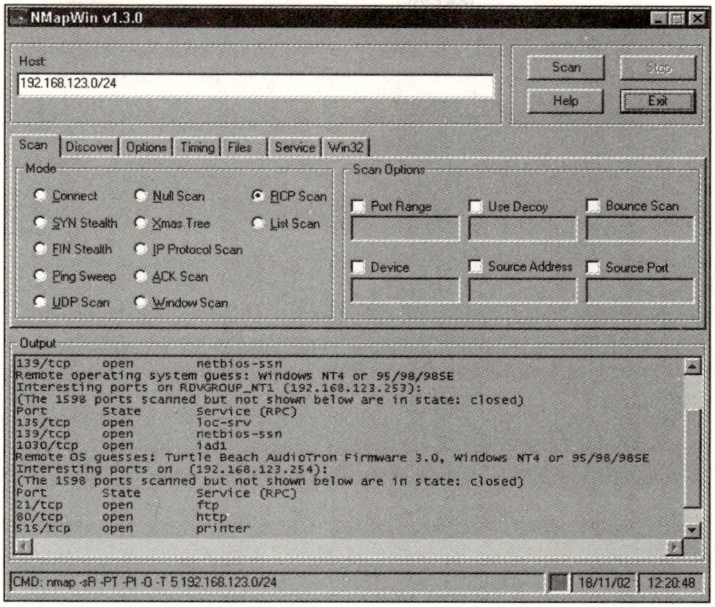

Figure 1.7 NMap RCP scan

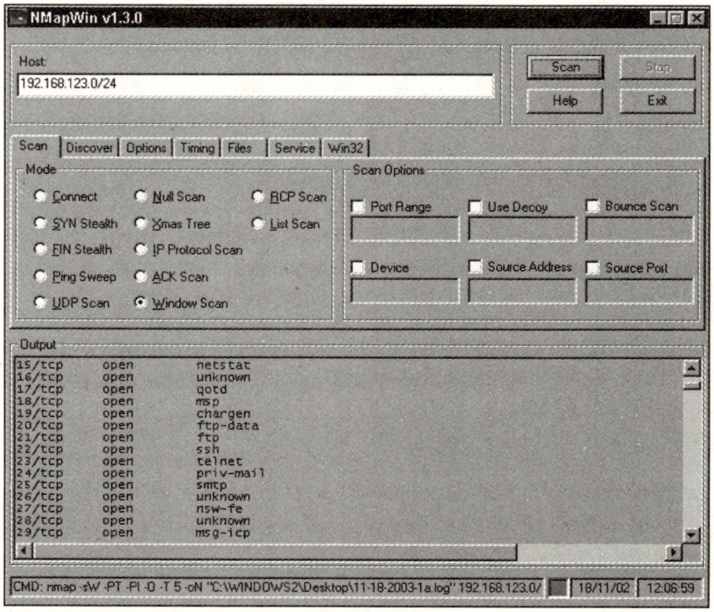

Figure 1.8 NMap Windows port scan

Vulnerable Ports

Although the complete listing of well-known and registered ports is extensive, some ports are attacked more than others. Table 1.4 lists the ports that present the greatest risk to networked systems.

Table 1.4
Commonly Attacked Ports

Port #	Service Name	Service Description
21	FTP	File Transfer Protocol
23	TELNET	TELNET virtual terminal
25,109,110 143	SMTP POP3 IMAP	Simple Mail Protocol, POP2, POP3 and IMAP Messaging
53	DNS	Domain Name Services
80, 8000, 8080	HTTP	Hyper-Text Transfer Protocol and HTTP proxy servers
118	SQLSERV	SQL database service
119	NNTP	Network News Transfer Protocol
161	SNMP	Simple Network Management Protocol
194	IRC	Internet Relay Chat
389,636	IDAP	Lightweight Directory Access Protocol
2049	NFS	Networking File Systems
5631	PCAnywhere	PCAnywhere Remote Control

Issues with Vulnerability Scanning

Some precautions must be taken when the security administrator begins a program of vulnerability scanning in his own network. Some of the issues could cause a system crash or create unreliable scan data.

- **False positives**—Some legitimate software uses port numbers registered to other software, which can cause false alarms when port scanning. This may block legitimate software, which appears to be intrusions.

- **Heavy traffic**—Port scanning can adversely affect WAN links and even effectively disable slow links. Because heavy port scanning generates a lot of traffic, it is usually preferable to perform the scanning outside normal business hours.

- **False negatives**—Port scanning can sometimes exhaust resources on the scanning machine, creating false negatives and resulting in improper identification of vulnerabilities.
- **System crash**—Port scanning has been known to render needed services inoperable or actually crash systems. This can happen when systems have not been currently patched or the scanning process exhausts the targeted system's resources.
- **Unregistered port numbers**—Many port numbers in use are not registered, which complicates the act of identifying what software is using them.

✦ ✦ ✦

SAMPLE QUESTIONS

1. Kerberos sets up secure communications between clients and other network resources through which of the following?

    a. Passwords

    b. Tokens

    c. Public keys

    d. Session keys

2. Access control must consider which of the following?

    a. Vulnerabilities, biometrics, and exposures

    b. Threats, assets, and safeguards

    c. Exposures, threats, and countermeasures

    d. Threats, vulnerabilities, and risks

3. Single sign-on (SSO) can be implemented by which of the following?

    a. Kerberos

    b. IDEA

    c. Hash functions

    d. RSA

4. Which choice is a scanning technique that uses ICMP?

    a. Ping-sweep

    b. FTP proxy bounce attack

    c. TCP FIN scan

    d. TCP half-open scan

5. Authentication using biometrics is which of the following?

    a. The Crossover Error Rate (CER)

    b. A "one-to-many" search of an individual's characteristics from a database

    c. A "one-to-one" search to verify an individual's claim to an identity

    d. Aggregation

6. Preventing the modification of information by unauthorized users, preventing the unauthorized or unintentional modification of information by authorized users, and preserving internal and external consistency are goals of what?

   a. Authentication

   b. Integrity

   c. Authorization

   d. Availability

7. The boundary where security controls are in effect to protect assets is called what?

   a. A security perimeter

   b. An enforced path

   c. A trusted computing base

   d. A trusted perimeter

8. Which of the following statements best describes a worm?

   a. Worms move from device to device.

   b. Worms create common network backdoors.

   c. Worms are programmed to execute on a particular date.

   d. Worms alter their appearance after infection.

9. Which of the following is an important control that should be in place for external connections to a network that uses Callback schemes?

   a. Breaking of a dial-up connection at the remote user's side of the line

   b. Call forwarding

   c. Call enhancement

   d. Breaking of a dial-up connection at the organization's computing resource side of the line

10. What is a protection domain?

    a. A group of processes that share access to the same resources

    b. A list denoting which users possess what privileges to a particular resource

    c. A database view

    d. A Trusted Computing Base (TCB)

11. What part of an access control matrix shows one user's capabilities in relation to multiple resources?

   a. Columns

   b. Rows

   c. Rows and columns

   d. Access control list

12. In biometrics, which of the following describes the activity of collecting images and extracting features from the image?

   a. Authentication

   b. Throughput

   c. Enrollment

   d. Identification

13. Content-dependent access control is defined as what?

   a. Access control that is based on positive access rights

   b. Access control that is a function of information contained in the item being accessed

   c. Access control that is a function of such factors as location, time of day, and previous access history

   d. Access control that is a function of the role of the subject

14. In a Kerberos exchange involving a message with an authenticator, the authenticator contains the client ID and which of the following?

   a. Ticket Granting Ticket (TGT)

   b. Timestamp

   c. Client/TGS session key

   d. Client network address

15. Which of the following security areas is directly addressed by Kerberos?

   a. Confidentiality

   b. Frequency analysis

   c. Availability

   d. Physical attacks

16. Access control in which the access rights to an object are assigned by the object's owner is called what?

   a. Mandatory

   b. Role-based

   c. Discretionary

   d. Rule-based

17. What is the BEST reason for the security administrator to initiate internal vulnerability scanning?

   a. Vulnerability scanning can replicate a system crash.

   b. Vulnerability scanning can identify exposed ports.

   c. Vulnerability scanning can return false positives.

   d. Vulnerability scanning can return false negatives.

18. A *reference monitor* is a system component that enforces access controls on an object. Specifically, the *reference monitor concept* is an abstract machine that mediates all access of subjects to objects. What do you call the hardware, firmware, and software elements of a Trusted Computing Base that implement the reference monitor concept?

   a. The authorization database

   b. Identification and authentication (I & A) mechanisms

   c. The auditing subsystem

   d. The security kernel

19. What is a passphrase?

   a. A password that changes with each logon

   b. A password that remains the same for each logon

   c. A long word or group of words that is converted by the authentication system to a password

   d. A long word or group of words that is used for identification

20. Which choice is NOT a property of a polymorphic virus?

   a. The polymorphic virus decryption routine varies from infection to infection.

   b. Polymorphic viruses execute when an Excel or Word application is started.

   c. Polymorphic viruses alter their appearance to evade detection.

   d. Polymorphic viruses contain an encrypted virus body, a decryption routine, and a mutation engine.

21. Which of the following is NOT a function of the frequency of use of a password and the criticality of the information it is protecting?

    a. The randomness of the password characters

    b. The password's length

    c. The frequency at which the password is changed

    d. The composition of the user's ID

22. Call forwarding is an attack that can be used against which one the following?

    a. Callback

    b. Challenge Handshake Authentication Protocol

    c. RADIUS

    d. Internet Service Providers (ISPs)

23. An attack in which a cracker intercepts messages and then forwards them to the intended receiver without the receiver's knowledge is called _____:

    a. Meet-in-the-middle

    b. Man-in-the-middle

    c. Dual messaging

    d. Call forwarding

24. Which property is useful in determining the scanning target's operating system?

    a. BackOrifice

    b. RAPS

    c. Trinoo

    d. TTL

25. The type of access control that is used in local, dynamic situations where subjects can specify what resources certain users can access is called _____:

    a. Mandatory access control

    b. Rule-based access control

    c. Sensitivity-based access control

    d. Discretionary access control

26. Kerberos provides an integrity check service for messages between two entities through the use of what?

   a. A checksum

   b. Credentials

   c. Tickets

   d. A trusted, third-party authentication server

27. Access control that is based on an individual's duties or title in an organization is known as _____:

   a. Rule-based access control

   b. Discretionary access control

   c. Role-based access control

   d. Mandatory access control

28. The * (Star) property of the Bell LaPadula model states what?

   a. Reading of information by a subject at a lower sensitivity level from an object at a higher sensitivity level is not permitted (no read up).

   b. Writing of information by a subject at a higher level of sensitivity to an object at a lower level of sensitivity is not permitted (no write down).

   c. An access matrix is used to specify discretionary access control.

   d. Reading or writing is permitted at a particular level of sensitivity, but not to either higher or lower levels of sensitivity.

29. An ATM card and a PIN are an example of what?

   a. Multi-factor identification

   b. Single-factor authentication

   c. Two-factor authentication

   d. Single-factor identification

30. Which statement describes a property of a logic bomb?

   a. Logic bombs replicate from device to device.

   b. Logic bombs alter their appearance to evade detection.

   c. Logic bombs do not activate until a preset trigger is reached.

   d. Logic bombs leave a backdoor Trojan, like NetBus.

Communication Security

Communication security describes the security concepts, protocols, and methods required to assure the confidentiality, integrity, and availability of transmitted sensitive data, either through a company local area network (LAN), intranet, or the Internet. This chapter examines the following communication security concepts:

- Remote access and virtual private networks (VPNs)
- E-mail security
- Web security issues
- Directory and certificate authority (CA) recognition
- File Transfer Protocols
- Wireless networking security

Remote Access

Remote access to internetworks requires a host of protocols, standards, and concepts to help ensure the data is protected. The most common communication security methods are as follows:

- Virtual private networks (VPNs)
- Remote access protocols
- RADIUS
- TACACS

Virtual Private Networking

A *virtual private network (VPN)* is created by building a secure communications link between two nodes by emulating the properties of a point-to-point private link. A VPN can be used to facilitate secure remote access into a network, securely connect two networks together, or create a secure data tunnel within a network.

The portion of the link in which the private data is encapsulated is known as the *tunnel*. It may be referred to as a secure, encrypted tunnel, although it's more accurately defined as an *encapsulated* tunnel because encryption may or may not be used. To emulate a point-to-point link, data is encapsulated, or wrapped, with a header that provides routing information. Most often, the data is encrypted for confidentiality. This encrypted part of the link is considered the actual virtual private network connection. Figure 2.1 shows a common VPN configuration for remote access into a company intranet through the Internet.

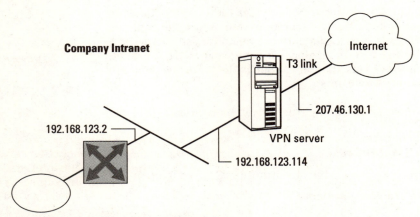

Figure 2.1 A common VPN configuration

VPN Examples

Common VPN configurations include the following:

- Remote access VPNs
- Network-to-network VPNs
- Intranet access VPNs

Remote Access VPNs

A VPN can be configured to provide remote access to corporate resources over the public Internet to maintain confidentiality and integrity. This configuration enables the remote user to utilize whatever local Internet Service Provider (ISP) is available to access the Internet, without forcing the user to make a long distance or 800 call to a third-party access provider. Using the connection to the local ISP, the VPN software creates a virtual private network between the dial-up user and the corporate VPN server across the Internet. Figure 2.2 shows a remote user VPN connection.

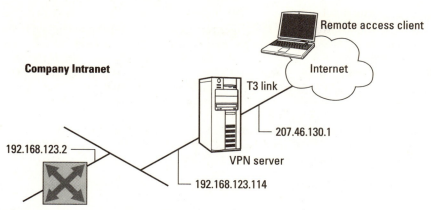

Figure 2.2 A remote access VPN

Network-to-Network VPNs

A VPN is commonly used to connect two networks (perhaps the main corporate LAN and a remote branch office LAN) through the Internet. This connection can either use dedicated lines to the Internet or dial-up connections to the Internet; however, the corporate hub router that acts as a VPN server must be connected to a local ISP with a dedicated line if the VPN server needs to be continuously available. The VPN software uses the connection to the local ISP to create a VPN tunnel between the branch office router and the corporate hub router across the Internet. Figure 2.3 shows a remote branch office connected to the corporate main office using a VPN tunnel through the Internet.

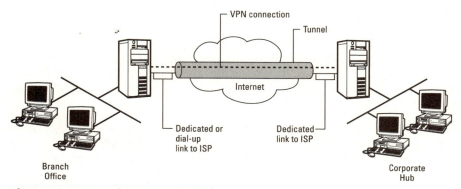

Figure 2.3 A network-to-network VPN

Intranet Access VPNs

If remote users need to access sensitive data on a LAN that is physically disconnected from the rest of the corporate network, a VPN may provide the solution. A VPN allows the LAN with the sensitive data to be physically connected to the corporate internetwork but separated by a VPN server, as shown in Figure 2.4. This ensures that only authorized users on the corporate network can establish a connection with the VPN server and thereby gain access to the sensitive data.

In this case, the VPN server is not acting as a router between the corporate internetwork and the department LAN because a router would connect the two networks, allowing everyone access to the sensitive LAN.

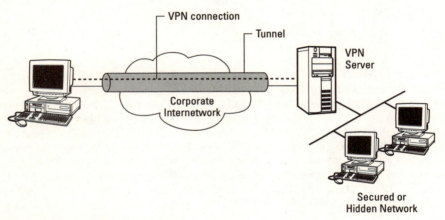

Figure 2.4 An intranet access VPN

VPN Tunneling

Tunneling is a method of transferring data from one network to another by encapsulating the packets in an additional header. The additional header provides routing information so that the encapsulated payload can traverse the intermediate networks, as shown in Figure 2.5.

Before a tunnel can be established, both the tunnel client and the tunnel server must be using the same tunneling protocol. Tunneling technology can be based on either a Layer 2 or a Layer 3 tunneling protocol. These layers correspond to the Open Systems Interconnection (OSI) reference model.

Tunneling, and the use of a VPN, is not intended as a substitute for encryption/decryption. In cases where a high level of security is necessary, the strongest possible encryption should be used within the VPN itself, and tunneling should serve only as a convenience.

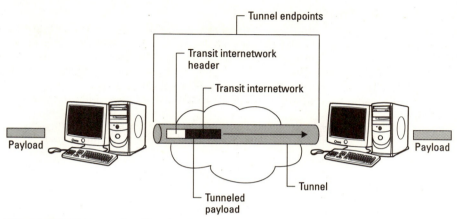

Figure 2.5 VPN tunnel and payload

VPN and Remote Access Protocols

Both the Point-to-Point Tunneling Protocol (PPTP) and the Layer Two Tunneling Protocol (L2TP) are Layer 2 tunneling protocols that use Data Link layer formatting and encapsulate the payload in a Point-to-Point Protocol (PPP) frame (see the remote access protocols later in this chapter). Layer 3 protocols correspond to the Network layer and use packets. IPSec tunnel mode is an example of a Layer 3 tunneling protocol that encapsulates IP packets in an additional IP header.

Refer to Chapter 3 for more information on IPSec tunnel mode.

Layer 3 tunneling technologies generally assume that all the configuration issues are preconfigured, often by manual processes. These protocols may have no tunnel maintenance phase. For Layer 2 protocols, however, a tunnel must be created, maintained, and then terminated.

Point-to-Point Tunneling Protocol

Point-to-Point Tunneling Protocol (PPTP) works at the Data Link layer of the OSI model. It is designed for individual client-to-server connections, as it allows only a single point-to-point connection per session. PPTP is commonly used by Windows clients for asynchronous communications. PPTP uses the native PPP authentication and encryption services.

PPTP allows IP, IPX, or NetBEUI traffic to be encrypted and then encapsulated in an IP header to be sent across a corporate IP internetwork or a public IP internetwork such as the Internet. PPTP uses a TCP connection for tunnel maintenance and a modified version of Generic Routing Encapsulation (GRE) to encapsulate PPP frames for tunneled data. Encapsulated PPP frame payloads can be encrypted and/or compressed.

Layer 2 Tunneling Protocol

Layer 2 Tunneling Protocol (L2TP) is a combination of PPTP and the earlier Layer 2 Forwarding Protocol (L2F) and also works at the Data Link layer. L2TP is an accepted tunneling standard for VPNs, and dial-up VPNs use this standard frequently. Like PPTP, it was designed for single point-to-point, client-to-server connections. Like PPTP, L2TP allows IP, IPX, or NetBEUI traffic to be encrypted, and then sent over any medium that supports point-to-point datagram delivery, such as the following:

- ✦ IP
- ✦ X.25
- ✦ Frame Relay
- ✦ ATM

L2TP supports TACACS+ and RADIUS, but PPTP does not.

L2TP over IP networks uses UDP and a series of L2TP messages for tunnel maintenance. L2TP also uses UDP to send L2TP-encapsulated PPP frames as the tunneled data. Encapsulated PPP frame payloads can be encrypted and/or compressed.

Internet Protocol Security

Internet Protocol Security (IPSec) operates at the Network layer and allows multiple simultaneous tunnels. IPSec contains the functionality to encrypt and authenticate IP data. While PPTP and L2TP are aimed more at dial-up VPNs, IPSec also encompasses network-to-network connectivity.

IPSec operates at the Network layer and enables multiple and simultaneous tunnels, but it is not multiprotocol. IPSec has the functionality to encrypt and authenticate IP data. It is built into the new IPv6 standard, and is used as an add-on to the current IPv4. IPSec tunnel mode enables IP packets to be encrypted, and then encapsulated in an IP header to be sent across a corporate IP internetwork or a public IP internetwork such as the Internet.

IPSec uses an authentication header (AH) to provide source authentication and integrity without encryption, and the Encapsulating Security Payload (ESP) to provide authentication and integrity along with encryption. With IPSec, only the sender and recipient know the key. If the authentication data is valid, the recipient knows that the communication came from the sender and that it was not changed in transit.

Serial Line Internet Protocol

Serial Line Internet Protocol (SLIP) is a TCP/IP protocol and early de facto standard for asynchronous dial-up communication. An ISP can provide a SLIP connection for Internet access.

Note   PPP is now preferred over SLIP because it can handle synchronous as well as asynchronous communication. PPP can share a line with other users and it has error detection that SLIP lacks.

Point-to-Point Protocol

The Point-to-Point Protocol (PPP) defines an encapsulation method to transmit multiprotocol packets over Layer 2 point-to-point links, such as a serial interface. PPP is a full-duplex protocol that can be used on various physical media, including twisted pair or fiber optic lines or satellite transmission. It uses a variation of High Speed Data Link Control (HDLC) for packet encapsulation.

A user can connect to a network access server (NAS) through integrated services digital network (ISDN), asymmetric digital subscriber line (ADSL), dial-up, or other remote access service, and runs PPP over that connection. Most PPP implementations provide limited authentication methods, including:

- Password Authentication Protocol (PAP)
- Challenge Handshake Authentication Protocol (CHAP)
- Microsoft Challenge Handshake Authentication Protocol (MS-CHAP)

Password Authentication Protocol

The Password Authentication Protocol (PAP) is a basic cleartext authentication scheme. The NAS requests the user name and password, and PAP returns them in cleartext, unencrypted. PAP user authentication is often used on the Internet, which simply sends a user name and password to a server, where they are compared with a database of authorized users. Although the user database may be kept in encrypted form, each ID and password is sent unencrypted.

This authentication scheme is not secure because a third party could capture the user's name and password and use it to get subsequent access to the NAS and all of the resources the NAS provides. PAP provides no protection against replay attacks or remote client impersonation once the user's password is compromised. A better variation on this method is the Challenge Handshake Authentication Protocol (CHAP).

Challenge Handshake Authentication Protocol

Challenge Handshake Authentication Protocol (CHAP) is an encrypted authentication mechanism that avoids transmission of the actual password across the connection. The NAS sends a challenge, which consists of a session ID and an arbitrary challenge string, to the remote client. The remote client must use the MD5 one-way hashing algorithm to return the user name and an encryption of the challenge, session ID, and the client's password. The user name is sent unhashed.

CHAP is an improvement over PAP because the cleartext password is not sent over the link. Instead, the password is used to create an encrypted hash from the original challenge. The server knows the client's cleartext password and can replicate the operation and compare the result to the password sent in the client's response. CHAP protects against replay attacks by using an arbitrary challenge string for each authentication attempt. CHAP protects against remote client impersonation by unpredictably sending repeated challenges to the remote client throughout the duration of the connection.

During the CHAP process, a three-way handshake occurs.

1. A link is established, and the server agent sends a message to the machine originating the link.
2. This machine then computes a hash function from the challenge and sends it to the server.
3. The server determines if this is the expected response and if so, authenticates the connection.

At any time, the server can request that the connected party send a new challenge message. Because CHAP identifiers are changed frequently and because the server can request authentication at any time, CHAP provides more security than PAP. Both CHAP and PAP are defined in RFC 1334.

MS-CHAP

Microsoft Challenge Handshake Authentication Protocol (MS-CHAP) is an encrypted authentication mechanism similar to CHAP. As in CHAP, the NAS sends a challenge, which consists of a session ID and an arbitrary challenge string, to the remote client. The remote client must return the user name and an encrypted form of the challenge string, the session ID, and the MD4-hashed password. This design, which uses a hash of the MD4 hash of the password, provides an additional level of security because it enables the server to store hashed passwords instead of cleartext passwords.

MS-CHAP also provides additional error codes, including a password-expired code, and additional encrypted client-server messages that permit users to change their passwords. In MS-CHAP, both the access client and the NAS independently generate an initial key for subsequent data encryption by using the Microsoft Point-to-Point Encryption protocol (MPPE). MS-CHAP authentication is required to enable MPPE-based data encryption.

MS-CHAP version 2

MS-CHAP version 2 (MS-CHAP v2) is an updated encrypted authentication mechanism that provides stronger security. The NAS sends a challenge to the access client that consists of a session identifier and an arbitrary challenge string. The remote access client sends a response that contains the following:

- The user name
- An arbitrary peer challenge string
- An encrypted form of the received challenge string
- The peer challenge string
- The session identifier
- The user's password

The NAS checks the response from the client and sends back a response that indicates the success or failure of the connection attempt and an authenticated response based on the sent challenge string, the peer challenge string, the client's encrypted response, and the user's password. The remote access client verifies the authentication response and, if correct, uses the connection. If the authentication response is not correct, the remote access client terminates the connection.

Using this process, MS-CHAP v2 provides mutual authentication: the NAS verifies that the access client has knowledge of the user's password, and the access client verifies that the NAS has knowledge of the user's password. MS-CHAP v2 also determines two encryption keys, one for data sent and one for data received.

Extensible Authentication Protocol

Because most implementations of PPP provide very limited authentication methods, the Extensible Authentication Protocol (EAP) was designed to allow the dynamic addition of authentication plug-in modules at both the client and server ends of a connection.

EAP is an extension to PPP that allows for arbitrary authentication mechanisms for the validation of a PPP connection. This allows vendors to supply a new authentication scheme at any time, providing the highest flexibility in authentication uniqueness and variation. EAP is supported in Microsoft Windows 2000 and defined in RFC 2284.

EAP Transport Level Security

EAP Transport Level Security (EAP-TLS) is an IETF standard (RFC 2716) for a strong authentication method based on public key certificates. With EAP-TLS, a client presents a user certificate to the dial-in server, and the server presents a server certificate to the client. The client provides strong user authentication to the server, and the server provides assurance that the user has reached the server that he or she expected. Both systems rely on a chain of trusted authorities to verify the validity of the offered certificate.

EAP-TLS is the specific EAP method implemented in Microsoft Windows 2000. Like MS-CHAP and MS-CHAP v2, EAP-TLS returns an encryption key to enable subsequent data encryption by MPPE.

Wireless VPNs

Wireless LANs can especially benefit from a VPN. A VPN can act as a gateway between the WLAN and the network, and can supplement the WEP's authentication and encryption functions. All traffic between the wired and wireless network should travel through the VPN tunnel and be encrypted with the IPSec protocol. IPSec thwarts sniffer attacks launched using applications such as AirSnort.

When a VPN client needs to access the network, it connects to a VPN server and the server authenticates the client. Once authenticated, the VPN server provides the client with an IP address and an encryption key. All communications will be carried out through this IP address. Every packet that passes through this secure tunnel between the client and server will be encrypted.

Consequently, an attacker cannot simply highjack an IP address to gain access, because he or she will not possess the encryption key. The VPN server will simply reject all connections from the attacker.

Guidelines for wireless VPN implementation include the following:

✦ Use VPN clients on wireless devices to enforce strong encryption and require positive authentication via hardware tokens.

✦ For wireless applications within the company, use a wireless VPN solution that supports a Federal Information Processing Standards (FIPS)-approved data encryption algorithm to ensure data confidentiality in a WLAN environment.

✦ Ensure that each endpoint of the VPN remains under company control. When possible, install WLAN network access points and wireless VPN gateways behind network perimeter security mechanisms (firewall, IDS, and so on) so that wireless access to the internal wired network can be controlled and monitored.

RADIUS and TACACS

As the demand for large remote access networks has increased, remote access authentication systems have emerged to provide better network access security for remote clients. The two most common remote access authentication systems are *Remote Authentication Dial-In User Server (RADIUS)* and *Terminal Access Controller Access Control System+ (TACACS+)*, which is TACACS with additional features, including the use of two-factor authentication.

TACACS and RADIUS are "standards-based," which means that they are interoperable with other systems of the same type. Some of these systems provide a centralized database that maintains user lists, passwords, and user profiles that remote access equipment on a network can access to authenticate clients.

Remote Authentication Dial-in User Service

The Remote Authentication Dial-in User Service (RADIUS) protocol is a lightweight, UDP-based protocol used for managing remote user authentication and authorization. It is a fully open protocol, is distributed in source code format, and can be modified to work with any security system that is currently available on the market.

RADIUS is a distributed client/server system wherein the clients send their authentication requests to a central RADIUS server that contains all of the user authentication and network service access information (network ACLs). RADIUS servers can be located anywhere on the network and provide authentication and authorization for network access servers and VPNs.

RADIUS can be used with TACACS+ and Kerberos to provide CHAP remote node authentication. It provides user authentication (including the use of dynamic passwords) and password management similar to that of a TACACS+-enabled system.

Because RADIUS does not support all protocols, it is often used as a stepping-stone to a more robust TACACS+ system. RADIUS does not provide two-way authentication and is not commonly used for router-to-router authentication. Figure 2.6 shows a RADIUS server performing authentication within a company intranet for VPN and remote access server (RAS) clients.

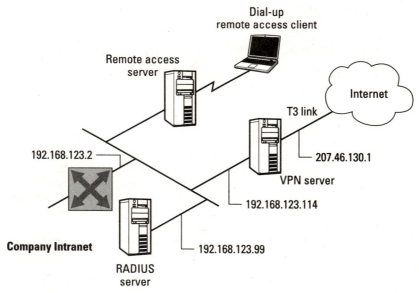

Figure 2.6 A RADIUS VPN

Wireless RADIUS

Several 802.11 access points offer RADIUS authentication, which gives wireless clients access to network resources after supplying a user name and password to a RADIUS server. Such user-based authentication provides a centrally managed method of verifying users who attempt to access the wireless network. Most RADIUS servers can handle this VPN client authentication functionality.

Some RADIUS implementations also allow the user to be authenticated via a digital key system and restrict access to preauthorized areas by user. For example, Cisco's RADIUS server makes it possible to establish access by time and date.

Terminal Access Controller Access Control System

TACACS is an authentication protocol that provides remote access authentication and related services, such as event logging. In a TACACS system, user passwords are administered in a central database rather than in individual routers, which provides an easily scalable network security solution. A TACACS-enabled network device prompts the remote user for a user name and static password; then, the TACACS-enabled device queries a TACACS server to verify that password. TACACS does not support prompting for a password change or for the use of dynamic password tokens.

TACACS+ superseded TACACS. TACACS+ provides the following additional features:

- The use of two-factor password authentication
- The user's ability to change his or her password
- The capability for resynchronizing security tokens
- Better audit trails and session accounting

E-mail

E-mail is the primary means of virus and malicious code distribution. It is also one of the main ways that Trojan horses and other executable code are distributed. The virus danger from e-mail stems from attachments containing active executable program files with extensions such as CLASS, OCX, EXE, COM, and DLL, and from macro-enabled data files. These attachments do not even need to be opened, because many mail clients automatically display all attachments. These attachments could contain malicious code that could be masquerading as another file type. Virus detection and removal is — and will continue to be — a major industry.

E-mail Protocols

The following are the three main ways of exchanging e-mail over the Internet:

- Simple Mail Transfer Protocol (SMTP)
- Post Office Protocol 3 (POP3)
- Internet Message Access Protocol (IMAP)

Simple Mail Transfer Protocol

Simple Mail Transfer Protocol (SMTP) is a TCP/IP protocol used in sending and receiving e-mail. SMTP typically sends e-mail, and either POP3 or IMAP receives e-mail. On UNIX-based systems, sendmail is the most widely used SMTP server for e-mail. SMTP is usually implemented to operate over Transmission Control Protocol port 25.

Post Office Protocol 3

Post Office Protocol 3 (POP3) is the most recent version of a standard protocol for receiving e-mail. POP3 is a client/server protocol in which e-mail is received and held by the server. The user or client e-mail receiver checks the mailbox on the server and downloads any mail. Think of POP as a "store-and-forward" service. The conventional port number for POP3 is 110.

IMAP

An alternative protocol to POP3 is Internet Message Access Protocol (IMAP). With IMAP, the e-mail is viewed at the server as though it was on the user's computer. IMAP (the latest version is IMAP4) is a client/server protocol in which e-mail is received and held on the Internet server. The user's e-mail client can view just the heading and the source of the e-mail or download the mail. IMAP requires continual access to the server during the e-mail session. Think of IMAP as a remote file server.

Spam and Hoaxes

Internet users are constantly being flooded with computer virus hoaxes and unwanted commercial advertisements. Virus hoaxes are false reports about nonexistent viruses, often claiming to do impossible things. While these hoaxes do not infect systems, they are still time-consuming and costly to handle. Spam is electronic "junk mail," often sent from a spoofed address, which constitutes a major expense and annoyance for companies to filter and remove.

Corporations usually spend much more time handling virus hoaxes than real virus incidents. Furthermore, it is estimated that virus hoaxes cost more than genuine virus incidents. No antivirus product will detect hoaxes because they are not viruses, and users may panic when they receive a hoax virus.

S/MIME

Although S/MIME and PGP both offer privacy and authentication services for e-mail, they are quite different. Secure Multipurpose Internet Mail Extensions (S/MIME) is a specification that adds secure services to e-mail in a MIME format. S/MIME provides authentication through digital signatures and the confidentiality of encryption. S/MIME follows the Public Key Cryptography Standards (PKCS) and uses the X.509 standard for its digital certificates.

The S/MIME specification consists of two documents: S/MIME Message Specification and S/MIME Certificate Handling. Both of these are Internet drafts. The S/MIME community has submitted them to the IETF. The goal is to form a working group and produce an Internet standard.

S/MIME uses a hybrid approach to providing security, often referred to as a *digital envelope*. The bulk message encryption is done with a symmetric cipher, and a public key algorithm is used for key exchange. A public key algorithm is also used for digital signatures.

S/MIME recommends three symmetric encryption algorithms:

- DES
- Triple-DES
- RC2

The adjustable key size of the RC2 algorithm makes it especially useful for applications intended for export outside the U.S. RSA is the required public key algorithm.

PGP

To bring e-mail security to the "masses," Phil Zimmerman developed the Pretty Good Privacy (PGP) software (Zimmerman, Philip R., *The Official PGP User's Guide*, Cambridge, MA: MIT Press, 1995). Zimmerman derived the PGP name from Ralph's Pretty Good Groceries, which sponsored Garrison Keillor's *Prairie Home Companion* radio show. In PGP, the symmetric cipher IDEA is used to encipher the message, and RSA is used for symmetric key exchange and for digital signatures.

Instead of using a CA, PGP uses a "web of trust." Users can certify each other in a mesh model. PGP relies on users to exchange keys and establish trust in each other. This informal "web of trust" works well for small workgroups, but can become unmanageable for large numbers of users.

Since S/MIME utilizes hierarchies in which the roles of the user and the certifier are formalized, S/MIME is both more secure and more scalable than PGP implementations. S/MIME has flexible guidelines for establishing hierarchies of users and is scalable from small groups to large enterprises. S/MIME is also well integrated into many e-mail applications, making it simple for users and ubiquitous.

Web

With the transformation of the Internet from a network used primarily by universities and research laboratories to a worldwide communications medium, attacks on the World Wide Web and Internet can produce serious consequences. These attacks can involve nuisance attacks, criminal exploits and, in information warfare, incapacitation of a nation's critical infrastructure. There is a need for protecting nodes on the Internet and for providing the confidentiality, integrity, and authentication of information utilizing these networks. Some of the important mechanisms for providing these protections are discussed in this section.

SSL/TLS

The Secure Sockets Layer (SSL) Protocol was developed by Netscape in 1994 to protect the confidentiality of information transmitted between two applications, to verify the integrity of the communications, and to provide an authentication means in both directions. SSL implements these functions using public and private key encryption and a message authentication code (MAC).

A newer version of SSL called *Transport Layer Security (TLS)* has been developed by Microsoft. As with SSL, TLS implements confidentiality, authentication, and integrity above the Transport layer and is application-independent. Because SSL and TLS ride on the Transport layer protocol, they are independent of the application. SSL and TLS can be used with applications such as TELNET, FTP, HTTP, and e-mail protocols.

Both SSL and TLS use certificates for public key verification that are based on the X.509 standard.

SSL 3.0

The design goals of SSL 3.0 were to provide the following:

- **Cryptographic security** — Protection of the confidentiality of transmitted messages.
- **Interoperability** — The ability to develop applications without knowing each other's code.
- **Extensibility** — The ability to incorporate different encryption algorithms into SSL 3.0 without major changes to SSL 3.0.
- **Relative efficiency** — Efficient utilization of computing and network resources.

Session keys generated during SSL private key cryptography transactions are either 40 bits or 128 bits in length. Newer browsers support 128-bit encryption.

The SSL Protocol comprises two layers: the SSL Record Protocol and the SSL Handshake Protocol. The SSL Record Protocol is layered above a transport protocol, such as TCP. This Record Protocol is used for encapsulation of higher-level protocols, such as the SSL Handshake Protocol. The latter protocol is used for client/server mutual authentication, negotiation of a cryptographic algorithm, and exchange of cryptographic keys.

Through these mechanisms, SSL provides the following:

- Mutual authentication using pubic key cryptography based on algorithms such as the Digital Signature Standard (DSS) and RSA
- Encryption of messages using private key cryptography based on algorithms such as IDEA, 3DES, and RC4
- Integrity verification of the message using a keyed MAC based on hash functions such as MD5 and SHA

One example of a secure exchange of information between a client and a server using SSL is given as follows:

1. The client sends [Client name,C; Transaction Serial #, C#; and Nonce, Nc] to the server.
2. The server sends [Server name,S; Transaction Serial #, S#; Nonce, Ns; and the server's certificate, Cs, containing the server's public key, Ks] to the client.
3. The client verifies that the certificate, Cs, is valid by checking it against a root certificate issued by a trusted CA.
4. The client sends [pre-master secret key, Km, encrypted with server's public key, Ks] to the server.
5. The client sends [finished message with keyed message authentication code (MAC) generated from all messages sent to date] to the server. The MAC key is the *master secret key, Kmac,* generated by hashing the pre-master secret key, Km, with the client and server nonces, [Kmac = H (Km, Nc, Ns)].
6. The server sends [finished message with keyed message authentication code (MAC) generated from all messages sent to date] to the client.
7. Encrypted messages are now sent between the server and client using master secret keys successively generated by hashing the pre-master secret key with new nonces.

TLS 1.0

Similar to SSL, the TLS Protocol comprises the TLS Record and Handshake Protocols. The TLS Record Protocol is layered on top of a transport protocol, such as TCP, and provides privacy and reliability to the communications. The privacy is implemented by encryption using symmetric key cryptography such as DES or RC4. The secret key is generated anew for each connection; however, the Record Protocol can be used without encryption. Integrity is provided through the use of a keyed MAC using hash algorithms such as SHA or MD5.

The TLS Record Protocol is also used to encapsulate a higher-level protocol such as the TLS Handshake Protocol. The server and client use this Handshake Protocol to authenticate each other. The authentication can be accomplished using asymmetric key cryptography such as RSA or DSS. The Handshake Protocol also sets up the encryption algorithm and cryptographic keys to enable the application protocol to transmit and receive information.

Because TLS is based on SSL, they have similar functionality and goals; however, SSL and TLS have enough differences that they cannot interoperate. To address this situation, TLS has a built-in mechanism that can be used to make TLS compatible with SSL 3.0.

HTTP/S

Web pages using the SSL Protocol start with HTTPs, denoting the Hypertext Transfer Protocol with SSL.

S-HTTP

Secure HTTP (S-HTTP) is a communications protocol designed to provide secure messaging over HTTP. S-HTTP provides equal and symmetric capabilities to both client and server, but one entity that is S-HTTP-enabled can communicate with another entity that is not S-HTTP capable. In that instance, the security features would not be operable. S-HTTP implements secure, end-to-end transactions.

S-HTTP supports a symmetric key encryption–only mode and does not require public key encryption for key exchanges. It is flexible, however, and permits the clients and servers to use different forms of transactions related to the signing of messages, encryption of messages, algorithms used, and certain types of certificates.

In summary, S-HTTP is a protocol that supports the following:

- ✦ Option negotiations for defining the type of transactions desired
- ✦ A variety of key management approaches
- ✦ Different trust models
- ✦ Multiple cryptographic algorithms
- ✦ Multiple operation modes
- ✦ Different encapsulation formats

Instant Messaging

Instant messaging (IM) goes a step beyond e-mail in that it supports the real-time exchange of messages between two parties using the Internet. To use this service, the user must have IM client software on his or her computer. The client software then communicates with an IM server. The user provides the server with a contact, or "buddy," list of people with whom he or she desires to set up instant messaging.

To use instant messaging, the user logs on to the IM server with the user's ID and password. The server authenticates the user. Then, the client sends the server the user's IP address and the port number on the user's computer that is being used by the IM client. The server stores this information as well as identical information from any other individuals on the user's contact list that are logged in at that time. Once an individual, A, is logged on to the server, the server sends the IP addresses and port numbers of all the others logged on to the server at that time to A's client software. All people on the contact list who are logged on to the IM server at that time are notified of the "online" presence and contact information of the others who are also logged on.

A user can send a message to another individual on the contact list who is logged on and that message will instantly appear on the receiving individual's screen. Because a user's client knows the IP address and port number of the receiving individual, the user's message is sent directly to the intended recipient — it does not have to go through the IM server.

With instant messaging, communication only takes place between two individuals. If the situation requires instant conferencing among more than two individuals, a chat room can be set up. A *chat room* is similar to instant messaging, but everyone logged on to the "room" can see a message that is sent by one individual.

When an individual, A, wants to terminate the IM session, A closes their message window and exits the IM client. The client then sends a message to the IM server indicating that A has logged off. The server, in turn, sends a message to all the active participants of the contact list indicating that A has exited the session. The members of the contact list who are still logged on will see A's status on their windows change from "online" to "offline."

IM software packages also offer other services, including the following:

- ✦ Setting up chat rooms
- ✦ Transmitting images and sounds
- ✦ Voice communication
- ✦ Streaming content

Some of the more popular IM utilities are the freeware ICQ (for "I seek you" at www.icq.com), AIM (America Online's Instant Messenger), Microsoft's instant messaging utility in MSN Explorer, and Yahoo Instant Messenger.

One problem with instant messaging is lack of interoperability. An individual with an IM utility from one source or vendor may not be able to communicate with a person using a different IM package. To address this situation, the Internet Engineering Task Force (IETF) has developed a standard protocol for instant messaging — the Instant Messaging Presence Protocol.

Vulnerabilities

Messages sent by means of instant messaging are not inherently secure and safe from prying eyes. The instant messaging server is particularly vulnerable because it contains both the messages and the connection information of the participants. Thus, instant messaging servers should be secure servers located in protected and limited access areas. Additional security features that are provided by some instant messaging software utilities include:

- Encryption, integrity, and authentication services using SSL
- Authentication against proprietary databases, domains, or LDAP
- Secure file transfer
- Ability to use any TCP port
- Web-based tools for administration of the instant messaging network on the instant messaging server, including tools for user account administration, logging of critical data, and analysis of log information

8.3 Naming Conventions

Web servers that respond to requests for files in their DOS 8.3 file names are vulnerable to attacks that can cause the server to reveal source code. The Microsoft New Technology File System (NTFS) can generate file names in the DOS 8.3 naming convention to service 16-bit applications that access files that do not conform to DOS 8.3 naming. Windows 2000, Windows NT Server, and Windows NT Workstation support the NTFS file system. The earlier File Allocation Table (FAT) file system along with the newer version, FAT 32, is supported by Windows 95 and 98. The NFTS enhancements over FAT and FAT 32 include optimization of available disk space, fault tolerance, and improved security features.

In Windows, file names that are not in the DOS 8.3 format are converted to short names in DOS 8.3 format. The algorithm for the conversion is as follows:

1. If the part of the file name before the extension is more than six characters, truncate that portion to six letters. (Another approach is taken if the name is only one or two characters long.)
2. Append a ~1 to the result. (If there is another file with this alternate name in the directory, increment to ~2 or ~3 or until there is no conflict.)
3. If needed, reduce the extension to three letters.

For example, the file name `semestergrades.txt` would be converted by NTFS to the DOS 8.3 format `semest~1.txt`.

Another example that demonstrates a security vulnerability is the conversion of a file name such as `calculate.jhtml`. Using the above algorithm, this name would be converted by NTFS to `calcul~1.jht`. A vulnerable Web server would not realize that the `calcul~1` was an alternate representation of *calculate*. The server would attempt to associate a handler with the extension `jht`. Since there is no such handler, the server would use a default handler. The default handler will be unable to open the file and will return the script's source code to the requesting client. In other situations involving the DOS 8.3 naming convention on an NTFS file system, requesting the converted, truncated DOS 8.3 name file may permit the client to bypass some server security functions.

One fix to this problem is to disable DOS 8.3 file name creation on the NTFS server — although this can lead to difficulties in using 16-bit applications.

Packet Sniffing

Packet sniffing is akin to tapping a telephone wire, but involves tapping into digital transmissions over networks. Computers connected to Ethernet LANs have a Network Interface Card (NIC) that monitors the LAN message traffic to see if they have been targeted as the recipients of a particular message. To route the message to the correct computer on the LAN, each computer is given a unique address called a *media access control* (MAC) address. The MAC address is a 48-bit number, comprised of a 24-bit number identifying the NIC's vendor and a 24-bit, unique serial number provided by the vendor.

The header of each message traveling on the LAN contains the MAC address of the destination computer; so, as a message travels past each computer on the Ethernet, each computer checks to see if the message contains its MAC address. If it does, that computer takes in the message and processes it to retrieve the information that it contains. If the MAC address is different from the computer's MAC address, the computer ignores the message and it continues on to the LAN to be inspected by other computers on the network. If a NIC is programmed to acquire all messages that it sees on the LAN regardless of the addresses, the NIC is said to be operating in *promiscuous mode*. It is, essentially, "sniffing" all packets on the network and gathering all messages being sent on the network. Sniffers decode the messages and display the text of the message for review.

An alternative sniffing method to tapping into the LAN is to surreptitiously install software on a person's computer. This software can monitor messages being sent and received by that computer and can also capture passwords and e-mail them to the person that installed the sniffing program.

A good defense against sniffing is to encrypt messages so that they cannot be read when acquired by a sniffer. This encryption can be accomplished by using protocols such as Secure Sockets Layer (SSL), Transport Layer Security (TLS), Pretty Good Privacy (PGP), Secure Shell (SSH), and virtual private networks (VPNs).

Privacy

Messages sent over the Internet are vulnerable to interception. As discussed in earlier sections, encryption is a good defense against unauthorized capture of message traffic.

Another aspect of privacy is determining the policy of Web sites that gather information from the site's visitors and how the sites handle that information. On the other end, the user should have the means to indicate his or her privacy preferences to visited Web sites. One approach to satisfying these requirements is the *Platform for Privacy Preferences 1.0 (P3P1.0)*, developed by the World Wide Web Consortium (W3C). P3P provides a standard format for Web sites to impart their privacy policies to users through a machine-readable syntax. It also allows users to specify privacy preferences to their browsers for comparison with a Web site's privacy practices.

At a Web site, P3P policies are encoded in a machine-readable XML format using the P3P vocabulary. User agents then issue standard HTTP requests to retrieve the P3P policy reference file from the Web site. P3P-enabled browsers can obtain a Web site's privacy policy and automatically compare it to thresholds set into the browser by the user. The browser can also block cookies based on the Web site's privacy policy.

The specification of P3P1.0 contains the following items:

- A standard vocabulary for describing a Web site's data practices
- A set of data elements that Web sites can refer to in their P3P privacy policies
- A standard schema for data that a Web site might wish to collect, known as the *P3P base data schema*
- A standard set of uses, recipients, data categories, and other privacy disclosures
- An XML format for expressing a privacy policy
- A means of associating privacy policies with Web pages or sites, and cookies
- A mechanism for transporting P3P policies over HTTP

A useful consequence of implementing P3P on a Web site is that Web site owners are required to answer multiple-choice questions about their privacy practices. This activity causes the organization sponsoring the Web site to think about and evaluate their privacy policy and practices in the event that they have not already done so. After answering the necessary P3P privacy questions, an organization can develop its policy. A number of sources provide free policy editors and assistance in writing privacy policies, such as `www.w3.org/P3P/` and `http://p3ptoolbox.org/`.

The following items comprise the Web site's privacy policy statements, which must be published on the Web site:

- XML documents indicating the data the site will collect and its intended use
- A reference file, in XML format, that provides the URL for the site's policy statements; this file also indicates which policy statements apply to specific parts of the Web site and the Web site's cookies
- A human-readable form of the privacy policy
- A machine-readable XML version of the privacy policy
- Pointers to the policy reference file for use by Web browsers

Microsoft's Internet Explorer 6 (IE6) Web browser supports P3P. IE6 is used primarily for filtering and blocking cookies, but it can also be used to generate and display a report describing a particular Web site's P3P-implemented privacy policy.

Another P3P implementation is provided by AT&T's Privacy Bird software, which is an add-on to a browser that inserts a bird icon in the top-right corner of a user's Web browser. The AT&T software reads the XML privacy policy statements from a Web site and causes the bird to chirp and change color to inform the user if the user's listed privacy preference settings are satisfied by the Web site's P3P policy statements. Clicking on the bird provides more detailed information concerning mismatches between the Web site's policy practices and the user's provided preferences. Clicking on the bird also provides a summary of the site's privacy policy.

Vulnerabilities

This section reviews the major vulnerabilities of Web-based systems. The reasons for these vulnerabilities range from flaws in software design to the improper application of normally useful capabilities.

JavaScript

The Java programming language was developed by Sun Microsystems and is widely used to create animated and dynamic Web pages. Basic, static Web pages are developed using HTML files that do not require the programming skills needed to write Java programs. Small application programs, or *applets,* written in Java code can be downloaded from a Web server and run on a user's Web browser that is accessing the Web site. Java offers protection from this *mobile code* running on the user's computer by establishing a *sandbox*: a virtual barrier that "surrounds" the Java program as it is executing. The sandbox, implemented by software in the client's browser, restricts applets from accessing any files in the client computer. If the sandbox software is working properly, an applet containing malicious code cannot contaminate or destroy files on the client computer.

Scripting languages, such as JavaScript, do not use compilers; instead, they run on the client-side browser. Scripting statements are embedded with HTML statements. Script programs, or scripts, are much easier to write than code in a programming language such as Java, and they are also used to create interactive and dynamic Web pages.

Because Script programs run on a client's browser, they have the potential to cause damage or violate the user's privacy. For example, JavaScripts can do the following:

- Forge e-mail
- Read a user's history file
- Access the user's local files
- Take e-mail addresses from the user's address book
- Read the user's cookie file
- Remotely monitor a user's Web visits

JavaScripts can also run on the server-side as compiled, executable files.

JavaScript Details

As previously discussed, JavaScript client applications run in a browser, such as Netscape Navigator, and server applications run on a server, such as Netscape Enterprise Server. JavaScript supports the development of dynamic HTML pages as well as access to Java distributed-object applications.

Both the server and client JavaScript applications use the same core language. This language corresponds to ECMA-262, a standardized European scripting language.

JavaScript on the client-side is contained in HTML pages and is interpreted by the browser at runtime. It has additional features over the core language to support its browser environment. JavaScript running on the server-side adds capabilities related to execution on the server, such as predefined objects and functions. JavaScript server applications are compiled before they are needed.

When a browser requests an HTML page from a server, the server transmits the page to the browser, including JavaScript instructions embedded in the HTML statements. JavaScript can be embedded in HTML using statements and functions within a <SCRIPT> tag or by specifying a file as the JavaScript source. The client software displays the HTML-defined Web page and executes the embedded JavaScript instructions. Such JavaScript instructions can respond to user inputs, such as Web page navigation or mouse clicking. JavaScript programs can also perform checks on data entered on the client-side.

On the server-side, JavaScript instructions can access files on the server, access relational databases, and communicate with other applications. HTML pages that use server-side JavaScript are compiled into bytecode executable files.

Even though client- and server-side JavaScripts are different, they display the following common characteristics:

- Rules for expressions, variables, and literals
- Basic object model
- Keywords, statement syntax, and grammar
- Predefined objects and functions

Differences between JavaScript and Java

Some similarities exist between JavaScript and the Java programming language, but a number of significant differences exist. For example, Java has strong type checking and static typing, while JavaScript does not have these controls. JavaScript does support most Java expression syntaxes and basic control-flow constructs. JavaScript uses a runtime system with numeric, Boolean, and string values. Java is based on a system of classes built by declarations, while JavaScript supports dynamic inheritance and functions without any special declarative requirements. Java's strong typing and class inheritance require more programming skills to implement than those needed to author JavaScripts.

ActiveX

The ActiveX environment can attach programs to Web pages to make these Web pages interactive and dynamic. ActiveX is not a programming language like Java, but an environment under which programs are managed and run. While Java applets are downloaded from a Web site and are executed on the Java Virtual Machine on the user's browser in a sandbox, ActiveX programs are downloaded to the user's hard drive. This paradigm poses potential security problems. To protect the user, ActiveX provides security-level and authentication mechanisms for downloaded programs. An ActiveX program, or *component*, carries a security-level designation that defines when an ActiveX component can be safely run. An ActiveX *control* is a type of program that is used by other programs in the Windows environment to perform particular functions.

ActiveX components that have restricted access to a user's computer resources are called *sandbox components*. These components cannot access the user's hard drive and may include Java applets. Conversely, ActiveX components that run outside of the sandbox are called *trusted*, or *full access*, components. ActiveX relies on the digital signing of trusted components to verify that these components are safe to execute and do not contain malicious code. The validity of this approach requires that the source of the component authentication be trustworthy and reliable.

Buffer Overflow

A *buffer overflow* occurs when a process receives more data than it can store in allocated buffer space in memory. When the buffer overflows, erratic program activity can sometimes occur if the control software is not equipped to handle such a development. Buffer overflow attacks are possible because of poor programming methods.

In a typical buffer overflow attack, the program used to load the incoming data into the buffer or stack does not perform parameter checking and is not aware that the incoming data will exceed the allotted buffer storage space. In this type of attack, the incoming data is actually a program that is loaded onto the stack. When the overflow occurs, the return address that specifies the location of the next instruction to be executed by the computer is modified to point to the beginning of the attack program loaded into the buffer. The malicious code is executed instead of the proper code in the sequence that was interrupted prior to the loading of the buffer.

Cookies

A *cookie* is a text file containing information about a user's Web browsing experience that is gathered by the Web site and stored on the user's hard disk through his or her Web browser. Passwords, IDs, the frequency of visits to a particular site, and network addresses for ISPs are typical types of information stored in cookies. Unscrupulous Web sites may read personal information from your cookie file as well as information on what Web sites you visit, how often you visit them, and so on. One way for a user to avoid a Web site's ability to access cookies is to use an *anonymizer server* to access a Web site. An anonymizer server is a third-party server that sits between the user and other Web sites and screens the user's information from these sites.

Signed Applets

Recall that the Java security model uses a sandbox for executing Java applets to prevent malicious code from accessing files on the user's machine. This model severely restricts the utility of applets, and an alternate mode of operation is necessary to permit the applets to access files to perform necessary functions. To accommodate this situation where the user desires the applet to have access to local computer disks, a model similar to ActiveX is used for Java applets.

To ensure that the applets are safe to use, Java-enabled products are incorporating digital signatures, resulting in *signed applets*. Based on the trustworthiness of the signing agent, a user can decide whether or not the applet should be permitted to run outside of the sandbox environment.

Java Development Kit (JDK) releases provided by Sun Microsystems include Application Programming Interfaces (APIs) for digital signatures, message digests, and support for X.509 v3 certificates. A tool called *javakey* is also provided that can be used to digitally sign *Java Archive (JAR) files*. A JAR file may contain images and Java classes. JAR files that are signed by a trusted source are not constrained to run in the Java sandbox. These digitally signed files can run on the local computer and have access rights to the computer's files.

A signed applet can be developed using the RSA public encryption algorithm by using the Netscape Browser signing tools to digitally sign the directory structure of applet files. Then, an Object Signing Certificate must be obtained from a trusted RSA Certificate Authority and installed on the system.

When a signed applet is downloaded, the user plug-in software determines if the Certificate Authority is a valid, trusted entity and if the applet is properly signed. If these verifications are successfully completed, the user is presented with a dialog that lists the following four options of permissions to run on the local computer:

- Full permission, which is always granted to the applet
- Permission for a browser session
- Denial of permission
- Additional information required to make a decision

When the user selects one of these options, the applet runs according to the permissions associated with that option.

CGI

The *Common Gateway Interface (CGI)* is a standard that defines how HTTP or Web servers interface with client applications. A CGI program runs on the server and is invoked when a client requests information from the server. For example, a CGI program can access information from a database on a Web server and present the data to the user running a client program. A CGI program is executed in real time when a client requests service from a Web server and the CGI program can generate dynamic information. For example, a user requesting information from a database residing on a server can, through CGI, be presented with a dynamically generated HTML document displaying the information.

Because a CGI program is executable and runs on the server in real time to respond to requests for service from external clients, a potential information security vulnerability exists. To indicate to the Web server that a CGI program must be executed and not treated as data to be displayed, the CGI program must reside in a special directory. In the NCSA HTTP'd server distribution, all CGI programs are stored in directory `/cgi-bin`.

A CGI program can be written in a variety of languages, including C, C++, PERL, TCL, Fortran, and Visual Basic. A language such as C must be compiled to generate object code that will run on the server. A scripting language such as PERL, however, is easier to use and requires no compilation. PERL is widely used to implement CGI programs. CGI scripts can pose a security risk to Web servers in that they execute directly on the server.

When a CGI script is run on the server, the following activities take place:

- The server provides the script with any necessary data that it needs to run. The user's browser on the client machine usually provides this data to the server.
- The server supplies values for any environmental variables that the script requires.

♦ The server processes the script's output, including adding the proper header, for presentation to the user's browser. The header is necessary to enable the browser to interpret the information returned from the server.

PERL

Practical Extraction and Report Language (PERL) is an interpreted language that is well suited to text processing applications. PERL was developed by Larry Wall to operate on text files on UNIX platforms. PERL instructions are interpreted and are referred to as *scripts*. Some of the salient capabilities of PERL include the following:

- ♦ Automatic array sizing
- ♦ Binary date conversion operations
- ♦ Automatic type conversion
- ♦ Support of associative arrays
- ♦ Support of C operators
- ♦ Formatted output functions
- ♦ Rich control structures
- ♦ File I/O

In PERL, string variables can grow automatically to hold the characters that the script has assigned to those variables. This characteristic supports security in that one variable cannot be overwritten by another.

SMTP Relay

The *Simple Mail Transfer Protocol (SMTP)* specifies a method of transferring e-mail messages over the Internet. By default, port 25 is monitored for e-mail messages and then the mail is acquired and sent to the destination mailboxes. When a TCP connection is made to port 25, the transmitting client listens for the receiving server entity to send a response identifying the server and indicating that the server is prepared to accept e-mail messages. The TCP connection is broken after the message exchange has been completed. Typical attacks against SMTP are Denial-of-Service, spamming, and e-mail bombs.

If the SMTP server receives mail that is destined for another host, it implements its *relay* function and forwards the e-mail message to that host. A concern associated with this functionality is that an SMTP server can be used as an agent in forwarding bulk or spam mail to other hosts. To counter this type of attack, SMTP offers options that restrict the addresses to which a host can relay e-mail messages. These options include the following:

- ♦ **No mail relay** — All users send and receive e-mail from the local host running the SMTP server
- ♦ **Relay mail for local hosts only** — Limits relay forwarding to mail hosts on the local server

- **Relay mail for local users only** — Limits relay forwarding to users on the local hosts
- **Relay mail for** — Provides the host with the specification of the range of IP addresses to which e-mail can be forwarded

In addition, SMTP has a *kill file* into which a domain name or spam e-mail source address can be entered to stop messages originating from those locations. Another security practice is to change the SMTP welcome message to eliminate the default identification of the mail server vendor, mail server version, and the operating system. Some SMTP implementations offer virus scanning, backup of e-mails, and retry of unsuccessful e-mail delivery.

Directory/CA Recognition

Certificate authorities (CAs) can apply for recognition from governmental agencies or entities designated and/or approved by the governmental agency. Recognition may be granted to the CA and/or to all certificates, or a particular type, class, or description of certificates issued or to be issued by the CA.

Recognition of the CA

The recognition-granting entity requires the CA to meet a specified standard of performance and operation to receive recognition. Examples of items considered in making the recognition decision include:

- The CA's financial status
- The methods, standards, and procedures used by the CA to issue certificates to its subscribers
- The information security standards, procedures, and guidelines used by the CA in association with the CA's issuance of certificates to its subscribers
- The CA's establishment of coverage for any liability issues that may arise
- The ability of the CA to comply with the governmental legal requirements and established Code of Practices for a recognized CA
- The background and qualifications of the CA's officers

The recognition of the CA is valid for a period of time, after which the CA is required to apply for recognition renewal.

Recognition of Certificates

A recognized CA may apply for recognition of some or all of its certificates. Recognition of a CA's certificates is only granted if the CA itself has met the requirements and been awarded recognition. The status of a recognized certificate depends on the CA's ability to maintain its recognition by the appropriate entity.

The following list provides typical examples of areas considered in granting recognition to certificates:

- ✦ Whether the certificate(s) are issued in accordance with the recognized CA's certification practice statement
- ✦ The reliance limit set for a certificate or a type or class of certificate
- ✦ The arrangements established by the recognized CA to cover any liability that may arise from the issuance of certificates

SSL/TLS

SSL/TLS-enabled clients step through the following activities to authenticate a server using digital certificates:

- ✦ Verify that the current date and time fall within the certificate's validity period
- ✦ Verify that the issuing CA is on the list of trusted CAs maintained by the client by checking the CA's distinguished name (DN) and matching it to the DN of CAs on the trusted list
- ✦ Use the CA's public key (obtained from the list in the preceding step) to validate the CA's digital signature for the server's certificate; the CA's public key should "open" the digital signature developed using the CA's private key
- ✦ Verify that the domain name in the server's certificate corresponds to the domain name of the server

With the server authenticated, the client continues with the SSL/TLS handshaking process.

LDAP

The Lightweight Directory Access Protocol (LDAP) is an IETF standard that was originally developed at the University of Michigan to support client-server access to online directory services. LDAP is a successor to the X.500 protocol.

In typical applications, a client accesses a directory server running on a host computer to locate entries in the directory. LDAP exhibits the following characteristics:

- It contains client, gateway, and server programs.
- It is platform-independent.
- Directory services based on LDAP are in the form of a tree structure.
- Searches are based on an entry's object class and attributes.
- A distinguished name (DN) is used as a unique identifier for each LDAP entry.
- LDAP supports confidentiality, authentication, and integrity.

Figure 2.7 provides an example of the LDAP hierarchical tree structure.

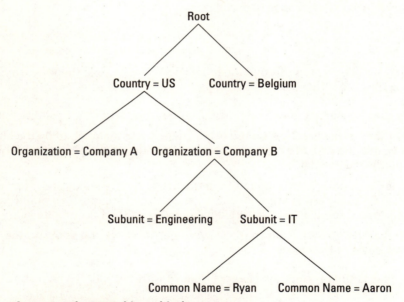

Figure 2.7 The LDAP hierarchical tree structure

LDAP became a standard in 1995 as RFC 1777 of the IETF. LDAP was initially designed to be a front-end to X.500 directories, but can now function as a stand-alone directory as well as work with other directory servers. LDAP is implemented on servers at the following three levels:

- Large public servers (Bigfoot)
- Organizational servers (companies and universities)
- Workgroup servers (small groups)

LDAP employs a data structure known as an *entry*. An LDAP entry is composed of attributes. An *attribute* has a Distinguished Name (DN), a type, and a set of values corresponding to the type. For example, an entry might have a "part" attribute that has a type of "partNumber." The type defines the kinds of data that can be used, such as integers. An entry also has an attribute called objectClass that has multiple values and determines which attribute values are required and which are optional for a particular entry. LDAP is object-oriented and can thus employ predefined standard object classes to construct new entries. Because LDAP was developed from database structures, a collection of object classes that specify attributes for the entries in an LDAP server is called a *schema*.

See additional discussions of LDAP and X.509 certificates in Chapter 4.

File Transfer Protocols

A server providing File Transfer Protocol (FTP) services can allow fully anonymous login without requiring passwords, or it can be set up to require a valid user name/password pair. FTP servers provide a simple interface resembling a standard UNIX file directory. Users can retrieve files and view or execute the files later, if they have the appropriate applications.

However, if an FTP server is not configured correctly, it can provide access to any file found on the host computer, or even on the network connected to the host computer. FTP servers should be limited to accessing a limited directory space, and should require the use of passwords whenever feasible.

Sometimes, an organization may want to support an anonymous FTP server to allow all external users the ability to download nonsensitive information without using strong authentication. In this case, FTP should be hosted outside the firewall or on a service network not connected to corporate networks that contain sensitive data. Table 2.1 shows a sample of such an FTP policy.

FTP and Firewall Proxy

Application gateways may require a proxy for FTP services to be supported through the firewall. All incoming requests for FTP network services should go through the appropriate proxy on the firewall regardless of which host on the internal network is the final destination. These application-level firewalls should be configured so that outbound network traffic appears as if the traffic originated from the firewall (only the firewall is visible to outside networks). In this manner, direct access to network services on the internal network is not allowed.

Table 2.1
Sample FTP Service Policy

Policy Statement	Non-Anonymous FTP Service	Anonymous FTP Service
Require FTP server outside the firewall	No	Yes
Require FTP server on the service network	No	Yes
Require FTP server on protected network	Yes	No
Require FTP server on the firewall itself	No	No
FTP server will be accessed by Internet	No	Yes

SFTP

Secure File Transfer Protocol (SFTP) is replacing FTP because it includes strong encryption and authentication. SFTP is an FTP-style client that can be used to exchange files over a network, and is an encryption-based replacement for the insecure FTP. SFTP provides secure file transfer functionality using Secure Shell (SSH) or Secure Shell version 2 (SSH-2); it is the standard file transfer protocol for use with the SSH-2 protocol.

Although SFTP is designed to primarily provide file transfer services, it can provide secure file system access to a remote server. An SFTP server can be designed to provide only file transfer access, or system command access as well. SFTP can restrict users to their home directories, is not vulnerable to the "flashfxp" transfer utility (which allows an unknown third party to use the network for file transfer to a remote location), and is much less vulnerable to remote exploitation than standard FTP. It can be configured to authorize users with certificates as well as passwords. MacSFTP is a Macintosh application used to transfer files over TCP/IP using SFTP.

SSH/SSH-2

SSH is a set of protocols that are primarily used for remote access over a network by establishing an encrypted tunnel between an SSH client and an SSH server. This protocol can be used to authenticate the client to the server. In addition, it can also provide confidentiality and integrity services. It consists of a Transport layer protocol, a user authentication protocol, and a connection protocol. A number of SSH software programs, such as OPENSSH, are available on the Internet for free.

SSH-2 contains security enhancements over the original SSH and should therefore be used in place of SSH. SSH-2 is not strictly a VPN product, but it can be used like one. SSH opens a secure, encrypted shell (command line) session from the Internet through a firewall to the SSH server. After the connection is established, it can be used as a terminal session or for tunneling other protocols.

SSH-2 should be used instead of TELNET when connecting to remote hosts. Tunneling features available in SSH-2 can be utilized for providing secure connections to applications that are connected to a remote server, such as connecting to a POP3 e-mail server.

TFTP

Trivial File Transfer Protocol (TFTP) is a stripped-down version of FTP. TFTP has no directory browsing abilities; it can do nothing but send and receive files. TFTP is commonly used to capture router configuration files by logging a terminal session during a configuration session and then storing that configuration on a TFTP server. The TFTP server is then accessed during the configuration session to save or retrieve configuration information to the network device. However, unlike FTP, session authentication does not occur, so it is insecure. Some sites choose not to implement TFTP due to the inherent security risks.

Wireless Security

Wireless is one of the newest communications technology frontiers, offering the possibility of always-on, instant mobile communications. However, the vulnerabilities inherent in wireless computing present daunting hurdles. These vulnerabilities, which include the threat of eavesdropping, session highjacking, and data alteration and manipulation in conjunction with an overall lack of privacy, are major challenges posed by wireless technologies.

Typically, when a new technology emerges, standards are created and a rush commences to develop the technology without a thorough security vetting. This has been the case with wireless, too. The result is that much work is now devoted to retrofitting security into the existing models and protocols, and designing new models and protocols with better security features. Progress is being made as standards like 802.1x and newer versions of WAP emerge. Network infrastructure design, such as implementation of VPNs and RADIUS, can also create secure pipes for wireless sessions.

802.11 Standards

IEEE 802.11 refers to a family of specifications for wireless local area networks (WLANs) developed by a working group of the Institute of Electrical and Electronics Engineers (IEEE). This standards effort began in 1989, with a focus on effectively deploying a wireless equivalent to Ethernet in large enterprise networking environments. The IEEE accepted the specification in 1997.

802.11 also generically refers to the IEEE committee responsible for setting the various wireless LAN standards.

The 802.11 specification identifies an over-the-air interface between a mobile device wireless client and a base station, or between two mobile device wireless clients. All the existing standards in the 802.11 family use the Ethernet protocol and Carrier Sense Multiple Access with Collision Avoidance (CSMA/CA) for path sharing.

The current specifications in the 802.11 family, include the following:

- **802.11** — The original IEEE wireless LAN standard that provides 1 or 2 Mbps transmission speed in the 2.4 GHz band, using either FHSS or DSSS. The modulation used in 802.11 is commonly phase-shift keying (PSK).

- **802.11b** — An extension to the 802.11 wireless LAN standard. 802.11b provides 11 Mbps transmission speed, but that automatically slows down to 5.5 Mbps, 2 Mbps, or 1 Mbps speeds in the 2.4 GHz band, based on the strength of the signal. 802.11b uses only DSSS. 802.11b, a 1999 ratification to the original 802.11 standard, allows wireless functionality comparable to Ethernet; it is also referred to as *802.11 High Rate*, or *Wi-Fi*.

The term *Wi-Fi* is used by the Wireless Ethernet Compatibility Alliance (www.weca.net) to specify products that conform to the 802.11b standard.

- **802.11a** — An extension to the original IEEE 802.11 wireless LAN standard that provides up to 54 Mbps in the 5 GHz band. 802.11a uses an orthogonal frequency division multiplexing encoding scheme rather than FHSS or DSSS.

- **802.11g** — A new IEEE wireless standard that applies to wireless LANs, 802.11g provides 20 Mbps to 54 Mbps in the 2.4 GHz band.

- **802.11e** — A IEEE draft extension to provide quality-of-service (QoS) features and multimedia support for home and business wireless environments.

Each of these specs is defined more fully in the following sections.

Original IEEE 802.11 LAN Standard

The IEEE 802.11 wireless LAN standard provides for 1 Mbps or 2 Mbps wireless communications in the 2.4 GHz industrial, scientific, medical (ISM) band using either FHSS or DSSS. The modulation used in 802.11 is commonly phase-shift keying (PSK).

In a typical WLAN installation, wireless stations (STAs) are associated with a fixed access point (AP), which provides a bridging function to the wired network. The combination of the AP and its associated STA is referred to as a *Basic Service Set (BSS)*. BSS is described later in the chapter.

The 802.11 standard is aimed at medium-range, higher-data-rate applications. This technology can be used in shop-floor areas in factory environments or in other enterprises in which the wireless interaction is confined to a limited range and can tolerate 1 Mbps to 2 Mbps wireless connectivity.

802.11b

In 1999, the Institute of Electrical and Electronics Engineers ratified an extension to the IEEE 802.11 standard and called it *IEEE 802.11b*. The IEEE 802.11b standard addresses transmission for WLANs in the 2.4 GHz range. It offers 1 Mbps, 2 Mbps, and 5.5 Mbps, and a peak data rate of 11 Mbps, transmission speeds. Most implementations of 802.11b allow for slow-down of the transmission speeds when the client is farther away from the AP, allowing the communications to continue uninterrupted, albeit at a slower speed.

IEEE 802.11b is the most commonly implemented wireless networking communications standard, with the largest number of vendor implementations available to the business, home, or small office home office (SOHO) consumer. IEEE 802.11b, like HomeRF and Bluetooth, uses the 2.4 GHz band, and uses a linear modulation known as *complementary code keying (CCK)* with a coding variation of DSSS.

The 802.11b standard, also called Wi-Fi, is backward-compatible with 802.11. The modulation used in 802.11 has historically been PSK, but the modulation method selected for 802.11b, as just noted, is CCK, which allows higher data speeds and is less susceptible to multipath-propagation interference.

The 11 Mbps data rate makes wireless LAN technology viable in enterprises and other large organizations. It is thus the current de facto standard for wireless business LANs. The home market has also seen an explosion in the use of 802.11b LANs, with many traditional wired LANs component vendors hopping on the 802.11b bandwagon.

Interoperability of wireless LAN products from different vendors is overseen by an independent organization called the *Wireless Ethernet Compatibility Alliance*, or *WECA* (www.wi-fi.com), which brands compliant products as "Wi-Fi."

802.11a

802.11a came after 802.11b. The IEEE 802.11a standard was passed in an attempt to remedy some of the major problems that arose in early 802.11 and 802.11b implementations. It operates at radio frequencies between the 5 GHz and 6 GHz range. It uses a modulation scheme known as *orthogonal frequency-division multiplexing (OFDM)* that makes data speeds as high as 54 Mbps possible (though most current implementations transmit at 6 Mbps, 12 Mbps, or 24 Mbps).

One advantage of 802.11a is that it largely quiets many of the current interference concerns about 802.11b and somewhat mitigates the network density limitations of 802.11b by operating in the 5 GHz range and using OFDM, rather than the spread spectrum technology.

802.11g

The newly proposed standard, IEEE 802.11g, offers wireless transmission over relatively short distances at speeds from 20 Mbps to 54 Mbps, compared with the 11 Mbps of the 802.11b standard. Like 802.11b, 802.11g operates in the 2.4 GHz range and is backward-compatible with existing 802.11b-based networks, a major advantage for the standard over 802.11a.

However, the IEEE working group has been divided for some time over which coding technology is preferable for the new standard. At last report, the IEEE's new standard was slated to borrow from Intersil's OFDM modulation technology, touted as one of the key components of 802.11g, as well as Texas Instruments' rival technology, PBCC.

IEEE 902.11g is expected to see vendor implementations by late 2002, using OFDM, and CCK modulation, which is complementary code keying from 802.11b.

802.11e

The latest IEEE draft specification for wireless networks, 802.11e, will focus on interoperability between business, home, and public environments, such as airports and hotels. Unlike other wireless initiatives, 802.11e is the first wireless standard that intentionally spans home and business environments.

It also adds QoS features and multimedia support to the existing 802.11b and 802.11a wireless standards, while maintaining full backward-compatibility with these standards. QoS and multimedia support are essential ingredients to offering residential customers video-on-demand, audio-on-demand, voice over IP (VoIP), and high-speed Internet access.

802.16

Another wireless 802 standard, called *IEEE 802 Broadband Wireless Access (802.WBA,* or *802.16),* is under development. IEEE 802.16 standardizes the air interface and related functions associated with the wireless local loop (WLL) for wireless broadband subscriber access. Three working groups have been chartered to produce standards:

- **IEEE 802.16.1** — Air interface for 10 to 66 GHz
- **IEEE 802.16.2** — Coexistence of broadband wireless access systems
- **IEEE 802.16.3** — Air interface for licensed frequencies, 2 to 11 GHz

802.1x

The 802.1x Port Based Network Access Control standard was drafted in 2001 by the IEEE to provide enhanced security for users of 802.11b wireless LANs. It provides port-level authentication for any wired or wireless Ethernet client system. This supplement to ISO/IEC 15802-3:1998 (IEEE Std 802.1D-1998) defines the changes necessary to the operation of a MAC bridge to provide port-based network access control capability.

Originally designed as a standard for wired Ethernet, 802.1x is applicable to WLANs. It leverages many of the security features used with dial-up networking; it uses encryption keys that are unique for each user and each network session and supports 128-bit key lengths. It has a key management protocol built into its specification, which provides keys automatically. Keys can also be changed rapidly at set intervals. It also supports the use of Remote Authentication Dial-In User Service (RADIUS) and Kerberos. The 802.1x standard can be used to provide link-layer authentication, making employee authentication by active directories and databases easier.

A good source for 802.1x information can be found at www.drizzle.com/~aboba/IEEE/.

The standard defines a client/server-based access control and authentication protocol that restricts unauthorized devices from connecting to a LAN through publicly accessible ports. The authentication server verifies each client connected to a switch port before making any services offered by the switch or the LAN available. Until the client has been authenticated, 802.1x access control allows only Extensible Authentication Protocol over LAN (EAPOL) traffic through the port to which the client is connected. After the client has been authenticated, normal traffic can pass through the port.

Cisco Systems has implemented 802.1x in its Aironet series of cards, and Microsoft has added the feature to WinXP. The goal of 802.1x is to provide a level of authentication comparable to that of the wired network. Using 802.1x, any appropriated wireless Network Interface Cards (NICs) no longer pose a threat because the network authenticates the user, not the hardware.

When the user (called the supplicant) wants to use the network service, he or she connects to the access point (called the *authenticator*), and a RADIUS server (the authentication server) at the other end receives the request and issues a challenge. If the supplicant can provide a correct response, it is allowed access.

Cisco has already introduced the Lightweight Extensible Authentication Protocol (LEAP) for its Aironet devices. Using LEAP, client devices dynamically generate a new WEP key, instead of using a static key as part of the log-in process. In the Cisco model, the supplicant and authentication server change roles and attempt mutual communication. Using this authentication method minimizes the risk of authenticating to a rogue access point. After authentication, the authentication server and the supplicant determine a WEP key for the session. This gives each client a unique WEP for every session.

Wireless Application Protocol

Wireless Application Protocol (WAP) was developed as a set of technologies related to HTML but tailored to the small screens and limited resources of handheld, wireless devices. The most notable of these technologies is the *Handheld Device Markup Language (HDML)*. HDML looks similar to HTML but has a feature set and programming paradigm tailored to wireless devices with small screens. HDML and other elements of this architecture eventually became the *Wireless Markup Language (WML)* and the architecture of WAP.

Since its initial release, WAP has evolved twice. Releases 1.1 and 1.2 of the specification have the same functionality as 1.0, but with added features to align with what the rest of the industry is doing. As of this writing, version 1.3 is used most often in WAP products.

In August 2001, the WAP Forum approved and released the specifications for WAP 2.0 for public review, and Ericsson, Nokia, and Motorola all announced support for WAP 2.0. The WAP 2.0 specification contains new functionality that enables users to send sound and moving pictures over their telephones, among other things. WAP 2.0 also provides a toolkit for easy development and deployment of new services, including XHTML.

The WAP architecture is loosely based on the OSI model. However, unlike the seven layers of OSI or the four layers of the TCP/IP model, WAP has five layers:

- Application
- Session
- Transaction
- Security
- Transport

Application Layer

The WAP Application layer is the direct interface to the user and contains the wireless application environment (WAE). This top layer consists of several elements, including a microbrowser specification for Internet access, WML, WMLScript, and wireless telephony applications (WTAs).

It encompasses devices, content, development languages (WML and WMLScript), wireless telephony APIs (WTAs) for accessing telephony functionality from within WAE programs, and some well-defined content formats for phone book records, calendar information, and graphics.

Session Layer

The WAP Session layer contains the Wireless Session Protocol (WSP), which is similar to the Hypertext Transfer Protocol (HTTP) because it is designed for low-bandwidth, high-latency wireless networks. WSP facilitates the transfer of content between WAP clients and WAP gateways in a binary format. Additional functionalities include content push and the suspension/resumption of connections.

The WAP Session layer provides a consistent interface to WAE for two types of session services: a connection mode and a connectionless service. This layer provides the following:

- Connection creation and release between the client and server
- Data exchange between the client and server by using a coding scheme that is much more compact than traditional HTML text
- Session suspend and release between the client and server

Transaction Layer

The WAP Transaction layer provides the Wireless Transactional Protocol (WTP), which provides functionality similar to TCP/IP in the Internet model. WTP is a lightweight transactional protocol that provides reliable request and response transactions and supports unguaranteed and guaranteed push.

WTP provides transaction services to WAP. It handles acknowledgments so that users can determine whether a transaction has succeeded. It also provides a retransmission of transactions in case they are not successfully received and removes duplicate transactions. WTP manages different classes of transactions for WAP devices: unreliable one-way requests, reliable one-way requests, and reliable two-way requests. An unreliable request from a WAP device means that no precautions are taken to guarantee that the information request makes it to the server.

Security Layer

The Security layer contains Wireless Transport Layer Security (WTLS). WTLS is based on Transport Layer Security (TLS, similar to the Secure Sockets Layer, or SSL) and can be invoked similarly to HTTPS in the Internet world. It provides data integrity, privacy, authentication, and DoS protection mechanisms. See the next section for more detail on the function of WTLS.

WAP privacy services guarantee that all transactions between the WAP device and gateway are encrypted. Authentication guarantees the authenticity of the client and application server. DoS protection detects and rejects data that comes in the form of unverified requests.

Transport Layer

The bottom WAP layer, the Transport layer, supports the Wireless Datagram Protocol (WDP), which provides an interface to the bearers of transportation. It supports the following protocols:

- CDPD
- GSM
- iDEN

- ◆ CDMA
- ◆ TDMA
- ◆ SMS
- ◆ FLEX

WDP provides a consistent interface to the higher layers of the WAP architecture, meaning that it does not matter which type of wireless network the application is running on. Among other capabilities, WDP provides data error correction. The bearers, or wireless communications networks, are at WAP's lowest level.

Figure 2.8 shows the WAP layers.

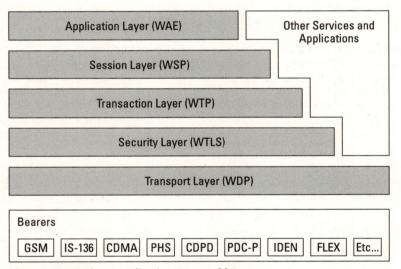

Figure 2.8 Wireless Application Protocol layers

Wireless Transport Layer Security Protocol

The Wireless Transport Layer Security Protocol (WTLS) is WAP's communications security protocol. It operates above the Transport protocol layer and provides the upper-level layer of the WAP with a secure transport service interface. The interface preserves the transport interface below it and presents methods to manage secure connections. WTLS's primary purpose is to provide privacy, data integrity, and authentication for WAP applications, to enable safe connections to other clients.

The WTLS supports a group of algorithms to meet privacy, authentication, and integrity requirements.

Currently, privacy is implemented using block ciphers, such as DES-CBC, IDEA, and RC5-CBC. RSA- and Diffie-Hellman-based key exchange suites are supported to authenticate the communicating parties. Integrity is implemented with SHA-1 and MD5 algorithms.

For secure wireless communications, the client and the server must be authenticated and the connection must be encrypted. WTLS provides three security classes:

- **Class 1: Anonymous Authentication** — In this mode, the client logs on to the server, but neither the client nor the server can be certain of the other's identity.
- **Class 2: Server Authentication** — The server is authenticated to the client, but the client is not authenticated to the server.
- **Class 3: Two-Way Client and Server Authentication** — The server is authenticated to the client, and the client is authenticated to the server.

WTLS is based on the Transport Layer Security (the TLS security layer used on the Internet, but with a number of modifications to accommodate the nature of wireless networks). For one, it has been optimized for low-bandwidth networks with relatively long latency. Because of the limited processing power and memory of mobile devices, fast algorithms are implemented in the algorithm suite. In addition, restrictions on export and the use of cryptography must be observed.

WTLS is the first attempt to provide a secure end-to-end connection for the WAP. The most common protocols, such as TLS v1.0 and SSL v3.0, were adopted as a basis of the WTLS. WTLS incorporates features such as datagram support, optimized packet size and handshake, and dynamic key refreshing.

Wired Equivalent Privacy

The IEEE 802.11b standard defines an optional encryption scheme called *Wired Equivalent Privacy (WEP)*, which includes a mechanism for securing wireless LAN data streams. WEP was part of the original IEEE 802.11 wireless standard. This standard's algorithms enable RC4-based, 40-bit data encryption to prevent an intruder from accessing the network and capturing wireless LAN traffic.

Originally intended only to supply privacy-type security on a par with a wired network, the objective of WEP is to provide a level of security and privacy equivalent to that provided in a wired Ethernet 802.3 LAN. WEP uses a symmetric scheme wherein the same key and algorithm are used for both data encryption and decryption.

The features of WEP include the following:

- **Access control** — To prevent users without the correct WEP key (who are, therefore, unauthenticated) from gaining access to the network
- **Privacy** — To protect wireless LAN data streams by encrypting them and allowing decryption only by users who have the correct WEP keys

Although any support for WEP in a mobile device is optional, support for WEP with 40-bit encryption keys is a requirement for Wi-Fi certification by WECA, so its members invariably support WEP. Some vendors implement their encryption and decryption routines in software, while others use hardware accelerators to minimize the performance degradation inherent in encrypting and decrypting the data stream.

WEP Encryption

When WEP encrypts data, two processes are applied to the plaintext data: one to encrypt the plaintext, the other to protect against unauthorized data modification. Here's the procedure:

1. The 40-bit secret key is concatenated with a 24-bit initialization vector (IV), resulting in a 64-bit total key size.
2. The resulting key is input to the pseudo-random number generator (PRNG).
3. The PRNG (RC4; described later) outputs a pseudo-random key sequence based on the input key.
4. The resulting sequence is used to encrypt the data by doing a bitwise XOR.

To protect against unauthorized data modification, an integrity algorithm (CRC-32) operates on the plaintext to produce the ICV. Figure 2.9 shows the WEP encryption algorithm.

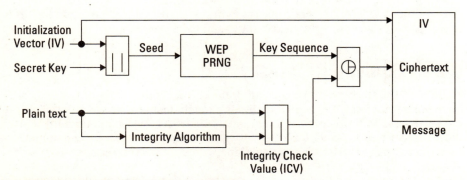

Figure 2.9 The WEP encryption algorithm

WEP Decryption

To decrypt the data stream, WEP follows this process:

1. The IV of the incoming message is used to generate the key sequence necessary to decrypt the incoming message.
2. The ciphertext, combined with the proper key sequence, yields the original plaintext and ICV.

3. The decryption is verified by performing the integrity check algorithm on the recovered plaintext and comparing the output ICV[1] to the ICV transmitted with the message.

4. If ICV[1] is not equal to ICV, the received message is in error, and an error indication is sent back to the sending station. Mobile units with erroneous messages are not authorized.

Figure 2.10 shows the WEP decryption algorithm.

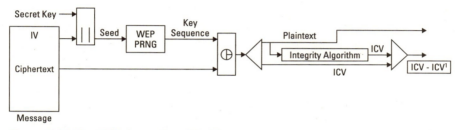

Figure 2.10 The WEP decryption algorithm

WEP RC4

WEP is implemented using the RC4 encryption engine, a stream cipher that takes a fixed-length key and produces a series of pseudo-random bits that are XOR'ed with the plaintext to produce ciphertext, and vice versa. RC4 is used in Secure Sockets Layer (SSL) and many other cryptography products.

The WEP RC4 PRNG is the critical component of the WEP process, as it is the actual encryption engine. The IV extends the useful lifetime of the secret key and provides the self-synchronous property of the algorithm. The secret key remains constant, while the IV changes periodically.

Because a one-to-one correspondence exists between the IV and the output, the data in higher-layer protocols like IP is usually predictable. An eavesdropper can readily determine portions of the key sequence generated by the key-IV pair. Using the same pair for successive messages may reduce the degree of privacy. Changing the IV after each message is a simple method of preserving the effectiveness of WEP; but several new products that use different algorithms, such as 3DES and ECC, are becoming available, and they will provide better communications security.

Also, RC4 will likely be dropped in favor of the aforementioned Advanced Encryption Standard (AES). It's believed that a block cipher such as AES better protects traffic from attacks that attempt to modify data in transit.

WEP Authentication Methods

A client cannot participate in a wireless LAN until that client has been authenticated. The authentication method must be set on each client, and the setting should match that of the AP with which the client wants to associate. The IEEE 802.11b standard defines two types of authentication methods: open and shared key.

Open System Authentication

Open system authentication is the default authentication protocol for 802.11. As its name implies, open system authentication authenticates anyone who requests authentication. With open authentication, the entire authentication process is performed in cleartext, and a client can associate with an AP even if the correct WEP key hasn't been supplied.

The open system authentication is considered a "null" authentication; that is, the station can associate with any AP and listen to all plaintext data that is sent. It is usually implemented where ease of use is the main issue and the network administrator does not want to deal with security at all. In open system mode, stations and APs are essentially using WEP as an encryption engine only.

Shared Key Authentication

Shared key authentication involves a shared secret key to authenticate the station to the AP. It uses a standard challenge and response, along with a shared secret key, to provide authentication to the station that's attempting to join the network. It enables a mobile station to encrypt data using a common key.

WEP allows an administrator to define a shared key for authentication. Access is denied to anyone who does not have an assigned key. The shared key used to encrypt and decrypt the data frames is also used to authenticate the station, but this is considered a security risk. However, the shared key authentication approach provides a better degree of authentication than the open system approach. In order to use shared key authentication, a station must implement WEP.

Four frames are exchanged in the authentication process:

1. The new station sends an authentication frame to the access point with the WEP bit = 1.
2. The AP returns an authentication frame with challenge text.
3. The new station uses the shared key and initialization vector to encrypt the challenge text and generates an integrity check value. This frame is sent to the AP with the IV and ICV. The AP decrypts the text and compares its ICV with the one it received.
4. If they match, it sends an authentication frame to indicate success. If it does not match, it returns an authentication frame indicating the reason for failure.

Figure 2.11 illustrates the operation of shared key authentication.

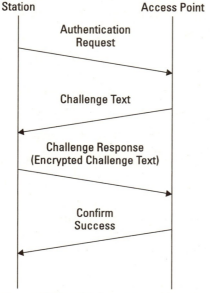

Figure 2.11 WEP shared key authentication

With shared key authentication, the access point sends the client a challenge text packet that the client must encrypt with the correct WEP key and return to the AP. If the client has the wrong key or no key, it fails authentication and is not allowed to associate with the AP.

Remember that stations are being authenticated here, not users. This authentication method can only verify that particular users belong to a certain group with access rights to the network; it cannot distinguish one mobile user from another.

Media Access Control Authentication
In certain implementations, WLAN vendors support authentication based on the Ethernet physical address, or MAC address, of a client. An AP allows association by a client only if that client's MAC address matches an address in an authentication table used by the AP. Each AP can limit the network's clients to those using a listed MAC address. If a client's MAC address is listed, he or she is permitted access to the network. If the address is not listed, access to the network is prevented.

WEP Key Management

The secret shared key resides in each station's management information database. Though the IEEE 802.11 standard does not specify how to distribute the keys to each station, it does provide two schemes for managing the WEP keys on a wireless LAN:

- All stations, including the wireless clients and their access points, share a set of four default keys.
- Each client establishes a key mapping relationship with another station.

The first method provides a window with four keys. When a client obtains the default keys, that client can communicate securely with all other stations in the subsystem. A station or AP can decrypt packets encrypted with any one of the four keys. Transmission is limited to one of the four manually entered keys. The problem with this scheme is that when the default keys become widely distributed, they are more likely to be compromised.

In the second scheme, each client establishes a key-mapping relationship with another station, called a *key mappings table*. In this method, each unique MAC address can have a separate key; this is thought to be a more secure form of operation because fewer stations have the keys.

Having a separate key for each user helps reduce the chance of cryptographic attacks, but enforcing a reasonable key period remains a problem because the keys can only be changed manually, and distributing keys becomes more difficult as the number of stations increases.

WEP2

The new IEEE 802.11i working group is developing a series of patches that address WEP's vulnerable encryption methodology. Modifications address, for example, the way systems create and use the initialization vector (IV) and key used in encrypting network traffic, which have become the basis for widely publicized WEP cracks. Other modifications are aimed at protecting the system against replay attacks, forged packets, and IV collision attacks. Additional changes to both WEP and the overall 802.11 security framework are expected over the long-term. RSA Security has released a patch that can be used in current WEP implementations. The technology, known as *fast-packet keying*, reduces the similarity of WEP keys used to encrypt successive packets, a flaw that is widely exploited to crack WEP-encrypted traffic. The IEEE approved the patch in December 2001.

Note   Recent URLs for WEP crack activity can be found at http://lists.anti-dmca.org/pipermail/dmca_discuss/2001-August/000044.html, www.lava.net/~newsham/wlan, and http://sourceforge.net/projects/wepcrack.

Wireless Vulnerabilities

Many vulnerabilities exist in wireless networks. This section addresses some of those vulnerabilities.

Denial-of-Service Attacks

A Denial-of-Service (DoS) attack is an example of the failure of the tenet of availability. A DoS attack occurs when an adversary causes a system or a network to become unavailable to legitimate users, or causes services to be interrupted or delayed. Consequences can range from a measurable reduction in performance to complete system failure. An example from the wireless world would be an external signal jamming the wireless channel. Little can be done to keep a determined adversary from mounting a DoS attack, because wireless LANs are susceptible to interference and interception and can be easily jammed.

Due to the nature of the wireless transmission medium, wireless networks are vulnerable to DoS attacks. If an attacker makes use of a powerful transceiver, enough interference can be generated to prevent wireless devices from communicating with one another. DoS attack devices do not need to be next to the devices being attacked, either; they only need to be within range of the wireless transmissions.

The following are examples of techniques used to deny service to a wireless device:

- Requests for authentication at a frequency that disrupts legitimate traffic
- Requests for deauthentication of legitimate users (these requests may not be refused according to the current 802.11 standard)
- Mimicking the behavior of an access point and convincing unsuspecting clients to communicate with it
- Repeatedly transmitting RTS/CTS frames to silence the network

The 2.4 GHz frequency range, within which 802.11b operates, is shared with other wireless devices such as cordless telephones, baby monitors, and Bluetooth-based devices. All of these devices can contribute to the degradation of and interruption to wireless signals. In addition, a determined and resourceful attacker with the proper equipment can flood the frequency with artificial noise and completely disrupt wireless network operation.

The "WAP GAP"

A specific security issue associated with WAP is the "WAP GAP." A WAP gap results from the requirement to change security protocols at the carrier's WAP gateway from the wireless WTLS to SSL for use over the wired network. At the WAP gateway, the transmission, which is protected by WTLS, is decrypted and then re-encrypted for transmission using SSL. The data is temporarily in the clear on the gateway and can be compromised if the gateway is not adequately protected (see Figure 2.12).

To address this issue, the WAP Forum has developed specifications that reduce this vulnerability and support e-commerce applications. These specifications are defined in WAP 1.2 as WMLScript Crypto Library and the WAP Identity Module (WIM). The WMLScript Crypto Library supports end-to-end security by providing for cryptographic functions to be initiated on the WAP client from the Internet content server. These functions include digital signatures originating with the WAP client and encryption and decryption of data. The WIM is a tamper-resistant device, such as a smart card, that cooperates with WTLS and provides cryptographic operations during the handshake phase.

Take special precautions to avoid the compromise of sensitive information caused by the WAP gap. WAP-enabled Personal Electronic Devices (PEDs) should not use commercial wireless network service provider gateways to access company Web servers unless end-to-end data encryption is provided.

However, a WAP gateway is implemented in the safest manner when companies install the gateway in their own networks. A company WAP gateway reduces the risk of data compromise, because the WTLS-to-SSL conversion required to access company Web servers occurs on a company-controlled and protected network, and connections may be monitored by IDS.

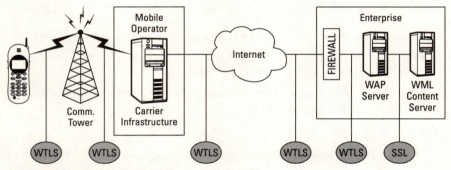

Figure 2.12 A WAP gateway

Insertion Attacks

In an insertion attack, unauthorized devices are deployed to gain access to an existing network. Laptops or Personal Digital Assistants (PDAs) can be configured to attempt access to networks simply by installing wireless network cards and setting up near a target network. If password authentication is not enabled on the network, it's a simple matter to get a connection to an AP and network resources.

Rogue Access Points

An insertion attack could be facilitated by the deployment of rogue access points, either by a hacker or by well-meaning internal employees seeking to enhance wireless coverage. Hacker-controlled APs can be used to entice authorized wireless clients to connect to a hacker's AP rather than to the network's intended APs. In addition, APs not authorized by the network administrator could be improperly configured and thus vulnerable to outside attack. This raises the risk of the interception of login IDs and passwords for future direct attacks on a network. The risk can be magnified if rogue APs are deployed behind the corporate firewall.

Typically, an AP employs one or several methods to control access to a wireless LAN, including use of a common Service Set Identifier (SSID) to allow access based on MAC address and WEP. Because the default authentication in 802.11 is open authentication, most systems will authenticate any user who requests connection. Shared key authentication is described but not mandated in 802.11, and it can be defeated.

Another common issue with 802.11b networks is that the APs have been designed for easy installation. So, although security features may be present, in most cases the features are turned off in their default state so that the network can be up and running as quickly as possible. Network administrators who leave their equipment with the default settings intact are particularly vulnerable, as hackers are likely to try known passwords and settings when attempting to penetrate wireless networks.

Also, even when password authentication is implemented on wireless network APs, unauthorized access is still possible through the use of brute force dictionary attacks. Password-cracking applications can methodically test passwords in an attempt to break into a network AP.

WEP Weaknesses

Most WEP products implement a 64-bit shared key, 40 bits of which are used for the secret key and 24 bits for the initialization vector. The key is installed at the wired network AP and must also be entered into each client.

WEP was not designed to withstand a directed cryptographic attack. WEP has well-known flaws in the encryption algorithms used to secure wireless transmissions. Two programs capable of exploiting the RC4 vulnerability, AirSnort and WEPCrack, both run under Linux and require a relatively small amount of captured data.

A number of researchers have investigated attacks on WEP:

- ✦ University of California, Berkeley, and Zero-Knowledge Systems researchers released a paper outlining the vulnerability of key stream reuse caused by the mismanagement of IVs. Their paper (posted at www.isaac.cs.berkeley.edu/isaac/wep-draft.pdf) noted that all possible IVs could be exhausted in as little as five hours.

- ✦ A paper written in 2000 by Scott Fluhrer, Itsik Mantin, and Adi Shamir (posted at www.securityfocus.com/cgi-bin/library.pl?cat=154&offset=10) exposed two significant weaknesses of RC4 in the key scheduling algorithm (KSA). They found that a small portion of the secret key determines a large portion of the initial KSA output, and the secret key can be easily derived by looking at the key stream used with multiple IVs.

- Rice University and AT&T Lab researchers put the aforementioned Fluhrer theory into practice by cracking encrypted packets and successfully demonstrating the severity of the flaw.
- In 2001, Nikita Borisov and a group of researchers from the University of California, Berkeley, published a paper regarding weaknesses in the WEP RC4 stream cipher (posted at www.isaac.cs.berkeley.edu/isaac/wep-faq.html). They found that if two messages used the same key stream, information about both messages might be revealed.
- Adam Stubblefield, an intern at AT&T Labs, was the first person to implement the Fluhrer attack mentioned above. He noted that an extra 802.2 header is added in IP traffic, making the attack easier, as every IP packet has the same first plaintext byte.

WEP Encryption Workarounds

To address WEP encryption issues, some vendors have implemented several enhanced 802.11b security methods, such as the following:

- **Secure key derivation** — The original shared secret secure key derivation is used to construct responses to the mutual challenges. It undergoes irreversible one-way hashes that make password-replay attacks impossible. The hash values sent over the wire are useful one time, at the start of the authentication process, but never again.
- **Initialization vector changes** — The Cisco Aironet wireless security solution also changes the initialization vector (IV) on a per-packet basis so that hackers can find no predetermined sequence to exploit. This capability, coupled with the reduction in possible attack windows, greatly mitigates exposure to hacker attacks due to frequent key rotation. In particular, this makes it difficult to create table-based attacks based on the knowledge of the IVs seen on the wireless network.
- **Dynamic WEP keys** — Several vendors offer products that eliminate the use of static keys, instead implementing per-user/per-session keys combined with RADIUS authentication. Clients must authenticate with a RADIUS server using network credentials, and WEP keys are dynamically distributed securely to the client.

Service Set Identifier Issues

The service set identifier (SSID) is an identification value programmed in the AP or group of APs to identify the local wireless subnet. This segmentation of the wireless network in multiple networks is a form of an authentication check. If a wireless station does not know the value of the SSID, access is denied to the associated AP. When a client computer is connected to the AP, the SSID acts as a simple password, which provides a measure of security.

War Driving

War driving (also known as *war walking*) is a term used to describe a hacker, who, armed with a laptop and a wireless adapter card and traveling in a car, bus, subway train, or other form of transport, goes around sniffing for WLANs.

The concept of war driving is simple: Using a device capable of receiving an 802.11b signal, a device capable of locating itself on a map, and software that logs data from the second a network is detected, the hacker moves from place to place, letting these devices do their job. Over time, the hacker builds up a database that comprises the network name, signal strength, location, and ip/namespace in use. Via SNMP, the hacker may even log packet samples and probe the AP for available data. The hacker may also mark the location of the vulnerable wireless network with chalk on the sidewalk or building itself. This is called war chalking, and it alerts other intruders that an exposed WLAN is nearby.

Common war driving exploits find many wireless networks with WEP disabled and using only the SSID for access control. And, as previously noted, the SSID for wireless networks can be found quickly. This vulnerability makes these networks susceptible to what's called the "parking lot attack," where, at a safe distance from the building's perimeter, an attacker gains access to the target network.

The wireless AP is configured to broadcast its SSID. When enabled, any client without an SSID can receive it and then access the AP. Users can also configure their own client systems with the appropriate SSID, because they are widely known and easily shared. A problem caused by the fact that most APs broadcast the SSID in their signals is that several of these APs use default SSIDs provided by the manufacturers, and a list of those default SSIDs is available for download on the Internet. This means that a hacker can easily determine a network's SSID and gain access to it using software tools.

Wireless Scanning and Eavesdropping

Wireless technology is also vulnerable to eavesdropping, especially because intruders do not have to physically tap into a network. It doesn't matter whether the intruder is on a different floor, across the room, or outside the building—as long as he possesses a WLAN network card with a promiscuous mode (that is, the capability to capture every packet on the segment of the LAN), he can passively "sniff" your network traffic without gaining physical access. Covert monitoring of wireless LANs is simple. Unless specifically configured to prevent another WLAN device from joining the network, a WLAN device will accept communications from any device within its range.

Furthermore, the 802.11 protocol inherently leaves the Physical layer header unencrypted, providing critical information to the attacker. Data encryption is the critical layer of defense, but data is often transmitted unencrypted. Using wireless packet sniffers, an attacker can passively intercept wireless network traffic and, through packet analysis, determine login IDs and passwords, as well as collect other sensitive data.

Wireless Packet Sniffers and Scanners

Wireless packet analyzers, or sniffers, work pretty much the same way as wired network packet analyzers: They capture packets from the data stream and allow the user to open them up and look at, or decode, them. Some wireless scanners don't employ full decoding tools, but show existing WLANs and SSIDs.

The figures in the next section show the same wireless network scanned with AirMagnet, NetStumbler, and AiroPeek.

AirMagnet

AirMagnet (www.airmagnet.com) is a full-featured wireless tool originally developed for WLAN inventory, but quickly developed into a useful wireless security assessment utility. The version of AirMagnet used for this demonstration was the latest Windows beta version, usable on a Win2K and later laptop. AirMagnet was primarily designed to operate from a PocketPC; the Windows version of the software is more recent. One of the major differences between the Win build and the PPC build is that the Win build allows more information to be displayed on a single screen, rather than alternating between screens in the PPC version. Figure 2.13 shows the AirMagnet product installed on a Compaq iPAQ Pocket PC.

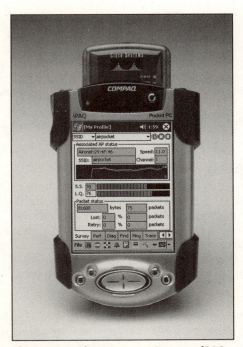

Figure 2.13 AirMagnet on Compaq iPAQ

Figure 2.14 shows the initial screen generated at the start of the session capture. It identifies two likely 802.11b WLANs, on channels 6 and 11. This screen in the Win version is actually a composite of three PPC screens: Expert mode, Survey mode, and Access Point List.

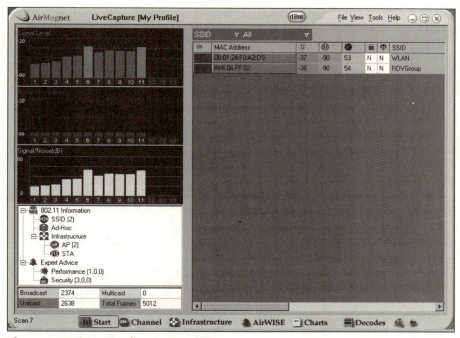

Figure 2.14 AirMagnet live capture scan

Figure 2.15 shows the AirWISE screen. This screen provides a cursory security examination of the APs, pointing out any major security issues, such as factory-default APs or WEP disabled.

AirMagnet helps determine the intensity and source of the WLAN transmissions, as well as the intensity and source of any RFI competing with the signal. AM also shows the type and speed of the packets, separating them between data, control, and management frames.

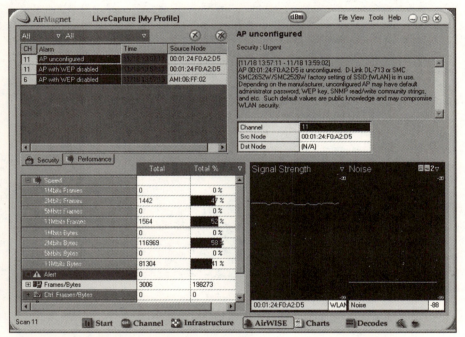

Figure 2.15 AirMagnet AirWISE screen

Figure 2.16 shows the session decode in Chart mode. This mode can display all channels in bar graph format, showing the channel's differentiation between 802.11 frame types, frame speed, or address type. This figure shows the breakdown of each channel's broadcast, multicast, and unicast transmissions.

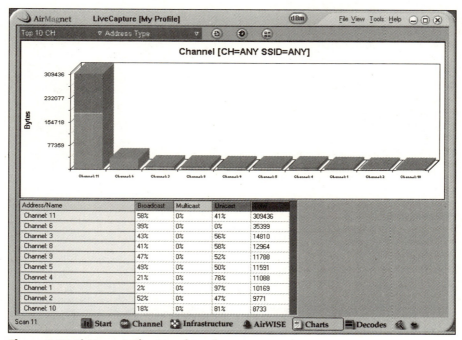

Figure 2.16 AirMagnet Chart mode

Finally, Figure 2.17 shows the session captured in full Decode mode. Packets can be filtered and saved for later analysis, and a single channel can be selected for decoding.

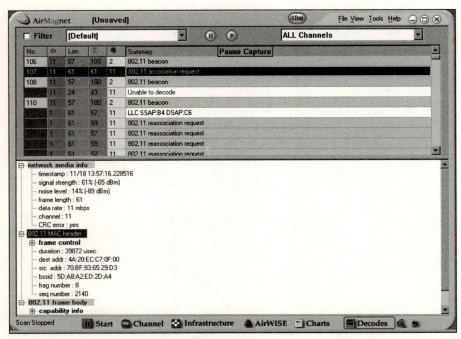

Figure 2.17 AirMagnet Decode mode

NetStumbler

Figure 2.18 shows the same WLAN scanned with NetStumbler (www.netstumbler.com). NetStumbler is a shareware program for locating WLAN SSIDs. NetStumbler doesn't provide the detail AirMagnet does, because it only shows the actual 802.11b WLANs found, not the spurious radiation from other channels. It attempts to identify the WLAN vendor, and when coupled with a GPS, it can provide directional information.

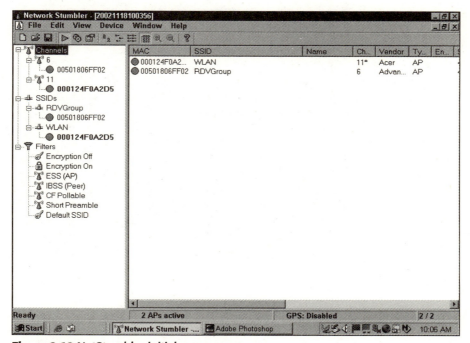

Figure 2.18 NetStumbler initial scan screen

NetStumbler can also provide signal-to-noise information over time, as shown in Figure 2.19.

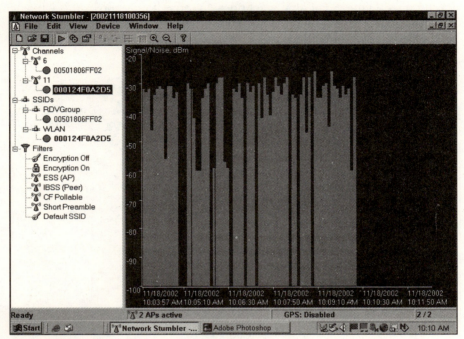

Figure 2.19 NetStumbler signal-to-noise screen

AiroPeek

AiroPeek (www.wildpackets.com) is a comprehensive packet analyzer for IEEE 802.11b wireless LANs, supporting all higher-level network protocols such as TCP/IP, AppleTalk, NetBEUI, and IPX. AiroPeek contains all of the network troubleshooting features of EtherPeek, WildPackets' Ethernet packet analyzer. AiroPeek is used to isolate security problems by decoding 802.11b WLAN protocols and analyzing wireless network performance with an identification of signal strength, channel, and data rates.

The following figures show the same WLAN scanned previously, using the AiroPeek NX product. Figure 2.20 shows the packet capture screen at the initiation of the sniffing session. Airopeek provides quite a bit of information, including source and destination of the packet, data rate, channel, signal strength, and protocol.

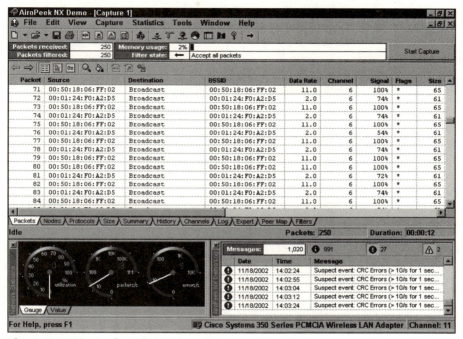

Figure 2.20 AiroPeek packet capture screen

Figure 2.21 shows the protocols screen from the same capture. This can identify the various protocols communicated, and the percentage of management, data, and control frames exchanged.

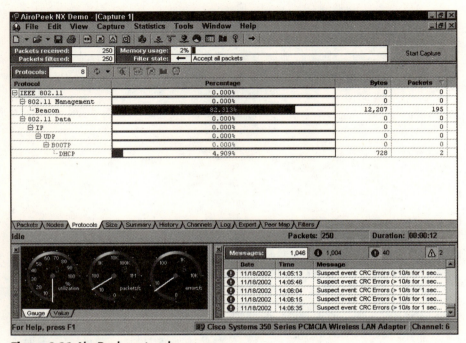

Figure 2.21 AiroPeek protocols screen

Figure 2.22 shows a summary screen from the capture session. It displays a detailed analysis of each type of frame exchanged, including error types.

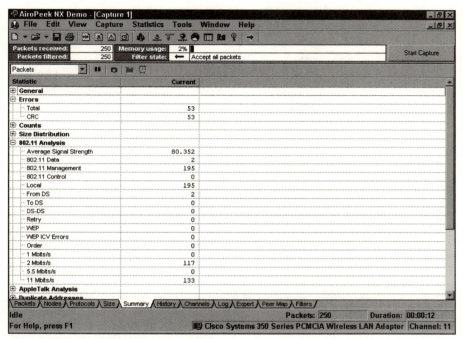

Figure 2.22 AiroPeek summary screen

The expert screen, shown in Figure 2.23, is useful for troubleshooting error conditions during specific node-to-node conversations.

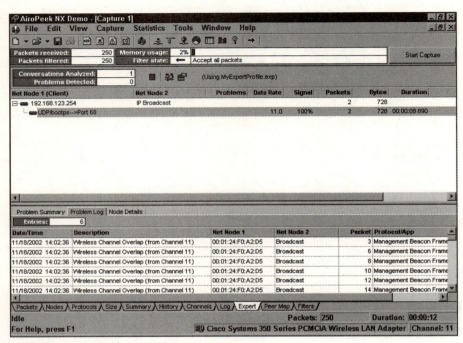

Figure 2.23 AiroPeek expert screen

✦   ✦   ✦

SAMPLE QUESTIONS

1. The protocol within the Wireless Application Protocol (WAP) that performs functions similar to SSL in the TCP/IP protocol is called the _____.

    a. Wireless Session Protocol (WSP)

    b. Wireless Transport Layer Security Protocol (WTLS)

    c. Wireless Transaction Protocol (WTP)

    d. Wireless Application Environment (WAE)

2. Which IEEE standard uses the Extensible Authentication Protocol to offer authentication and key management for wireless LANs?

    a. 802.15

    b. 802.1x

    c. 802.11g

    d. 802.11a

3. What protocol adds digital signatures and encryption to Internet Multipurpose Internet Mail Extensions (MIME)?

    a. S/MIME

    b. PGP

    c. SET/MIME

    d. IPSEC

4. Which of the following statements is *not* correct about the difference between Layer 2 and Layer 3 tunneling protocols?

    a. Layer 2 tunneling supports multiple payload protocols.

    b. Layer 3 tunneling supports multiple payload protocols.

    c. Layer 3 tunneling protocols typically support only IP networks.

    d. Layer 2 tunneling supports dynamic assignment of client addresses.

5. The Wired Equivalency Privacy (WEP) algorithm of the 802.11 Wireless LAN Standard uses which of the following to protect the confidentiality of information being transmitted on the LAN?

    a. A public/private key pair that is shared between a mobile station (for example, a laptop with a wireless Ethernet card) and a base station access point

    b. A digital signature that is sent between a mobile station (for example, a laptop with a wireless Ethernet card) and a base station access point

c. A secret key that is shared between a mobile station (for example, a laptop with a wireless Ethernet card) and a base station access point

d. Frequency shift keying (FSK) of the message that is sent between a mobile station (for example, a laptop with a wireless Ethernet card) and a base station access point

6. The vulnerability associated with the requirement to change security protocols at a carrier's Wireless Application Protocol (WAP) gateway from the Wireless Transport Layer Security Protocol (WTLS) to SSL or TLS over the wired network is called the _____.

   a. Wired Equivalency Privacy (WEP) gap

   b. Wireless Transaction Protocol (WTP) gap

   c. Wireless Transport Layer Security Protocol (WTLS) gap

   d. Wireless Application Protocol (WAP) gap

7. Which of the following choices is *not* a Layer 2 tunneling protocol?

   a. PPTP

   b. L2TP

   c. IPSec

   d. L2F

8. Which statement about Layer 2 tunneling technologies is *not* correct?

   a. Both of the Layer 2 tunnel endpoints must agree to the tunnel and must negotiate configuration variables.

   b. Layer 2 tunnels must be created, maintained, and then terminated.

   c. Layer 2 tunneling technologies generally assume that all of the configuration issues are preconfigured.

   d. Layer 2 tunnels require a tunnel maintenance phase.

9. Which statement best describes PPP?

   a. PPP uses Link Control Protocol (LCP).

   b. PPP was the de facto standard before SLIP.

   c. PPP is a half-duplex protocol.

   d. PPP only uses asynchronous communication.

10. Which of the following statements about CHAP is incorrect?

    a. CHAP sends the password in cleartext.

    b. The password is used to create an MD5 encrypted hash.

    c. CHAP protects against replay attacks.

    d. CHAP protects against remote client impersonation.

11. Which of the following choices is *not* considered a basic VPN requirement?

    a. Multiprotocol support

    b. Data encryption

    c. Cleartext passwords

    d. User authentication

12. Which PPP authentication method sends passwords in cleartext?

    a. PAP

    b. CHAP

    c. MS-CHAP

    d. MS-CHAP v2

13. Which statement best describes a replay attack?

    a. A third party takes over an authenticated connection.

    b. An intruder tries many passwords.

    c. The intruder waits until the connection has been authenticated.

    d. An intruder resends captured packets to create an authenticated connection.

14. The algorithm of the 802.11 Wireless LAN Standard that is used to protect transmitted information from disclosure is called the _____.

    a. Wireless Application Environment (WAE)

    b. Wireless Transaction Protocol (WTP)

    c. Wired Equivalency Privacy (WEP)

    d. Wireless Transport Layer Security Protocol (WTLS)

15. Which statement about a VPN tunnel is *not* correct?

    a. A VPN tunnel can be created by installing software or hardware agents on the client or network.

    b. A VPN tunnel can be created by implementing key and certificate exchange systems.

    c. A tunnel maintenance protocol is used as the mechanism to manage the tunnel.

    d. A VPN tunnel can be created by implementing IPSec devices only.

16. Which of the following statements describing SSL is *not* true?

    a. SSL uses public key cryptography for secret key exchange.

    b. SSL uses a message authentication code (MAC) to verify integrity.

c. SSL uses private key encryption to ensure the confidentiality of transmitted information.

d. SSL provides authentication in one direction only.

17. The SSL/TLS protocol comprises two layers. Which choice correctly names these two layers?

    a. Record Protocol and Handshake Protocol

    b. Record Protocol and Authentication Protocol

    c. Exchange Protocol and Authentication Protocol

    d. Exchange Protocol and Handshake Protocol

18. Which of the following designations on a Web page indicates that HTTP is being used with SSL?

    a. S-HTTP

    b. HTTPs

    c. SSL/TLS

    d. HTTP/SSL

19. Which of the following statements is *not* true regarding instant-messaging (IM)?

    a. It supports the real time exchange of messages on the Internet.

    b. A user logs on to an instant messaging server and is authenticated by the server.

    c. Communication takes place only between two individuals at a time.

    d. Messages from one user to another are routed through the instant messaging server.

20. If an Ethernet Network Interface Card (NIC) is programmed to read all messages that it sees on the network, it is said to be operating in what?

    a. Acquisition mode

    b. Broadcast mode

    c. Promiscuous mode

    d. Monitoring mode

21. Which choice refers to a standard format whereby Web sites can impart their privacy policies to users through a machine-readable syntax?

    a. Platform for Privacy Preferences

    b. Pretty Good Privacy

    c. Post Office Protocol

    d. Privacy Practices Protocol

22. Which of the following statements is *not* true regarding JavaScript?

  a. On the client-side, JavaScript is embedded in HTML pages and is interpreted by the browser at runtime.

  b. JavaScript programs running on the server-side are compiled into bytecode executable files.

  c. JavaScript has strong type checking and static typing.

  d. JavaScripts are easier to author than Java programs.

23. Which of the following statements regarding ActiveX is *not* true?

  a. ActiveX is an environment under which programs are managed and run.

  b. ActiveX programs are downloaded directly to a user's hard drive.

  c. ActiveX does not rely on the digital signing of trusted components.

  d. An ActiveX component carries a security level designation that defines if and when the component can be safely executed.

24. A component that is used to allow a Java plug-in to access a user's hard drive is called a _____.

  a. Signed applet

  b. Cookie

  c. Buffer

  d. Gateway interface

25. Which of the following statements regarding the Common Gateway Interface (CGI) is *not* true?

  a. CGI is a standard that defines how HTTP or Web servers interface with client applications.

  b. A CGI program is executable and runs on the server in real time.

  c. CGI does not support the dynamic generation of HTML documents.

  d. A CGI program is invoked when a client requests information from a server.

26. What is PERL?

  a. A compiled language that is commonly used to write CGI programs

  b. A scripting language that is commonly used to write CGI programs

  c. A compiled language that is suited to text processing

  d. A protocol used to transmit e-mail messages over the Internet

27. Which of the following items is *not* a restricted forwarding option provided by the SMTP Relay protocol?

    a. Relay mail for local hosts only

    b. No mail relay

    c. All mail relay

    d. Relay mail for

28. Which of the following is *not* a valid step that is performed by SSL/TLS-enabled clients to authenticate a server using digital certificates?

    a. Verifying that the current date and time are within the certificate's validity period

    b. Verifying that the domain name in the server's certificate corresponds to the domain name of the server

    c. Using the CA's private key to validate the CA's digital signature for the server's certificate

    d. Verifying that the issuing CA is on the list of trusted CAs maintained by the client

29. Which choice is *not* a component of an LDAP attribute?

    a. A Distinguished Name

    b. A Designated Name

    c. A type

    d. A set of values corresponding to a type

30. Which of the following items is *not* a characteristic of LDAP?

    a. It is platform-independent.

    b. It supports confidentiality, authentication, and integrity.

    c. Searches are based on an entry's object class and attributes.

    d. It is not suitable for implementation at small, workgroup levels.

CHAPTER 3

Infrastructure Security

This chapter examines the elements of networking infrastructure that require security consideration, including the following:

- Protocol models
- Network devices, such as firewalls, hubs, and routers
- Wireless devices
- Data media, such as cables and removable media
- Network address translation and tunneling
- Intrusion detection and response
- Various hardening techniques

Protocol Models

Before the various infrastructure devices and elements are discussed, this section takes a quick look at the OSI model and the TCP/IP protocol suite. These devices use many different protocols at varying OSI model layers, and the candidate will need to know one from another.

Open Systems Interconnect Model

The Open Systems Interconnect (OSI) model was created in the early 1980s by the International Standards Organization (ISO) to help vendors develop interoperable network devices. The OSI model describes how data and network information is communicated from one computer to another through the network media. The model breaks this information into seven distinct layers, each with a unique set of properties. Each layer directly interacts with its adjacent layers.

The seven OSI layers are shown in Figure 3.1.

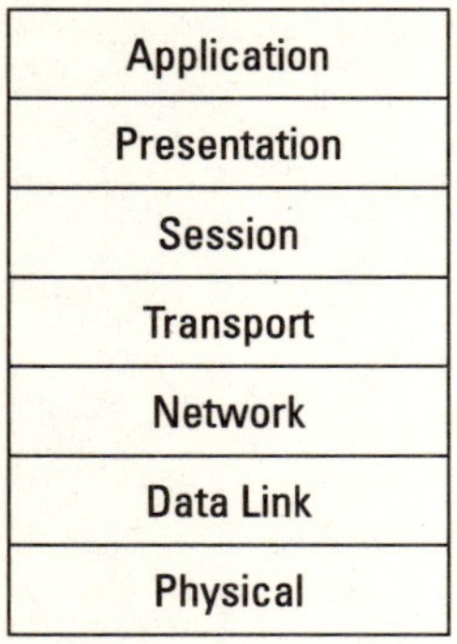

Figure 3.1 The OSI seven-layer reference model

Application
Presentation
Session
Transport
Network
Data Link
Physical

- **Application layer (Layer 7)** — The Application layer is the highest level of the OSI model and the direct interface to the user. It supports the processes that deal with the communication aspects of an application. The Application layer is responsible for identifying and establishing the availability of the intended communication partner. This layer is also responsible for determining whether sufficient resources exist for the intended communication.

- **Presentation layer (Layer 6)** — The Presentation layer presents data to the Application layer. Essentially, it's a translator. Tasks such as data compression, decompression, encryption, and decryption are associated with the Presentation layer. It also defines how applications can enter the network.

- **Session layer (Layer 5)** — The Session layer makes the initial contact with other computers and sets up lines of communication. It formats the data for transfer between end nodes, provides session restart and recovery, and performs general maintenance of the session from end to end. It also splits up a communication session into three different phases: connection establishment, data transfer, and connection release.

- **Transport layer (Layer 4)** — The Transport layer is responsible for maintaining the end-to-end integrity and control of the session. It defines how to address the physical locations and/or devices on the network, makes connections between nodes, and handles the internetworking of messages. Services located in the Transport layer segment and reassemble data from upper-layer applications and unite it onto the same data stream, provide end-to-end data transport services, and establish a logical connection between the sending host and destination host on a network.

- **Network layer (Layer 3)** — The Network layer defines how the small packets of data are routed and relayed between end systems on the same network or on interconnected networks. At this layer, message routing, error detection, and control of node data traffic are managed. Sending packets from the source network to the destination network is the Network layer's primary function. The IP protocol operates at this layer.

- **Data Link layer (Layer 2)** — The Data Link layer defines the protocol that computers must follow to access the network for transmitting and receiving messages. Token Ring and Ethernet operate within this layer, which establishes the communications link between individual devices over a physical link or channel. The Data Link layer ensures that messages are delivered to the proper device, and translates messages from above into bits for the Physical layer (layer 1) to transmit. The Data Link layer formats the message into data frames and adds a customized header that contains the hardware destination and source address. It also contains the logical link control and the media access control (MAC) sublayers.

- **Physical layer (Layer 1)** — The Physical layer has only two responsibilities: to send and receive bits. The Physical layer defines the physical connection between the computer and the network and converts the bits into voltages or light impulses for transmission. It defines the electrical and mechanical aspects of the device interface to a physical transmission medium, such as twisted pair, coax, or fiber.

Transmission Control Protocol/ Internet Protocol Model

Transmission Control Protocol/Internet Protocol (TCP/IP) is the common name for the suite of protocols developed by the Department of Defense in the 1970s to support the construction of worldwide networks. The Internet is based on TCP/IP, the two best-known protocols in the suite.

As shown in Figure 3.2, TCP/IP adheres roughly to the bottom four layers of the OSI model. This figure reflects the original Department of Defense (DoD) concept of the TCP/IP model.

Application
Host-to-Host
Internet
Network Access

Figure 3.2 TCP/IP layers

- **Application layer** — This layer isn't really in TCP/IP. It's made up of whatever application is trying to communicate using TCP/IP. TCP/IP views everything above the three bottom layers as the responsibility of the application, so the Application, Presentation, and Session layers of the OSI model are considered folded into this top layer. The TCP/IP suite primarily operates in the Transport and Network layers of the OSI model.

- **Host-to-Host layer** — The Host-to-Host layer is comparable to the OSI Transport layer. It defines protocols for setting up the level of transmission service. It provides for reliable end-to-end communications, ensures that data is delivered error-free, handles packet sequencing of the data, and maintains data integrity.
- **Internet layer** — The Internet layer corresponds to the OSI Network layer. It designates the protocols relating to the logical transmission of packets over the network. It gives network nodes an IP address and handles the routing of packets among multiple networks. It also controls the communication flow between hosts.
- **Network Access layer** — At the bottom of the TCP/IP model, the Network Access layer monitors the data exchange between the host and the network. The equivalent of the Data Link and Physical layers of the OSI model, it oversees hardware addressing and defines protocols for the physical transmission of data.

TCP/IP Protocols

Table 3.1 lists some important TCP/IP protocols that populate the TCP/IP model, and their related layers.

Table 3.1
TCP/IP Protocols

Layer	Protocol
Host-to-host	Transmission Control Protocol (TCP)
Host-to-host	User Datagram Protocol (UDP)
Internet	Internet Protocol (IP)
Internet	Address Resolution Protocol (ARP)
Internet	Reverse Address Resolution Protocol (RARP)
Internet	Internet Control Message Protocol (ICMP)

- **Transmission Control Protocol (TCP)** — TCP provides a full-duplex, connection-oriented, reliable connection. Incoming TCP packets are sequenced to match the original transmission sequence numbers. Any lost or damaged packets are retransmitted.
- **User Datagram Protocol (UDP)** — UDP is similar to TCP but gives only a "best effort" delivery, which means it offers no error correction, does not sequence the packet segments, and does not care in which order the packet segments arrive at their destination. Consequently, it's referred to as an unreliable protocol. It's also considered a connectionless protocol. Table 3.2 illustrates the differences between the TCP and the UDP protocols.

Table 3.2
TCP versus UDP Protocol

TCP	UDP
Sequenced	Unsequenced
Connection-oriented	Connectionless
Reliable	Unreliable
High overhead	Low overhead
Slower	Faster

✦ **Internet Protocol (IP)** — IP provides an unreliable datagram service, meaning that it does not guarantee that the packet will be delivered at all, that it will be delivered only once, or that it will be delivered in the order in which it was sent.

On the Internet, and in networks using the IP protocol, each data packet is assigned the IP address of the sender and the IP address of the recipient. Each device then receives the packet and makes routing decisions based on the packet's destination IP address.

✦ **Address Resolution Protocol (ARP)** — IP needs to know the hardware address of the packet's destination in order to send it. ARP is used to match an IP address to an Ethernet address. An Ethernet address is a 48-bit address that is hard-wired into the network interface card (NIC) of the network node. ARP is used to match the 32-bit IP address to this hardware address, technically referred to as the *media access control (MAC)* address, or *physical address*.

Figure 3.3 shows a flow chart of the ARP decision process.

✦ **Reverse Address Resolution Protocol (RARP)** — In some cases, the MAC address is known but the IP address must be discovered, as when diskless machines are booted onto the network. The RARP protocol sends out a packet that includes its MAC address and a request to be informed which IP address should be assigned to that MAC address. A RARP server responds with the answer.

✦ **Internet Control Message Protocol (ICMP)** — ICMP's primary function is to send messages between network devices regarding the health of the network. It can inform hosts of a better route to a destination if an existing route is problematic, and help identify the problem with a route. The Packet INternet Groper utility (PING) uses ICMP messages to check the physical connectivity of machines on a network.

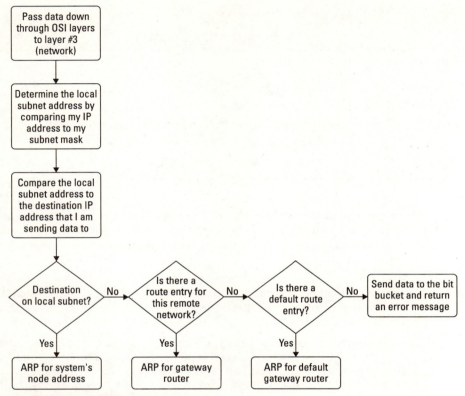

Figure 3.3 The ARP decision process

Figure 3.4 shows how TCP/IP layers correspond to the OSI model layers.

OSI	TCP/IP			
Application	FTP	Telnet	SMTP	Other
Presentation	FTP	Telnet	SMTP	Other
Session				
Transport	TCP		UDP	
Network	IP			
Data Link	Ethernet	FDDI	x.25	Other
Physical	Ethernet	FDDI	x.25	Other

Figure 3.4 OSI model layers mapped to TCP/IP layers

Network Devices

This section examines those devices that interact with the infrastructure in some way, and present unique challenges to the security professional.

Firewall Types

The Security+ candidate should know the basic types of firewalls and their functions, which firewall operates at which protocol layer, and the basic variations of firewall architectures.

Firewalls act as perimeter access control devices and are classified into three common types:

- Packet-level filtering firewalls
- Proxy firewalls, such as application-level or circuit-level
- Stateful inspection firewalls

Packet Filtering Firewalls

The packet filtering firewall examines both the source and destination address of the incoming data packet. This firewall either blocks or passes the packet to its intended destination network. The firewall can allow or deny access to specific applications and/or services based on Access Control Lists (ACLs). ACLs are database files that reside on the firewall, are maintained by the firewall administrator, and tell the firewall specifically which packets can and cannot be forwarded to certain addresses.

The firewall can also be configured to allow access for only authorized application port or service numbers. It looks at the data packet to get information about the source and destination addresses of an incoming packet, the session's communications protocol (TCP, UDP, or ICMP), and the source and destination application port for the desired service.

A packet-level firewall doesn't keep a history of the communications session. It operates at the Network layer of the OSI model and offers good performance. Ongoing maintenance of the ACLs can become an issue. Figure 3.5 shows an external router being used as a simple packet filtering firewall.

Figure 3.5 A packet filtering router

Application-Level Firewalls

An application-level firewall (see Figure 3.6) is commonly a host computer that is running proxy server software, making it a proxy server. This firewall works by transferring a copy of each accepted data packet from one network to another, masking the data's origin. A proxy server can control which services a workstation uses on the Internet, and aids in protecting the network from outsiders who may be trying to get information about the network's design.

Also called an *application-layer gateway*, this firewall is commonly used with a dual-homed host. It operates at OSI protocol layer seven, the Application layer, and is more secure because it examines the packet at the Application layer, albeit at the expense of performance.

Unlike packet firewalls, proxy firewalls capture some session history. Proxy firewalls have higher protocols carried on low-level protocols, such as e-mail or HTML.

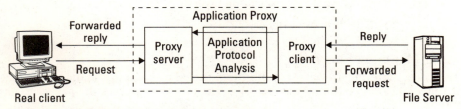

Figure 3.6 Application-level proxy firewall process

Circuit-Level Firewalls

Like an application-level firewall, a circuit-level firewall is used as a proxy server. It is similar to the application-level firewall in that it functions as a proxy server, but differs in that special proxy application software is not needed.

This firewall creates a virtual circuit between the workstation client (destination) and the server (host). It also provides security for a wide variety of protocols and is easier to maintain.

Stateful Inspection Firewalls

A stateful inspection firewall intercepts incoming packets at the Network level, then uses an "inspection engine" to extract state-related information from upper layers. It maintains the information in a dynamic state table and evaluates subsequent connection attempts. Stateful inspection firewalls keep low-protocol records at the IP level.

The packets are queued and then analyzed at all OSI layers against the state table. By examining the "state" and "context" of the incoming data packets, protocols that are considered "connectionless," such as UDP-based applications and Remote Procedure Calls (RPCs), can be tracked more easily.

Dynamic Packet Filtering Firewalls

A *dynamic packet filtering firewall* employs a technology that enables the modification of the firewall security rule. This type of technology is mostly used for providing limited support for UDP. For a short period of time, this firewall remembers all of the UDP packets that have crossed the network's perimeter, and it decides whether to enable packets to pass through the firewall.

Firewall Architectures

The four basic types of firewall architectures are as follows:

- Packet filtering
- Screened hosts
- Dual-homed hosts
- Screened subnet firewalls

Keep in mind that some of these architectures are specifically associated with one of the previously discussed firewall types, while other architectures can be a combination of types.

Packet Filtering Routers

A packet filtering router is the most common and oldest firewall device in use. A packet filtering router sits between the private "trusted" network and the "untrusted" network or network segment. This firewall architecture is used as a packet filtering firewall (described in the previous section). A packet filtering router is sometimes used to directly manage access to a demilitarized zone (DMZ) network segment.

Screened Host Firewalls

Like a dual-homed host, a screened host firewall uses two network cards to connect to the trusted and untrusted networks, but adds a screening router between the host and the untrusted network (see Figure 3.7). It provides both network-layer (routing) and application-layer (proxy) services. This type of firewall system requires an intruder to penetrate two separate systems before he or she can compromise the trusted network.

The host is configured between the local "trusted" network and "untrusted" network. Because the firewall can be the focus of external attacks, it is sometimes called the "sacrificial lamb."

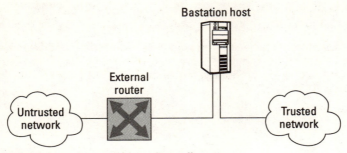

Figure 3.7 A screened host firewall

Dual-Homed Host Firewalls

Another very common firewall architecture configuration is the dual-homed host (see Figure 3.8). A dual-homed host has two NICs but no screening router. It uses two NICs to attach to two separate networks, commonly a trusted network and an untrusted network.

This architecture is a simple configuration that consists of a single computer (the host) with two NICs: One is connected to the local "trusted" network and the other is connected to the Internet or an "untrusted" external network. A dual-homed host firewall usually acts to block or filter some or all of the traffic trying to pass between the networks.

IP traffic forwarding is usually disabled or restricted—all traffic between the networks and the traffic's destination must pass through some kind of security inspection mechanism.

The host's routing capabilities must be disabled so the host does not unintentionally enable internal routing, which will connect the two networks together transparently and negate the firewall's function. Many systems come with routing enabled by default, such as IP Forwarding, which makes the firewall useless.

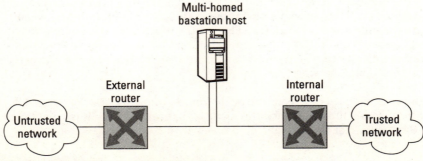

Figure 3.8 A dual-homed firewall

Screened Subnet Firewalls

One of the most secure implementations of firewall architectures is the screened subnet firewall. Like a dual-homed host firewall, a screened subnet firewall uses two NICs but also has two screening routers with the host acting as a proxy server on its own network segment. One screening router controls traffic local to the network while the second monitors and controls incoming and outgoing Internet traffic.

It employs two packet filtering routers and a bastion host. Like a screened host firewall, this firewall supports both packet filtering and proxy services, yet it can also define a DMZ.

A DMZ, or *demilitarized zone*, is a network added between an internal network and an external network to provide an additional layer of security. In some cases, it is also called a *perimeter network*. The DMZ creates a small network between the untrusted network and the trusted network where the bastion host and other public Web services exist. The outside router provides protection against external attacks, while the inside router manages the private network access to a DMZ by routing it through the bastion host.

Many firewalls allow you to place a network in the DMZ. Figure 3.9 shows a common firewall implementation employing a DMZ.

SOCKS

A SOCKS server provides another variation of firewall protection. Socket Security (SOCKS) is a Transport-layer, secure networking proxy protocol. SOCKS replaces the standard network system's calls with its own calls. These calls open connections to a SOCKS proxy server for client authentication transparently to the user. Common network utilities, such as TELNET or FTP, need to be SOCKS-ified, or have their network calls altered to recognize SOCKS proxy calls.

A SOCKS server is a circuit-level proxy server that does not require the server resource overhead of conventional proxy servers. SOCKS uses port 1080 and is used both for outbound host access by a workstation and to allow a host outside of a firewall to connect transparently and securely through the firewall. Consequently, some sites may have port 1080 open for incoming connections to a system running a SOCKS daemon. One of the more common uses of SOCKS is to allow ICQ traffic to hosts that are behind a firewall.

Bastion Hosts

A *bastion host* is any computer that is fully exposed to attack by being on the public side of the demilitarized zone (DMZ), unprotected by a firewall or filtering router. Firewalls and routers, or anything that provides perimeter access-control security, can be considered a bastion host. Other types of bastion hosts can include Web, mail, DNS, and FTP servers. A bastion host is often used as a sacrificial lamb. Due to their exposure, a great deal of effort must be put into designing and configuring bastion hosts to minimize the chance of penetration.

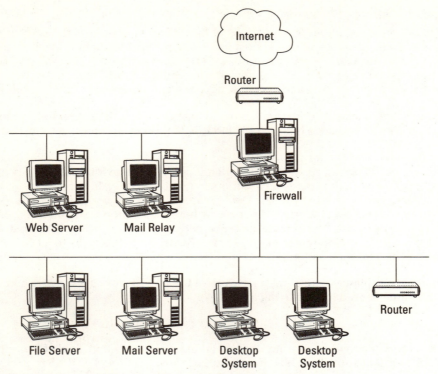

Figure 3.9 A common firewall implementation employing a DMZ

Hubs and Repeaters

Repeaters and hubs operate at the Physical layer of the OSI model. They amplify the data signal to extend the length of a network segment, and they help compensate for signal deterioration due to attenuation.

Hubs are more ubiquitous than repeaters. They are used to connect multiple LAN devices, such as servers and workstations. Hubs do not add much intelligence to the communications process, however, because they don't filter packets, examine addressing, or alter the data packet.

Figure 3-10 shows a repeater amplifying the network signal.

Bridges

Bridges amplify the data signals like hubs, but make intelligent decisions as to where to forward the data. A bridge forwards the data to all other network segments if the destination computer's MAC address is not on the local network segment. If the destination computer is on the local network segment, the bridge does not forward the data.

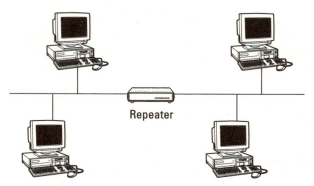

Figure 3.10 Repeater

Because bridges operate at the Data Link layer (Layer 2), they do not use IP addresses (IP information is attached in the Network layer, Layer 3). Because a bridge automatically forwards any broadcast traffic to all ports, an error state known as a *broadcast storm* can develop, overwhelming the network devices.

Figure 3.11 shows a bridged network.

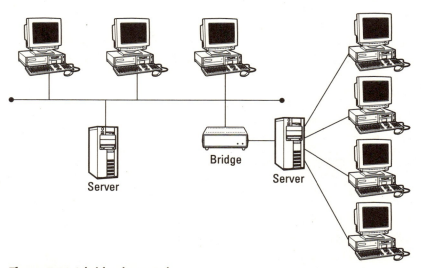

Figure 3.11 A bridged network

Spanning Tree

To prevent broadcast storms and other unwanted side effects of looping, Digital Equipment Corporation created the *Spanning Tree Protocol (STP)*, which has been standardized as the 802.1d specification by the Institute of Electrical and Electronic Engineers (IEEE).

A spanning tree uses the *Spanning Tree Algorithm (STA)*, which senses that the switch has more than one way to communicate with a node and determines which way is best. It blocks out the other paths, but keeps track of them in case the primary path becomes unavailable.

Switches

A *switch* is similar to a bridge or a hub, except that it only sends the data packet to the specific port where the destination MAC address is located, rather than to all ports that are attached to the hub or bridge. A switch relies on the MAC addresses to determine the source and destination of a packet, which is Layer 2 networking.

Switches primarily operate at the Data Link layer (Layer 2), although intelligent Layer 3 switching techniques (combining switching and routing) are being more frequently used (see the section called "Layer 3 Switching," later in this chapter).

Figure 3.12 shows a switched network.

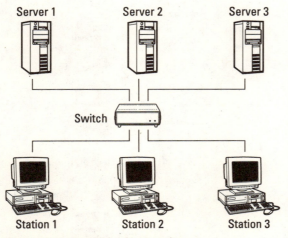

Figure 3.12 A switched network

Most Ethernet LAN switches use transparent bridging to create their address lookup tables. Transparent bridging allows a switch to learn everything it needs to know about the location of nodes on the network.

The five steps of the transparent bridging process are as follows:

1. Learning
2. Flooding
3. Filtering
4. Forwarding
5. Aging

Routers

Routers add more intelligence to the process of forwarding packets. When a router receives a packet, it looks at the Network layer source and destination addresses (IP address) to determine the path the packet should take, and only forwards the packet to the network to which the packet was destined. This prevents unnecessary network traffic from being sent over the network by blocking broadcast information and traffic to unknown addresses. Routers operate at the Network layer (Layer 3) of the OSI protocol model. Routers are necessary when communicating between VLANs.

Figure 3.13 shows a routed network.

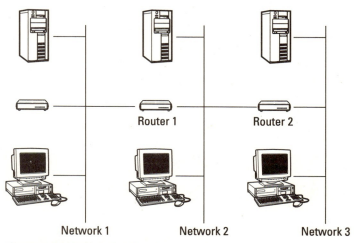

Figure 3.13 A routed network

Routing Methodologies

Three fundamental routing methodologies exist, and other routing protocols and methods expand on this process.

- Static routing
- Distance vector routing
- Link state routing

Static routing refers to the definition of a specific route in a configuration file on the router and does not require the routers to exchange route information dynamically.

Distance vector routing uses the Routing Information Protocol (RIP) to maintain a dynamic table of routing information that is updated regularly. RIP bases its routing path on the distance (number of hops) to the destination. RIP maintains optimum routing paths by sending out routing update messages if the network topology changes (see Figure 3.14).

For example, if a router finds that a particular link is faulty, it updates its routing table and sends a copy of the modified table to each of its neighbors. RIP is the oldest and most common type of dynamic routing, and commonly broadcasts its routing table information to all other routers every minute.

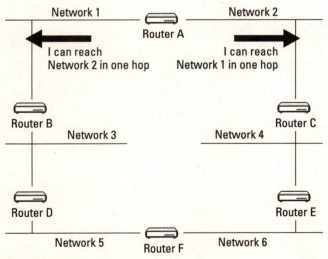

Figure 3.14 Distance vector routing

Link state routers function like distance vector routers, but only use first-hand information when building routing tables by maintaining a copy of every other router's

Link State Protocol (LSP) frame. This helps eliminate routing errors and considerably lessens convergence time.

The Open Shortest Path First (OSPF) is a link-state hierarchical routing algorithm intended as a successor to RIP. It features least-cost routing, multipath routing, and load balancing.

Layer 3 Switching

Although most standard switches operate at the Data Link layer, Layer 3 switches operate at the Network layer and function like a router by incorporating some router features. The pattern matching and caching on Layer 3 switches is similar to the pattern matching and caching on a router. Both use a routing protocol and routing table to determine the best path. However, Layer 3 switches have optimized hardware to pass data as fast as Layer 2 switches.

A Layer 3 switch can also reprogram the hardware dynamically with the current Layer 3 routing information, providing much faster packet processing. The information received from the routing protocols is used to update the hardware caching tables.

Within the LAN environment, a Layer 3 switch is usually faster than a router because it is built on switching hardware. Many of Cisco's Layer 3 switches, like the Cisco Catalyst 6000, are actually routers that operate faster because they are built on "switching" hardware with customized chips inside the box.

Wireless Devices

Wireless devices and technologies deliver on the promise of quick establishment of ad hoc connections and automatic connectivity between devices. Unfortunately, these devices also present the organization with a whole new level of security concerns.

Spread Spectrum Technologies

The de facto communication standard for wireless LANs is *spread spectrum*, a wideband radio frequency technique originally developed by the military for use in secure, mission-critical communications systems. Spread spectrum uses a radio transmission mode that broadcasts signals over a range of frequencies. The receiving mobile device must know the correct frequency of the spread spectrum signal being broadcast.

 Note An interesting URL about the actress Hedy Lamar's involvement with spread spectrum technology can be found at: `www.inventions.org/culture/female/lamarr.html`.

Two different spread spectrum technologies for 2.4 GHz wireless LANs currently exist: *direct-sequence spread spectrum (DSSS)* and *frequency-hopping spread spectrum (FHSS)*.

Direct-Sequence Spread Spectrum

DSSS is a wideband spread spectrum transmission technology that generates a redundant bit pattern for each bit to be transmitted. DSSS spreads the signal over a wide frequency band in which the source transmitter maps each bit of data into a pattern of chips. At the receiving mobile device, the original data is re-created by mapping the chips back into a data bit. The DSSS transmitter and receiver must be synchronized to operate properly. A DSSS signal appears as low-power wideband noise to a non-DSSS receiver and is ignored by most narrowband receivers.

Because DSSS spreads across the spectrum, the number of independent, non-overlapping channels in the 2.4 GHz band is small (typically only three); therefore, only a very limited number of collocated networks can operate without interference. Some DSSS products enable users to deploy more than one channel in the same area by separating the 2.4 GHz band into multiple sub-bands, each of which contains an independent DSSS network.

Frequency-Hopping Spread Spectrum

FHSS uses a narrowband carrier that continually changes frequency in a known pattern. The FHSS algorithm spreads the signal by operating on one frequency for a short duration and then "hopping" to another frequency. The minimum number of frequencies engaged in the hopping pattern and the maximum frequency dwell time (how long the signal stays on each frequency before it changes) are restricted by the FCC, which requires that 75 or more frequencies be used with a maximum dwell time of 400 ms.

The source mobile device's transmission and the destination mobile device's transmission must be synchronized so that they are on the same frequency at the same time. When the transmitter and receiver are properly synchronized, a single logical communications channel is maintained. Similar to DSSS, FHSS appears to be noise of a short duration to a non-FHSS receiver and is thus ignored.

FHSS makes it possible to deploy many non-overlapping channels. Because a large number of sequences are possible in the 2.4 GHz band, FHSS products enable users to deploy more than one channel in the same area by implementing separate channels with different hopping sequences.

WLAN Operational Modes

The IEEE 802.11 wireless networks operate in one of two operational modes: *ad hoc* or *infrastructure*. Ad hoc mode is a peer-to-peer type of networking, whereas infrastructure mode uses access points to communicate between the mobile devices and the wired network.

Ad Hoc Mode

In ad hoc mode, each mobile device client communicates directly with the other mobile device clients within the network. That is, no access points are used to connect the ad hoc network directly with any WLAN. Ad hoc mode is designed so that only the clients within transmission range (within the same cell) of each other can communicate. If a client on an ad hoc network wants to communicate outside the cell, a member of the cell must operate as a gateway and perform a routing service. Figure 3.15 shows a wireless session in ad hoc mode.

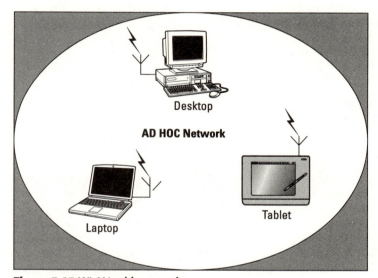

Figure 3.15 WLAN ad hoc mode

Infrastructure Mode

Each mobile device client in infrastructure mode sends all of its communications to a network device called an *access point (AP)*. The access point acts as an Ethernet bridge and forwards the communications to the appropriate network, either the WLAN or another wireless network. Figure 3.16 shows wireless connectivity using infrastructure mode.

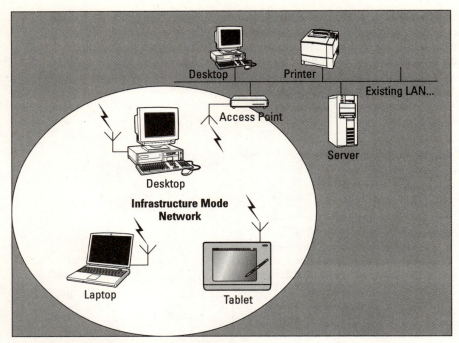

Figure 3.16 WLAN infrastructure mode

WLAN Devices

WLAN computing is an interesting example of a technology that was introduced into the home environment first, and migrated to the workplace through the proliferation of cheap, easy-to-configure WLAN devices and routers. Since then, vendors have been scrambling to add security elements that were not originally considered necessary for home or small office/home office (SOHO) use.

Figure 3.17 shows an example of an 802.11b access point (AP) manufactured by SMC Networks (`www.smc.com`), which employs relatively sophisticated security elements for an inexpensive consumer product. Some of its features include the following:

- ✦ Support for Static IP, Dynamic IP, PPPoE, PPTP, and Dial-up
- ✦ Print Server, DHCP Server, VPN, NAT, and Firewall
- ✦ Supports IEEE 802.3, 802.3u, and 802.11 standards

Figure 3.17 SMC Barricade wireless broadband router *(Courtesy of SMC Networks)*

A recent product introduced by SMC, the Barricade Plus Cable/DSL Broadband Router, adds integrated stateful packet inspection (SPI) and a VPN tunneling feature that supports up to five VPN tunnels.

Another recent vendor with an entry into the 802.11b home or SOHO market is Belkin Components (www.belkin.com), perhaps better known as a maker of cables and PC accessories. Like several other WLAN vendors, it offers several WLAN products, including a wireless Cable/DSL gateway router and a wireless USB network adapter, as shown in Figure 3.18.

Personal Electronic Devices

The product category known as *personal electronic devices (PEDs)* includes many types of products, though our focus is on those that offer some kind of wireless or Internet mobile communications technology. These wireless devices usually subscribe to a commercial Internet or message service provider that is not under the full control of the company providing the device to the employee.

Examples of mobile communications devices and systems meeting this criterion include the following:

- **Personal digital assistants (PDAs)** — Windows handhelds, Palm OS handhelds, and other operating systems commonly using wireless modems for Internet connectivity

- **Web-enabled cellular phones** — Internet-enabled cell phones using WAP, and Symbian OS, or other systems

- **Digital text devices** — BlackBerry and two-way pagers

Figure 3.18 The Belkin USB network adapter
(Courtesy of Belkin Components)

PDAs

PDA use has increased significantly in the past few years. PDAs comprise one of the fastest-growing areas of consumer electronics, and many companies and government agencies have issued them to their employees to increase productivity. However, although PDAs can enhance productivity, they can also introduce security vulnerabilities that must be addressed by company PDA policies.

Two classes of PDAs are found:

- ✦ Those using the Palm operating system (Palm OS), such as PalmPilot (shown in Figure 3.5) and the Handspring Visor
- ✦ Windows OS handhelds, such as Compaq, HP Jornada, and Casio, which run Windows CE or Microsoft Pocket PC 2002

The Palm OS and Windows OS operating systems represent the largest segment of the current PDA market. There are others, but they constitute a very small share of the PDA market.

The Palm OS

The Palm OS is a proprietary system available on PalmPilot devices and a few other PEDs. The Palm OS is optimized for a specific hardware platform. There is very little functional difference between the two main Palm OS platform vendors, 3Com and Handspring.

As just stated, Palm OS performance has been optimized for vendor-specific hardware, but it is limited as to the number of functions it can execute. Its ROM can support very few tasks because there are only enough task slots for the ROM's needs. To support more tasks, the ROM would have to be rebuilt.

The OS is written very compactly, but it does not address major areas of security, such as auditing or object reuse. It supports an optional use of passwords, but does not have a fully developed data protection security scheme.

Windows Handhelds

Windows OS handhelds currently run either a version of Windows CE or the newer Microsoft Pocket PC 2002 OS.

Windows CE

Microsoft Windows CE originated as a stripped-down version of Windows95 and was targeted at the PED market, primarily PDAs. Unlike Palm, however, Windows CE was designed to support a much wider range of hardware. Compared to the single-version Palm OS, Windows CE is a general-purpose OS, designed to support a number of hardware platforms, and not optimized for a specific hardware platform.

Many different versions of the Windows CE kernel are built for various CPUs, such as NEC MIPS, Intel or AMD x86, and Sega Dreamcast. Also, CE isn't just for PDAs; it was adapted to operate on Windows terminals, light notebook PCs, and even car computers.

Microsoft Pocket PC 2002 OS

In October 2001, Microsoft introduced the Pocket PC 2002 (PPC 2002), the company's third major PDA OS release. PPC 2002 features many significant improvements over the CE platform; its design tries to capture the look and feel of Microsoft Windows XP OS on a PDA screen.

PPC 2002 includes a terminal services client and integrated VPN support for remote operation, and access to corporate systems. Password support with encryption, Windows 2000 password rules, and a user-configurable active period (after which authentication stops) help improve security over that of the CE platform.

Other PDA devices

Other PDA devices include the Psion Series 7, devices using PsiWin 2.3, and various EPOC devices using EPOC release 5.

PDA Security Issues

PDAs have not been designed to the same standards nor exposed to the same rigorous examination as desktop operating systems. For example, they are not required to comply with the functional requirements spelled out in the ISO standard 15408, the Common Criteria.

- PDA operating systems do not have provisions to separate one user's data from another, which are required to support Discretionary Access Control (DAC).
- They lack audit capabilities.
- They have no support for object reuse control through the implementation of Identification and Authentication (I&A).
- They do not provide data integrity protection.
- Even when the OS is password-locked, applications can be installed onto the Palm OS without the owner's knowledge.

Confidentiality Loss

Even if a PDA is password-protected, a malicious user can retrieve a target PDA's password by using the Palm debug mode. The password can then be decoded by using simple tools such as PalmCrypt.

Once the password has been bypassed, all the information on the PDA is fully readable by the malicious user. Security administrators currently are not able to determine whether this type of attack has occurred, nor do they have any way to determine who was responsible for the attack.

Physical Loss

The most common threat to a PDA is probably the physical loss of the device. Although some technical solutions are available to protect against some of the OS security deficiencies just mentioned, none provide a countermeasure to the physical security concerns associated with the use of PDAs. The devices are so small and portable that loss of the device and any information contained on it is common. They are smaller and lighter, and their mode of use puts them at a greater risk because they are generally used in uncontrolled environments.

Internet-Enabled Cell Phones

Various Internet-enabled cell phones use WAP, include the Symbian OS or other operating systems, and employ many common digital transmission schemes, such as time division multiple access (TDMA), code division multiple access (CDMA), and the global system for mobile communication (GSM).

TDMA was the first U.S. digital standard to be developed by the Telecommunications Industry Association (TIA) in 1992. TDMA is further described in the following iDEN section. CDMA was adopted by the TIA in 1993. Although the U.S. military has used CDMA as a digital transport since the 1940s, as a commercial wireless transport, it is considered the new kid on the block compared to TDMA. GSM is similar to TDMA. It is the first digital cellular system to be used commercially, and has been adopted in Europe and many Pacific Rim countries.

WAP-Enabled Phones

A wide variety of WAP-enabled phones are on the market today, but primarily for use in the United States. For example, AT&T subscribers can only use their WAP phone in the United States and only through AT&T. Ericsson, Mitsubishi, and Nokia all manufacture phones for AT&T using TDMA. Similarly, Sprint subscribers can access only Sprint for their service; they cannot use Sprint phones through AT&T, because Sprint uses CDMA for its digital mode of communication. Motorola, Samsung, and Sanyo manufacture WAP-enabled phones for Sprint.

Most of these manufacturers also manufacture GSM-only WAP phones for use in Europe. New global standards are not expected to be in place until 2004 at the earliest, and the adoption curve will add a few years before all cellular phones and WAP phones are standardized for global use.

i-Mode

First introduced in Japan in February 1999 by NTT DoCoMo, i-mode is one of the world's most successful services, offering wireless Web browsing and e-mail from mobile phones. i-mode phones also allow users to use their handsets to access various information services and communicate via e-mail. In Japan, i-mode is most popular among young users, 24 to 35 years of age. The heaviest users of i-mode are women in their late 20s. As of November 2000, i-mode had an estimated 14.9 million users. When using i-mode services, you do not pay for the time you are connected to a Web site or service; you are charged only according to the volume of data transmitted.

iDEN

The iDEN digital technology developed by Motorola integrates four network communications services into one device. This effort marks Motorola's attempt to bring the following features together in one product:

- ✦ Dispatch radio
- ✦ Full-duplex telephone interconnect
- ✦ Short message service
- ✦ Data transmission

iDEN phones incorporate a number of messaging services, such as voice messaging, text messaging, numeric paging, and alphanumeric messaging.

iDEN utilizes time division multiple access (TDMA), which divides a channel into different slots. Each slot can carry one voice or data transmission. TDMA utilizes GPS satellites to reference a synchronized time, and divides the channel into time slots. By concerting one channel to multiple voice or data transmission pipelines, channel capacity can be increased by as much as six times their current analog networks, according to estimates.

iDEN also employs Vector Sum Excited Linear Prediction (VSELP), which digitally codes and compresses voice signals, increasing radio channel capacity by reducing the amount of information that must be transmitted. VSELP provides iDEN systems with the capability to fit voice transmission into the smaller transmissions pipeline that results from TDMA.

BlackBerry

One of the faster-growing consumer communications products is the BlackBerry device from Research In Motion Limited (RIM), a designer, manufacturer, and marketer of wireless solutions for the mobile communications market. RIM's products include the following:

- The RIM Wireless Handheld line
- The BlackBerry wireless e-mail solution
- Embedded radio modems
- Software development tools

BlackBerry is an integrated package device that provides mobile access to e-mail, contacts, calendars, and task lists. It is offered in two basic varieties: BlackBerry Internet Edition and BlackBerry Enterprise Edition.

IrDA

The Infrared Data Association (IrDA) is a non-profit trade association with a membership of more than 160 companies representing computer and telecommunications hardware, software, components, and adapters. The term *IrDA* is also commonly used to refer to infrared communications that comply with IrDA standards.

The Infrared Data Association international organization creates and promotes interoperable, low-cost infrared data interconnection standards. IrDA has a set of protocols covering all layers of data transfer, including some limited network management and interoperability.

More information on infrared can be found at www.irda.com.

IrDA provides wireless connectivity technologies for devices that would normally use cables. It is a point-to-point, narrow angle (30-degree radiation cone), ad hoc data transmission standard that uses infrared and is designed to operate over a distance of 0 to 1 meter at speeds of 9600 Bps to 16 Mbps. Infrared devices can be found in cordless keyboards, television remote controls, printers, watches, and serial PC adapters.

IrDA protocols have IrDA DATA as the vehicle for data delivery and IrDA CONTROL for sending control information. Adapters now include traditional upgrades to serial and parallel ports.

IrDA exhibits the following features:

- ✦ Transmission range up to 1 meter, plus extensions of up to 2 meters. A low-power version relaxes the range objective for operation from contact to at least 20 centimeters between low-power devices and 30 centimeters between low-power and standard-power devices. This implementation affords lower power consumption.
- ✦ Bi-directional communication.
- ✦ Primary data transmission speed of 9600 bps, with the capability to step up to 115 Kbps and even 4 Mbps in some implementations.
- ✦ Protected data packets, using a CRC-16 for speeds up to 1.152 Mbps and CRC-32 for speeds up to 4 Mbps.

Media Types

Various types of media also present challenges to the security professional. Cabling, removable and magnetic media, object reuse and data remanence, and access cards all add to these challenges.

Cable

Network cabling commonly comes in three types: twisted pair, coaxial, and fiber optic, as shown in Figure 3.19.

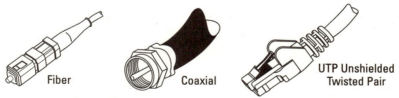

Fig 3.19 Cable types

Coaxial Cable

Coaxial cable (or coax) consists of a hollow outer cylindrical conductor that surrounds a single, inner wire conductor. Two types of coaxial cable are currently used in LANs: 50-ohm cable, which is used for digital signaling, and 75-ohm cable, which is used for analog signaling and high-speed digital signaling.

Coax is more expensive but more resistant to electromagnetic interference (EMI) than twisted pair cabling and can transmit at a greater bandwidth and distance. However, twisted pair cabling is so ubiquitous that most installations rarely use coax except in special cases, such as broadband communications.

Coax comes in two types for LANs:

- Thinnet (RG58 size)
- Thicknet (RG8 or RG11 size)

The following are the two common types of coaxial cable transmission methods:

- **Baseband** — The cable carries only a single channel.
- **Broadband** — The cable carries several usable channels, such as data, voice, audio, and video.

Twisted Pair Cabling

Twisted pair comes in shielded (STP) or unshielded (UTP) formats. The most commonly used format is UTP. UTP cabling is a four-pair wire medium used in a variety of networks.

UTP comes in several categories. The category rating is based on how tightly the copper cable is wound within the shielding; the tighter the wind, the higher the rating and its resistance against interference and attenuation. UTP Category 3 wire was often used for phone lines, but now the Category 5 wire is the standard, and even higher categories are available.

The categories of UTP are as follows:

- **Category 1 UTP** — Used for telephone communications and not suitable for transmitting data
- **Category 2 UTP** — Specified in the EIA/TIA-586 standard to be capable of handling data rates of up to 4 million bits per second (Mbps)
- **Category 3 UTP** — Used in 10BaseT networks and specified to be capable of handling data rates up to 10 Mbps
- **Category 4 UTP** — Used in Token Ring networks and capable of transmitting data at speeds up to 16 Mbps
- **Category 5 UTP** — Specified to be capable of handling data rates up to 100 Mbps; currently, the UTP standard for new installations
- **Category 6 UTP** — Specified to be capable of handling data rates up to 155 Mbps
- **Category 7 UTP** — Specified to be capable of handling data rates up to 1 billion bits per second (Gbps)

Fiber Optic

Fiber optic cable is a physical medium capable of conducting modulated light transmission. Fiber optic cable carries signals as light waves, creating higher transmission speeds and greater distances due to less attenuation. This type of cabling is much more difficult to tap than other cabling and is the most resistant to interference, especially EMI. It is sometimes called *optical fiber*.

Fiber optic cable is usually reserved for the connections between backbone devices in larger networks. In some very demanding environments, however, fiber optic cable connects desktop workstations to the network or links to adjacent buildings. Fiber optic cable is the most reliable cable type, but it is also the most expensive to install and terminate.

Fiber optic cable has three basic physical elements:

- **The core** — The core is the innermost transmission medium. It can be glass or plastic.
- **The cladding** — The next outer layer, the cladding is also made of glass or plastic, but has different properties, and helps to reflect the light back into the core.
- **The jacket** — The outermost layer, the jacket, provides protection from heat, moisture, and other environmental elements.

Figure 3.20 shows the three layers in fiber optic cable.

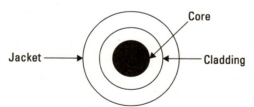

Figure 3.20 Fiber optic cable layers

Cabling Vulnerabilities

Coaxial cabling is vulnerable in regards to cable failure and length. All network devices attached to the same length of coax in a bus topology are vulnerable to disconnection from the network if the cable is broken or severed. This was one reason the star and ring topologies overtook the bus topology in installed base. In addition, exceeding the specified effective cable length can be a source of cabling failures.

The two categories of twisted pair cable in common usage are CAT3 and CAT5. The fundamental difference between these two types is how tightly the copper wires are wound. This tightness determines the cable's resistance to interference, the allowable distance it can be pulled between points, and the data's transmission speed before attenuation begins to affect the signal. CAT3 is an older specification with a shorter effective distance, and can contribute to failure due to exceeding the specified effective cable length (100 meters, in most cases).

UTP does not require the fixed spacing between connections that is necessary with some coaxial-type connections. UTP is also not as vulnerable to failure from cable breaks as coax, but eavesdroppers can more easily tap UTP cabling than either coax or fiber.

Fiber optic cable is immune to the effects of electromagnetic interference (EMI) and has a much longer effective usable length (up to 2 kilometers in some cases). It can carry a heavy load of activity much more easily than the copper types, and is thus commonly used for infrastructure backbones, server farms, or connections that need large amounts of bandwidth. The primary drawbacks of this cable type are its cost of installation and the high level of expertise needed to have it properly terminated.

Figure 3.21 demonstrates EMI radiation from copper cable.

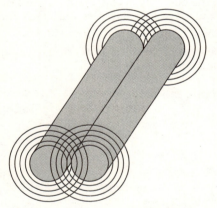

Figure 3.21 Copper cable signal radiation

Copper wire conducting AC signal

Removable and Magnetic Media

Removable media presents several unique security issues. Each tenet of confidentiality, integrity, and availability can be affected by loss or corruption. Removable media is vulnerable to the following:

- ✦ Loss of confidentiality through data remanence, object reuse, and inventory loss
- ✦ Loss of integrity through data degradation of magnetic media, software and hardware incompatibility, and ineffective operator controls
- ✦ Loss of availability through improper inventory control and logging

Media Storage and Reuse Control

Media storage control and the proper disposal of media is a serious security concern. An organization may devote large resources to perimeter protection but dispose of reports improperly or reuse laptops or diskettes before wiping the data fully.

The following types of media commonly require storage, destruction, or reuse:

- Data backup tapes
- CD-ROM/CDR/CDRW
- Floppy diskettes and zip disks
- Hard drives
- Paper printouts, reports, and sensitive documentation

Effective storage media controls must consider the following:

- Environmental controls, such as fire and water protections
- Physical access control to the storage areas
- Inventory controls, such as checkout logs

Transportation controls are also often overlooked, such as data backup vault services, partners and vendors, and disposal systems. Transportation to or from an external data vault services vendor is a security concern, and should be examined for problems relating to theft, copying, alteration, or destruction of data.

Data Destruction and Reuse

Magnetic media that is no longer needed or in use should be destroyed by degaussing or overwriting. Formatting a disk once does not completely destroy all data, so the entire media must be overwritten or formatted several times to conform to standards for object reuse.

Paper reports should be shredded by personnel with the proper level of security clearance. Some shredders cut in straight lines or strips; others crosscut or disintegrate the material into pulp. Care must be taken to limit access to the reports prior to disposal and those stored for long periods. Reports should never be disposed of without shredding. Burning is also sometimes used to destroy paper reports.

Object Reuse

Object reuse (A Guide to Understanding Object Reuse in Trusted Systems, NCSC-TG-018, Light Blue Book) is the concept of reusing data storage media after its initial use. Object reuse controls ensure that storage media are reallocated or reassigned to users in a way that prevents the unintentional release of sensitive information.

Object reuse is defined as "the reassignment to some subject of a storage medium (for example, page frame, disk sector, magnetic tape) that contained one or more objects. To be securely reassigned, no residual data can be available to the new subject through standard system mechanisms" (*A Guide to Understanding Data Remanence in Automated Information Systems*, NCSC-TG-025, National Computer Security Center, September 1991). The object reuse requirement of the TCSEC is intended to assure that system resources, in particular storage media, are allocated and reassigned among system users in a manner that prevents the disclosure of sensitive information.

Object reuse controls apply to all primary and secondary storage media, such as removable media, fixed media, real and virtual main memory (including registers), and cache memory.

Data Remanence

Data remanence is the problem of residual information remaining on storage media after erasure that may be subject to restoration by another user, resulting in a loss of confidentiality. Diskettes, hard drives, tapes, and any magnetic or writable media are susceptible to data remanence. Data remanence is the residual physical representation of data that has been erased in some way. After storage media is erased, some physical characteristics may still allow data to be reconstructed.

Anytime storage media is reused or discarded, the possibility that residual information may be retrieved exists. Methods must be employed to properly destroy the existing data to ensure that no residual data is available to new users.

Retrieving the bits and pieces of data that have not been thoroughly removed from storage media is a common method of computer forensics, and is often used by law enforcement personnel to preserve evidence and to construct a trail of misuse. The Orange Book standard recommends that magnetic media be formatted seven times before discard or reuse.

Techniques of data erasure include the following:

- **Clearing** — The overwriting of data media (primarily magnetic) intended to be reused in the same organization or monitored environment.
- **Purging** — Degaussing or overwriting media intended to be removed from a monitored environment, such as during resale (laptops) or donations to charity.
- **Destruction** — Completely destroying the media, and therefore the residual data. Paper reports, diskettes, and optical media (CD-ROMs) need to be physically destroyed before disposal.

The Forest Green book

The Forest Green book is a Rainbow series book that defines the secure handling of sensitive or classified automated information system memory and secondary storage media, such as degaussers, magnetic tapes, hard disks, floppy disks, and cards. The book details procedures for clearing, purging, declassifying, or destroying automated information system (AIS) storage media to prevent data remanence.

Common problems with magnetic media erasure that may cause data remanence include the following:

- ✦ Erasing the data through an operating system does not remove the data; it just changes the File Allocation Table and renames the first character of the file. This is the most common way computer forensics investigators can restore files.

- ✦ Damaged sectors of the disk may not be overwritten by the format utility. Degaussing may need to be used, or formatting seven times is recommended.

- ✦ Rewriting files on top of the old files may not overwrite all data areas on the disk, because the new file may not be as long as the older file, and data could be retrieved past the file end control character.

- ✦ Degausser equipment failure or operator error may result in an inadequate erasure.

- ✦ An inadequate number of formats may exist. Magnetic media containing sensitive information should be formatted seven times or more.

Degaussing

Degaussing is recommended as the best method for purging most magnetic media. Degaussing is a process whereby the magnetic media is erased (that is, returned to its initial virgin state). Erasure via degaussing may be accomplished in two ways:

- ✦ In AC erasure, the media is degaussed by applying an alternating field that is reduced in amplitude over time from an initial high value (that is, AC-powered).

- ✦ In DC erasure, the media is saturated by applying a unidirectional field (that is, DC-powered or by employing a permanent magnet).

Degaussed magnetic hard drives generally require restoration of factory-installed timing tracks, so data purging is recommended. Also, physical destruction of CD-ROM or WORM media is required.

Purging

To purge the media, the DoD requires overwriting with a pattern, then its complement, and finally with another pattern (that is, overwrite first with 0011 0101, followed by 1100 1010, then 1001 0111). The number of times an overwrite must be accomplished depends on the storage media, sometimes on its sensitivity, and sometimes on differing DoD component requirements, but seven times is often recommended. To satisfy the DoD clearing requirement, it is sufficient to write any character to all data locations in question. Purging media before submitting it for destruction is good practice.

Destruction

Destruction is the only approved disposal method for CD-ROM, CDR, CDRW, or paper reports. Media may generally be destroyed by one of the following five methods:

- Destruction at an approved metal destruction facility (smelting, disintegration, or pulverization).
- Incineration.
- Application of an abrasive substance (emery wheel or disk sander) to a magnetic disk or drum recording surface. Make certain that the entire recording surface is completely removed before disposal. Also, ensure that you are properly protected from the inhalation of abraded dust.
- Application of concentrated hydriodic acid (55 percent to 58 percent solution) to a gamma ferric oxide disk surface. Acid solutions should be used in a well-ventilated area by qualified personnel only.
- Application of acid activator Dubais Race A (8010 181 7171) and stripper Dubais Race B (8010 181 7170) to a magnetic drum recording surface. Technical acetone (6810 184 4796) should then be applied to remove residue from the drum surface. The above should be done in a well-ventilated area, and personnel must wear eye protection. Extreme caution must be observed when handling acid solutions. This procedure should be performed only by qualified and approved personnel.

Although the last two methods listed above have been approved, they use acid, which is dangerous and excessive, to remove recording surfaces. Thus, the first three methods are preferable.

Smart and Smarter Cards

A smart card is a plastic card with an embedded microchip. Magnetic stripe cards (cards with magnetically encoded strips) are also sometimes called *smart cards*, although later smart cards contain more information than magnetic stripe cards.

Both cards contain intelligence, and may require knowledge of a password or Personal Identification Number (PIN). A bank ATM card is an example of a magnetic stripe card.

A smart card may contain a processor encoded with the host system's authentication protocol, read-only memory storage of programs and data, and even some kind of user interface. Smart cards can be loaded with data, used for telephone calling, electronic cash payments, and other applications, and then periodically refreshed for additional use. Some cards can be programmed for different applications and be updated to add new applications.

Facility Access Cards

Smart cards are frequently used for facility access, and have become extremely sophisticated. Smart entry cards can either have a magnetic stripe or a small Integrated Circuit (IC) chip embedded in them, often including a photo of the bearer, and, in some cases, containing personal or medical information.

These cards may be able to create various multi-level access groups. The card reader can be programmed by an online access control computer to accept facility entry and provide information about the date and time of entry.

Some smart cards can be coupled with an authentication token that generates a one-time or challenge-response password or PIN. While two-factor, or dual-factor, authentication is most often used for logical access to network services, it can be combined with an intelligent card reader to provide extremely strong facility access control.

Wireless Proximity Readers

A proximity reader does not require the user to physically insert the access card. The card reader senses that the card is in a user's possession in the general area (proximity) and enables access. Proximity readers fall into two general categories: *user-activated* and *system-sensing*.

A user-activated proximity card transmits a sequence of keystrokes to a wireless keypad on the reader. The keypad on the reader contains either a fixed preset code or a programmable unique key pattern. A system-sensing proximity card recognizes the presence of the coded device in the reader's general area.

The three common types of system-sensing cards are defined by the way the power is generated for these devices:

- ✦ **Passive devices** — Contain no battery or power on the card, but sense the electromagnetic field transmitted by the reader and transmit at different frequencies using the reader's power field.

- ✦ **Field-powered devices** — Contain active electronics, a radio frequency transmitter, and a power supply circuit on the card.

- ✦ **Transponders** — The card and reader each contain a receiver, transmitter, active electronics, and a battery. The reader transmits an interrogating signal to the card, which in turn causes it to transmit an access code.

These systems are often used as portable devices for dynamically assigning access control.

Infrastructure Topologies

This section covers various infrastructure topologies, and the ways they interact with security.

Local Area Networks

A *local area network*, or *LAN* (see Figure 3.22), is a discrete network that is designed to operate in a specific, limited geographic area like a single building or floor. LANs connect workstations and file servers so that they can share network resources such as printers, e-mail, and files. LAN devices are connected by using a type of connection medium (such as copper wire or fiber optics), and they use various LAN protocols and access methods to communicate through LAN devices (such as bridges or routers). LANs can also be connected to a public switched network.

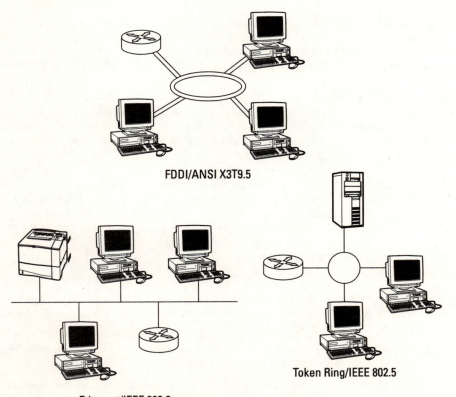

Figure 3.22 Local area networks

Two common types of LANs are:

- **Campus area network (CAN)** — A typically large campus network that connects multiple buildings with each other across a high-performance, switched backbone on the main campus.
- **Metropolitan area network (MAN)** — A MAN is essentially a LAN that extends over a city-wide metropolitan area.

Both CANs and MANs can have connections to a wide area network, or WAN.

Wide Area Networks

A wide area network (WAN) is a network of subnetworks that physically or logically interconnect LANs over a larger geographic area. A WAN is basically everything outside of a LAN. A WAN might be privately operated for a specific user community, might support multiple communication protocols, or might provide network connectivity and services via interconnected network segments (extranets, intranets, and VPNs).

Internet

The Internet is a WAN that was originally funded by the DoD and that uses TCP/IP for data interchange. The term *Internet* refers to any and all kinds of Advanced Research Projects Agency Network (ARPANET), Department of Defense Research Projects Agency Network (DARPANET), Defense Data Network (DDN), or DoD Internets. It specifically refers to the global network of public networks and Internet service providers (ISPs) throughout the world. Either public or private networks (with a VPN) can utilize the Internet.

Intranet

An intranet is an Internet-like logical network that uses a firm's internal, physical network infrastructure. Because it uses TCP/IP and HTTP standards, it can use low-cost Internet products such as Web browsers. One common usage for an intranet

Broadcast Domains

A *broadcast domain* is a network (or portion of a network) that receives a broadcast packet from any node located within that network. Normally, everything on the same side of the router is all part of the same broadcast domain.

would involve a human resource department electronically publishing employee guidelines that are accessible by all company personnel. An intranet provides more security and control than a public posting on the Internet.

Extranet

Like an intranet, an extranet is a private network that uses Internet protocols. Unlike an intranet, users outside the company (such as partners and vendors) can access an extranet, but the general public cannot. For example, using an extranet, a supplier may be able to access a company's private network via a VPN or authenticated Internet connection. The supplier would then have access only to the information it needs.

VLANs

A Virtual LAN (VLAN) is a collection of nodes that are grouped together in a single broadcast domain in a switch, and based on something other than physical segment location. A VLAN creates an isolated broadcast domain, and a switch with multiple VLANs creates multiple broadcast domains, similar to a router. However, VLANs can't route between each other. Such routing would defeat the purpose of the VLAN, to isolate the traffic from the general traffic flow.

VLANs provide the following advantages:

+ They can aid in isolating segments with sensitive data from the rest of the broadcast domain and increase security assurance.
+ They can reduce the number of router hops and increase the usable bandwidth.
+ A VLAN reduces routing broadcasts as ACLs control what stations receive what traffic.
+ They may be created to segregate job or department functions that require heavy bandwidth, without affecting the rest of the network.

A single VLAN can span across multiple switches, and more than one VLAN can exist on a single switch. For multiple VLANs on multiple switches to communicate via a single link between the switches, a process called *trunking* must be used. Trunking is the technology that allows information from multiple VLANs to be carried over just one link between switches. The VLAN Trunking Protocol (VTP) is the protocol used by switches to communicate among themselves about VLAN configuration.

Network Address Translation

Generically, Network Address Translation (NAT) describes the process of converting an IP address valid within one network to a different IP address valid within another network. More specifically, NAT converts a private IP address on the inside, trusted network to a registered "real" IP address seen by the untrusted, outside network.

The Internet Assigned Numbers Authority (IANA) has reserved three blocks of the IP address space for private Internets:

+ 10.0.0.0 to 10.255.255.255
+ 172.16.0.0 to 172.31.255.255
+ 192.168.0.0 to 192.168.255.255

Employing these internal addresses through NAT enhances security by hiding the true IP address of the origination of the packet. As each incoming or outgoing packet is converted by NAT, the request can be authenticated.

NAT also helps conserve the number of global IP addresses that a company requires, and allows the company to use a single IP address for its outside communications.

NAT can be statically defined, or it can be configured to dynamically use a group of IP addresses. For example, Cisco's version of NAT lets an administrator create policies that define the following:

+ A static one-to-one relationship between one local IP address and one global IP address
+ A relationship between a local IP address to any of one of a dynamic group of global IP addresses
+ A relationship between a local IP address and a specific TCP port to a static or dynamic group of global IP addresses
+ A conversion from a global IP address to any one of a group of local IP addresses on a round-robin basis

NAT is described in general terms in RFC 1631, which discusses NAT's relationship to Classless Interdomain Routing (CIDR) as a way to reduce the IP address depletion problem. NAT is often included as part of a router, and most firewall systems now include NAT capability. Figure 3.23 shows the NAT process.

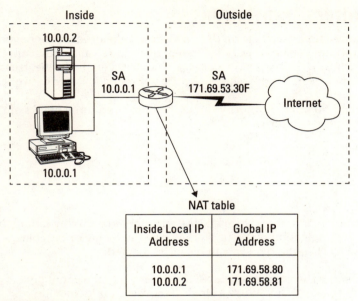

Figure 3.23 Network Address Translation

VPN Tunneling

A Virtual Private Network (VPN) tunnel is created by dynamically building a secure communications link between two nodes by using a secret encapsulation method (see Figure 3.24). This link is commonly called a *secure encrypted tunnel*, although it is more accurately defined as an encapsulated tunnel because encryption may or may not be used.

Cross-Reference   VPN protocols and standards are described in more detail in Chapter 2.

This tunnel can be created by using methods such as the following:

+ Installing software or hardware agents on the client or a network gateway
+ Implementing various user or node authentication systems
+ Implementing key and certificate exchange systems

VPN Protocol Tunneling Standards

The following are the three most common VPN communications protocol standards.

+ **Point-to-Point Tunneling Protocol (PPTP)** — PPTP works at the Data Link layer of the OSI model. This standard is very common with asynchronous connections that use Win9*x* or NT clients. PPTP uses native Point-to-Point Protocol (PPP) authentication and encryption services.

- **Layer 2 Tunneling Protocol (L2TP)** — L2TP is a combination of PPTP and the earlier Layer 2 Forwarding (L2F) Protocol that works at the Data Link layer like PPTP. It has become an accepted tunneling standard for VPNs. L2TP supports TACACS+ and RADIUS, but PPTP does not.
- **IPSec** — IPSec, which operates at the Network layer, enables multiple and simultaneous tunnels, unlike the single connection of the previous standards. IPSec has the functionality to encrypt and authenticate IP data, but is not multi-protocol.

VPN Devices

VPN devices are hardware or software devices that utilize the previously discussed VPN standards to create a secure tunnel. The VPN devices are primarily grouped into two types: *IPSec-compatible* and *non-IPSec-compatible*.

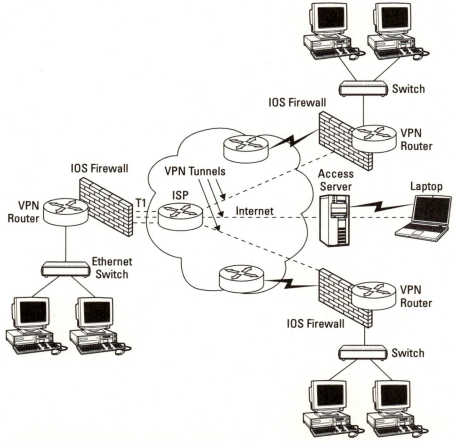

Figure 3.24 An example of a Cisco VPN

IPSec-Compatible VPN Devices

IPSec-compatible VPN devices are installed on a network's perimeter and encrypt the traffic between networks or nodes by creating a secure tunnel through the unsecured network. Because they employ IPSec encryption, they only work with IP (they are not multiprotocol). These devices operate at the Network layer (Layer 3). They operate in two modes:

- **Tunnel** — The entire data packet is encrypted and encased in an IPSec packet.
- **Transport** — Only the datagram is encrypted, leaving the IP address visible.

Non-IPSec-Compatible VPN Devices

Common VPN devices that are not compatible with IPSec include SOCKS-based proxy servers and L2TP/PPTP-compatible devices.

SOCKS-based proxy servers were described earlier. SOCKS-based proxy servers can be used in a VPN configuration as well as in a firewall configuration. While not a traditional VPN protocol, SOCKS-based systems contain authentication and encryption features, which are similar to strong VPN protocols.

Intrusion Detection and Response

Intrusion Detection (ID) and Response is the task of monitoring systems for evidence of an intrusion or an inappropriate usage and then responding to the intrusion. ID is the detection of inappropriate, incorrect, or anomalous activity. ID is not a preventative control; it is a detective control.

Types of ID Systems

ID systems that operate on a specific host and detect malicious activity only on that host are called *host-based ID systems*. ID systems that operate on network segments and analyze that segment's traffic are called *network-based ID systems*. Because there are pros and cons with each, an effective IDS should use a combination of both network- and host-based intrusion detection systems.

Host-Based ID Systems

Host-based ID systems use small software programs called *intelligent agents*. They reside on a host computer, monitor the operating system, and continually write to log files and trigger alarms. They detect inappropriate activity only on the host computer — they do not monitor the entire network segment.

Host-based ID systems accomplish the following:

- Monitor accesses and changes to critical system files and changes in user privileges
- Detect trusted-insider attacks better than network-based IDS
- Are relatively effective for detecting attacks from the outside
- Can be configured to look at all network packets, connection attempts, or login attempts to the monitored machine, including dial-in attempts or other non-network-related communication ports

Figure 3.25 shows the host-based intrusion detection software RealSecure, from ISS (www.iss.net). This screen shows the discovery of critical vulnerabilities on the server after performing a baseline audit.

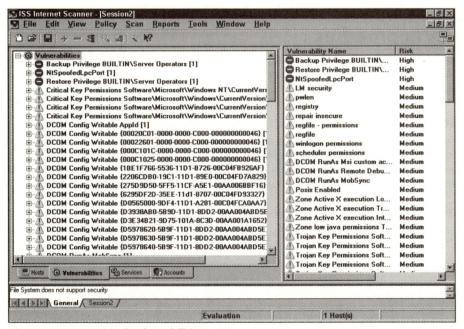

Figure 3.25 ISS critical vulnerabilities

Network-Based ID Systems

Network-based ID systems commonly reside on a discrete network segment and monitor the traffic on that network segment. They usually consist of a network appliance with a Network Interface Card (NIC) that is operating in promiscuous mode and is intercepting and analyzing the network packets in real time.

Network-based ID involves looking at the packets on the network as they pass by a sensor. The sensor can only see the packets that happen to be carried on the network segment to which it's attached. Network traffic on other segments, and traffic on other means of communication (such as phone lines) can't be monitored properly by network-based IDS.

Packets are identified of interest if they match a signature. Three primary types of signatures are as follows:

- **String signatures**—String signatures look for a text string that indicates a possible attack.
- **Port signatures**—Port signatures watch for connection attempts to well known, frequently attacked ports.
- **Header condition signatures**—Header signatures watch for dangerous or illogical combinations in packet headers.

IDS Approaches

The most common approaches to ID are *statistical anomaly detection* (also known as *behavior-based detection*) and *pattern-matching* (also known as *knowledge-based* or *signature-based*) *detection*.

Knowledge-Based ID Systems

Knowledge-based ID systems use a database of previous attacks and known system vulnerabilities to look for current attempts to exploit their vulnerabilities, and trigger an alarm if an attempt is detected. Most IDSs today are knowledge-based, and the accuracy of knowledge-based intrusion detection systems is considered good.

The following are advantages of a knowledge-based ID system:

- The system is characterized by low false alarm rates (positives).
- Alarms are standardized and are clearly understandable by security personnel.

The following are disadvantages of knowledge-based ID systems:

- The system is resource-intensive. The knowledge database continually needs maintenance and updating with new vulnerabilities and environments to remain accurate.
- Because knowledge about attacks is very focused (dependent on the operating system, version, platform, and application), new, unique, or original attacks often go unnoticed.
- Detection of insider attacks involving an abuse of privileges is deemed more difficult because no vulnerability is actually exploited by the attacker.

Behavior-Based ID Systems

Behavior-based ID systems dynamically detect deviations from the learned patterns of user behavior; an alarm is triggered when an activity that is considered intrusive (outside of normal system use) occurs. Behavior-based ID systems are less common than knowledge-based ID systems.

Behavior-based ID systems learn normal or expected behavior of the system or the users and assume that an intrusion can be detected by observing deviations from this norm.

The following are advantages of behavior-based ID systems:

- They dynamically adapt to new, unique, or original vulnerabilities.
- They are not as dependent upon specific operating systems as a knowledge-based ID system.
- They help detect "abuse of privileges" types of attacks that do not actually involve exploiting any security vulnerability.

The following are disadvantages of behavior-based ID systems:

- Systems are characterized by high false alarm rates. High positives are the most common failure of behavior-based ID systems and can create data noise that can make the system unusable or difficult to use.
- Activity and behavior of the users while in the networked system might not be static enough to effectively implement a behavior-based ID system.
- The network may experience an attack at the same time the intrusion detection system is learning the behavior.

Honey Pots

A *honey pot* is a system on the network intentionally configured to lure intruders. Honey pots simulate one or more network services hoping that an attacker will attempt an intrusion. Honey pots are most successful when run on known servers, such as HTTP, mail, or DNS servers, because these systems advertise their services and are often the first point of attack. They are often used to augment the deployment of an IDR system.

A honey pot is configured to interact with potential hackers in such a way as to capture the details of their attacks. These details can be used to identify what the intruders are after, their skill level, and what tools they use.

Honey pots should be physically isolated from the real network and are commonly placed in a DMZ. All traffic to and from the honey pot should also be routed through a dedicated firewall.

A honey pot is usually configured by installing the operating system using defaults, no patches, and the application designed to record the intruders' activities.

Evidence of an intrusion into a honey pot can be collected through the following:

- The honey pot's firewall logs
- The honey pot's system logs
- Intrusion detection systems or other monitoring tools

A properly configured honey pot monitors traffic passively, doesn't advertise its presence, and provides a preserved prosecution trail for law enforcement agencies.

You should be aware of legal issues that arise from the implementation of a honey pot. Some organizations discourage the use of honey pots, citing the legal concerns of luring intruders, and feel that no level of intrusion should be encouraged.

Before the intrusion occurs, local law enforcement authorities should be consulted to determine the type and amount of data they need in order to prosecute, and how to properly preserve the chain of evidence.

Also, because the honey pot must be vigilantly monitored and maintained, some organizations feel it is too resource-intensive for practical use.

Intrusion Response

Response involves notifying the appropriate parties to take action to determine the severity of an incident and to remediate the incident's effects.

It can include the creation of a Computer Incident Response Team (CIRT), which is charged with the following tasks:

1. Analysis of an event notification
2. Response to an incident if the analysis warrants it
3. Escalation path procedures
4. Resolution, post-incident follow-up, and reporting to the appropriate parties

Every CIRT's prime directive is incident response management: management of a company's response to events that pose a risk to its computing environment.

This management often consists of the following processes:

- Coordinating the notification and distribution of information pertaining to the incident to the appropriate parties (those with a need to know) through a pre-defined escalation path
- Mitigating risk to the enterprise by minimizing the disruptions to normal business activities and the costs associated with remediating the incident (including public relations)

- Assembling teams of technical personnel to investigate the potential vulnerabilities and to resolve specific intrusions
- Additional examples of CIRT activities include the following:
    - Management of the network logs, including collection, retention, review, and analysis of data
    - Management of the resolution of an incident, management of the remediation of a vulnerability, and post-event reporting to the appropriate parties

IDS and a Layered Security Approach

Computer security is most effective when multiple layers of security are used within an organization, and ID is best utilized when implemented in a "layered security" approach. This concept implies that multiple steps are taken to secure the data, increasing the workload and time required for an intruder to penetrate the network.

While a firewall is an excellent perimeter security device, it is just one element of an effective security strategy. The more elements, or layers, of security you can add to protect the data, the more secure the infrastructure will remain.

Elements of an effective layered security approach include the following:

- Security policies, procedures, standards and guidelines, including high-level security policy
- Perimeter security, such as routers, firewalls, and other edge devices
- Hardware and/or software host security products
- Auditing, monitoring, intrusion detection, and response

Each of these layers may be implemented independently of the others, yet are interdependent when functioning. An IDS that alerts to unauthorized access attempts or port scanning is useless without a response plan to react to the problem. Since each layer provides elements of protection, the defeat of any one layer should not lead to a failure of protection.

IDS and Switches

One serious issue with IDS is the proper implementation of IDS sensors in a switched environment. This issue arises from the basic differences between standard hubs and switches. Hubs exclude only the port the packet came in on and echo every packet to every port on the hub. In networks employing only hubs, IDS sensors can be placed almost anywhere in the infrastructure.

However, when a packet comes into a switch, a temporary connection in the switch is first made to the destination port, after which the packets are forwarded. This means that more care must be exerted when placing IDS sensors in a switched environment to assure that the sensor can see all of the network traffic. Figure 3.26 shows an IDS employed on its own subnet.

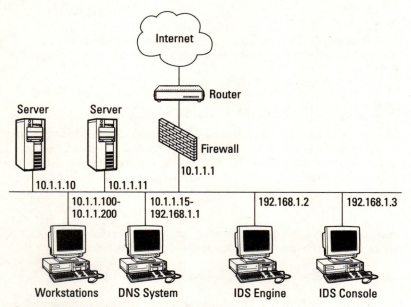

Figure 3.26 An IDS on its own subnet

Some switches permit spanning port configuration, which configures the switch to behave like a hub only for a specific port. The switch can be configured to span the data from a specific port to the IDS port. Unfortunately, some switches cannot be guaranteed to pass all the traffic to the spanned port, and most switches only allow one port to be spanned at a time.

Another partial solution is to place a hub between the monitored connections (between two switches, a router and switch, or a server and switch, for example). This allows traffic to flow between the switch and the target while allowing traffic to be copied to the IDS. This solution, however, spells the beginning of the end for the switched network, and removes the benefits of a switched solution.

IDS Performance

Another issue with the implementation of intrusion detection systems is the performance of the IDS when the network bandwidth begins to reach saturation levels. There is a limit to the number of packets that a network intrusion detection sensor can accurately analyze in any given time period. The higher the network traffic level and the more complex the analysis, the more the IDS may experience high error rates, such as the premature discard of copied network packets.

Hardening

One important facet of infrastructure security is called *hardening*. Hardening refers to the steps taken to make sure that workstations, servers, routers, applications, and any other element of the infrastructure are configured securely.

Workstation Hardening

As most unauthorized intrusion or abuse of system privilege occurs from inside the organization, implementing security policies and controls at the workstation level is very important.

Generally accepted principles of securing network workstations include the following:

- Run virus-detection software on every workstation, in addition to server-based detection mechanisms.
- Implement and monitor user privilege levels. Institute the principle of least privilege by creating a policy that initially grants minimal privilege, then increases privilege on a case-by-case basis as need-to-know is proven.
- Discourage local storage, especially of sensitive files. Data with a higher level of sensitivity should be stored on servers with security controls and backup services.
- Provide security auditing. Workstations in critical operational environments may need to be monitored and audited as frequently as networked servers.
- Limit cached logons by limiting the number of authentication contexts in which cached logons occur, to lessen the threat of retrieving domain password hashes.
- Remove backdoor access into the network via RAS or PCAnywhere. Workstations in critical operational environments should not have modems, infrared, or wireless access.
- Workstations in critical operational environments may need to be included in the backup process.

Server Hardening

Although there are many opinions about how best to increase a server's ability to withstand intrusions, a few standard guidelines exist. Common WinNT and Win2K security practices include the following:

- Isolating the boot partition
- Restricting permissions and accounts
- Disabling unneeded services and protocols
- Closing unneeded ports

- Enabling auditing
- Maintaining service packs
- Implementing bastion host hardening

Boot Partition

Use the NT file system (NTFS), especially for the boot partition. C2 Security requires that the boot partition and the data directories reside on physically separate hard drives. Only NTFS supports Discretionary Access Control to the files and directories. Consequently, only NTFS volumes should be allowed on the system to provide secure and auditable access to the files. FAT volumes do not provide the necessary security functions to support C2 Level security.

Also, allowing other operating systems, such as MS-DOS, to run on a secure system can provide an avenue to circumvent security. The primary Network Operating System (NOS) should be the only operating system on the computer.

Do not install system files in the \WINNT directory; rename the directory. This will prevent attacks hard-coded to refer to files in the \WINNT directory.

Enable a screen saver, password-protect it, and set it for some short interval like five minutes.

Permissions and Accounts

Default permissions on Windows NT system files and registry keys are overly permissive. Rebuild the NTFS permissions to remove any occurrence of "EVERYONE." Replace the Everyone group with the Authenticated Users group on critical system folders and files (for example, WinNT, system32) and registry keys (for example, `HKLM\Software\Microsoft\Windows\Run` and `HKLM\Software\Microsoft\Windows NT\CurrentVersion\AEDebug`). Remove the Everyone group from the "Access this Computer from the Network" user right.

Limit the information available from a null connection. Null connections (anonymous users) are included in the built-in Everyone security group, so anonymous users can access any resources that the Everyone group can access. Windows NT Service Pack 6a limits much of what an anonymous user can do.

Do not allow remote registry access. Many registry keys allow the Everyone group, and therefore anonymous users, read and/or set value permissions. If an unauthorized user were able to remotely edit the registry, he could modify registry keys in an attempt to gain elevated privileges. Restricting remote registry access is accomplished by setting security permissions on the `HKLM\SYSTEM\CurrentControlSet\Control\SecurePipeServers\winreg` key. It is highly recommended that only Administrators and System have remote access to the registry.

Disable the Guest account and give it a very strong password. Ensure that all accounts (service and user) have passwords regardless of the account being enabled or disabled. Create a very strong password for the Administrator account during the installation.

Restrict permissions on network shares. When a share is created, the default access control is Everyone having Full Control. Restrict the share permissions to only those groups that need access.

Review trust relationships between domains and remove unnecessary trusts.

Disable Unneeded Services

Remove all services that are not required. Ensure proper placement of services on the network. For example, RAS should not be on a Domain Controller. Disable any unnecessary or unused services.

Commonly unused services include the following:

- DHCP Client
- Remote Registry Service
- Simple TCP/IP Services
- TELNET
- Terminal Services
- Utility Manager
- FTP/TFTP
- RAS

Disable Unneeded Protocols

Unbind protocols like IPX and NetBIOS from interfaces where they are not required.

Disable LanMan authentication. LanMan passwords are used for backwards compatibility with older Windows operating systems (for example, Windows 9x) and are simply the NT/2000 password converted to all uppercase and encrypted in a different way. LanMan passwords are easier to crack than NTLM hash because they are treated as two 7-character passwords.

It is recommended that LanMan passwords be disabled. If Windows 9x boxes reside on the network, Directory Client Services (available on the Windows 2000 CD) must be installed on these systems to allow NTLM version 2 authentications.

Close Unneeded Ports

Close ports 135, 137, 138, and 139 either at the premise router or firewall. For networks containing Windows 2000 systems, also block port 445. These ports are needed in an internal network, but not externally. Blocking these ports will stop many attacks against Windows NT and Windows 2000. Review all ports for access control.

Enable Auditing

At a minimum, audit logons and logoffs, failed attempts at exercising user privileges, and system events such as shutdowns. Increase the maximum size of the Application, Security and System logs to at least 10,048KB each and configure them to overwrite events as needed.

Maintain Service Packs

Regularly monitor and update the server with current service packs, patches, and hot fixes.

It is not advisable to apply service packs immediately upon release, unless the service pack addresses an urgent vulnerability that has been identified in the production environment. Install the service pack or hot fix first in a test environment to see the impact on applications, then install on a production server.

Bastion Host Hardening

If a server functions as a bastion host, additional configuration concerns apply. It's important that bastion hosts do not share authentication services with trusted hosts within the network. Bastion hosts should not have much information about the infrastructure to give away to intruders.

Generic steps that are often taken to harden a bastion host are similar to those taken for a server, and may include the following:

- Secure all network applications on the host.
- Remove unused utilities and system configuration tools.
- Disable all unnecessary ports, especially tcp and udp.
- Disable all unnecessary protocols.
- Enable logging of all security-related events and preserve those logs against tampering.
- Encrypt any local user account and password databases.
- Remove all non-critical services, programs, and daemons.
- Install all appropriate service packs, hot fixes, patches, and application updates.

DHCP

Dynamic Host Configuration Protocol (DHCP) is a communications protocol that lets administrators centrally manage and automate the assignment of Internet Protocol (IP) addresses in an organization's network.

 DHCP is identified in RFC 2131.

DHCP Lease Periods

DHCP uses the concept of a "lease period," during which time a given IP address is valid for a client, providing hosts that do not need permanent IP addresses an IP address from a limited pool of addresses. The lease period can range from 1 minute to 99 years, and depends on how long a host is likely to require the Internet connection at a particular location. When the lease period expires, the server can assign the IP address to another client on the network. DHCP also supports static addresses for computers containing hosts that need a permanent IP address.

Security policy usually recommends that the lease period be shorter (no longer than 24 hours), rather than longer (one month or one year).

DHCP and BOOTP

DHCP is an alternative to an older network IP management protocol, Bootstrap Protocol (BOOTP), but both protocols are commonly used. Because the DHCP packet format is based on a BootP packet, DHCP uses the BootP relay agent to forward DHCP packets, and the BootP relay agent uses the same criteria and methods for forwarding both DHCP and BootP packets. This provides interoperability between the existing BootP clients and DHCP servers.

Although both DHCP and BootP use the same UDP port numbers (67 and 68), they differ in the following ways:

+ As previously mentioned, DHCP defines a lease period, allowing for reassignment of expired IP network addresses to different clients.

+ DHCP provides a mechanism for clients to acquire all of the IP configuration parameters needed to communicate on a network. DHCP's additional packet length allows a DHCP server to provide the client with all the IP configuration parameters that it needs to operate.

+ DHCP is a more complicated protocol than BootP, as DHCP has seven message types; BootP uses only two (Acquiring a New IP Address and New Configuration Parameters).

The DHCP process involves four steps:

1. Identifying DHCP servers
2. Requesting IP information
3. Receiving IP information
4. Accepting IP information

To identify DHCP servers, the client broadcasts a DHCPDISCOVER packet. Figure 3.27 shows the DHCPDISCOVER process.

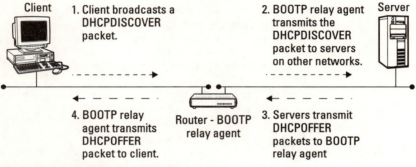

Fig 3.27 The DHCPDISCOVER process

◆ ◆ ◆

SAMPLE QUESTIONS

1. Which two TCP/UDP ports does FTP use?

    a. 22 and 23

    b. 23 and 25

    c. 20 and 21

    d. 67 and 65

2. What is one of the most common drawbacks to using a dual-homed host firewall?

    a. The examination of the packet at the Network layer introduces latency.

    b. The examination of the packet at the Application layer introduces latency.

    c. The ACLs must be manually maintained on the host.

    d. Internal routing may accidentally become enabled.

3. Which TCP/UDP port range should a security administrator be concerned about intruders scanning?

    a. 1–512

    b. 0–65535

    c. 513–1023

    d. 1025–65535

4. Which LAN topology listed is least vulnerable to a single point of failure?

    a. Ethernet Bus

    b. PPTP

    c. LDAP

    d. FDDI

5. Which choice below is *not* an element of a fiber optic cable?

    a. Core

    b. Medium

    c. Jacket

    d. Cladding

6. Which type of cabling is most commonly installed in new LAN infrastructures?

   a. ThickNet

   b. Token Ring

   c. Twinax

   d. Twisted pair

7. Which protocol is used to resolve a known MAC address to an unknown IP address?

   a. ARP

   b. RARP

   c. ICMP

   d. TFTP

8. Which choice defines an interface to the first commercially successful connection-oriented packet-switching network?

   a. X.25

   b. Frame Relay

   c. SMDS

   d. ATM

9. Which statement below is *not* correct regarding VLANs?

   a. A VLAN restricts flooding to only those ports included in the VLAN.

   b. A VLAN is a network segmented physically, not logically.

   c. A VLAN is more secure when implemented in conjunction with private port switching.

   d. A "closed" VLAN configuration is a very secure configuration.

10. Which protocol below pertains to e-mail?

    a. SMTP

    b. SNMP

    c. CHAP

    d. PPTP

11. Which statement is true about the SOCKS protocol?

    a. It is sometimes referred to as a stateful inspection firewall.

    b. It uses an ESP for authentication and encryption.

    c. It operates in the Data Link layer of the OSI model.

    d. Network applications need to be SOCKS-ified to operate.

12. Which level of RAID actually lessens fault tolerance?

    a. RAID 0

    b. RAID 1

    c. RAID 3

    d. RAID 5

13. Which choice is a link-state hierarchical routing algorithm intended as a successor to RIP?

    a. RIP

    b. OSPF

    c. IGRP

    d. EAP

14. Which category of UTP wiring was originally rated for 16 Mbps Token Ring LANs?

    a. Category 1

    b. Category 3

    c. Category 4

    d. Category 5

15. Which process below operates primarily at the Data Link layer?

    a. Internetwork packet routing

    b. LAN bridging

    c. SMTP Gateway services

    d. Signal regeneration and repeating

16. In the DoD reference model, which layer conforms to the OSI Network layer?

    a. Process/Application layer

    b. Host-to-Host layer

    c. Internet layer

    d. Network Access layer

17. Which IEEE protocol defines wireless connectivity?

    a. IEEE 802.5

    b. IEEE 802.3

    c. IEEE 802.11

    d. IEEE 802.1D

18. Which type of routing maintains a copy of every other router's Link State Protocol (LSP) frame?

   a. Static routing

   b. Distance vector routing

   c. Link state routing

   d. Dynamic control protocol routing

19. Which TCP/IP protocol operates at the OSI Transport layer?

   a. FTP

   b. IP

   c. TCP

   d. Bridging

20. Which statement is true regarding the difference between TCP and UDP?

   a. UDP is considered a connectionless protocol and TCP is connection-oriented.

   b. TCP is considered a connectionless protocol, and UDP is connection-oriented.

   c. UDP acknowledges the receipt of packets, and TCP does not.

   d. TCP is sometimes referred to as an unreliable protocol.

21. Which media control is the least secure method to prevent data remanence on magnetic tapes or floppy disks?

   a. Formatting the media at least seven times

   b. Degaussing the media

   c. Applying a concentration of hydriodic acid (55 percent to 58 percent solution) to the a gamma ferric oxide disk surface

   d. Making sure the disk is re-circulated as quickly as possible to prevent object reuse

22. Which choice is an example of a personnel control?

   a. Sanitizing the media before disposition

   b. Printing to a printer in a secured room

   c. Physically protecting copies of backup media

   d. Conducting background checks on individuals

23. When should a service pack be installed on a production server?

    a. Immediately when released

    b. After testing on a test server

    c. Only if the service pack addresses a known vulnerability in the system

    d. Never, if the production server is operating properly

24. Which choice *best* describes coaxial cable?

    a. Coax consists of two insulated wires wrapped around each other in a regular spiral pattern.

    b. Coax consists of a hollow outer cylindrical conductor surrounding a single, inner conductor.

    c. Coax does not require the fixed spacing between connections that UTP requires.

    d. Coax carries signals as light waves.

25. Which firewall type uses a dynamic state table to inspect the content of packets?

    a. A packet filtering firewall

    b. An application-level firewall

    c. A circuit-level firewall

    d. A stateful inspection firewall

26. Which statement is *not* accurate in describing the difference between 802.11b WLAN ad hoc and infrastructure modes?

    a. Infrastructure mode uses an Access Point to communicate to the wired network.

    b. Wireless nodes can only communicate peer-to-peer in the infrastructure mode.

    c. Wireless nodes can communicate peer-to-peer in the ad hoc mode.

    d. Access points are a vulnerability to the wired LAN.

27. Which statement is *not* accurate about the concept of object reuse?

    a. Object reuse protects against physical attacks on the storage medium.

    b. Object reuse ensures that users do not obtain residual information from system resources.

    c. Object reuse applies to all primary and secondary storage media.

    d. Data remanence vulnerability can result from improperly controlled object reuse.

28. Which of the choices is an OSI reference model Presentation layer protocol, standard, or interface?

   a. RPC

   b. MIDI

   c. ASP

   d. SQL

29. Which IEEE protocol defines wireless transmission in the 2.4 GHz band with data rates up to 54 Mbps?

   a. IEEE 802.11a

   b. IEEE 802.11b

   c. IEEE 802.11g

   d. IEEE 802.15

30. Which choice relates to analog dial-up hacking?

   a. War dialing

   b. War walking

   c. War driving

   d. War chalking

Basics of Cryptography

This chapter covers the fundamentals of cryptography, including the following:

- ✦ Cryptographic algorithms
- ✦ Applications of cryptography to protect the confidentiality and integrity of information
- ✦ Digital signatures
- ✦ Authentication
- ✦ Non-repudiation
- ✦ Access control
- ✦ Public Key Infrastructure
- ✦ Digital Certificates
- ✦ Standards and Protocols
- ✦ Key Management

Cryptography is used to scramble messages so that an unintended receiver cannot read them. No attempt is made to hide the fact that a message is being sent; the idea is to make the message so difficult to unscramble that the unintended receiver cannot retrieve the contents in time to make use of them. To use the proper terminology, a *plaintext message* is *enciphered,* or *encrypted,* by some means to become scrambled *ciphertext*. To return the message to its original form, the message must be *deciphered,* or *decrypted*. A *key,* or *cryptovariable,* is used to control the enciphering and deciphering of the message.

Cryptography is the art and science of hiding the meaning of a communication from unintended recipients. The word *cryptography* derives from the Greek: *kryptos* (hidden) and *graphein* (to write). An unintended receiver of a message tries to obtain the plaintext from the ciphertext or tries to determine the key used to encipher the plaintext message. These acts are defined as *cryptanalysis*. The amount of effort that is required to recover the plaintext from the ciphertext is called the *work factor*. The higher the work factor, the more difficult the recovery process.

Cryptography and cryptanalysis comprise the field of *cryptology*. The encryption and decryption processes can be summarized with the equations shown in Table 4.1, where E is the encryption transformation, D is the decryption transformation, M is the plaintext message, and C is the ciphertext. The letter K shows that encryption and decryption are a function of the key, or cryptovariable, K.

Table 4.1
Cryptography Equations

Function	Equation
Encryption	$E(M, K) = C$
Decryption	$D(C, K) = D[E(M, K), K] = M$

The transformations described in these equations are called a *cryptosystem*.

It is important to notice the difference between a cipher and a code. A *cipher* is a transformation that operates on bits, and a *code* operates on phrases or words.

If the encrypted message is sent from the point of origin to its final destination, it is termed *end-to-end encryption*. In *link encryption,* on the other hand, each sender/receiver has keys in common with its two neighboring nodes in a transmission chain. In operation, a node receives an encrypted message from its predecessor node, decrypts the message, and re-encrypts it with a different key that is common to the successor node. Then, the encrypted message is sent to the successor node, where the process is repeated until the final destination is reached. Link encryption does not protect the information if the nodes along the transmission path are compromised.

Algorithms

As one might expect, a message can be encrypted in numerous ways using different procedures or algorithms. These algorithms have evolved over centuries and, in some periods, the technology has favored those encrypting messages and, in other periods, the technology has favored those attempting to "break" the encrypted messages.

Exclusive Or

A straightforward means of encryption uses the Exclusive Or (XOR) function. In binary logic systems, the XOR function operates as follows:

- If two input bits are identical, the output of the XOR function is a logical 0.
- If two input bits are different, the output of the XOR function is a logical 1.

If a plaintext message is composed of the string of bits 11010110, and you apply the cryptovariable string 11101101 to the plaintext message through an XOR function, the ciphertext is produced as follows:

If

    Plaintext   11010110

    Cryptovariable   11101101

Then

    Ciphertext   00111011

A useful characteristic of the XOR function is that if the XOR function using the same cryptovariable is applied to the ciphertext, the original plaintext is generated. Using the previous example, this feature is illustrated as follows:

If

    Ciphertext   00111011

    Cryptovariable   11101101

Then

    Plaintext   11010110

The same hardware and/or software can be used for encryption and decryption. The XOR function lends itself to hardware implementation because it is simple to implement using basic Boolean operations.

Hash Functions

The hash function has been used extensively in computer science applications. It takes an input of variable length and generates an output of fixed length, called a *message digest (MD)*. Symbolically, this operation can be represented as:

$H(M) = MD,$

where M is the message, H is the hash function applied to the message, and MD is the output message digest.

For a hash function to be useful in cryptography, the output should uniquely represent the input. If the message input to the hash function changes, the message digest should also change. In addition, the hash function should be one-way in that it should be easy to generate the MD from the message, but very difficult or impossible to generate the message from the MD. In summary, a strong hash algorithm should possess the following characteristics:

1. It should be computationally infeasible to find two messages that produce a common message digest (that is, H(M1) ≠ H(M2)).
2. If a message and its corresponding message digest exist, it should be computationally infeasible to find another message that generates that specific message digest.
3. It should be computationally infeasible to find a message that corresponds to a given message digest.
4. The message digest should be calculated using all the data in the original message.

The first two statements seem to be identical, but there is a subtle difference. The first statement describes a case where two messages can hash to ANY common message digest. This situation is usually referred to as a *collision*. The second statement refers to a situation in which a message and its specific message digest exist and an attacker attempts to find another message that hashes to that specific message digest. These two statements are important because message digests are used in digital signatures to uniquely represent the messages from which they were generated. If another message could be found that generates the same message digest as the original message, this message could be substituted for the original message to deceive the intended receiver. In the third statement, the message digest is generated by a one-way function in that it should not be possible to generate the original message from its corresponding message digest.

Attacks relating to the first two statements are referred to as *birthday attacks*. The birthday analogy to the first statement would state that "If a room is filled with N number of people, what value of N would result in a better than 50/50 chance of two people having a common birthday?" Again, you are not looking for a specific birth date, but *any* birth date that is shared by two individuals. The answer to the question is that N equals 23. With 23 people in a room, there are N(N-1)/2, or 253, pairs of individuals in the room.

Similarly, the attack represented by the second statement would require 253 people in the room to have a better than 50/50 chance that another person will have the same birthday as a specific individual in the room.

To resist birthday attacks, a hash function should generate a message digest of at least 128 bits. For example, the Secure Hash Algorithm-1 (SHA–1) defined in FIPS

180 (National Institute of Standards and Technology, NIST FIPS PUB 180, "Secure Hash Standard, " U.S. Department of Commerce, May 1993) generates a message digest of 160 bits for any message less than 2^{64} bits in length. Another example of a hash algorithm is Message Digest 5 (MD5), developed by Ron Rivest (R.L. Rivest, "The MD5 Message Digest Algorithm," RFC 1321, Apr 1992). MD5 generates a 128-bit message digest. A third hash algorithm that produces a variable length message digest is HAVAL (Y. Zheng, J Pieprzyk, and J. Seberry, "HAVAL-A One-Way Hashing Algorithm with Variable Length of Output," *Advances in Cryptology-AUSCRYPT '92 Proceedings,* Springer-Verlag, 1993). HAVAL can produce message digests of 128, 160, 192, 224, or 256 bits in length.

Keyed Hash Algorithms

Hash algorithms can also use keys to control the generation of the message digest from the input message. Then, only an individual with the key used in the generation of the message digest can verify that the hash function sent with an original message is correct. An example of a keyed hash algorithm is a message authentication code (MAC). MACs are used to verify that files sent between users have not been altered en route. To accomplish this authentication, a hash or MAC of a message is generated using a keyed hash algorithm and the MAC is appended to the message prior to transmission. At the receiving end, the MAC is generated from the received message and compared to the MAC sent with the message. If the MACs generated at the transmitting and receiving ends are identical, the message is authenticated.

Symmetric Algorithms

Symmetric algorithms use a secret key to encrypt a message, and the same secret key must be used by the receiver to decrypt the message. The key is a shared secret between the sender and the receiver. Symmetric encryption is sometimes referred to as *private key encryption*. It exhibits the following general characteristics:

- ✦ Faster than asymmetric (public key) encryption, which will be discussed in the next section (approximately 1,000 to 10,000 times faster)
- ✦ Useful in encrypting large volumes of data
- ✦ Because the sender and receiver must share the same secret key, the sender must have a different secret key for use with each receiver
- ✦ A secure means must be used to transmit the secret key from the sender to the receiver

Symmetric algorithms have evolved and gained in sophistication over the centuries. The following discussions provide an overview of the most common symmetric algorithms, including the latest cryptosystems, in use today.

Substitution

This basic cipher simply involves substituting one letter of the alphabet for another. In the classic Caesar cipher, the key is shifting the alphabet three letters to the right. For example, the letter A would be encrypted into the letter D, the letter B would be encrypted into the letter E, and so on. Thus, the word BAG would be encrypted into the word EDJ. To decrypt the message, the reverse procedure would be followed. Because only one alphabet is used, this type of substitution is called a *monoalphabetic substitution*. A substitution cipher is attacked using frequency analysis. In this approach, the frequency of occurrence of particular letters in a language can be used to deduce the letters in the plaintext message from the ciphertext.

In an improvement over the monoalphabetic substitution cipher, the *polyalphabetic* substitution cipher uses multiple alphabets in the substitution process. The French diplomat Blaise de Vigenère, born in 1523, developed a very effective polyalphabetic cipher consisting of 26 alphabets. Because multiple alphabets are used, the polyalphabetic cipher counters frequency analysis since the same letter in the plaintext is not always converted into the same letter in ciphertext. However, attacks on polyalphabetic ciphers are based on determining the period when the substitution repeats by starting over with the first alphabet.

The German Enigma rotor machine that was used in World War II employed rotors to affect a polyalphabetic substitution cryptosystem.

Transposition

Transposition, or *permutation* as it is sometimes called, involves the transposition of the plaintext letters. Transposing the letters generates an anagram. In a simple example of transposition, you can rearrange the letters of the plaintext I AM HAPPY into PIMAYAHP. Deciphering this short sentence is fairly easy, but rearranging the transposed text back to its original order becomes increasingly difficult as the sentences get longer and longer. Keep in mind that the longer the plaintext that is subject to transposition, the more difficult it is to communicate the key to the intended receiver. Three examples of transposition in which the key is easy to understand are the *rail fence transposition*, the *columnar transposition,* and the *Spartan scytale*.

Rail Fence Transposition

In rail fence transposition, the plaintext is written on two lines. For example, applying the rail fence transposition to the plaintext message ONLY THE ADAPTABLE SHALL SURVIVE yields the following:

```
O L T E D P A L S A L U V V
 N Y H A A T B E H L S R I E
```

The lower part of the text is concatenated onto the upper text to yield the following enciphered message:

O L T E D P A L S A L U V V N Y H A A T B E H L S R I E

The ciphertext is converted back into the plaintext by reversing the process.

Columnar Transposition
In columnar transposition, the plaintext message is written in horizontal fashion and read vertically to generate the ciphertext. The sentence ONLY THE ADAPTABLE SHALL SURVIVE can be written horizontally as follows:

O N L Y T H E A D
A P T A B L E S H
A L L S U R V I V
E

Reading the letters vertically produces the ciphertext of OAAENPLLTLYAST-BUHLREEVASIDHV.

Spartan Syctale
The third example of transposition is the Spartan syctale. Used by the Spartans around 400 B.C., this device consisted of a cylinder of wood around which a strip of parchment or leather was wound. The plaintext message was written across the wound strips along the long axis of the cylinder. When the message was completed, the strip was unwound and appeared to contain a series of meaningless letters. When the strip was delivered to the receiver and wrapped around a cylinder of the same diameter as the originating cylinder, the plaintext message was visible.

One-Time Pad
The *one-time pad* is an unbreakable cipher that exhibits the following characteristics:

- ✦ The key is a series of letters as long as the message.
- ✦ The sequence of letters in the key is truly random and has no repeating patterns.
- ✦ A particular key should be used once and only once.

If each letter of the alphabet is given a numerical value, with A being equal to 0, B equal to one, and so on, and Z equal to 25; each letter of the one-time pad's key can be added modulo 26 to each letter of the plaintext. The resultant number can be converted back into a letter to become the ciphertext. For example, if the random key is ADFHOL and the plaintext message is HEAVEN, the one-time pad encipherment would proceed as follows:

ADFHOL converted to numbers is   0   3   5   7   14   11
HEAVEN converted to numbers is   7   4   0   21   4   13

Adding the random key to the plaintext modulo 26 yields   7 7 5 2 18 24

Converting these numbers back into letters yields   H H F C J Y

Thus, using the one-time pad key ADFHOL, the plaintext HEAVEN is encrypted into ciphertext HHFCJY.

The principle of the one-time pad was developed around 1918 by Major Joseph Mauborgne, who was in charge of cryptographic research for the U.S. Army. Vernam at AT&T developed a machine that implemented the one-time pad. The machine performed an exclusive Or function of the message bits in Baudot code with the key bits. The one-time pad is sometimes known as the *Vernam cipher*.

Modern Symmetric Key Encryption Algorithms

Modern approaches to symmetric or secret key cryptography use complex algorithms that essentially comprise a series of substitutions, transpositions, Exclusive Or operations, and various shifting and rotation of key components and plaintext. Most symmetric key cryptosystems assume the public knows the following information:

- The algorithm used to encrypt the plaintext message
- A copy of plaintext and the associated ciphertext
- In some cases, an encipherment of plaintext chosen by a possible attacker

Information that must be protected from disclosure is the key, or cryptovariable, and the particular cryptographic transformation that is used out of the many possible transformations using the specified algorithm. In secret key cryptography, the same key is used to encipher and decipher the message.

The Data Encryption Standard

The Data Encryption Standard (DES) was adopted in 1977 as the U.S. government cryptosystem for use in commercial, non-classified applications. DES uses a symmetric key algorithm called the Data Encryption Algorithm (DEA). DEA is based on the Lucifer algorithm developed by Horst Feistel and his team at IBM. DES and DEA are described in the U.S. Federal Information Processing Standard (FIPS) Publication 46-1.

DES is a block cipher because it segregates the plaintext into 64-bit blocks and applies the key and encryption algorithm to each block. The DEA of DES uses a 56-bit key plus 8 additional parity bits.

DES uses 16 rounds of substitution and transposition in the DEA. Substitution implements the concept of *confusion*, proposed by Claude Shannon. Confusion hides the statistical connection between the plaintext and the ciphertext. Non-linear substitution is accomplished in DES by S-boxes that take a 6-bit input string and convert it to a 4-bit output string. Permutations in DES P-boxes accomplish Shannon's other concept of *diffusion*. Diffusion spreads the influence of a plaintext character over many ciphertext characters.

DES was recertified by the U.S. National Institute of Standards and Technology (NIST) in 1993, but has not been used by the U.S. government since 1998. DES has been replaced by the Advanced Encryption Standard (AES) as a result of DES's vulnerability to brute force attacks. With a 56-bit key, one would have to try 2^{56}, or 70 quadrillion, possible keys in this attack. This trial-and-error approach can be accomplished by using networks of very large numbers of computers. Even though DES has been replaced by AES, DES variants are still in use and DES employs many fundamental concepts of symmetric key algorithms. A version of DES, called triple DES, uses three encryptions. Triple DES is very secure and is used in many, non-classified applications.

DES Modes

DES operates in the following modes:

- Electronic Code Book (ECB)
- Cipher Feedback (CFB)
- Output Feedback (OFB)
- Cipher Block Chaining (CBC)

The *Electronic Code Book* mode operates on 64-bit length blocks and is normally used to encrypt encryption keys or initializing vectors used in the other DES modes. ECB is usually applied to small amounts of data. ECB's name derives from the concept of a codebook, where a plaintext word has a corresponding cipher text string of characters. For example, the code for ATTACK may be 78532.

Cipher Feedback operates as a stream cipher, where the input plaintext string of characters is Exclusive Or'd with a key stream of the same length as the plaintext stream to produce the ciphertext stream. Because the ciphertext is fed back to interact with the key to generate the ensuing characters of the key stream, this mode is referred to as *Cipher Feedback*. The disadvantage of this feedback arrangement is that errors propagate to the following generated ciphertext. Figure 4.1 illustrates the DES Cipher Feedback mode.

DES's *Output Feedback* mode operates in a similar fashion to CFB, except that the keystream is fed back instead of the ciphertext. Therefore, errors do not propagate in the OFB mode. OFB is illustrated in Figure 4.2.

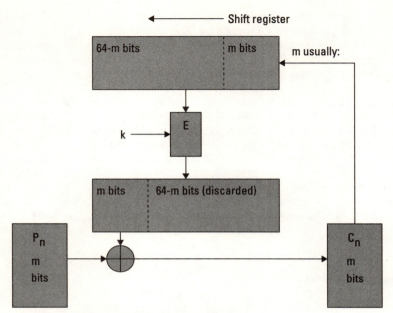

Figure 4.1 DES Cipher Feedback mode

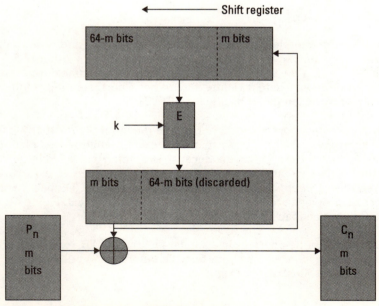

Figure 4.2 DES Output Feedback mode

Cipher Block Chaining performs the Exclusive Or of the plaintext with the generated ciphertext and operates on 64-bit blocks. To start the process, a 64-bit, randomly generated initialization vector is Exclusive Or'd with the first 64 bits of the plaintext. This result is encrypted with the DES key and fed into the next stage to be Exclusive Or'd with the next, 64-bit block of plaintext. Errors propagate in this operation, similar to the way they do in the Cipher Feedback mode. CBC is illustrated in Figure 4.3.

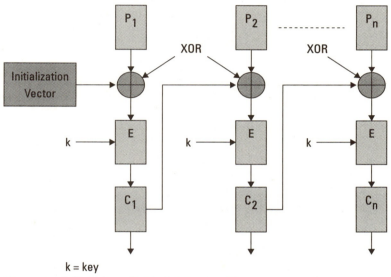

k = key

Figure 4.3 DES Cipher Block Chaining mode

Triple DES

In triple DES, a combination of three consecutive encryptions and/or decryptions is used to increase the security level of the plaintext message. Triple DES is specified in FIPS 46-3. In addition, the ANSI X9.52 standard defines a version of triple DES encryption with keys k1, k2, and k3 as follows:

$$C = E_{k3} [D_{k2} [E_{k1} [M]]]$$

This equation describes the triple DES EDE mode and performs an encryption E of plaintext message M with key k1 a decryption (D) with key k2 (essentially, another encryption), and a third encryption (E) with key k3. Another option, DES in the EEE mode, is written as follows:

$$C = E_{k3} [E_{k2} [E_{k1} [M]]]$$

Here, the three consecutive encryptions are performed on plaintext message M with three independent keys (k1, k2, k3).

Merkle and Hellman have shown that implementing two DES encryptions does not provide the additional security anticipated over a single DES encryption. A double DES encryption is vulnerable to a known plaintext, *meet-in-the-middle* attack that can break the double encryption in 2^{n+1} attempts. Consider a DES cipher with a key size of p. A double encryption results in an effective key size of 2p and yields the final result R. You would anticipate that you would have to search a key space of 2^{2p} in an exhaustive search of the keys. However, Merkle and Hellman have proved that a search of the key space on the order of 2^p is all that is necessary using the meet-in-the-middle attack. This search is the same size as that required for a single DES encryption. This situation is summarized as follows:

If you have available ciphertext R, where $R = E_{k2}[E_{k1}[M]]$ for a pair of secret keys k1 and k2, for each key, m, there is only one key, k, such that $D_m[R] = E_k[M]$, where D is the decipherment of R back from the second DES encipherment. In other words, 2^p possible keys will result in the pair [M,R] and can be found in a search of order 2^p.

The Advanced Encryption Standard

The Advanced Encryption Standard (AES) is a block cipher that has replaced DES, but it is anticipated that Triple DES will remain an approved algorithm for U.S. Government use. The AES initiative was announced in January 1997 by the National Institute of Standards and Technology (NIST) and candidate encryption algorithm submissions were solicited. On August 29, 1998, a group of 15 AES candidates was announced by NIST. In 1999, NIST announced five finalist candidates. These candidates were MARS, RC6, Rijndael, Serpent, and Twofish. NIST closed Round 2 of public analyses of these algorithms on May 15, 2000.

On October 2, 2000, NIST announced the selection of the Rijndael Block Cipher, developed by the Belgian cryptographers Dr. Joan Daemen and Dr. Vincent Rijmen, as the proposed AES algorithm. Rijndael was formalized as the Advanced Encryption Standard (AES) on November 26, 2001 as Federal Information Processing Standard Publication 197. FIPS PUB 197 states: "This standard may be used by Federal departments and agencies when an agency determines that sensitive (unclassified) information (as defined in P.L. 100–235) requires cryptographic protection. Other FIPS-approved cryptographic algorithms may be used in addition to, or in lieu of, this standard." AES consists of the three key sizes, 128, 192, and 256-bits, with a fixed block size of 128 bits. Depending on which of the three keys is used, the standard may be referred to as "AES-128", "AES-192", or "AES-256." It is expected that AES will be adopted by other private and public organizations inside and outside the United States.

Instead of a Feistel network that takes a portion of the modified plaintext and transposes it to another position, the Rijndael Cipher employs a round transformation that comprises three layers of distinct and invertible transformations. The number of rounds used in the Rijndael cipher is a function of the key size, as shown in Table 4.2.

Table 4.2
Rijndael Cipher Function

Bits	Number of Rounds
256-bit key	14 rounds
192-bit key	12 rounds
128-bit key	10 rounds

The Rijndael algorithm exhibits the following properties:

- Resistance against all known attacks
- Design simplicity
- Code compactness and speed on a wide variety of platforms

The Rijndael Block Cipher is suited for use in high-speed chips and in a compact coprocessor on a smart card.

Rijndael exhibits a symmetric and parallel structure that provides for flexibility of implementation and resistance to cryptanalytic attacks. Attacks on Rijndael would involve the use of differential and linear cryptanalysis.

In decimal terms, the Rijndael algorithm has approximately 3.4×10^{38} possible 128 bit keys, 6.2×10^{57} possible 192-bit keys, and 1.1×10^{77} possible 256-bit keys.

As a measure of the relative strength of the Rijndael encryption algorithm, if a computer could crack the DES encryption by trying 2^{56} keys in one second, the same computer would require 149 trillion (149×10^{12}) years to crack Rijndael. By comparison, the universe is estimated to be less than 20 billion (20×10^9) years old.

The International Data Encryption Algorithm

The International Data Encryption Algorithm (IDEA) cipher is another symmetric key cryptosystem. It operates on 64-bit plaintext blocks, uses a 128-bit key, and implements confusion and diffusion. It employs a block encryption algorithm that was developed by James Massey and Xuejia Lai (X. Lai, "On the Design and Security of Block Ciphers," *ETH Series on Information Processing, v.1*, Konstanz: Hartung-Gorre Verlag, 1992).

The IDEA algorithm performs eight rounds and operates on 16-bit subblocks using algebraic calculations that are amenable to hardware implementation. With its 128-bit key, an IDEA cipher is much more difficult to crack than DES. IDEA operates in the modes described for DES and is applied in the Pretty Good Privacy (PGP) e-mail encryption system that was developed by Phil Zimmerman.

Other Symmetric Key Algorithms

Covering the multitude of symmetric key algorithms that are currently in use is beyond the scope of this text, but some of the most popular ones are listed here for informational purposes.

- BLOWFISH
- FEAL
- GOST
- LOK
- RC4
- RC5
- SAFER
- SEAL
- TWOFISH

Asymmetric Algorithms

As previously noted, symmetric key cryptosystems are problematic in terms of key distribution (that is, securely sending the common secret key from the sender to the receiver). For years, cryptographers had been speculating about the possibility of having two separate, different keys — one held by the sender and one held by the receiver — that could be used to encrypt and decrypt the same message. If this scenario were possible, the problem of secure key distribution would be eliminated. Because the sender and receiver would each have different keys, this type of cryptography would be known as *asymmetric key cryptography*.

In 1976, Whitfield Diffie and Martin Hellman published a seminal paper (Whitfield Diffie and Martin Hellman, "New Directions in Cryptography," *IEEE Transactions on Information Theory, Vol. IT-22*, November 1976, pp. 644–54). This paper described a method whereby two users could securely exchange a secret key over a non-secure medium.

To accomplish this exchange, two system parameters, p and g, are required. Both parameters are public and can be used by all the system's users. Parameter p is a prime number, and parameter g (which is usually called a generator) is an integer less than p with the following property: For every number n between 1 and p – 1 inclusive, there is a power k of g such that g^k = n mod p.

For example, assume the following public parameters:

- p = prime number
- g = generator
- Generating Equation y = g^x mod p

Using these parameters, the following sequence illustrates the process in which Alice and Bob exchange a common secret key:

1. Alice calculates $y_a = g^a \bmod p$ using the value "a" of her private key.
2. Bob calculates $y_b = g^b \bmod p$ using his private value "b".
3. Alice sends y_a to Bob.
4. Bob can send y_b to Alice.
5. Knowing her private value, "a", Alice can calculate $(y_b)^a$, which yields $g^{ba} \bmod p$.
6. Knowing his private value, "b", Bob can calculate $(y_a)^b$, which yields $g^{ab} \bmod p$.

Because $g^{ba} \bmod p$ is equal to $g^{ab} \bmod p$, Bob and Alice have securely exchanged the secret key.

In its development of the key exchange method over a non-secure medium, the Diffie-Hellman paper provided the foundation for the development of asymmetric or, as it is also known, *public key cryptography*.

A fundamental concept in public key cryptography is that of the *one-way function*.

One-Way Functions

A one-way function is a function that is easy to compute in one direction, but very difficult or impossible to reverse. If the function $y = f(z)$ is a one-way function, it would be very easy to compute y, given z, but very difficult to compute z, given y.

Note   For some one-way functions, a *trapdoor* exists that enables one to easily calculate z, given y.

Public and Private Keys in Public Key Cryptography

As previously discussed, in asymmetric or public key cryptography, the sender and receiver have two different keys. However, these keys are related mathematically. For example, if Alice and Bob want to send encrypted messages to each other, Alice will have a public key known to everybody and a private key known only to her. Similarly, Bob will have his own private key, known only to him, and a corresponding public key that is known to everyone. The public and private keys display this property: if a plaintext message is encrypted with one of the keys, the message can be decrypted using the other key. However, because the public and private keys are generated using a one-way function, it is very difficult or impossible to derive a private key from its corresponding public key.

To send a secret message to Bob, Alice would encrypt the message with Bob's public key, which is known to everybody, and send it to Bob. Because Bob has the private key that is mathematically related to his public key, he can decrypt the message. No one else can decrypt the message unless they know Bob's private key. Also, the encryption process using the public key is a one-way function in that the public key cannot decrypt the message that was encrypted with the public key. In thinking about this process, a number of questions and issues arise. For example, how do you know that the public key posted for everyone to read as Bob's public key is really Bob's? The key could belong to someone else claiming to be Bob and who has the corresponding private key to read messages that people think they are sending to Bob. One solution is to use a certification authority that verifies Bob's identity and his corresponding public key. This topic will be discussed later in the chapter. The relationship between a public and private key can also serve to authenticate the source of a message. If Bob uses his private key to encrypt a plaintext message, his public key is the only other key that can decrypt the message. Therefore, if his public key does decrypt the message, it had to be sent by Bob. Again, the assumption is that Bob's public key has been certified to be his public key. This operation does not protect the message because anyone can read it using Bob's public key, but it does authenticate Bob as the source of the message.

If Bob wants to send an encrypted message to Alice and verify to Alice that he is really the sender, he can do the following:

1. Encrypt the message with Alice's public key — $E_{APUB}(M)$
2. Encrypt $E_{APUB}(M)$ with his private key — $E_{BPRV}[E_{APUB}(M)]$
3. Send the message to Alice
4. Alice uses Bob's public key to "open" the message and obtain $[(E_{APUB}(M)]$. If this step is successful, it verifies that Bob is the sender because his public key has "opened" the message.
5. Alice decrypts $[(E_{APUB}(M)]$ using her private key, E_{APRV}, to obtain M.

Digital Signatures

In addition to encryption and authentication, public key encryption can provide integrity protection to messages. Digital signatures, which are implemented with public key algorithms, can detect unauthorized or accidental modifications of the transmitted message. They can also authenticate the sender's identity. Digital signatures support non-repudiation. Bob uses the following process to send Alice a digitally signed message:

1. Using a one-way hash algorithm, Bob generates a message digest (MD) of the plaintext message. Recall that a strong hash algorithm will generate a fixed-length MD that uniquely characterizes the message from a message input of variable length. Typical message digests are 128, 160, or 256 bits in length.
2. Bob encrypts MD with his private key.
3. Bob attaches MD to his original plaintext message.
4. Bob sends the message with the appended MD digest to Alice.

5. Alice decrypts MD using Bob's public key. If Bob's public key "opens" the message digest, it verifies that Bob was the originator of the message (assuming that Bob's public key was certified to be his by an independent certification agency).

6. Alice takes the message that was sent with MD and generates a message digest, MD', using the same hash algorithm used by Bob to generate MD at the transmitting end.

7. If MD' = MD, the message integrity has been preserved, indicating that the message was not modified en route.

The NIST Digital Signature Standard and the Secure Hash Standard

NIST describes its digital signature standard (DSS) in FIPS PUB 186, "Digital Signature Standard," U.S. Department of Commerce, May 1994. The Standard states the following:

> Digital signatures are used to detect unauthorized modifications to data and to authenticate the identity of the signatory. In addition, the recipient of signed data can use a digital signature in proving to a third party that the signature was in fact generated by the signatory.

DSS uses either the RSA digital signature algorithm or the Digital Signature Algorithm (DSA). DSA was developed by Claus Schnorr circa 1989 (C.P. Schnorr, "Efficient Signature Generation for Smart Cards," *Advances in Cryptology-CRYPTO '89 Proceedings,* Springer-Verlag, 1990, pp. 239–252).

The RSA digital signature algorithm and the DSA use the Secure Hash Algorithm (SHA-1), as described in FIPS 180 (National Institute of Standards and Technology, NIST FIPS PUB 180, "Secure Hash Standard," U.S. Department of Commerce, May 1993).

SHA-1 sequentially processes blocks of 512 bits and generates a message digest of 160 bits in length when any message less than 2^{64} bits is provided as an input. As with any good strong, hash algorithm, SHA-1 exhibits the following properties:

- ✦ It is computationally infeasible to find a message that corresponds to a given message digest.
- ✦ It is computationally infeasible to find two different messages that produce the same message digest.

Public Key Algorithms

A number of popular algorithms are used to generate the public and private keys that exhibit the desired properties for use in public key cryptography. The most popular are discussed in the following sections.

RSA

The RSA algorithm is based on the difficulty of factoring a number that is the product of two prime numbers. As a one-way function, it is easy to multiply two large prime numbers to obtain their product, but it is difficult to factor a very large number to obtain its prime factors. The difficulty of obtaining the public key from the private key is based on the difficulty of obtaining the prime factors of a large number. A general-purpose, factoring algorithm, the Number Field Sieve (NFS), can be used to factor large numbers. A version of NFS has successfully factored a 155-digit number. So, if the product of two prime factors is on the order of 200 digits, the RSA algorithm (as of this writing, at least) is safe from factoring attacks.

RSA is derived from the last names of its inventors: Rivest, Shamir, and Addleman (R. L. Rivest, A. Shamir, and L. M. Addleman, "A Method for Obtaining Digital Signatures and Public-Key Cryptosystems," *Communications of the ACM, v. 21, n.2*, Feb 1978, pp. 120–126).

The RSA algorithm for generating the public and private keys is given as follows:

1. Choose two large prime numbers, p and q, of equal length, compute $p \times q = n$, which is the public modulus.
2. Choose a random public key, e, so that e and $(p-1)(q-1)$ are relatively prime.
3. Compute $e \times d = 1 \mod (p-1)(q-1)$, where d is the private key.
4. Thus, $d = e^{-1} \mod [(p-1)(q-1)]$

From these calculations, (d, n) is the private key and (e, n) is the public key.

The plaintext, P, is thus encrypted to generate ciphertext C as:

```
C [equals] Pe mod n,
```

and is decrypted to recover the plaintext, P, as:

```
P [equals] Cd mod n.
```

RSA can be used for encryption, key exchange, and digital signatures.

El Gamal Public Key Algorithm

Building on the Diffie-Hellman key exchange method, Dr. T. El Gamal developed a public key cryptosystem based on the difficulty of finding discrete logarithms in a finite field. In a simplified example, given g and x, it is not difficult to find $y = g^x$. However, given y and g, it is much more difficult to find x. The El Gamal algorithm can be used for encryption and digital signatures. It is described in El Gamal, "A Public-Key Crypto System and a Signature Scheme Based on Discrete Logarithms," *Advances in Cryptography: Proceedings of CRYPTO 84*, Springer-Verlag, 1985, pp. 10–18. An example of encryption using the El Gamal algorithm follows:

1. Given the prime number, p, and the integer, g, Alice uses her private key, a, to compute her public key as $y_a = g^a \bmod p$.

2. To send a message, M, to Alice, Bob would:

   a. Generate random #b < p.

   b. Compute $y_b = g^b \bmod p$ and $y_m = M \text{ XOR } y_{ab} = M \text{ XOR } g^{ab} \bmod p$.

   c. Send y_b, y_m to Alice; Alice would then compute $y_{ba} = g^{ab} \bmod p$.

3. Therefore, $M = y_{ba} \text{ XOR } y_m = g^{ab} \bmod p \text{ XOR } M \text{ XOR } g^{ab} \bmod p$.

Elliptic Curve

The elliptic curve algorithm is another approach to a one-way function that implements public key cryptography. It is based on the following equation for an elliptic curve:

```
y² [equal] x³ [plus] ax [plus] b along with a single point O, the
point at infinity
```

The elliptic curve is shown graphically in Figure 4.4.

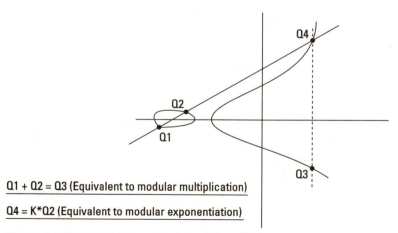

Q1 + Q2 = Q3 (Equivalent to modular multiplication)

Q4 = K*Q2 (Equivalent to modular exponentiation)

Figure 4.4 Graphical representation of the elliptic curve

Elliptic curves are analogous to the discrete logarithm problem and are usually defined over finite fields. The elliptic curve has the following properties:

- The operation of addition performed in the elliptic curve space is analogous to modular multiplication.
- The operation of multiplication is analogous to modular exponentiation.

The elliptic curve public key cryptography system was developed independently by Neal Koblitz (N. Koblitz, Elliptic Curve Cryptosystems," *Mathematics of Computation, v. 48, n. 177,* 1987, pp. 203–209) and V.S. Miller (V.S. Miller, "Use of Elliptic Curves in Cryptography," *Advances in Cryptology-CRYPTO '85 Proceedings*, Springer-Verlag, 1986, pp. 417–426).

One of the main advantages of elliptic curve systems is that equivalent levels of security to RSA and discrete logarithm implementations can be achieved with a smaller key size. This characteristic is a result of the increased difficulty in finding discrete logarithms using elliptic curves, as opposed to finding conventional discrete logarithms or factoring the product of prime numbers. For example, a 160-bit key using the elliptic curve cryptosystem is equivalent to a 1024-bit key in the RSA cryptosystem. The elliptic curve approach lends itself to implementation in hardware in applications such as smart cards.

Public Key Cryptography Function Summary

The two major classes of strong, one-way functions that are applied to public key cryptography are solving for the discrete logarithm in a finite field and factoring the product of large prime numbers. RSA uses the factoring approach and Diffie-Hellman, El Gamal, and elliptic curve are based on the discrete logarithm one-way function.

Other mathematical functions are useful as hard, one-way functions. For example, the Merkle-Hellman Knapsack is a one-way function that is based on the difficulty of determining which combination of available weights will total a specific weight. A good way to visualize this problem is to assume the existence of a fixed set of balls of different weights. If a subset of the balls is placed into a knapsack, the total weight of the knapsack is easily determined by summing the weights of those balls. However, the reverse operation can be much more difficult. Given the total weight of the balls in the knapsack, the problem would be to find which subset of balls must be in the knapsack. This concept is illustrated in Figure 4.5, using a set of balls with weights 3, 4, 8, 16, 32, and 64. This set can be described as *superincreasing*, in that each succeeding weight is greater than the sum of the previous weights.

In Figure 4.5, the problem has a small number of balls. Imagine very large numbers of these balls, each with different weights. The function becomes more difficult in the reverse direction as the number of balls increases.

The Merkle-Hellman Knapsack one-way function is described in R.C. Merkle and M. Hellman, "Hiding Information and Signatures in Trapdoor Knapsacks," *IEEE Transactions on Information Theory, v.24, n. 5,* September 1978, pp. 525–530.

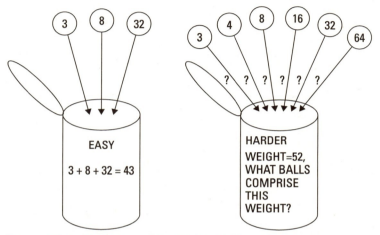

Figure 4.5 An illustration of the Merkle-Hellman Knapsack one-way function

Public Key Infrastructure

Public Key Infrastructure (PKI) is the integration of digital certificates, digital signatures, and other services required for e-commerce. These services provide the following for e-commerce transactions:

- Access control
- Integrity
- Confidentiality
- Authentication
- Non-repudiation

Digital Certificates

Major components of PKI include the digital certificate and management of the certificate. Remember: the purpose of a digital certificate is to verify to all that an individual's public key—posted on a public "key ring"—is actually his. A trusted, third-party certification authority (CA) can verify that the public key is that of the named individual and then issue a certificate attesting to that fact. The CA accomplishes the certification by digitally signing the individual's public key and associated information.

A certificate authority (CA) acts as notary by verifying a person's identity and issuing a certificate that vouches for a public key of the named individual. This certification agent signs the certificate with its own private key. The certificate is then sent to a repository, which holds the certificates and certificate revocation lists (CRLs) that denote the revoked certificates. To verify the CA's signature, its public key must be cross-certified with another CA's.

Certificates and CRLs can be held in a repository with responsibilities defined between the repository and the CA. The repository access protocol determines how these responsibilities are assigned. In one protocol, the repository interacts with other repositories, CAs, and users. The CA deposits its certificates and CRLs into the repository. The users can then access the repository for this information.

Directories and X.500

In PKI, a repository is usually referred to as a *directory*. The directory contains entries associated with an object class. An object class can refer to individuals or other computer-related entities. The class defines the attributes of the object. Attributes for PKI are defined in RFC 2587, *Internet X.509 Public Key Infrastructure LDAP v2 Schema* by Boeyen, Howes, and Richard, published in 1999. Additional information on attributes can be found in RFC 2079, *Definition of an X.500 Attribute Type and an Object Class to Hold Uniform Resource Identifiers (URLs)*, by M. Smith, published in January 1997.

The X.509 certificate standard defines the authentication bases for the X.500 directory. The X.500 directory stores information about individuals and objects in a distributed database residing on network servers. Some of the principal definitions associated with X.500 include the following:

- Directory User Agents (DUAs) — clients
- Directory Server Agents (DSAs) — servers
- Directory Service Protocol (DSP) — enables information exchanges between DSAs
- Directory Access Protocol (DAP) — enables information exchanges from a DUA to a DSA
- Directory Information Shadowing Protocol (DISP) — used by a DSA to duplicate or "shadow" some or all of its contents

DSAs accept requests from anonymous sources as well as authenticated requests. They share information through a *chaining* mechanism.

The Lightweight Directory Access Protocol

The Lightweight Directory Access Protocol (LDAP) was developed as a more efficient version of DAP and has evolved into a version 2 (Yeong, Y., T. Howes, and S. Killie, *Lightweight Directory Access Protocol*, RFC 1777, 1995). LDAP servers communicate through referrals (that is, a directory receiving a request for information it does not have will query the tables of remote directories). If it finds a directory with the required entry, it sends a referral to the requesting directory. LDAP v2 does not have chaining and shadowing capabilities, but additional protocols can be obtained to provide these functions.

LDAP provides a standard format to access the certificate directories. These directories are stored on network LDAP servers and provide public keys and corresponding X.509 certificates for the enterprise. A directory contains information, such as individuals' names, addresses, phone numbers, and public key certificates. The standards under X.500 define the protocols and information models for computer directory services that are independent of the platforms and other related entities. LDAP servers are subject to attacks that affect availability and integrity. For example, Denial of Service attacks on an LDAP server could prevent access to the CRLs and thus permit the use of a revoked certificate.

The DAP protocol in X.500 was unwieldy and led to most client implementations using LDAP. LDAP version 3 is under development, with extensions that will provide shadowing and chaining capabilities.

X.509 Certificates

The original X.509 certificate (CCITT, *The Directory—Authentication Framework*, Recommendation X.509, 1988) was developed to provide the authentication foundation for the X.500 directory. Since then, a version 2, version 3, and recently, a version 4 have been developed. Version 2 of the X.509 certificate addresses the reuse of names, version 3 provides for certificate extensions to the core certificate fields, and version 4 provides yet additional extensions. These extensions can be used as needed by different users and different applications. A version of X.509 that takes into account the requirements of the Internet was published by the IETF (Housley, R., W. Ford, W. Polk, and D. Solo, *Internet X.509 Public Key Infrastructure Certificate and CRL Profile, RFC 2459, 1999*).

The basic format of an X.509 certificate has been defined by the Consultation Committee, International Telephone and Telegraph, International Telecommunications Union (CCITT-ITU)/International Organization for Standardization (ISO). This structure is outlined in Figure 4.6.

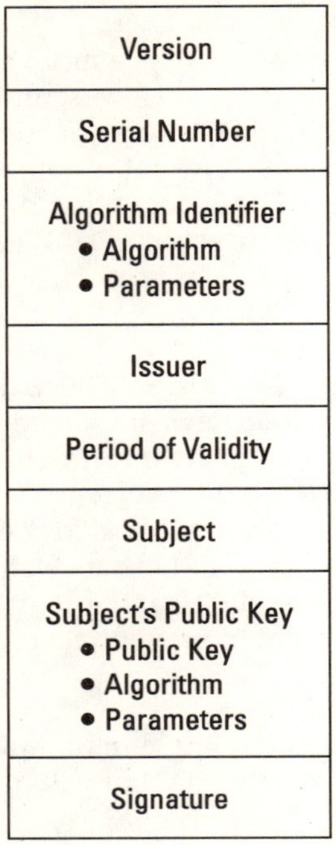

Figure 4.6 The CCITT-ITU/ ISO X.509 certificate format

```
┌─────────────────────┐
│      Version        │
├─────────────────────┤
│   Serial Number     │
├─────────────────────┤
│ Algorithm Identifier│
│   • Algorithm       │
│   • Parameters      │
├─────────────────────┤
│       Issuer        │
├─────────────────────┤
│  Period of Validity │
├─────────────────────┤
│       Subject       │
├─────────────────────┤
│ Subject's Public Key│
│   • Public Key      │
│   • Algorithm       │
│   • Parameters      │
├─────────────────────┤
│      Signature      │
└─────────────────────┘
```

If version 3 certificates are used, the optional extensions field can be used. It comes before the signature field components in the certificate. Some typical extensions are the entity's name and supporting identity information, the attributes of the key, certificate policy information, and the type of the subject. The digital signature serves as a tamper-evident envelope.

Some of the different types of certificates that are issued include the following:

- **CA certificates** — Issued to CAs, these certificates contain the public keys used to verify digital signatures on CRLs and certificates.
- **End entity certificates** — Issued to entities that are not CAs, these certificates contain the public keys that are needed by the certificate's user in order to perform key management or verify a digital signature.
- **Self-issued certificates** — These certificates are issued by an entity to itself to establish points of trust and to distribute a new signing public key.
- **Rollover certificates** — These certificates are issued by a CA to transition from an old public key to a new one.

Certificate Revocation Lists

Users check the certificate revocation list (CRL) to determine if a digital certificate has been revoked. They check for the serial number of the signature. The CA signs the CRL for integrity and authentication purposes. A CRL is shown in Figure 4.7 for an X.509 version 2 certificate.

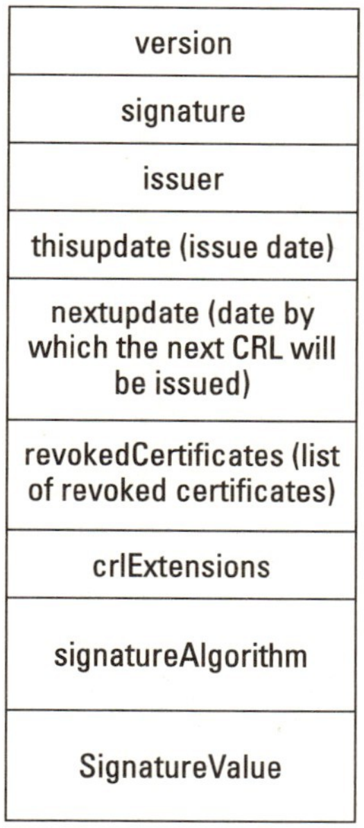

Figure 4.7 CRL format (version 2)

version
signature
issuer
thisupdate (issue date)
nextupdate (date by which the next CRL will be issued)
revokedCertificates (list of revoked certificates)
crlExtensions
signatureAlgorithm
SignatureValue

The CA usually generates the CRLs for its population. If the CA generates the CRLs for its entire population, the CRL is called a *full CRL*.

PKI Component Summary

The following list summarizes the major components of PKI:

- Digital certificates
- Certificate authority
- Certificate revocation
- Cross-certification
- Registration authorities
- Policies and procedures

- Non-repudiation support
- Timestamping
- Security-enabled applications
- Lightweight Directory Access Protocol

Key Distribution

As noted earlier, distributing secret keys in symmetric key encryption poses a problem. Secret keys can be distributed using asymmetric key cryptosystems. Other means of distributing secret keys include face-to-face meetings to exchange keys, sending the keys by secure messenger, or some other, secure, alternate channel. Another method is to encrypt the secret key with another key, called a *key encryption key*, and send the encrypted secret key to the intended receiver. These key encryption keys can be distributed manually, but need not be distributed often. The X9.17 Standard (ANSI X9.17 [Revised], "American National Standard for Financial Institution Key Management [Wholesale]," American Bankers Association, 1985) specifies key encryption keys as well as data keys for encrypting the plaintext messages.

Key distribution can also be accomplished by splitting the keys into different parts and sending each part by a different medium.

In large networks, key distribution can become a serious problem because in an N-person network, the total number of key exchanges is $N(N-1)/2$. Using public key cryptography or the creation and exchange of session keys that are valid only for a particular session and time are useful mechanisms for managing the key distribution problem.

Keys can be *updated* by generating a new key from an old key. If, for example, Alice and Bob share a secret key, they can apply the same transformation function (a hash algorithm) to their common secret key and obtain a new secret key.

Key Revocation

A digital certificate contains a timestamp or period for which the certificate is valid. Also, if a key is compromised or must be made invalid because of business or personnel-related issues, it must be revoked. The CA maintains a CRL of all invalid certificates. Users should regularly examine this list.

Key Recovery

A system must be put in place to decrypt critical data if the encryption key is lost or forgotten. One method is *key escrow:* the key is subdivided into different parts, each of which is encrypted and then sent to a different trusted individual in an organization. Keys can also be escrowed onto smart cards.

Key Renewal

Obviously, the longer a secret key is used without changing it, the more it is subject to compromise. The frequency with which you change the key is a direct function of the value of the data being encrypted and transmitted. Also, if the same secret key is used to encrypt valuable data over a relatively long period of time, you risk compromising a larger volume of data when the key is broken. Another important concern if the key is not changed frequently is that an attacker can intercept and change messages and send different messages to the receiver.

Key encryption keys, because they are not used as often as encryption keys, provide some protection against attacks.

Typically, private keys used for digital signatures are not frequently changed and may be kept for years.

Key Destruction

Keys that have been in use for long periods of time and are replaced by others should be destroyed. If the keys are compromised, older messages sent with those keys can be read.

Keys that are stored on disks or EEPROMS should be overwritten numerous times. The disks can also be destroyed by shredding and burning. However, in some cases, it is possible to recover data from disks that were put into a fire. Any hardware device storing the key, such as an EPROM, should also be physically destroyed.

Older keys stored by the operating system in various locations in memory must also be searched out and destroyed.

Multiple Keys

Usually, an individual has more than one public/private key pair. The keys may be of different sizes for different levels of security. A larger key size may be used for digitally signing documents and a smaller key size may be used for encryption. A person may also have multiple roles or responsibilities wherein they want to sign messages with a different signature. One key pair may be used for business matters, another for personal use, and another for some other activity, such as being a school board member.

Distributed versus Centralized Key Management

A CA is a form of centralized key management. It is a central location that issues certificates and maintains CRLs. An alternative is distributed key management, in which a "chain of trust" or "web of trust" is set up among users who know each other. Because they know each other, they can trust that each one's public key is valid. Some of these users may know other users and can verify their public key. The "chain" spreads outward from the original group. This arrangement results in an informal verification procedure that is based on people knowing and trusting each other.

Escrowed Encryption

For national security and crime fighting purposes, governments desire the ability to "listen-in" to encrypted transmissions. To avoid privacy and civil liberties issues, the escrowing of encryption keys with "trusted" agencies has been proposed. The keys could then only be retrieved to monitor encrypted transmissions after obtaining a valid court order. Most approaches involve dividing the secret key into multiple parts and escrowing each part with a different agency.

A specific example of escrowed encryption is the U.S. Escrowed Encryption Standard (National Institute of Standards and Technology, NIST FIPS PUB 185, "Escrowed Encryption Standard", U.S. Department of Commerce, Feb 1994). This standard proposed the adoption of the *clipper cryptosystem* for telephone communications and the *capstone cryptosystem* for computer communications. The telephone-related standard is implemented in tamper-proof hardware as the *clipper chip*. The clipper chip uses the declassified *Skipjack* symmetric key algorithm for encryption. The Skipjack key is 80 bits in length, which is weak compared to the computational power available with today's technology.

The U.S. government used the clipper and capstone standards for its own communications and required organizations doing business with the U.S. government to use these standards. The U.S. government hoped that other businesses would adopt the standards on a voluntary basis. However, because of privacy and civil liberty concerns, the Escrowed Encryption Standard did not become widespread. The obvious concern related to escrowed encryption in general is the possibility that the escrow agencies would divulge the private keys under government pressure or by corrupt employees.

To address some of these concerns, Sylvio Micali proposed a key escrow system that would be administered by voluntary trustees or businesses in different countries rather than by government agencies. His approach (S. Micali, "Fair Cryptosystems", MIT/LCS/TR-579.b, MIT Laboratory for Computer Science, Nov 1993) also provides for a validity test of each escrowed portion of the key without requiring the other parts of the key.

Hybrid Systems

Because symmetric key cryptosystems are faster than asymmetric key cryptosystems, they are excellent for encrypting and transmitting large volumes of data (for example, a digitized motion picture). However, symmetric key cryptosystems suffer from the problem of securely distributing the secret key(s). Asymmetric key cryptosystems have eliminated the problem of secret key distribution because two keys, public and private, are used for encrypting and decrypting the transmissions. The drawback of the asymmetric key cryptosystem is that it is computationally intensive and not well suited for transmitting large amounts of data. By combining private and public key cryptosystems in one application, you can have the best of both worlds. The public key cryptosystem can be used to securely distribute a symmetric key cryptosystem's secret key. Then, the data can be encrypted and decrypted using the symmetric key algorithm.

An excellent example of such a hybrid system is *Pretty Good Privacy (PGP)*, developed by Phil Zimmerman in the late 1980s. The name was derived from Ralph's Pretty Good Groceries, a sponsor of the *Prairie Home Companion* radio show hosted by Garrison Keillor.

Zimmerman designed a hybrid system using the RSA asymmetric key algorithm to encrypt and distribute the secret key of the IDEA symmetric key cipher that, in turn, was used to encrypt and transmit the data. Zimmerman developed a user-friendly interface that did not require the user to understand cryptography in detail and that handled the key generation issues in a manner transparent to the user. Zimmerman was concerned about the ability of governments to monitor the transmissions of ordinary citizens and saw PGP as a tool by which citizens could protect their privacy. In 1991, Zimmerman gave his PGP system to a friend to post on a Usenet bulletin board. From there, it spread all over the world and was praised by human rights groups as a godsend in protecting private information from government monitoring. However, in 1993, Zimmerman was investigated by the U.S. government and accused of illegally exporting software that was on the government's munitions list. Items on this list required an export license from the U.S. State Department. Eventually, the issue was resolved and Zimmerman was not punished since, technically, he had not exported the software but rather given it to a friend who had posted it on an Internet bulletin board.

Instead of using a certification agency to validate a person's public key, PGP uses a "web of trust" where users and groups can certify keys to each other.

Cryptographic Attacks

An attacker applies cryptanalysis to obtain the plaintext or the key from the ciphertext. The following is a list of some common attacks:

✦ **Birthday attack**—Refers to the probability of two different messages using the same hash function that produces a common message digest; or, given a message and its corresponding message digest, finding another message that when passed through the same hash function generates the same specific message digest. The term *birthday* comes from the fact that in a room with 23 people, the probability of two or more people having the same birthday is greater than 50 percent.

- **Brute force** — Trying every possible combination of key patterns — the longer the key length, the more difficult it is to find the key with this method.
- **Chosen ciphertext** — Portions of the ciphertext are selected for trial decryption with the code breaker having access to the corresponding decrypted plaintext.
    - Adaptive chosen ciphertext — A form of a chosen ciphertext attack where the selection of the portions of ciphertext for the attempted decryption is based on the results of previous attempts.
- **Chosen plaintext** — Chosen plaintext is encrypted and the output ciphertext is obtained.
    - Adaptive chosen plaintext — A form of a chosen plaintext attack where the selection of the plaintext is altered according to the previous results.
- **Ciphertext only** — Only the ciphertext is available.
- **Differential cryptanalysis** — Applied to private key cryptographic systems by looking at ciphertext pairs (that were generated through the encryption of plaintext pairs) with specific differences and analyzing the effect of these differences.
- **Linear cryptanalysis** — Using pairs of known plaintext and corresponding ciphertext to generate a linear approximation of a portion of the key.
- **Differential linear cryptanalysis** — Using both differential and linear approaches.
- **Factoring** — Using a mathematical approach to determine the prime factors of large numbers.
- **Known plaintext** — The attacker has a copy of the plaintext corresponding to the ciphertext.
- **Man-in-the-middle** — An attacker takes advantage of the store-and-forward nature of most networks by intercepting messages and forwarding modified versions of the original message while in between two parties attempting secure communications.
- **Meet-in-the-middle** — Applied to double encryption schemes by encrypting known plaintext from one end with each possible key (K) and comparing the results "in the middle" with the decryption of the corresponding ciphertext with each possible K.
- **Statistical** — Exploiting the lack of randomness in key generation.

Steganography

Where cryptography attempts to protect a message by encryption, *steganography* attempts to pass information by hiding the existence of a message. The word *steganography* comes from the Greek words *steganos*, meaning "covered," and *graphein*, meaning "to write." Examples of steganography are the use of invisible ink; the microdot, which compresses a message into the size of a period or dot; and changing the least significant bit of each word in a digital image. The image is essentially unaffected, but the secret information is transmitted. Steganography can also be used to make a digital "watermark" to detect the illegal copying of digital images.

One major problem with steganography is that if the hidden message is somehow found, it is easily read and the secret information is available to anyone.

✦ ✦ ✦

SAMPLE QUESTIONS

1. Which of the following statements is *not* true regarding the Exclusive Or function?

    a. 1 + 1 = 0

    b. 1 + 0 = 1

    c. 0 + 0 = 0

    d. 1 + 1 = 1

2. The Secure Hash Algorithm–1 (SHA–1) is specified in the _____.

    a. Data Encryption Standard

    b. Digital Signature Standard

    c. Digital Encryption Standard

    d. Advanced Encryption Standard

3. The Digital Signature Standard (DSS) uses which digital signature algorithm(s)?

    a. Either the RSA digital signature algorithm or the Digital Signature Algorithm (DSA)

    b. DSA only

    c. RSA only

    d. Either the El Gamal digital signature algorithm or the Digital Signature Algorithm (DSA)

4. The RSA digital signature algorithm and the DSA use which of the following hash algorithms?

    a. MD5

    b. MD4

    c. SHA–1

    d. HAVAL

5. Elliptic curve algorithms in public key cryptography are based on _____.

    a. Prime factors of very large numbers

    b. The discrete logarithm problem

    c. Modular addition

    d. The Knapsack problem

6. The U.S. Escrowed Encryption Standard employed which of the following symmetric key algorithms?

    a. IDEA

    b. DES

    c. 3 DES

    d. SKIPJACK

7. Key clustering is _____.

    a. The condition where many keys in use are very similar

    b. When one key encrypts a plaintext message into two different ciphertexts

    c. When two different keys encrypt a plaintext message into the same ciphertext

    d. Escrowing of keys

8. A cipher that breaks a message into fixed length units for encryption is called a _____.

    a. Block cipher

    b. An asymmetric key algorithm

    c. Message digest

    d. Hash function

9. Digital signatures are created using _____.

    a. Private key cryptography

    b. Public key cryptography

    c. DES

    d. 3 DES

10. Which of the following is *not* an asymmetric key algorithm?

  a. Knapsack

  b. RSA

  c. Diffie-Hellman

  d. Rijndael

11. A hybrid cryptosystem employs which of the following methodologies?

  a. Private key encryption to encrypt and send the secret key that will be used to encrypt and send the message using public key encryption.

  b. Public key encryption to encrypt and send the secret key that will be used to encrypt and send the message using private key encryption.

  c. Public key encryption to encrypt and send the secret key that will be used to encrypt and send the message using public key encryption.

  d. Private key encryption to encrypt and send the secret key that will be used to encrypt and send the message using private key encryption.

12. In public key cryptography, which of the following statements is *not* true?

  a. A message encrypted with Bob's public key can only be decrypted with Bob's private key.

  b. A message encrypted with Bob's private key can only be decrypted with Bob's public key.

  c. A message encrypted with Bob's public key can be decrypted with Bob's public key.

  d. Given Bob's public key, it is very difficult or impossible to determine his private key.

13. What is the block length of Advanced Encryption Standard (AES)?

  a. 64 bits

  b. 128 bits

  c. Variable

  d. 256 bits

14. Which of the following is *not* one of the AES key sizes?

  a. 128 bits

  b. 512 bits

  c. 192 bits

  d. 256 bits

15. A polyalphabetic cipher is also known as _____.

   a. One-time pad

   b. Vernam cipher

   c. Steganography

   d. Vigenère cipher

16. A method that is used to securely transmit secret messages and is based on keeping the existence of the messages unknown is called _____.

   a. Private key encryption

   b. Blind signatures

   c. Steganography

   d. A zero-knowledge proof

17. Confusion in block cipher algorithms does which of the following?

   a. Hides the relationship between the plaintext and ciphertext

   b. Spreads the influence of the plaintext over many ciphertext characters

   c. Disguises the fact that a cipher is being used

   d. Hides the relationship between the plaintext and the key

18. Which of the following modes is *not* a DES mode?

   a. Cipher Block Chaining

   b. Electronic Code Book

   c. Output Feedback

   d. Electronic Feedback

19. Which of the following is true?

   a. The work factor of triple DES is the same as for double DES.

   b. The work factor of single DES is the same as for triple DES.

   c. The work factor of double DES is the same as for single DES.

   d. No successful attacks have been reported against double DES.

20. Which of the following characteristics does *not* apply to a one-time pad, if it is used properly?

   a. The key is truly random with no repeating sequences or patterns.

   b. It can be used, carefully, more than once.

   c. It is unbreakable.

   d. The key must be of the same length as the message to be encrypted.

21. The key length of the DES key is _____.

   a. 128 bits

   b. 56 bits

   c. 64 bits

   d. 256 bits

22. In generating a digitally signed message using a hash function, _____.

   a. The message is encrypted in the public key of the sender.

   b. The message digest is encrypted in the private key of the sender.

   c. The message digest is encrypted in the public key of the sender.

   d. The message is encrypted in the private key of the sender.

23. The difficulty of finding the prime factors of very large numbers is the strong, one-way function used in which of the following public key cryptosystems?

   a. El Gamal

   b. Diffie-Hellman

   c. RSA

   d. Elliptic curve

24. Elliptic curve cryptosystems _____.

   a. Have a higher strength per bit than an RSA cryptosystem

   b. Have a lower strength per bit than an RSA cryptosystem

   c. Cannot be used to implement digital signatures

   d. Cannot be used to implement encryption

25. Digital certification, certification authority, timestamping, Lightweight Directory Access Protocol (LDAP), and non-repudiation support a portion of what services?

   a. Cryptanalysis

   b. Public Key Infrastructure

   c. Steganography

   d. Disaster recovery

26. In an X.500 directory, the Directory Server Agents (DSAs) exchange and share information through which of the following mechanisms?

   a. Shadowing

   b. Chaining

   c. Transitioning

   d. Depositing

27. Version 2 of the X.509 certificate is concerned with _____.

   a. The reuse of names

   b. Certificate extensions

   c. Message digests

   d. Revoked certificates

28. Version 3 of the X.509 certificate is concerned with _____.

   a. The reuse of names

   b. Certificate extensions

   c. Message digests

   d. Revoked certificates

29. Which of the following is *not* a type of X.509 certificate?

   a. Rollover certificate

   b. End entity certificate

   c. Confidential certificate

   d. CA certificate

30. A Certificate Revocation List (CRL) that is generated by a CA that covers its entire population is known as what type of CRL?

   a. Critical

   b. Global

   c. Complete

   d. Full

Operational/ Organizational Security

This chapter looks at the operational and organizational elements of security, including the following:

- ✦ Physical security
- ✦ Disaster recovery
- ✦ Business continuity
- ✦ Policy and procedures
- ✦ Privilege management
- ✦ Forensics
- ✦ Risk identification
- ✦ Security awareness and education
- ✦ Documentation

Physical Security

Securing physical access to the facility is often overlooked. In the realm of physical security, we look at the following components:

- ✦ Physical access control
- ✦ Electrical power
- ✦ Fire detection and suppression

Physical Access Control

Elements of security that control physical access to a facility include the following:

- Guards
- Dogs
- Fencing
- Lighting
- Locks
- Facility access devices
- CCTV
- Intrusion detectors and alarms
- Auditing access

Guards

Guards play a very important function in facility access control. Advantages to using guards are as follows:

- Guards can use discriminating judgment and make determinations that hardware or other automated security devices cannot.
- Guards can provide intrusion deterrent and response capability.
- Guards can provide escort functions.
- Well-trained guards are a good resource during emergencies for tasks such as crowd control and evacuation assistance.

The drawbacks to using guards are as follows:

- Guards cannot exist in environments that do not support human intervention.
- Pre-employment screening and bonding of guards is not foolproof.
- Guards can be socially engineered, and they may not be trained properly or have accurate access authorization lists.
- Maintaining a guard either internally or through an external service is expensive.

Dogs

Using dogs to guard is another very old concept. Dogs are loyal and reliable. They also have a keen sense of smell and hearing, which makes them valuable for tasks unsuited to humans. However, using dogs presents some drawbacks. They lack discretionary judgment, are costly to maintain, and present certain insurance and liability issues.

Fencing

Fencing is the standard way to control access at the facility's perimeter. Fencing and other barriers (gates, turnstiles, and mantraps) control entrance access and provide crowd control.

Common fencing height requirements are as follows:

- **3' to 4' high** — Used to deter casual trespassers
- **6' to 7' high** — Deters most opportunistic intruders
- **8' high with 3 strands of razor wire** — Deters most intruders

Lighting

Lighting is used to assist in facility perimeter protection. Lighting external entrances or parking areas may help discourage prowlers or casual intruders. Outside facility lighting, such as floodlights, streetlights, and in-ground fresnel lighting, should illuminate protected buildings up to 8 feet high with 2 feet candlepower.

Locks

Locks are commonly divided into two types: preset locks and programmable locks. Preset locks include key-in-knob, mortise, and rim locks, and consist of variations of latches, cylinders, and dead bolts.

Programmable locks are either mechanically- or electronically-based. An example of a mechanical programmable lock is the common five-key pushbutton lock that requires the user to enter a combination of numbers. An electronic programmable lock requires the user to enter a pattern of digits on a numerical-style keypad. It may display the digits in random order each time to prevent shoulder surfing for input patterns. Programmable locks are better suited for high-security areas than preset locks.

Mantraps

A *mantrap* is a guarded double door or set of doors used to control facility access. Personnel entering the facility are routed through a set of double doors monitored by a guard. *Piggybacking* describes an unauthorized person entering a facility through a door by following an authorized person who has opened the door using an access card or key.

Facility Access Devices

There are a few types of facility access devices. Smart access cards were discussed in chapter three.

- **Photo image cards** — Photo-image cards are simple identification cards with the photo of the bearer for identification.
- **Digitally-encoded cards** — Digitally-encoded cards contain chips or magnetically-encoded strips that are programmed with unique user information.
- **Wireless proximity readers** — A proximity reader does not require the user to physically insert the access card. It senses the card in the general proximity.
- **Biometric devices** — Biometric access control devices and techniques, such as fingerprinting or retinal scanning, are becoming more accepted as facility access control devices.

Closed-Circuit Television

Closed-circuit television (CCTV) may be used to provide visual surveillance or record events for analysis and/or prosecution. CCTV can monitor live events that occur in an area remote to the guard, or it can be used in conjunction with a VCR for a cost-effective method of recording.

Intrusion Detectors and Alarms

The following types of intrusion detectors identify unauthorized facility access attempts and respond with an alarm:

- **Perimeter intrusion detectors** — Two common perimeter detector types are photoelectric sensors and dry contact switches.
    - Photoelectric sensors receive a beam of light from a light-emitting device creating a grid of either visible, white light, or invisible, infrared light. An alarm is activated when the beams are broken.
    - Dry contact switches consist of metallic foil tape on windows or metal contact switches on doorframes.
- **Motion detectors** — Motion detectors are designed to detect the physical presence of an intruder and sound an alarm. Four systems for detecting an intruder's physical presence are as follows:
    - **Photometric** — Detect changes in the level of light.
    - **Wave motion** — Detect changes in the frequency of energy waves. Three kinds of wave motion detectors exist: sonic, ultrasonic, and microwave. Sonic detection systems operate in the audible range, ultrasonic detection systems operate in the high frequency range, and microwave detection systems utilize radio frequencies.

- **Acoustical-seismic** — Detect changes in the ambient noise level (vibrations).
- **Proximity** — Detect the approach of an intruder into an electrical field.

✦ **Alarm systems** — After an intrusion is detected, an alarm is generated. The four general types of alarm systems are:
- **Local alarm system** — Rings an audible alarm on the local premises.
- **Central station system** — Monitored by a private security firm.
- **Proprietary system** — Similar to the central station system except that it's owned and operated by the customer.
- **Auxiliary station system** — Any of the previous three systems may have auxiliary alarms that ring at the local fire or police stations.

Auditing Access

Access control auditing is used to locate the attempted access and identify who attempted it. Facility or entrance access audit trails should log the following:

✦ Date and time of the access attempt

✦ The entrance at which the access was attempted

✦ Whether the attempt was successful or not

✦ Who attempted the access

Audit trails help an administrator reconstruct the details of a physical facility intrusion for forensic analysis.

Social Engineering

Social engineering has been previously discussed in this book, but here are three examples of common techniques used by an intruder to gain physical access:

✦ **Asserting authority or pulling rank** — Professing to have the authority, perhaps supported with altered identification, to enter the facility

✦ **Intimidating or threatening** — Browbeating the access control subjects with harsh language or threatening behavior to permit access or release information

✦ **Praising, flattering, or sympathizing** — Using positive reinforcement to induce the subject into giving access or information for access

Electrical Power

The continued supply of clean, steady electrical power is needed to maintain the proper personnel environment and to sustain operations. Many elements can threaten power systems, including noise, power fluctuations, humidity, and static.

Noise

Electrical noise is the presence of interference in the electrical system. Electromagnetic interference (EMI) is noise that is caused by the generation of radiation due to the charge difference between the three electrical wires: the hot, neutral, and ground wires. Radio frequency interference (RFI) is generated by the components of a nearby electrical system, such as radiating electrical cables, fluorescent lighting, and electric space heaters. RFI can be so serious that it cannot only interfere with computer operations, but it can also permanently damage sensitive components.

Protection against noise interference can include the following:

- Power line conditioning
- Proper grounding
- Cable shielding

Table 5.1 lists various electrical power terms and descriptions.

Table 5.1 Electrical Power Definitions

Element	Description
Fault	Momentary power loss
Blackout	Complete loss of power
Sag	Momentary low voltage
Brownout	Prolonged low voltage
Spike	Momentary high voltage
Surge	Prolonged high voltage
Inrush	Initial surge of power at the beginning
Noise	Steady interfering disturbance
Transient	Short duration of line noise disturbances
Clean	Nonfluctuating pure power
Ground	One wire in an electrical circuit must be grounded

Power Fluctuations

Sags and brownouts can do serious harm to electronic components. A prolonged brownout can lower the supplied voltage more than 10 percent. Power surges and spikes from an inrush after a brownout can also damage components. All computer equipment should be protected by surge suppressors, and critical equipment should have an Uninterruptible Power Supply (UPS). Unlike a plain battery backup, a UPS can provide a source of filtered and steady power. Intelligent UPS systems can automatically shut down devices, notify personnel that a power outage has occurred, and restart the system after the outage has been remedied. The American National Standards Institute (ANSI) standards permit a maximum 8 percent drop between the power source and the building's meter, and a 3.5 percent drop between the meter and the wall.

Humidity and Static

The recommended optimal relative humidity level is 40 to 60 percent for computer operations. Electrostatic discharges from static electricity can damage sensitive electronic equipment, even in small amounts. Even though a static charge may be too low to harm humans, electronic components are sensitive to static charges. Dry air, below 40 percent relative humidity, increases the chance of static electricity being generated.

Conversely, when the relative humidity is too high for a prolonged period, electrical connections can start to corrode and condensation can form on a computer's components. A process similar to electroplating occurs, causing the silver particles to migrate from the connectors onto the copper circuits, impeding the electrical efficiency of the components.

Fire Detection and Suppression

Fire detection and suppression is necessary for the safe and continued operation of information systems. This section looks at differing types of combustibles, fire detection, extinguishing systems, suppression mediums, contamination and damage, and computer room fire safety.

Classes and Combustibles

Fire combustibles are rated as either Class A, B, C, or D based on their material composition, which determines which type of extinguishing system or agent is used. Table 5.2 shows the different combustibles and their related classes.

Table 5.2
Combustible Materials Fire Class Ratings

Fire Class	Combustible Materials
A	Wood, cloth, paper, rubber, most plastics, and ordinary combustibles
B	Flammable liquids and gases, oils, greases, tars, oil-based paints, and lacquers
C	Energized electrical equipment
D	Flammable chemicals such as magnesium and sodium

Fire Detection

Fire detectors respond to heat, flame, or smoke by sending an alarm.

- **Heat-actuated devices** — Detect one of two conditions: the temperature reaches a predetermined level, or the temperature rises quickly regardless of the initial temperature.
- **Flame-actuated devices** — Sense either the infrared energy of a flame or the pulsation of the flame.
- **Smoke-actuated devices** — Are commonly either photoelectric devices (triggered by the variation in the light hitting the photoelectric cell as a result of the smoke), or radioactive (triggered when the smoke disturbs the ionization current of the radioactive material).

Extinguishing Systems

An automatic sprinkler system must be provided to protect the computer room or computer areas when any of the following conditions exist ("NFPA 75 Standard for the Protection of Electronic Computer/Data Processing Equipment," National Fire Protection Association, 1999 Edition):

- The enclosure of a computer system is built entirely or in part of a significant quantity of combustible materials.
- The operation of the computer room or area involves a significant quantity of combustible materials.
- The building is otherwise required to have a sprinkler system.

Common computer room fire extinguishing systems utilize either water sprinkler or gas discharge systems. Water sprinkler systems come in various types, such as wet pipe, dry pipe, and preaction. In a wet pipe system, water is standing in the pipe and is released when heat breaks the sprinkler head seal.

In a dry pipe system, air pressure is maintained until the sprinkler head seal is ruptured. The air then escapes and the water enters the room. One advantage of the dry pipe system over the wet pipe system is that the wet pipe system is vulnerable to broken pipes due to freezing. A preaction pipe sounds an alarm and delays the water release, allowing the computer operations to shut down before the release of water.

Gas discharge systems employ a pressurized inert gas and are usually installed under the computer room raised floor. The fire detection system typically activates the gas discharge system to quickly smother the fire, either under the floor, in the cable areas, or throughout the room.

Typical agents in a gas discharge system are carbon dioxide (CO_2), Halon, or inert gas agents. Halon 1211 is used in portable extinguishers, and Halon 1301 is used in fixed total flooding systems. Common inert gas agents are IG-01, IG-100, IG-55, and IG-541. They are examined later in this chapter.

Suppression Mediums

Rapid oxidation (fire) can occur only if three elements are present: oxygen, heat, and fuel. Each suppression medium affects a different element of the fire and is therefore better suited for different types of fires.

- **Carbon dioxide (CO_2)** — A colorless and odorless gas that is very effective in fire suppression. It quickly removes any oxygen that could be used to sustain the fire. However, CO_2 is fatal to personnel when used in large concentrations, such as the level required to flood a computer room during a fire. CO_2 is generally used for direct fire suppression at the source.

- **Halon** — A medium that is not harmful to the equipment, mixes thoroughly with the air, and spreads extremely fast. It does not leave liquid or solid residues when discharged. It is preferred for sensitive areas, such as computer rooms and data storage areas. However, Halon 1301 was banned by the 1987 Montreal Protocol because it contributes to the depletion of the ozone layer. No new Halon 1301 installations are allowed.

- **IG-01** — An inert gas that doesn't contain hydrogen fluoride, a toxic byproduct of hydrocarbon agents after discharge. Inert gas does, however, create a danger to personnel by removing most of the breathable oxygen in a room when flooded, and precautions must be taken before its use.

Contamination and Damage

Damage to electronic components can be caused by many elements other than the direct damage caused by the fire, such as smoke, heat, water, and suppression medium contamination (Halon or CO_2).

Water-based damage can result from pipe breakage or sprinklers. When electronic equipment or media has been exposed to water, the following steps should be taken in this order:

1. Turn off all electrical power to the equipment.
2. Open cabinet doors and remove panels and covers to allow water to run out.
3. Place all affected equipment or media in an air-conditioned area, if portable.
4. Wipe the equipment with alcohol or Freon-alcohol solutions or spray with water-displacement aerosol sprays.

As with water damage, smoke damage can be mitigated with a quick response. Immediate smoke exposure to electronic equipment does little damage. However, the remaining particulate residue contains active byproducts that corrode metal contact surfaces in the presence of moisture and oxygen. If the recovery is prompt and successful, data can probably be removed from the system after stabilization. Also, like water or other types of damage, the treated systems should never be re-used once all usable data has been recovered.

The proper order of steps to be taken after electronic equipment or media has been exposed to smoke contaminants is as follows:

1. Turn off power to equipment.
2. Move equipment into an air-conditioned and humidity-controlled environment.
3. Spray connectors, backplanes, and printed circuit boards with Freon or Freon-alcohol solvents.
4. Spray corrosion-inhibiting aerosol to stabilize metal contact surfaces.

Computer Room Fire Safety

The National Fire Protection Association (NFPA) defines risk factors to consider when designing fire and safety protection for computing environments. The factors to be used when assessing the impact of damage and interruption resulting from a fire, in priority order, are as follows:

1. The life safety aspects of the function, such as air traffic controls or safety processing controls
2. The fire threat of the installation to the occupants or property of the computing area
3. The economic loss incurred from the loss of computing function or loss of stored records
4. The economic loss incurred from the loss of the value of the equipment

As in all evaluations of risk (not only fire risk), life safety is always the number one priority.

The fire-resistant rating of construction materials is a major factor in determining the fire safety of a computer operations room. The term *fire-resistant* refers to materials or construction that have a fire resistance rating of not less than the specified standard. For example, the computer room must be separated from other occupancy areas by construction with a fire-resistant rating of not less than one hour. Also, the room should not be vented to the outside unless damping elements are installed to prevent smoke from the computer room from entering other offices.

The NFPA recommends that only the absolute minimum essential records, paper stock, inks, unused recording media, or other combustibles be housed in the computer room. Because of the threat of fire, these combustibles should not be stored in the computer room or under raised flooring, including old, unused cabling. Under-floor abandoned cables can interfere with airflow and extinguishing systems. Cables that are not intended to be used should be removed from the room. The NFPA also recommends that tape libraries and record storage rooms be protected by an extinguishing system and separated from the computer room by wall construction fire-resistant rated for not less than one hour.

Disaster Recovery

To preserve the tenets of confidentiality, integrity, and especially availability, disaster recovery and business continuity are vital security concerns.

Disaster recovery planning involves preparing, testing, and updating the actions required to protect critical business processes from the effects of major system and network failures to quickly recover from an emergency with the minimal impact to the organization.

The following are examples of natural events that can create a continuity-threatening event:

- Fires, explosions, or hazardous material spills of environmental toxins
- Earthquakes, storms, floods, and fires due to acts of nature
- Power outages or other utility failures

Examples of man-made events include the following:

- Bombings, sabotage, or other attacks
- Strikes and job actions
- Communications infrastructure failures or testing-related outages (including a massive failure of configuration management controls)

Continuity and Recovery Definitions

- **Contingency plans (CP)** — The documented, organized plan for emergency response, backup operations, and recovery maintained by an activity as part of its security program that ensures the availability of critical resources and facilitates the continuity of operations in an emergency situation.
- **Disaster recovery plans (DRP)** — The plans and procedures that have been developed to recover from a disaster that has made the system operations impossible.
- **Continuity of operations plans (COOP)** — The plans and procedures documented to ensure continued critical operations during any period where normal operations are impossible.
- **Business continuity plans (BCP)** — The plans and procedures developed that identify and prioritize the critical business functions that must be preserved; the procedures for continued operations of those critical business functions during any disruption (other than a disaster) to normal operations.

Disaster Recovery Planning

A disaster recovery plan (DRP) is a comprehensive statement of consistent actions to be taken before, during, and after a disruptive event that causes a significant loss of information systems resources. The major goal of a disaster recovery plan is to provide an organized way to make decisions if a disruptive event occurs. The purpose of the disaster recovery plan is to reduce confusion and enhance the organization's ability to deal with the crisis. When a disruptive event occurs, the organization does not have the luxury to create and execute a recovery plan on the spot, so the amount of planning and testing performed beforehand will determine the organization's capability to withstand a disaster.

Disaster recovery plans are the procedures for responding to an emergency, providing extended backup operations during the interruption, and managing recovery and salvage processes afterwards should an organization experience a substantial loss of processing capability. A properly executed DRP also provides the capability to implement critical processes at an alternate site and return to the primary site and normal processing within a time frame that minimizes the loss to the organization.

DRP objectives include the following:

- Protecting an organization from major computer services failure
- Minimizing the risk to the organization from delays in providing services
- Guaranteeing the reliability of standby systems through testing and simulation
- Minimizing the decision-making required by personnel during a disaster

Fundamentally, the DRP process follows these steps:

1. Creating the DRP
2. Testing and adjusting the DRP
3. Executing the DRP in the event of an emergency

Creating the DRP

This phase of the DRP process involves developing and creating the recovery plans and defining the steps needed to protect the business in the event of an actual disaster.

Several vendors distribute automated tools to create disaster recovery plans. These tools can improve productivity by providing formatted templates customized to the particular organization's needs. In addition, some vendors offer specialized recovery software focused on a particular type of business or vertical market.

Testing and Adjusting the DRP

Regular drills and tests are fundamental to a disaster recovery plan. Since no demonstrated recovery capability exists until the plan is tested, the plan must be tested on a regular basis.

Some reasons for regularly testing the DRP are as follows:

- ✦ Testing verifies the accuracy of the recovery procedures and identifies deficiencies.
- ✦ Testing prepares and trains the personnel to execute their emergency duties.
- ✦ Testing verifies the processing capability of the alternate backup site.

DRP Testing Types

Some common DRP tests are as follows:

- ✦ **Checklist review** — The plan is distributed and reviewed by business units for its thoroughness and effectiveness.
- ✦ **Tabletop exercise or structured walk-through test** — Members of the emergency management group meet in a conference room setting to discuss their responsibilities and the ways they would react to emergency scenarios, by stepping through the plan.
- ✦ **Walk-through drill or simulation test** — The emergency management group and response teams actually perform their emergency response functions by walking through the test, without actually initiating recovery procedures (this is a more thorough test than the table-top exercise).

- **Functional drill** — Tests specific functions such as medical response, emergency notifications, warning and communications procedures and equipment, although not necessarily all at once. This also includes evacuation drills, where personnel walk the evacuation route to a designated area, where procedures for accounting for the personnel are tested.
- **Parallel test or full-scale exercise** — A real-life emergency situation is simulated as closely as possible. This involves all of the participants that would be responding to the real emergency, including community and external organizations. The test may involve ceasing some real production processing.

DRP Maintenance

Disaster recovery plans can become obsolete more quickly than you think. The company may reorganize, changing the critical business units. Most commonly, modifications in the network or computing infrastructure may change the location or configuration of hardware, software, and other components. The reasons might be administrative: complex disaster recovery plans are not easily updated, personnel lose interest in the process, or employee turnover might affect involvement.

Whatever the reason, plan maintenance techniques must be employed from the outset to ensure that the plan remains fresh and usable. It's important to build maintenance procedures into the organization by using job descriptions that centralize responsibility for updates. Also, create audit procedures that can report regularly on the state of the plan. Make sure that multiple versions of the plan do not exist, because this can create confusion during an emergency. Always replace older versions of the text with updated versions throughout the enterprise when a plan is changed or replaced.

Executing the DRP

Like life insurance, disaster recovery plans are the procedures that you hope you never have to implement. This part of the plan details what roles various personnel take on, what tasks must be implemented to recover and salvage the site, how the company interfaces with external groups, and financial considerations. The DRP should contain the steps necessary to operate at alternate sites and return to normal operations at the primary site.

There are three options for disaster recovery, based on the extent of the disaster and the organization's recovery ability:

- Recovery at the primary operating site
- Recovery to an alternate site for critical functions
- Restoring full system after a catastrophic loss

Two teams may be used to restore the system from a catastrophic loss:

- **The recovery team** — The recovery team's primary task is to get the pre-defined critical business functions operating at the alternate backup processing site. The recovery team is concerned with rebuilding production processing and determining the criticality of data, for example.
- **The salvage team** — The salvage team is different from the recovery team and has the mandate to quickly and safely clean, repair, salvage, and determine the viability of the primary processing infrastructure immediately after the disaster.

Other important elements of a DRP to be considered are as follows:

- Interfacing with external groups, such as police and the fire department
- Employee relations
- Fraud and crime
- Financial disbursement
- Media relations

Alternate Sites

The three most common types of remote off-site backup processing facilities are hot sites, warm sites, and cold sites. They are primarily differentiated by how much preparation is devoted to the site, and thus by how quickly the site can be used as an alternate processing site.

- **Cold site** — A designated computer operations room with heating, ventilation, and air conditioning (HVAC) that may have few or no computing systems installed and would require a substantial effort to install the hardware and software required to begin alternate processing. This type of site is rarely useful in an actual emergency.
- **Warm site** — An alternate processing facility with most hardware and software installed, which would need a minor effort to be up and running as an alternate processing center. It may use cheaper or older equipment and create a degradation in processing performance, but would be able to handle the most important processing tasks.
- **Hot site** — A site with all required hardware and software installed to begin alternate processing either immediately or within an acceptably short time frame. This site would be 100 percent–compatible with the original site and would probably only need an upgrade of the most current data to duplicate operations.

Table 5.3 shows a common scheme to classify the recovery timeframe needs of each business function.

Table 5.3
Recovery Timeframe Classification Scheme

Rating Class	Recovery Timeframe Needed
AAA	Immediate recovery needed; no downtime allowed
AA	Full functional recovery required within four hours
A	Same business day recovery required
B	Up to 24 hours downtime acceptable
C	24 to 72 hours downtime acceptable
D	Greater than 72 hours downtime acceptable

Other alternate processing concepts include the following:

- **Mutual aid agreement**—An arrangement with another company that may have similar computing needs. Both parties agree to support each other in the case of a disruptive event by providing alternative processing facilities. While appealing, this is not a good choice if the emergency affects both parties.
- **Rolling or mobile backup**—Contracting with a vendor to provide mobile power and HVAC facilities sufficient to stage the alternate processing.

Backups

The availability of a reliable backup/restoration system is a cornerstone of a viable disaster recovery process. The purpose of tape backup is to preserve and restore lost, corrupted, or deleted information, thereby preserving data integrity and ensuring network availability.

Most backup methods use the "archive" file attribute to determine whether the file should be backed up. The backup software determines which files need to be backed up by checking to see if the archive file attribute has been set, and then resets the archive bit value to null after the backup procedure.

The following are the three most common backup methods:

- **Full backup** — This backup method makes a complete backup of every file on the server every time it is run. It is used for system archive or level 0 baseline tape sets. The full or complete backup changes the archive file attribute.
- **Incremental backup** — This backup method only copies files that have been recently added or changed (that day) and ignores any other backup set. This method backs up only files that have been created or modified since the last backup was made because the archive file attribute is reset after backup.
- **Differential backup** — This backup method copies all files that have changed since the full backup was last performed. It does not reset the archive file attribute, so the changed file is backed up every time the differential backup is run.

All backup systems share common issues and problems, such as the following:

- **Slow data transfer** — The time required to restore the data must be factored into a disaster recovery plan.
- **Disk space expansion** — As the amount of data that needs to be copied increases, the length of time required to run the backup proportionally increases and the demand on the system grows as more tapes are required.

Backup Media Protection

Backup media protection encompasses two areas: security controls and viability controls. Security controls address threats to confidentiality, integrity, and availability by the unauthorized exposure of backup media. Viability controls are implemented to preserve the proper working state of the media, particularly to facilitate timely and accurate system restoration after a failure.

Backup Media Security Controls

Backup media security controls are implemented to prevent the exposure of sensitive information when the media is stored off-site.

- **Logging** — Logging the use of backup media provides accountability and helps facilitate the recovery process.
- **Access control** — Physical access control to the media is used to prevent unauthorized personnel from accessing the media.
- **Disposal** — Proper disposal of the media after use is required to prevent data remanence.

Media Librarian

A media librarian's job is to control access to the media library and to regulate the media library environment. All media must be labeled in a human and machine-readable form that should contain information such as the date and author of the media, the retention period, a volume name and version, and security classification.

Backup Media Viability Controls

Backup media viability controls should be used to protect the media from damage during handling and transportation or during short-term or long-term storage. Viability control ensures that the media is readily available and usable when needed for data restoration.

- **Marking and handling**—All backup storage media should be accurately marked or labeled. The labels can be used to identify media with special handling instructions or to log serial numbers or bar codes for retrieval during a system recovery. Proper handling of the media is important, especially to protect the media from physical damage during transportation to the archive sites.

- **Off-site storage**—A proper heat- and humidity-free, clean storage environment should be provided for the media. Data media is sensitive to temperature, liquids, magnetism, smoke, and dust. The media controls must extend to areas outside of the facility, such as data backup vault services, partners and vendors, and external disposal systems. Transportation to or from an external data vault services vendor is a security concern.

Business Continuity Planning

Business continuity planning (BCP) is a strategy that minimizes the effect of disturbances and allows for the resumption of business processes. The aim of BCP is to minimize the effects of a disruptive event on a company.

Business continuity plans are designed to protect critical business processes from natural or manmade failures or disasters and the resulting loss of capital due to the unavailability of normal business processes. The BCP should also help minimize the cost associated with the disruptive event and mitigate the risk associated with it.

The BCP process comprises four major phases:

1. **Scope and plan initiation**—Creating the scope of the plan and the other elements needed to define its parameters.

2. **Business impact assessment**—A process to help business units understand the impact of a disruptive event.
3. **Business continuity plan development**—Developing the BCP. This process includes the areas of plan implementation, plan testing, and ongoing plan maintenance.
4. **Plan approval and implementation**—Final senior management signoff, enterprise-wide awareness of the plan, and implementation of a maintenance procedure for updating the plan, as needed.

Step two, a business impact assessment (BIA) is an attempt to measure the effect of resource loss and escalating losses over time to provide the entity with reliable data upon which to base decisions on hazard mitigation and continuity planning. A BIA is similar to a risk assessment.

A BIA creates a document that explains what impact a disruptive event would have on the business. A BIA generally takes these four steps:

1. Gathering the needed assessment materials
2. Performing the vulnerability assessment
3. Analyzing the information compiled
4. Documenting the results and presenting recommendations

High Availability and Fault Tolerance

The concept of high availability refers to a level of fault tolerance and redundancy in transaction processing and communications. While these processes are not used solely for disaster recovery, they are often elements of a larger disaster recovery plan. If one or more of these processes are employed, the ability of a company to get back online is greatly enhanced.

Some concepts employed for high availability and fault tolerance are as follows:

+ **Electronic vaulting**—Refers to the transfer of backup data to an off-site location. This is primarily a batch process of dumping the data through communications lines to a server at an alternate location.

+ **Remote journaling**—Consists of parallel processing of transactions to an alternate site, as opposed to a batch dump process like electronic vaulting. A communications line is used to transmit live data as it occurs. This feature enables the alternate site to be fully operational at all times and introduces a very high level of fault tolerance.

- **Database shadowing** — Uses the live processing advantages of remote journaling, but creates even more redundancy by duplicating the database sets to multiple servers.
- **Server redundancy** — Uses the concept of RAID 1 (mirroring, discussed further in the following section) and applies it to a pair of servers. A primary server mirrors its data to a secondary server, enabling the primary to "roll over" to the secondary in the case of primary server failure (the secondary server steps in and takes over for the primary server). Figure 5.1 shows a common redundant server implementation.
- **Server clustering** — Creates a group of independent servers functioning as a single server to the user. The cluster provides fault tolerance and load balancing. Figure 5.2 shows the concept of server clustering.
- **Redundant communications lines** — T1 and other communications lines need redundancy, because the severing of a T1 line or other type of loss of the line can cause a failure of availability. An ISDN basic rate interface (BRI) connection is commonly used as a backup for a T1. An organization may use multiple vendors for fault tolerance.

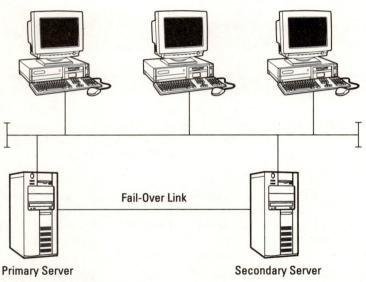

Figure 5.1 Redundant servers

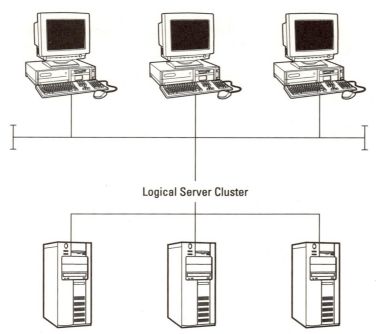

Figure 5.2 Server clustering

RAID

RAID stands for *Redundant Array of Inexpensive (or Independent) Disks*. RAID provides fault tolerance protection against hard failure, and the resultant availability and data loss.

RAID can be implemented in one or a combination of ways, called levels.

- ✦ **Level 0** — Creates one large disk by striping the data across several disks. This creates the maximum usable data volume size for storage, but provides no redundancy and no fault tolerance.
- ✦ **Level 1** — This level is commonly called *mirroring*, because it makes an exact copy of the data on one disk or set of disks on another disk or set of disks. Because this process is often implemented by a one-for-one disk-to-disk ratio, it is an expensive implementation of RAID.
- ✦ **Level 2** — Consists of bit-interleaved data on multiple disks. This level is not used in practice, as it defines a disk drive system with 39 disks.

- **Levels 3 and 4** — Data is striped across several drives and the parity check bit is written to a dedicated parity drive. Level 3 is implemented at the byte level and level 4 is usually implemented at the block level. If a hard disk fails, the data is reconstructed by using the bit information on the parity drive.
- **Level 5** — Similar to RAID 3 and 4, except that the parity information is written to the next available drive rather than to a dedicated drive by using an interleave parity.

Table 5.4 shows several levels of RAID.

Table 5.4 RAID Level Descriptions

RAID Level	Description
0	Striping
1	Mirroring
2	Hamming Code Parity
3	Byte-Level Parity
4	Block-Level Parity
5	Interleave Parity
6	Second Independent Parity
7	Single Virtual Disk
10	Striping across Multiple Pairs (levels 1+0)
15	Striping with Parity across RAID 5 Pairs (levels 1+5)
51	Mirroring RAID 5 Arrays with Parity (levels 5+1)

Policies and Procedures

An organizational security policy is a general statement of management's intent and its implementation is mandatory. This high level policy comprises the following:

- An acknowledgment of the importance of the computing resources to the business model
- A statement of support for the information security throughout the enterprise
- A commitment to authorize and manage the definition of the lower-level standards, procedures, and guidelines

Policies, standards, procedures, and guidelines fall into a hierarchy below the organizational security policy, as shown in Figure 5.3.

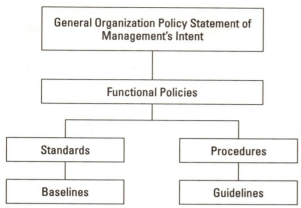

Figure 5.3 Hierarchical ordering of policies, procedures, standards, guidelines, and baselines

Below the general organizational policies are the *functional policies* guiding implementation. *Standards* are compulsory; they define the use of specific hardware and software technologies in a uniform manner. *Procedures*, detailed step-by-step actions, are also required, *Baselines* describe how to implement security mechanisms to ensure that security is being accomplished in a uniform manner on the various platforms and operating systems throughout the enterprise. The use of adopted baselines is compulsory. *Guidelines* are non-compulsory, recommended actions that take into account the different types of information systems.

In the information security arena, policies require administrative controls to protect information systems. These controls can be very effective in screening personnel, controlling access to sensitive information, and detecting violations of the security policies. The principal elements of these controls are described in the following sections.

Acceptable Use

An acceptable or appropriate use policy details the conditions that a user must agree to in order to use an account on an information system. The account might have access to an organization's network or be with an outside organization, such as an Internet Service Provider (ISP). Users signing up for an account must agree to the stated policy provisions. Examples of such provisions follow:

- ✦ The user must be at least 18 years of age and legally able to agree to the terms of the acceptable use policy.

- ✦ The user must agree to use the account for the uses permitted by the account. For example, a company employee must usually agree not to use the account for purposes other than company business.

- ✦ The user must take full responsibility for his or her actions in using the account and accept all recourses for their actions.

- The owner of the account is fully responsible for any charges incurred by the use of the account.
- The user must agree not to use the account to obtain materials that are found to be illegal or contravene acceptable use policies and standards.

Due Care

The concept of *due care*, or *due diligence*, requires that an individual or organization engage in good business practices relative to the organization's industry. The practice of due diligence for an individual is related to the legal, *prudent man rule* that requires senior officials to perform their duties with the care that ordinary, prudent people would exercise under similar circumstances.

Due care may be a legal requirement in some cases.

Privacy

Privacy is an individual's right to protection from unauthorized disclosure of his or her personally identifiable information (PII). This right is embodied in the following fundamental principles of privacy:

- Notice regarding collection, use, and disclosure of personally identifiable information (PII)
- Choice to opt out or opt in regarding disclosure of PII to third parties
- Access by consumers to their PII to permit review and correction of information
- Security to protect PII from unauthorized disclosure
- Enforcement of applicable privacy policies and obligations

Privacy Policy

Organizations develop and publish privacy policies that describe their approach to handling PII. Organizations' Web sites usually make a privacy policy available online. Privacy policies usually cover the following areas:

- Statement of the organization's commitment to privacy
- The type of information collected, such as name, address, credit card number, phone number, and so on
- The organization's ability to retain and use your e-mail correspondence
- Information gathered through cookies and Web server logs and how that information is used
- How information is shared with affiliates and strategic partners

- Mechanisms to secure information transmissions, such as encryption and digital signatures
- Mechanisms to protect PII stored by the organization
- Procedures for review of the organization's compliance with the privacy policy
- Evaluation of information protection practices
- Means for the user to access and correct PII held by the organization
- Rules for disclosing PII to outside parties
- Providing PII that is legally required

Privacy-Related Legislation and Guidelines

The following list summarizes some of the important legislation and recommended standards for privacy:

- **The Cable Communications Policy Act** — Provides for discretionary use of PII by cable operators internally, but imposes restrictions on disclosures to third parties.
- **The Children's Online Privacy Protection Act (COPPA)** — Aimed at providing protection to children under the age of 13.
- **Customer Proprietary Network Information Rules** — Rules that apply to telephone companies and restrict their use of customer information both internally and to third parties.
- **The Electronic Communications Privacy Act** — Protects exchanged information from being intercepted or disclosed by third parties, including law enforcement agencies.
- **The Financial Services Modernization Act (Gramm-Leach-Bliley)** — Requires financial institutions to provide customers with clear descriptions of the institution's polices and procedures for protecting the customers' PII.
- **Telephone Consumer Protection Act** — Restricts communications between companies and consumers, as in telemarketing.
- **The 1973 U.S. Code of Fair Information Practices** states the following:
  - There must not be personal data record keeping systems whose very existence is secret.
  - There must be a way for a person to find out how much of their personal information a record contains and how it is used.
  - There must be a way for a person to prevent their personal information, which was obtained for one purpose, from being used or made available for other purposes without their consent.
  - Any organization creating, maintaining, using, or disseminating records of identifiable personal data must ensure the reliability of the data for their intended use and must take precautions to prevent misuse of that data.

- **The Health Insurance Portability and Accountability Act (HIPAA), Administrative Simplification Title** — Includes privacy and security rules and standards for electronic transactions and code sets.
- **The 2001 U.S. Patriot Act** — Gives the U.S. government new powers to subpoena electronic records and to monitor Internet traffic.
- **The European Union (EU)** — Has defined privacy principles that include the following:
    - Data should be collected in accordance with the law.
    - Information collected about an individual cannot be disclosed to other organizations or individuals unless authorized by law or by consent of the individual.
    - Records kept on an individual should be accurate and up-to-date.
    - Individuals have the right to correct errors contained in their personal data.
    - Data should be used only for the purposes for which it was collected and it should be used only for a reasonable period of time.
    - Individuals are entitled to receive a report on the information that is held about them.
    - Transmission of personal information to locations where "equivalent" personal data protection cannot be assured is prohibited.
- **The Organization for Economic Cooperation and Development (OECD)** — Has issued guidelines that can be summarized as follows:
    - There should be limits to the collection of personal data, and any such data should be obtained by lawful and fair means.
    - Personal data should be relevant to the purposes for which they are to be used, and, to the extent necessary for those purposes, should be accurate, complete, and up-to-date.
    - The purpose for which personal data is collected should be specified no later than at the time of data collection.
    - Personal data should not be disclosed, made available, or otherwise used for purposes other than those specified.
    - Personal data should be protected by reasonable security safeguards against such risks as loss or unauthorized access, destruction, use, modification, or disclosure of data.
    - There should be a general policy of openness about developments, practices, and policies with respect to personal data.
    - An individual should have the right to obtain confirmation from a data controller as to whether or not the data controller has data relating to him or her.

- A member country should refrain from restricting transborder flows of personal data between itself and another member country except where the latter does not yet substantially observe these guidelines or where the re-export of such data would circumvent its domestic privacy legislation.
- A member country may also impose restrictions in respect of certain categories of personal data for which its domestic privacy legislation includes specific regulations in view of the nature of that data and for which the other member country provides no equivalent protection.

P3P

The Platform for Privacy Preferences (P3P) was developed by the World Wide Web Consortium (W3C) to implement privacy practices on Web sites. An excerpt of the W3C P3P specification states "P3P enables Web sites to express their privacy practices in a standard format that can be retrieved automatically and interpreted easily by user agents. P3P user agents will allow users to be informed of site practices (in both machine- and human-readable formats) and to automate decision-making based on these practices when appropriate. Thus, users need not read the privacy policies at every site they visit."

The latest W3C working draft of P3P is P3P 1.0, 28 January 2002 (www.w3.org/TR). With P3P, an organization can post its privacy policy in machine-readable form (XML) on its Web site. This policy statement includes the following information:

- Who has access to collected information
- The type of information collected
- How the information is used
- The legal entity making the privacy statement

P3P also supports user agents that allow a user to configure a P3P-enabled Web browser with the user's privacy preferences. Then, when the user attempts to access a Web site, the user agent compares the user's stated preferences with the privacy policy in machine-readable form at the Web site. Access is granted if the preferences match the policy. Otherwise, access to the Web site is blocked or a pop-up window appears, notifying the user that he must change his privacy preferences. Usually, this means that the user must lower his privacy threshold.

Separation of Duties

Separation of duties divides responsibility among a number of different individuals. For example, a check issued by a company for over a certain amount would require the signatures of three different individuals. For fraud to take place, collusion among the three individuals must occur. To put it in different terms, collusion must be forced to occur if a violation of policy is to take place.

In many organizations, the systems administrator and the information security director are one and the same person. This arrangement gives this person almost total control of the information systems and makes the systems vulnerable to any actions he may take. Following the doctrine of separation of duties, one individual should be assigned the systems administrator role and another should be assigned the information security responsibilities. Separation of duties is sometimes called *segregation of duties*.

A related concept is that of *least privilege*. The principle of least privilege states that an individual should be given the minimum amount of privileges required for the assigned job. Also, these privileges should be assigned for the minimum amount of time necessary to perform the assigned tasks.

Need-to-Know

The concept of need-to-know is usually associated with government classifications of materials and the clearances of individuals to access those materials. It is similar to *the least privilege principle*. Even though an individual has the proper clearance to access documents of a particular classification, that individual is not permitted to access that information if he or she does not have a need to know the information. For example, a military personnel officer may have a Secret clearance to access documents that are classified as Secret or below. However, if that officer does not have a need to know certain types of Secret information, the officer is not permitted to access that information. The military personnel officer might be authorized access to personnel records classified as Secret, but would not be authorized access to Secret information describing a new air defense weapons system. That officer does not have a need to know the Secret material describing the new weapons system to perform his or her job.

Password Management

Password management is key to the protection of sensitive information held on computers. Passwords are the primary means of authentication for most users. Best practices have evolved for managing and using passwords and these practices should be applied in a networked computing environment. The following list summarizes these practices:

- ✦ An organization should maintain a clear password policy and employees should know this policy.
- ✦ The organization should enforce the password policy.
- ✦ A password should be a minimum of eight random alphanumeric characters. No common words, names, or phrases should be used that are associated with the user.
- ✦ After a specified number of unsuccessful logon attempts (usually three), the logon session should be terminated or the time allowed before the next logon attempt should be increased.

- Passwords should be protected and not written down and placed in easily observable locations.
- Passwords should be changed at specified periods. The frequency at which passwords are changed is a function of the sensitivity of the information being protected. On average, a password should be changed every 90 days.
- When there is an extended period of inactivity in a session, the session should be terminated and the logon process repeated to regain entry into the system.
- The date and time of the last successful logon should be displayed. This information can alert the user to an unauthorized logon that occurred when the user was absent from the workstation.
- Passwords and IDs should not be shared and should be unique for each user.
- When an employee is terminated, her account on the system should be terminated. Also, the passwords of other employees who have worked with this individual should be changed because the terminated employee may know their passwords.
- For increased security, dynamic password generators should be used.
- For remote logon situations, authentication protocols such as CHAP should be used.

Service Level Agreements

Users running applications require and expect minimum levels of service to meet their job requirements. A critical requirement is that the information system is available when needed. A service level agreement (SLA) guarantees the quality of service to a subscriber by a network service provider. Defined service levels provide a basis for measuring the delivered services and are useful in anticipating, identifying, and correcting problems. Examples of areas that must be considered by the service provider are the number of users and transactions per unit time, average system response time, up time, and average CPU usage.

Agreements with the user for providing the required levels of service usually cover the following points:

- Average response times
- Turn-around times
- Number of online users
- System utilization rates
- System up-times
- Volume of transactions

Disposal/Destruction

Storage media such as disks or tapes can be a source of compromise of sensitive information if they are not disposed of in the correct manner. Proper disposal of media after use is required to prevent *data remanence*. Remanence is defined as the residual information remaining on the media after erasure, which may be subject to restoration by another user.

Computer forensics experts can retrieve data from disks that have been formatted, broken, or even burned. Law enforcement personnel use such techniques to discover evidence and to construct a trail of misuse. Anytime a storage medium is reused (and also when it is discarded), the media's information can potentially be recovered. Methods must be employed to properly destroy the existing data to ensure that no residual data is left on the media. Some definitions associated with removal of data are as follows:

- **Clearing**—Refers to the overwriting of data media (primarily magnetic) intended to be reused in the same organization or monitored environment.
- **Purging**—Degaussing or overwriting media intended to be removed from a monitored environment, such as during resale (laptops) or donations to charity.
- **Destruction**—Refers to completely destroying the media, and therefore, the residual data. Paper reports, diskettes, and optical media (CD-ROMs) must be physically destroyed before disposal.

Erasing data through an operating system does not remove the data; it just changes the File Allocation Table and renames the first character of the file. This is the primary method used by computer forensics investigators to restore files. Also, damaged sectors of a disk may not be overwritten by the format utility. Degaussing may have to be used. Formatting seven times is also recommended.

Another vulnerability associated with media is that rewriting files on top of old files may not overwrite all data areas on the disk. This situation may occur because the new file may not be as long as the older file, and data past the file end control character may be retrievable. Other concerns are the improper operation of degaussing equipment and the failure to format media-sensitive information at least seven times.

Human Resources Policy

Information security can be severely affected by human resource and administrative policies. For example, a good human resource policy states that an individual working in a sensitive area should take vacation time in large increments instead of one day here and there. If someone is involved in unauthorized activities, the chance of being discovered increases if that individual is away for an extended period and someone else must take over his or her duties. Similarly, background checks before hiring an individual are a must. Background checks are common sense, but the number of organizations that do not conduct these checks—or conduct weak ones—is startling. Individuals with criminal records, bad conduct at other places of employment, or other telltale signs should not be considered for work in places where they could access sensitive information.

It is important to develop well-thought-out policies and procedures regarding employee termination. The termination could be friendly or unfriendly. In the termination interview, the employee should be reminded of the conditions in the employment agreement document that they signed when they first started working for the organization. These conditions usually include non-disclosure of proprietary information, possible restrictions on working for a direct competitor for a period of time, returning all documents and related material to the organization when leaving, turning in keys, and so on. In particular, cryptographic keys must be taken into account. If the individual being terminated has encrypted files on his or her computer, he must provide the employer with the decryption keys so that the information can be retrieved. All computer accounts assigned to the individual must be closed, and passwords that the individual knows for information system accounts must be changed.

Code of Ethics

An individual's ethics are a function of his cultural heritage, his homeland, his religion, and numerous other intangibles. People violate ethical computing standards by making the assumption that they really are not harming anyone.

Many crackers rationalize intrusions and illegal access to proprietary information as harmless because no physical property is stolen. Their credo is "information should be free." Others believe that when they hack into an organization's information systems, they are performing a service by alerting the organization to weaknesses in their system safeguards. Such thinking is wrong because it is difficult to predict what can happen to information if unauthorized persons gain access to networks and browse files. Security breaches can result in an organization losing millions of dollars through the destruction or unavailability of critical data and resources or through stock devaluation. From a national perspective, destructive cracker behavior could seriously affect a nation's critical infrastructure, economic health, and security.

In an attempt to formalize ethical behavior relative to information systems and information systems security, a number of organizations have developed and published ethical guidelines. Certified professionals in the field of information systems security (or in any other field) are held to higher standards of ethical conduct. To instill proper computing behavior, ethics should be incorporated into an organizational ethical computing policy.

Some typical ethical codes follow.

The Computer Ethics Institute's Ten Commandments of Computer Ethics

In 1992, the Coalition for Computer Ethics incorporated as the Computer Ethics Institute (CEI) to focus on the interface of advances in information technologies, ethics, and corporate and public policy. CEI addresses industrial, academic, and public policy organizations. The Institute's founding organizations are as follows:

- The Brookings Institution
- IBM
- The Washington Consulting Group
- The Washington Theological Consortium

The Institute is concerned with the ethical issues associated with the advancement of information technologies in society and has generated the following ten commandments of computer ethics:

1. Thou shalt not use a computer to harm other people.
2. Thou shalt not interfere with other people's computer work.
3. Thou shalt not snoop around in other people's computer files.
4. Thou shalt not use a computer to steal.
5. Thou shalt not use a computer to bear false witness.
6. Thou shalt not copy or use proprietary software for which you have not paid.
7. Thou shalt not use other people's computer resources without authorization or proper compensation.
8. Thou shalt not appropriate other people's intellectual output.
9. Thou shalt think about the social consequences of the program you are writing for the system you are designing.
10. Thou shalt use a computer in ways that ensure consideration and respect for your fellow humans.

(ISC)² Code of Ethics

Certified Information Systems Security Professionals (CISSPs) should do the following:

1. Conduct themselves in accordance with the highest standards of moral, ethical, and legal behavior
2. Not commit or be a party to any unlawful or unethical act that may negatively affect their professional reputation or the reputation of their profession

3. Appropriately report activity related to the profession that they believe to be unlawful and cooperate with resulting investigations

4. Support efforts to promote understanding and acceptance of prudent information security measures throughout the public, private, and academic sectors of our global information society

5. Provide competent service to their employers and clients, and avoid any conflicts of interest

6. Execute responsibilities in a manner consistent with the highest standards of their profession

7. Not misuse the information with which they come into contact during the course of their duties, and maintain the confidentiality of all information in their possession that is so identified

The Internet Activities Board Ethics and the Internet (RFC 1087)

The Internet Activities Board (IAB) states that "Access to and use of the Internet is a privilege and should be treated as such by all users of the system."

Any activity is defined as unacceptable and unethical that purposely does the following:

1. Seeks to gain unauthorized access to Internet resources
2. Destroys the integrity of computer-based information
3. Disrupts the intended use of the Internet
4. Wastes resources such as people, capacity, and computers through such actions
5. Compromises the privacy of users
6. Involves negligence in the conduct of Internet-wide experiments

Incident Response Policy

Organizations should be prepared to detect and respond to incidents before they occur. This plan should be embodied in an incident response policy.

For example, the Carnegie Mellon University CERT Coordination Center (CERT/CC) recommends the following incident response practices:

✦ PREPARE

1. Establish policies and procedures for responding to intrusions.
2. Prepare to respond to intrusions.

✦ **HANDLE**

   3. Analyze all available information to characterize an intrusion.

   4. Communicate with all parties that need to be made aware of an intrusion and its progress.

   5. Collect and protect information associated with an intrusion.

   6. Apply short-term solutions to contain an intrusion.

   7. Eliminate all means of intruder access.

   8. Return systems to normal operation.

✦ **FOLLOW UP**

   9. Identify and implement security lessons learned.

Additional guidance on incident handling is provided by the Internet Engineering Task Force (IETF) RFC 2196, Site Security Handbook. The handbook recommends the following approach to handling incidents:

1. Preparing and planning (What are the goals and objectives in handling an incident?)
2. Notification (Who should be contacted in the case of an incident?)
   - Local managers and personnel
   - Law enforcement and investigative agencies
   - Computer security incidents handling teams
   - Affected and involved sites
   - Internal communications
   - Public relations and press releases
3. Identifying an incident (Is it an incident, and if so, how serious is it?)
4. Handling (What should be done when an incident occurs?)
   - Notification (Who should be notified about the incident?)
   - Protecting evidence and activity logs (What records should be kept from before, during, and after the incident?)
   - Containment (How can the damage be limited?)
   - Eradication (How can you eliminate the reasons for the incident?)
   - Recovery (How do you reestablish service and systems?)
   - Follow up (What actions should be taken after the incident?)
5. Aftermath (What are the implications of past incidents?)
6. Administrative response to incidents

Responding to incidents in an efficient and effective manner is extremely important. The following critical issues are involved:

- ✦ Protecting the assets that could be compromised
- ✦ Protecting resources that could be utilized more profitably if an incident did not require their services
- ✦ Complying with (government or other) regulations
- ✦ Preventing the use of your systems in attacks against other systems (which could cause you to incur legal liability)
- ✦ Minimizing the potential for negative exposure

Privilege Management

Determining what individuals, groups, or organizational roles are privileged to access sensitive information is a management responsibility. To properly assign privileges, personnel can be classified into different categories. The major categories are discussed in the following sections.

Users, Groups, and Roles

Organizational personnel can be divided into the three categories of users, groups, and their roles in the organization. Additional categories are used to determine the privileges assigned to individuals to access information. It is important to understand these categories and their respective characteristics.

Owner
The owner is a manager who is responsible for specific organizational information. The owner should not be an IT person, but a manager with business responsibilities. The owner is responsible for ensuring that the appropriate security controls are in place, for assigning the initial classification to the data to be protected, for approving access requests from other parts of the organization, and for periodically reviewing the data classifications and access rights.

Group
Relative to information system security, a group can be defined as a subset of the organization that operates under a common policy and management. For example, the organization's human resources department could be considered a group.

Role
A role refers to an individual's title, position, and responsibilities in the organization. The human resources director is a role in an organization.

Custodian

The information custodian is responsible for back up, retention, and recovery of data. The information owner delegates these responsibilities to the custodian.

User Supervisor

The user supervisor is the user's immediate manager. This manager is responsible for user information, including user IDs, informing other relevant organizational entities of a change in the individual's status, reporting security incidents, and security awareness training.

Single Sign-On

Single Sign-On (SSO) addresses a situation in which a user must enter multiple passwords and IDs to access the various resources in a networked environment. This capability can be implemented through the use of scripts that read the single password and generate the other multiple passwords required for the various servers and utilities on the network. In a Single Sign-On system such as Kerberos, a user provides one ID and password per work session and is automatically logged on to all the required applications. SSO in Kerberos is accomplished through the use of an authentication server (AS) and Key Distribution Center (KDC). A user is authenticated through a password and a ticket is granted to the user to access the networked resources. The ticket contains a session key that is used to encrypt communications and a timestamp that indicates the time period during which the ticket is valid.

Other approaches similar to Kerberos that implement SSO are SESAME, KryptoKnight, and NetSP.

SSO provides the ability to use stronger passwords and easier password administration (such as changing and deleting them); using it also means that less time is required to access resources. The major disadvantage of many SSO implementations is that once a user obtains access to the system through the initial logon, the user can freely roam the network resources without any restrictions.

Other SSO authentication mechanisms include items such as smart cards and magnetic badges.

Centralized versus Decentralized

Many examples of centralized control are associated with remote access requirements. For example, dial-up users can gain access privileges through one of the following five approaches:

- **Remote Authentication and Dial-In User Service (RADIUS)** — RADIUS incorporates an authentication server and dynamic passwords.
- **Callback systems** — In this method, a remote user dials in to an authentication server. The server requests an ID and password, which the user provides.

The server then hangs up. The authentication server looks up the caller's ID in a database of authorized users and obtains a phone number at a fixed location. The authentication server calls the phone number; the user answers and can then access the information system. In some Callback implementations, the user must enter another password upon receiving a Callback. The disadvantage of this system is that the user must be at a fixed location whose phone number is known to the authentication server. A threat to Callback is that a cracker can arrange to have the call automatically forwarded to his number, enabling access to the system.

- **The Challenge Handshake Authentication Protocol (CHAP)** — CHAP employs a challenge handshake in which the authentication server generates a challenge string and presents it to the user desiring to log on. The user enters this challenge number into a token, along with a PIN. The token then takes these two items and generates a response string. The user enters this response into the authentication server. The server verifies that this response is correct because it also knows the user's PIN and the token's response generation algorithm. CHAP protects the password from eavesdroppers and supports the encryption of communication.

- **The Terminal Access Controller Access Control System (TACACS)** — TACACS employs a user ID and a static password for networked applications.

- **The Terminal Access Controller Access Control System+ (TACACS+)** — TACACS+ provides even stronger protection through the use of tokens for two-factor, dynamic password authentication.

Kerberos is an excellent example of a decentralized approach to privilege and access management. Another common mechanism for controlling the access privileges to information in a decentralized environment is through the use of databases. Database models include relational, hierarchical, network, object-oriented, and object-relational. The relational model has been the focus of much research in providing access control privileges. A key feature of the relational model is the database *view*. A view is a virtual composition of the tables in the database, and the contents of the view are a function of the user's access privileges. A view implements the principle of least privilege in database access.

The relational and object-relational database models support queries, while the traditional file systems and the object-oriented database model do not. The object-relational and object-oriented models are better suited to managing complex data used in such applications as computer-aided design and imaging.

Auditing

The purpose of auditing is to provide information to management so that they are informed about the operation of the target systems. The audit function provides the ability to determine if the system is being operated in accordance with accepted industry practices and standards.

Auditing cannot provide information to completely eliminate risks. Risks can never be completely eliminated, but they can be mitigated and understood. Management must determine the level of risk it is willing to tolerate. This type of decision is based on the cost of addressing a specific risk versus the potential cost of the harm to the system if the risk is exploited.

Three types of risk are associated with an information system security audit:

- **Control risk** — The risk that controls put in place will not prevent, correct, or detect errors on a timely basis
- **Detection risk** — The risk that the procedures conducted by the audit team will not detect a material problem
- **Inherent risk** — The susceptibility of a business or process to commit relevant errors, assuming there were no internal controls in place

Relative to information system security, the audit is accomplished by collecting, storing, and reviewing system logs to determine what material events have occurred. This activity also entails a review of the system security and identification of potential breaches in security. If a breach is discovered, the audit attempts to reconstruct the events that lead to a security breach and reconstitute the activities performed during the breach. Information security auditing occurs at the network protection layer, at subnet gateways, at the servers (e-mail, file, application), and at the users' workstations. Events that should be logged include the following:

- Logon
- Logout
- Permission changes
- Sending information to removable media
- Invoking privileged commands
- Application initiation
- Repeated attempts to access sensitive files
- System startup and shutdown

Audit files should be protected at the highest level of security in an information system to prevent unauthorized access and modification or destruction of the files.

Mandatory Access Control

In mandatory access control (MAC), privileges are determined by labels assigned to sensitive material and clearances assigned to subjects seeking access to that material. If the subject's clearance is equal to or higher than the material's classification, the subject is authorized to access the material, with one other condition. The subject must have a "need-to-know" the material to perform the subject's assigned tasks. If the individual is cleared to access the material but the material is not needed by the subject to carry out its duties, access privileges are denied. "Need-to-know" is equivalent to the principle of least privilege.

Rule-based access control is a type of MAC in which access privileges are determined by rules and not by the identity of the subjects and objects alone.

Discretionary Access Control

In discretionary access control (DAC), administrators and/or owners of the information can specify the privileges assigned to a subject to access that information. These privileges are called "discretionary" because they are not based on a policy and are assigned at the discretion of the owner/administrator and not by labels and clearances. However, "need-to-know" also applies to DAC. An access control list (ACL) is one way of implementing DAC. An ACL is a list denoting which users have what privileges to a particular resource. For example, a tabular listing would show what subjects have access to a particular object. Subject A may have read only privileges to File Q, and subject B may have read and write privileges to File Y. DAC is used in local, dynamic situations where the administrators/owners must have the discretion to specify what resources certain users are permitted to access.

An identity-based access control is a type of DAC based on an individual's identity.

Role-Based Access Control

Role-based access control (RBAC) assigns privileges to individuals relative to certain objects, based on the individual's role in the organization (role-based) or the person's responsibilities and duties (task-based). RBAC is especially effective in an organization in which frequent personnel changes occur, eliminating the need to change access privileges whenever a new person assumes the same role.

Computer Forensics

Computer forensics refers information collection from and about computer systems that is admissible in a court of law. Because computer data is intangible, can be easily modified, and is a critical part of an organization's day-to-day operations, computer crime investigations have the following characteristics:

- ✦ Because the Internet and World Wide Web are global, computer crime can be committed from extremely diverse geographic locations. A perpetrator in Russia may be committing fraud in the U.S. using the Internet. Prosecution is impeded because of differences in laws, attitudes toward computer crimes, definitions of computer crimes, as well as difficulty in obtaining search warrants.

- ✦ A plan should be prepared beforehand on how to handle reports of suspected computer crimes.

- Investigators and prosecutors have a compressed time frame for the investigation.
- A computer crime investigation will involve an organization's computers. As a result, the investigation might interfere with the organization's business activities. In some cases, computers may be seized.
- In a corporate environment, an investigation will involve management, corporate security, human resources, the legal department, and other appropriate staff members.
- The act of investigating may also affect critical operations.
- Investigating may prompt a suspect to commit retaliatory acts that could compromise data, result in a Denial of Service (DoS) attack, generate negative publicity, or open individual privacy issues.
- A committee of appropriate personnel should be set up to address investigative issues in advance.

To accommodate the prosecution of computer crimes, many jurisdictions have expanded the definition of property to include electronic information.

Chain of Evidence

Evidence associated with a computer-related crime must be carefully acquired, handled, and preserved to be admissible in court. Specifically, one must follow and protect a chain of custody of evidence. The following are the major components of this chain of evidence:

- Location of the evidence when obtained
- Time that the evidence was obtained
- Identification of individual(s) who discovered the evidence
- Identification of individual(s) who secured the evidence
- Identification of individual(s) who controlled the evidence and/or who maintained possession of that evidence

Evidence Life Cycle

Similarly, evidence progresses through a life cycle that ranges from its discovery through its use in prosecution to its return to the evidence owner. The following list shows the major phases of the evidence life cycle:

1. Discovery and recognition
2. Protection
3. Recording

4. Collection
    - Collect all relevant storage media
    - Make image of hard disk before removing power
    - Print out screen
    - Avoid degaussing equipment
5. Identification (tagging and marking)
6. Preservation
    - Protect magnetic media from erasure
    - Store in proper environment
7. Transportation
8. Presentation in a court of law
9. Return of evidence to owner

To be admissible in a court of law, the evidence must be:

- **Relevant** — The evidence must be related to the crime in that it shows that the crime has been committed, can provide information describing the crime, can provide information to the perpetrator's motives, can verify what has occurred, and can fix the crime's time of occurrence.
- **Legally permissible** — The evidence was obtained in a lawful manner.
- **Reliable** — The evidence has not been tampered with or modified.
- **Identified** — The evidence is properly identified without changing or damaging it. In computer forensics, this process includes the following:
    - Labeling printouts with permanent markers
    - Identifying the operating system used, the hardware types, and so on
    - Recording serial numbers
    - Marking evidence without damaging it, or by placing it in sealed containers that are marked
- **Preserved** — The evidence is not subject to damage or destruction. For the computer investigation, take the following precautions:
    - Do not prematurely remove power.
    - Back up the hard disk image using disk imaging hardware or software.
    - Avoid placing magnetic media in the proximity of sources of magnetic fields.
    - Store media in a dust and smoke-free environment at proper temperature and humidity.
    - Write-protect the media.
    - Authenticate the file system by creating a digital signature based on the contents of a file or disk sector.

Types of Evidence

Legal evidence can be classified into the following types:

- **Direct evidence** — Proves or disproves a specific act through oral testimony based on information gathered through the witness's five senses
- **Conclusive evidence** — Incontrovertible; overrides all other evidence
- **Best evidence** — Original or primary evidence rather than a copy or duplicate of the evidence
- **Secondary evidence** — A copy of evidence or an oral description of its contents; not as reliable as best evidence
- **Opinions** — The following are the two types of opinions:
    - **Expert** — May offer an opinion based on personal expertise and facts
    - **Nonexpert** — May testify only as to facts
- **Hearsay evidence (third-party)** — Evidence that is not based on personal, first-hand knowledge of the witness, but was obtained from another source. Under the U.S. Federal Rules of Evidence (803), hearsay evidence is generally not admissible in court. Computer-generated records and other business records fall under the category of hearsay evidence because these records cannot be proven accurate and reliable. This inadmissibility is known as the *hearsay rule*. However, exceptions to the hearsay rule exist for records that are:
    - Made during the regular conduct of business and authenticated by witnesses familiar with their use
    - Relied upon in the regular course of business
    - Made by a person with knowledge of the records
    - Made by a person with information transmitted by a person with knowledge
    - Made at or near the time of occurrence of the act being investigated
    - In the custody of the witness on a regular basis
- **Circumstantial evidence** — Inference of information from other, intermediate, relevant facts

Law Enforcement and the 4th Amendment

If a computer crime is suspected, it is critical to determine if law or regulation requires disclosure to legal authorities. U.S. Federal Sentencing Guidelines require organizations to report criminal acts. A consequence of reporting the criminal act is that control passes from the organization to law enforcement. Negative publicity may result that adversely affects the organization.

The timing of requesting outside assistance from law enforcement is another major issue. In the United States, law enforcement personnel are bound by the Fourth Amendment to the U.S. Constitution and must obtain a warrant to search for evidence. Private citizens are not held to this strict requirement and, in some cases, a private individual can conduct a search for possible evidence without a warrant. However, if a private individual were asked by a law enforcement officer to search for evidence, a warrant would be required because the private individual would be acting as a law enforcement agent.

An exception to the search warrant requirement for law enforcement officers is the *Exigent Circumstances Doctrine*. Under this doctrine, if probable cause is present and destruction of the evidence is deemed imminent, the search can be conducted without the delay of having to obtain the warrant.

A standard discriminator used to determine whether a subject may be the perpetrator of a crime is to evaluate whether the individual had a motive, opportunity, and means to commit the crime. This test is known as MOM.

Liability

In 1997, the Federal Sentencing Guidelines were extended to apply to computer crime. Under these guidelines, senior corporate officers can be personally subject to up to 290 million dollars in fines if their organizations do not comply with the law. These guidelines also treat the possession of illegally acquired material without intent to resell as a crime.

Management is obligated to protect the organization from losses due to the following:

- ✦ Natural disasters
- ✦ Malicious code
- ✦ Compromise of proprietary information
- ✦ Damage to reputation
- ✦ Violation of the law
- ✦ Employee privacy suits
- ✦ Stockholder suits

Management must follow the *prudent man rule*, which "requires officers to perform duties with the diligence and care that ordinary, prudent people would exercise under similar circumstances." The officers must exercise *due care* or *reasonable care* to carry out their responsibilities to the organization.

The criterion for evaluating the legal requirements for implementing safeguards is to evaluate the cost (C) of instituting the protection versus the estimated loss (L) resulting from exploitation of the corresponding vulnerability. If C < L, a legal liability exists.

Risk Identification

Risk identification is important to the proper selection of security controls and safeguards. Risk is a function of the probability of a given threat agent exercising a particular vulnerability, and the resulting impact of that adverse event on the organization. It entails the potential for the realization of unwanted, adverse consequences to human life, health, property, or the environment.

Some risk-related definitions follow:

- **Risk reduction** — Taking measures to alter or improve the risk position of an asset throughout the company.
- **Risk transference** — Assigning or transferring the potential cost of a loss to another party (such as an insurance company).
- **Risk acceptance** — Accepting the level of loss that will occur and absorbing that loss.
- **Asset** — An *asset* is a resource, process, product, computing infrastructure, and so on that an organization wants to protect. The value of an asset is composed of all the elements related to that asset, including its creation, development, support, replacement, public credibility, considered costs, and ownership values.
- **Threat** — The potential for a threat-source to exploit a specific vulnerability. The presence of any potential event that causes an undesirable impact on the organization is called a *threat*. A threat can be manmade or natural, intentional or accidental, and have a small or large effect on a company's security.
- **Vulnerability** — Any weakness in an information system, system security procedures, internal controls, or implementation that could be exploited by a threat or threat agent. A minor threat can potentially become a greater threat, or a more frequent threat, because of a vulnerability.
- **Safeguard** — A *safeguard* is the control or countermeasure employed to reduce the risk associated with a specific threat or group of threats. Controls can be operational, technical, or administrative. Multiple layered controls that utilize all three control areas are the best defense against a threat.
- **Countermeasures** — Those controls put in place as a result of an analysis of a system's security posture. They are the same controls defined above, in Safeguards, but are implemented as a countermeasure to reduce a specific identified and measured risk.
- **Threat agent** — Any circumstance or event that could harm an information system through unauthorized access, destruction, disclosure, data modification, and/or denial of service.
- **Exposure** — The exposure subelement pertains to the openness of a source of information.

To mitigate risk, the organization needs to know the threat, the consequences of the realized threat, the frequency of the occurrence of the threat, and the likelihood that this threat will occur. To gather the information required to answer these questions, the organization must perform a risk assessment, including asset, threat, and vulnerability identification.

Risk Assessment

The main purpose of performing a risk analysis (RA) is to quantify the impact of potential threats—that is, to put a price on the cost of a lost business functionality. The two main results of an RA are the identification of risks and the cost/benefit justification of the countermeasures.

Performing an RA is beneficial because it:

- Creates a clear cost-to-value ratio for security protections.
- Influences the decision-making process dealing with hardware configuration and software systems design.
- Helps a company focus its security resources where they are needed most.
- Influences planning and construction decisions, such as site selection and building design.

Risk assessment is the first process in the risk management methodology. It helps organizations identify appropriate controls for reducing or eliminating risk during the risk mitigation process.

To determine the likelihood of a future adverse event, threats to an IT system must be analyzed in conjunction with the potential vulnerabilities and the controls in place for the IT system. The likelihood that a potential vulnerability could be exploited by a given threat-source can be described as high, medium, or low.

Any combination of the following techniques (from *NIST Special Publication 800-30, Risk Management Guide for Information Technology Systems*) can be used in gathering information relevant to the IT system within its operational boundary:

- **Questionnaire**—The questionnaire should be distributed to the applicable technical and nontechnical management personnel who are designing or supporting the IT system.
- **On-site interviews**—On-site visits also enable risk assessment personnel to observe and gather information about the physical, environmental, and operational security of the IT system.
- **Document review**—Policy documents, system documentation, and security-related documentation can provide good information about the security controls used by and planned for the IT system.
- **Use of automated scanning tools**—Proactive technical methods can be used to collect system information efficiently.

The three primary steps in performing a risk analysis are as follows:

- Estimate the potential losses to assets by determining their value.
- Analyze potential threats to the assets.
- Determine the threats' likelihood and regularity.

After performing the risk analysis, the final results should contain the following:

- Valuations of the critical assets in hard costs
- A detailed list of significant threats
- Each threat's likelihood and possible occurrence rate
- Loss potential of a threat (the dollar impact that the threat will have on an asset)
- Recommended remedial measures and safeguards or countermeasures

Automated risk analysis products can minimize the manual effort expended during the risk analysis and assist in forecasting expected losses quickly under differing scenarios. These products enable the users to perform calculations quickly to estimate future expected losses, thereby determining the benefit of their implemented safeguards.

Asset Identification

One of the most overlooked elements of a security strategy is the proper identification and valuation of the organization's assets. The proper and cost-effective implementation of security controls requires that the organization conduct a thorough asset identification. A common mistake made by organizations is not accurately identifying the information's value before implementing the security controls.

Some of the components that determine an information asset's value are as follows:

- The initial and ongoing cost (to an organization) of purchasing, licensing, developing, and supporting the information asset
- The asset's value to the organization's production operations, research and development, and business model viability
- The asset's value, established in the external marketplace, and the estimated value of the intellectual property (trade secrets, patents, copyrights, and so on)

Quantitative and qualitative risk analysis are two general methodologies used to determine the value of an asset and analyze risk.

Quantitative Risk Analysis

Quantitative RA attempts to assign independently objective numeric values (hard dollars, for example) to the components of the risk assessment and to the assessment of potential losses. When all elements (asset value, impact, threat frequency, safeguard effectiveness, safeguard costs, uncertainty, and probability) are measured, rated, and assigned values, the process is considered to be fully quantitative.

Estimating Potential Losses

To estimate the potential losses incurred during the realization of a threat, the assets are valued by common asset valuation procedures (quantitative or qualitative), and then the annual loss expectancy (ALE) is determined. The ALE is the expected cost of the loss to the organization annually and is determined using the exposure factor (EF), the single loss expectancy (SLE), and the annual rate of occurrence (ARO).

Typically, the results (quantity) are addressed in terms of dollars. Fully quantitative risk analysis is not possible, however, because qualitative determinations must be made in the process.

Qualitative Risk Analysis

Qualitative RA addresses the more intangible values of data loss and focuses on issues that go beyond the pure, hard cost of data loss. In a qualitative RA, the seriousness of threats and the relative sensitivity of the assets are given a ranking, or qualitative grading, by using a scenario approach and by creating an exposure rating scale for each scenario. This results in a subjective quality rating, such as high, medium, or low, or on a scale from 0 to 5.

During a qualitative RA scenario description, threats are matched to assets. This scenario describes the type of threat and the potential loss to each asset and selects the safeguards to mitigate risk. After creating the threat listing, defining the assets for protection, and assigning an exposure level rating, the qualitative risk assessment scenario begins. Table 5.5 lists some differences between quantitative and qualitative risk analysis.

Table 5.5
Quantitative versus Qualitative RA

Property	Quantitative	Qualitative
Cost/benefit analysis	Yes	No
Financial hard costs	Yes	No
Can be automated	Yes	No
Guesswork involved	Low	High
Complex calculations	Yes	No
Volume of information required	High	Low
Time/work involved	High	Low
Ease of communication	High	Low

Threat Identification

After the identification and valuation of the assets, the identification of the threats must occur as part of the risk assessment. Threats are often categorized for this process. Threat categories might include the following:

- **Criminal** — Physical destruction or vandalism, the theft of assets or information, organized insider theft, armed robbery, or physical harm to personnel
- **Personnel** — Unauthorized or uncontrolled system access, the misuse of technology by authorized users, tampering by disgruntled employees, or falsified data input
- **Environmental** — Utility failure, service outage, natural disasters, or neighboring hazards
- **Information warfare** — Technology-oriented terrorism, malicious code or logic, or emanation interception for military or economic espionage
- **Application/operational** — An ineffective security application that results in procedural errors or incorrect data entry
- **Computer infrastructure** — Hardware/equipment failure, program errors, operating system flaws, or a communications system failure
- **Data classification** — Data aggregation or concentration that results in data inference, covert channel manipulation, a malicious code/virus/Trojan horse/worm/logic bomb, or a concentration of responsibilities (lack of separation of duties)
- **Delayed processing** — Reduced productivity or a delayed funds collection that results in reduced income, increased expenses, or late charges

Vulnerability Definition

After identifying the threats, the vulnerabilities that those threats could impact are defined. A vulnerability assessment is a common method of matching potential threats to existing vulnerabilities in the organization.

Common steps that are performed in a vulnerability assessment might include the following:

- Listing potential emergencies, both internally to the facility and externally to the community; natural, man-made, technological, and human error are all categories of potential emergencies and errors.
- Estimating the likelihood that each emergency could occur.
- Assessing the potential impact of the emergency on the organization in the areas of human impact, property impact, and business asset impact.

♦ Assessing external and internal resources required to deal with the emergency, and determining if they are located internally or if external resources are required.

Figure 5.4 shows a sample vulnerability matrix. This can be used to create a subjective impact analysis for each type of emergency and its probability. The lower the final number, the better, as a high number means a high probability, impact, or lack of remediation resources.

TYPE OF EMERGENCY	Probability	Human Impact	Property Impact	Business Impact	Internal Resources	External Resources	Total
	High 5 ↔ 1 Low	High Impact 5 ↔ 1 Low Impact			Weak Resources 5 ↔ 1 Strong Resources		

Figure 5.4 Sample vulnerability assessment matrix

Security Awareness and Education

Computer security awareness and education is based on the following assumptions:

♦ Making computer system users aware of their security responsibilities and teaching them correct practices helps users change their behavior.

♦ Developing skills and knowledge helps computer users perform their jobs more securely

♦ Security education builds in-depth knowledge, as needed, to design, implement, or operate security programs for organizations and systems

An effective computer security awareness and education program requires proper planning, implementation, maintenance, and periodic evaluation. The program could follow these steps (taken from *NIST Special Publication 800-14 Generally Accepted Principles and Practices for Securing Information Technology Systems*):

- Identify program scope, goals, and objectives.
- Identify training staff.
- Identify target audiences.
- Motivate management and employees.
- Administer the program.
- Maintain the program.
- Evaluate the program.

Security awareness and education is often an overlooked element of security management, because most of a security administrator's time is spent proactively or reactively administering security. However, all employees must be aware of basic security concepts and their benefit to an organization. Employees must be aware of the need to secure information and to protect the information assets of the enterprise, and how their actions impact an organization's overall security posture.

Awareness

Awareness is used to reinforce the fact that security supports the organization's mission by protecting valuable resources. Security awareness supports individual accountability. Without the knowledge of necessary security measures and how to use them, users cannot be truly accountable for their actions. Management commitment is also necessary because of the resources used in developing and implementing the program and because the program affects their staff.

Security awareness programs have other benefits, including the following:

- Make a measurable reduction in the unauthorized actions attempted by personnel
- Significantly increase the effectiveness of the protection controls
- Help to avoid the fraud, waste, and abuse of computing resources

Personnel are considered "security-aware" when they clearly understand the need for security, how security impacts viability and the bottom line, and the daily risks to computing resources. It's also important to have periodic awareness sessions to orient new employees and refresh senior employees. A common awareness technique is to create a hypothetical security vulnerability scenario and to get the participants' input on possible solutions or outcomes.

Education and Training

Education and training is vital to the smooth operation of security controls, particularly the proper operation and maintenance of these controls by security personnel. Operators need training in the skills that are required to fulfill their job functions securely, and security practitioners need education to implement and maintain necessary security controls.

In-depth training and education for systems personnel, auditors, and security professionals is very important and considered necessary for career development. In addition, specific product training for security software and hardware is vital to the protection of the enterprise.

The following are types of security education:

- Security-related job training for operators and specific users
- Awareness training for specific departments or personnel groups with security-sensitive positions
- Technical security training for IT support personnel and system administrators
- Advanced InfoSec training for security practitioners and information systems auditors
- Security training for senior managers, functional managers, and business unit managers

A starting point for a security education program could be the topic of policies, standards, guidelines, and procedures that are used in the organization.

Documentation

A security system needs documentation controls. Documentation can include several things: security plans, contingency plans, risk analyses, and security policies and procedures. Policy documents, system documentation, and security-related documentation can provide good information about the security controls used by and planned for the IT system.

This documentation must be protected from unauthorized disclosure, kept current, and be made easily available in the event of a disaster.

Documentation Change Control

Update all relevant documentation when system changes occur. Such changes could include:

- Changes to the system infrastructure
- Changes to security policies or procedures

- Changes to the disaster recovery or business continuity plans
- Facility environment changes, such as office moves or HVAC and electrical changes

Documentation control is a cornerstone of configuration management. Configuration management specifies strict adherence to documenting system changes and the process of the documentation itself.

Configuration management applies technical and administrative direction to the following:

- Identifying and documenting the functional and physical characteristics of each configuration item for the system
- Managing all changes to these characteristics
- Recording and reporting the status of change processing and implementation

Configuration management involves process monitoring, version control, information capture, quality control, bookkeeping, and an organizational framework to support these activities, plus all documentation related to the configuration process.

Documentation control is a means of assuring that system changes are approved before being implemented, that only the proposed and approved changes are implemented, and that the implementation is complete and accurate. This involves strict procedures for proposing, monitoring, and approving system changes and their implementation. Documentation control assists the change process by supporting the personnel who coordinate analytical tasks, approve system changes, review the implementation of changes, and supervise other tasks such as documenting the controls.

Records Retention and Storage

Records retention refers to how long transactions, documentation, and other types of records should be retained according to management, legal, audit, or tax compliance requirements. The retention of data media (tapes, diskettes, and backup media) can be based on one or more criteria, such as the number of days elapsed, number of days since creation, hold time, or other factors. The retention of documentation is normally based on the standards and best practices of the organization's business. An example of documentation retention requirements could be the mandated retention periods for trial documentation or financial records.

Although data remanence refers to the data left on the media after the media has been erased, data remanence can also apply to discarded documentation. Dumpster diving is a very effective means of retrieving confidential information from improperly disposed documentation.

The destruction of documentation should be controlled under the tenets of data remanence, as discussed earlier. Burning is a common method of disposing of sensitive documentation, as is shredding multiple times with differing patterns.

In any case, the documentation should be handled only by personnel with the proper security clearance for the level of the information in the documentation. Systems administrators and security administrators should be aware of the risks of object reuse, declassification, destruction, and disposal of documentation.

✦ ✦ ✦

SAMPLE QUESTIONS

1. Which of the following statements is TRUE?

    a. An organizational security policy is a detailed and specific listing of management's requirements, and its implementation is mandatory.

    b. An organizational security policy is a general statement of management's intent, and its implementation is in the form of guidelines.

    c. An organizational security policy is a general statement of management's intent, and its implementation is mandatory.

    d. An organizational security policy is a detailed and specific listing of management's requirements, and its implementation is in the form of guidelines.

2. Which of the following definitions *best* describes standards?

    a. The compulsory use of specific hardware and software technologies in a uniform manner

    b. Non-mandatory guidelines for the use of specific hardware and software technologies in a uniform manner

    c. Detailed step-by-step actions that must be accomplished

    d. Detailed step-by-step actions that are presented as nonmandatory guidelines

3. The definition "describe how to implement security mechanisms to ensure that security is being accomplished in a uniform manner on the various platforms and operating systems throughout the enterprise" applies to which of the following terms?

    a. Baselines

    b. Guidelines

    c. Procedures

    d. Standard recommendations

4. The statement "The user must take full responsibility for his or her actions in using a computer account and accept all recourses for their actions." is an example of which of the following administrative policies?

    a. Prudent use

    b. Due diligence

    c. Due care

    d. Acceptable use

5. Privacy is defined as an individual's right to protection from unauthorized disclosure of his personally identifiable information (PII). Which of the following items is *not* one of the fundamental privacy principles?

   a. Notice

   b. Recount

   c. Choice

   d. Security

6. The following items are typical components of what type of policy?

   - The type of information collected, such as name, address, credit card number, phone number, and so on
   - Information gathered through cookies and Web server logs and how that information is used
   - How information is shared with affiliates and strategic partners
   - Mechanisms to secure information transmissions, such as encryption and digital signatures

   a. Fair use

   b. Transaction

   c. Security

   d. Privacy

7. Which of the following areas is *not* addressed in the Health Insurance Portability and Accountability Act (HIPAA), Administrative Simplification Title?

   a. Privacy

   b. Security

   c. Costs

   d. Electronic transactions and code sets

8. What specification defines how Web sites can express their privacy practices in a standard format that can be retrieved automatically and interpreted easily by user agents?

   a. The Platform for Privacy Preferences (P3P)

   b. Web Privacy Standard (WPS)

   c. Web Privacy Platform (WPP)

   d. European Union (EU) Privacy Principles

9. What administrative control divides responsibility among a number of different individuals?

   a. Need-to-know

   b. Separation of duties

   c. Least privilege

   d. Least authority

10. The overwriting of data media (primarily magnetic) intended to be reused in the same organization or monitored environment is known as what?

    a. Purging

    b. Destruction

    c. Removing

    d. Clearing

11. The Carnegie Mellon University CERT Coordination Center (CERT/CC) recommends which of the following sets of incident response practices?

    a. Prepare, notify, follow-up

    b. Prepare, handle, follow-up

    c. Notify, handle, follow-up

    d. Prepare, handle, notify

12. Which of the following classifications is best described as "responsible for ensuring that the appropriate security controls are in place, for assigning the initial classification to the data to be protected, for approving access requests from other parts of the organization, and for periodically reviewing the data classifications and access rights?"

    a. Custodian

    b. Security analyst

    c. Owner

    d. User supervisor

13. Which of the following is a potential vulnerability when using single sign-on (SSO)?

    a. The ability to use stronger passwords

    b. Easier administration of changing or deleting passwords

    c. The user can freely roam the network resources without any restrictions

    d. Requires less time to access resources

14. In what type of control can administrators and/or owners of information specify the privileges assigned to a subject to access that information?

    a. Role-based

    b. Discretionary

    c. Mandatory

    d. Supervisory

15. The type of evidence that proves or disproves a specific act through oral testimony based on information gathered through the witness's five senses is called what?

    a. Hearsay evidence

    b. Best evidence

    c. Conclusive evidence

    d. Direct evidence

16. Which choice describes a control?

    a. Competitive advantage, credibility, or good will

    b. Events or situations that could cause a financial or operational impact to the organization

    c. Personnel compensation and retirement programs

    d. Protection devices or procedures in place that reduce the effects of threats

17. Which backup method will probably require the backup operator to use the least number of tapes for a complete system restoration, if a different tape is used every night in a five-day rotation?

    a. Ad hoc backup method

    b. Differential backup method

    c. Incremental backup method

    d. Reactive backup method

18. Which statement is true about security awareness and educational programs?

    a. Awareness and training help users become more accountable for their actions.

    b. Security education assists management in determining who should be promoted.

    c. A security awareness and training program helps prevent the occurrence of natural disasters.

    d. Security awareness is not necessary for high-level senior executives.

19. Which choice is an example of an inert gas fire suppression agent?

  a. FC-3-1-10

  b. HFC-23

  c. HCFC-22

  d. IG-541

20. Which statement most accurately describes a "wet pipe" sprinkler system?

  a. Wet pipe is the most commonly used sprinkler system.

  b. Wet pipe contains air pressure.

  c. Wet pipe sounds an alarm and delays water release.

  d. Wet pipe may contain carbon dioxide.

21. Which choice is an example of a "dirty" fire-extinguishing agent?

  a. CO_2

  b. IG-55

  c. IG-01

  d. HCFC-22

22. Which statement accurately describes smoke exposure to electronic equipment?

  a. Smoke exposure for a relatively short period does little immediate damage.

  b. Continuing power to the smoke-exposed equipment won't increase the damage.

  c. Moisture and oxygen corrosion constitute less main damage to the equipment than smoke exposure.

  d. The primary damage done by smoke exposure is immediate.

23. Which choice describes a social engineering technique used to gain physical access to a secure facility?

  a. Asserting authority or pulling rank to intimidate

  b. Using a Trojan horse to create a network back door

  c. Eavesdropping on electronic emanations

  d. Employing the salami accounting fraud

24. Which choice is an example of an electronic physical access control method?

   a. Deadbolts

   b. Access tokens

   c. Key locks

   d. Pushbutton locks

25. Which statement about disaster recovery plan testing is incorrect?

   a. If no deficiencies were found during the test, the plan is probably perfect.

   b. Testing prepares and trains the personnel to execute their emergency duties.

   c. If no deficiencies were found during the test, the test was probably flawed.

   d. Testing identifies deficiencies in the recovery procedures.

26. Which statement is *not* true regarding company/employee relations during and after a disaster?

   a. The organization has a responsibility to continue salaries or other funding to the employees and/or families affected by the disaster.

   b. The organization's responsibility to the employees' families ends when the disaster stops the business from functioning.

   c. Employees do not have the right to obtain compensatory damages fraudulently if the organization cannot compensate them.

   d. The company must be insured to the extent it can properly compensate its employees and families.

27. Which choice is considered an appropriate role for senior management in the disaster recovery process?

   a. Continuously reassessing the recovery site's stability

   b. Recovering and constructing all critical data

   c. Remaining visible to employees and stakeholders

   d. Identifying and prioritizing mission-critical applications

28. In developing a recovery plan, which choice would be considered a long-term objective?

   a. Priorities for restoration

   b. Acceptable downtime before restoration

   c. Minimum resources needed to accomplish the restoration

   d. The organization's strategic plan

29. Which choice is considered an appropriate role for financial management in the business continuity and disaster recovery process?

   a. Providing appropriate retraining

   b. Providing employees and their families with counseling and support

   c. Formally notifying insurers of claims

   d. Monitoring productivity of personnel

30. Which choice is *not* a reason to control the humidity in computer operations areas?

   a. Computer operators do not perform at their peak if the humidity is too high.

   b. Electrostatic discharges can harm electronic equipment.

   c. Electrical connections become inefficient in high humidity.

   d. If the air is too humid, electroplating of conductors may occur.

Answers to Sample Questions

APPENDIX A

Chapter 1: General Security Concepts

1. Kerberos sets up secure communications between clients and other network resources through which of the following?

    a. Passwords

    b. Tokens

    c. Public keys

    d. Session keys

Answer: **d.** Session keys are temporary, secret keys assigned by the Kerberos Key Distribution Center and used during a time window between the client and other resources on the network. Answer a is incorrect because it is not a key, and answer b is incorrect because a token generates dynamic passwords. Answer c is wrong because it refers to asymmetric encryption that is not used in the basic Kerberos protocol.

2. Access control must consider which of the following?

    a. Vulnerabilities, biometrics, and exposures

    b. Threats, assets, and safeguards

    c. Exposures, threats, and countermeasures

    d. Threats, vulnerabilities, and risks

Answer: **d.** Threats are an event or situation that may cause harm to an information system; vulnerabilities describe weaknesses in the system that might be exploited by the threats; and the risk determines the probability of threats being realized. All three items must be considered to meaningfully apply access control. Therefore, the other answers are incorrect.

3. Single sign-on (SSO) can be implemented by which of the following?

   a. Kerberos

   b. IDEA

   c. Hash functions

   d. RSA

Answer: **a.** Kerberos is a third-party authentication protocol that can be used to implement SSO. Answer b is incorrect because it is a symmetric key algorithm. Answer c is a one-way transformation used to disguise passwords or to implement digital signatures, and answer d is a public key algorithm based on the difficulty of finding the prime factors of large numbers.

4. Which choice is a scanning technique that uses ICMP?

   a. Ping sweep

   b. FTP proxy bounce attack

   c. TCP FIN scan

   d. TCP half-open scan

Answer: **a.** The ICMP ping sweep scan uses the ICMP Echo and Reply values to find alive hosts. The other three choices are common TCP scanning techniques.

5. Authentication using biometrics is which of the following?

   a. The Crossover Error Rate (CER)

   b. A "one-to-many" search of an individual's characteristics from a database

   c. A "one-to-one" search to verify an individual's claim to an identity

   d. Aggregation

Answer: **c.** Answer a refers to the percentage in a biometric system where the False Rejection Rate equals the False Acceptance Rate. Answer b refers to identification using a biometric system, and answer d refers to obtaining higher-sensitivity information from a number of pieces of information of lower sensitivity.

6. Preventing the modification of information by unauthorized users, preventing the unauthorized or unintentional modification of information by authorized users, and preserving internal and external consistency are goals of what?

   a. Authentication

   b. Integrity

   c. Authorization

   d. Availability

Answer: **b.** Answer a, authentication, is the process of verifying that a person is who they claim to be. Answer c is concerned with the rights and permissions assigned to subjects to access objects, and availability is the reliable and timely access to computing and network resources.

7. The boundary where security controls are in effect to protect assets is called what?

    a. A security perimeter

    b. An enforced path

    c. A trusted computing base

    d. A trusted perimeter

Answer: **a.** Answer b, enforced path, prohibits the user from accessing a resource through a different route than is authorized to that particular user. Examples of controls to implement an enforced path include establishing Virtual Private Networks (VPNs) for specific groups within an organization, using firewalls with access control lists, restricting user menu options and providing specific phone numbers or dedicated lines for remote access. Answer c, a Trusted Computing Base (TCB), is the total combination of protection mechanisms within a computer system. These mechanisms include the firmware, hardware, and software that enforce the system security policy. Answer d is a distractor.

8. Which of the following statements best describes a worm?

    a. Worms move from device to device.

    b. Worms create common network backdoors.

    c. Worms are programmed to execute on a particular date.

    d. Worms alter their appearance after infection.

Answer: **a.** Worms attack a network by moving from device to device. Answer b describes a Trojan horse. Answer c describes a logic bomb, and answer d describes a polymorphic virus.

9. Which of the following is an important control that should be in place for external connections to a network that uses Callback schemes?

    a. Breaking of a dial-up connection at the remote user's side of the line

    b. Call forwarding

    c. Call enhancement

    d. Breaking of a dial-up connection at the organization's computing resource side of the line

Answer: **d.** One attack that can be applied when Callback is used for remote, dial-up connections is that the caller may not hang up. If the caller has been previously authenticated and has completed his/her session, a "live" connection into the remote network will still be maintained. Also, an unauthenticated remote user may hold the line open, acting as if Callback authentication has taken place. Thus, an active disconnect should be effected at the computing resource's side of the line. Answer a is not correct since it involves the caller hanging up. Answer b, call forwarding, is a feature that should be disabled, if possible, when used with Callback schemes. With Callback, a cracker can have a call forwarded from a valid phone number to an invalid phone number during the Callback process. Answer c is a distractor.

10. What is a protection domain?

    a. A group of processes that share access to the same resources

    b. A list denoting which users possess what privileges to a particular resource

    c. A database view

    d. A Trusted Computing Base (TCB)

Answer: **a.** Answer b refers to an access control list (ACL). Answer c refers to a database view mechanism that limits what a user can see in a relational database, depending on the user's authorization. It implements the principle of least privilege. Answer d, TCB, is the total combination of protection mechanisms within a computer system. These mechanisms include the firmware, hardware, and software that enforce the system security policy.

11. What part of an access control matrix shows one user's capabilities in relation to multiple resources?

    a. Columns

    b. Rows

    c. Rows and columns

    d. Access control list

Answer: **b.** The rows of an access control matrix indicate the capabilities that users have to a number of resources. An example of a row in the access control matrix showing the capabilities user JIM is given is provided in the following table.

Table Capabilities			
USER	PROGRAM X	FILE X	FILE Y
JIM	EXECUTE	READ	READ/WRITE

Answer a, columns in the access control matrix, define the access control list described in Question 4. Answer c is incorrect since capabilities involve only the rows of the access control matrix. Answer d is incorrect since an ACL, again, is a column in the access control matrix.

12. In biometrics, which of the following describes the activity of collecting images and extracting features from the image?

    a. Authentication
    b. Throughput
    c. Enrollment
    d. Identification

Answer: **c.** In biometrics, the image collection process and storage must be performed carefully with constant checking. In enrollment, images are collected and features are extracted, but no comparison occurs. The information is stored for use in future comparison steps. If an individual is being authenticated, answer a, the biometric system takes a sample of the individual's characteristic to be evaluated and compares it to a template. Recall that authentication is a "one-to-one" comparison of a person's physiological or behavioral characteristics with their corresponding template entry in an authentication database. Answer b, throughput, refers to the rate at which individuals, once enrolled, can be processed by a biometric system. Answer d, identification, is a "one-to-many" search, comparing an individual's physiological or behavioral characteristics to those in a database.

13. Content-dependent access control is defined as what?

    a. Access control that is based on positive access rights
    b. Access control that is a function of information contained in the item being accessed
    c. Access control that is a function of such factors as location, time of day, and previous access history
    d. Access control that is a function of the role of the subject

Answer: **b.** In content-dependent access control, for example, the manager of a hospital pharmacy may be authorized to access a patient's health records, but may not be permitted to view their billing records. In answer a, the term "positive" in access control refers to positive access rights, such as read or write. Denial rights, such as denial to write to a file, can also be conferred upon a subject. Answer c is the definition of context-dependent access control, and answer d defines role-based access control. In role-based access control, access rights are based on the role or title of an individual in an organization.

14. In a Kerberos exchange involving a message with an authenticator, the authenticator contains the client ID and which of the following?

   a. Ticket Granting Ticket (TGT)

   b. Timestamp

   c. Client/TGS session key

   d. Client network address

Answer: **b.** A *timestamp*, t, is used to check the validity of the accompanying request because a Kerberos ticket is valid for some time window, v, after it is issued. The timestamp indicates when the ticket was issued. Answer a, the TGT, is composed of the client ID, the client network address, the starting and ending time the ticket is valid (v), and the client/TGS session key. This ticket is used by the client to request the service of a resource on the network from the TGS. In answer c, the client/TGS session key, $K_{c, tgs}$, is the symmetric key used for encrypted communication between the client and TGS for this particular session. For answer d, the client network address is included in the TGT and not in the authenticator.

15. Which of the following security areas is directly addressed by Kerberos?

   a. Confidentiality

   b. Frequency analysis

   c. Availability

   d. Physical attacks

Answer: **a.** Kerberos directly addresses the confidentiality and also the integrity of information. For answer b, attacks such as frequency analysis are not considered in the basic Kerberos implementation. In addition, the Kerberos protocol does not directly address availability issues (answer c). For answer d, since the Kerberos TGS and the authentication servers hold all the secret keys, these servers are vulnerable to both physical attacks and attacks from malicious code. In the Kerberos exchange, the client workstation temporarily holds the client's secret key and this key is vulnerable to compromise at the workstation.

16. Access control in which the access rights to an object are assigned by the object's owner is called what?

   a. Mandatory

   b. Role-based

   c. Discretionary

   d. Rule-based

Answer: **c.** Answer a, mandatory access control, uses security labels or classifications assigned to data items and clearances assigned to users. A user has access rights to data items with a classification equal to or less than the user's clearance. Another restriction is that the user must have a "need-to-know" the information; this requirement is identical to the principle of least privilege. Answer b, role-based access control, assigns identical privileges to groups of users. This approach simplifies the management of access rights, particularly when members of the group change. Thus, access rights are assigned to a role, not to an individual. Individuals are entered as members of specific groups and are assigned the access privileges of that group. Answer d, rule-based access control, assigns access rights based on stated rules. An example of a rule is "Access to salary data is restricted to the payroll department and the data owner."

17. What is the *best* reason for the security administrator to initiate internal vulnerability scanning?

    a. Vulnerability scanning can replicate a system crash.

    b. Vulnerability scanning can identify exposed ports.

    c. Vulnerability scanning can return false positives.

    d. Vulnerability scanning can return false negatives.

Answer: **b.** Vulnerability scanning should be conducted on a periodic basis to identify compromised or vulnerable systems. Conducting scans is one way to identify and track several types of potential problems, such as unused ports or unauthorized software. The other three answers are distractors.

18. A *reference monitor* is a system component that enforces access controls on an object. Specifically, the *reference monitor concept* is an abstract machine that mediates all access of subjects to objects. What do you call the hardware, firmware, and software elements of a Trusted Computing Base that implement the reference monitor concept?

    a. The authorization database

    b. Identification and authentication (I & A) mechanisms

    c. The auditing subsystem

    d. The security kernel

Answer: **d.** The *security kernel* implements the reference model concept. The reference model must exhibit the following characteristics:

✦ It must mediate all accesses.

✦ It must be protected from modification.

✦ It must be verifiable as correct.

Answer a, the authorization database, is used by the reference monitor to mediate accesses by subjects to objects. When a request for access is received, the reference monitor refers to entries in the authorization database to verify that the operation requested by a subject for application to an object is permitted. The authorization database has entries, or authorizations, of the form subject, object, access mode. In answer b, the I & A operation is separate from the reference monitor. The user enters his/her identification to the I & A function. Then the user must be authenticated. Authentication is verification that the user's claimed identity is valid. Authentication is based on the following three factor types:

- **Type 1.** Something you know, such as a PIN or password
- **Type 2.** Something you have, such as an ATM card or smart card
- **Type 3.** Something you are (physically), such as a fingerprint or retina scan

Answer c, the auditing subsystem, is a key complement to the reference monitor. The auditing subsystem is used by the reference monitor to keep track of the reference monitor's activities. Examples of such activities include the date and time of an access request, identification of the subject and objects involved, the access privileges requested, and the result of the request.

19. What is a passphrase?

    a. A password that changes with each logon

    b. A password that remains the same for each logon

    c. A long word or group of words that is converted by the authentication system to a password

    d. A long word or group of words that is used for identification

Answer: c. Answer a defines a dynamic password, and answer b defines a static password. Answer d is incorrect because passphrases are used for authentication, not identification.

20. Which choice is *not* a property of a polymorphic virus?

    a. The polymorphic virus decryption routine varies from infection to infection.

    b. Polymorphic viruses execute when an Excel or Word application is started.

    c. Polymorphic viruses alter their appearance to evade detection.

    d. Polymorphic viruses contain an encrypted virus body, a decryption routine, and a mutation engine.

Answer: b. Answer b is a property of a macro virus. The other three answers are all properties of polymorphic viruses.

21. Which of the following is *not* a function of the frequency of use of a password and the criticality of the information it is protecting?

   a. The randomness of the password characters

   b. The password's length

   c. The frequency at which the password is changed

   d. The composition of the user's ID

Answer: **d.** The user's ID is usually known and is not used as an authentication mechanism. The password is an authentication mechanism.

22. Call forwarding is an attack that can be used against which one the following?

   a. Callback

   b. Challenge Handshake Authentication Protocol

   c. RADIUS

   d. Internet service providers (ISPs)

Answer: **a.** An attacker can have a person's call forwarded to another number to foil the Callback system. Answer b is incorrect because it refers to a challenge-response protocol in which the user desiring to remotely access an information system must provide a correct authentication string to the authentication server for the information system. This authentication string is a response to a challenge string sent by the authentication server to the user. Answer c, RADIUS, is the Remote Authentication and Dial-In User Service. RADIUS uses an authentication server and dynamic passwords. It is a distributed client/server protocol in which clients send their requests for authentication to a centralized RADIUS server that contains all the user authentication and network service access data. Answer d is a distractor.

23. An attack in which a cracker intercepts messages and then forwards them to the intended receiver without the receiver's knowledge is called _____.

   a. Meet-in-the-middle

   b. Man-in-the-middle

   c. Dual messaging

   d. Call forwarding

Answer: **b.** Answer a is a known plaintext attack that is mounted on cryptographic algorithms such as Double DES. Using this attack, Merkle and Hellman have shown that implementing two DES encryptions does not provide the additional security anticipated over a single DES encryption. Answer c is a distractor. Answer d is an attack used against Callback systems.

24. Which property is useful in determining the scanning target's operating system?

   a. BackOrifice

   b. RAPS

   c. Trinoo

   d. TTL

Answer: **d.** The Time To Live (TTL) value is a common way to find out a target host's operating system. The other three answers are distractors.

25. The type of access control that is used in local, dynamic situations where subjects can specify what resources certain users can access is called _____.

   a. Mandatory access control

   b. Rule-based access control

   c. Sensitivity-based access control

   d. Discretionary access control

Answer: **d.** Answers a and b require strict adherence to labels and clearances. Answer c is a distractor.

26. Kerberos provides an integrity check service for messages between two entities through the use of what?

   a. A checksum

   b. Credentials

   c. Tickets

   d. A trusted, third-party authentication server

Answer: **a.** A checksum that is derived from a Kerberos message is used to verify the integrity of the message. This checksum may be a message digest resulting from the application of a hash function to the message. At the receiving end of the transmission, the receiving party can calculate the message digest of the received message using the identical hash algorithm as the sender. Then the message digest calculated by the receiver can be compared with the message digest appended to the message by the sender. If the two message digests match, the message has not been modified en route and its integrity has been preserved. For answers b and c, credentials and tickets are authenticators used in the process of granting user access to services on the network. Answer d is the AS or authentication server that conducts the ticket granting process.

27. Access control that is based on an individual's duties or title in an organization is known as _____.

   a. Rule-based access control
   b. Discretionary access control
   c. Role-based access control
   d. Mandatory access control

Answer: c. Answer a, rule-based access control, is a type of mandatory access control where access is determined by specified rules. Answer b refers to access control where the user has the authority, within certain limitations, to specify access rights that can be assigned to an individual. Mandatory access control, answer d, is dependent on labels that indicate the subject's clearance level and the classification assigned to objects.

28. The * (Star) property of the Bell-LaPadula model states what?

   a. Reading of information by a subject at a lower sensitivity level from an object at a higher sensitivity level is not permitted (no read up).
   b. Writing of information by a subject at a higher level of sensitivity to an object at a lower level of sensitivity is not permitted (no write down).
   c. An access matrix is used to specify discretionary access control.
   d. Reading or writing is permitted at a particular level of sensitivity, but not to either higher or lower levels of sensitivity.

Answer: b. Answer a describes the simple security property, and answer c describes the discretionary security property. Answer d is the Strong *(Star) property.

29. An ATM card and a PIN are an example of what?

   a. Multi-factor identification
   b. Single-factor authentication
   c. Two-factor authentication
   d. Single-factor identification

Answer: c. A PIN and ATM card are something you know and something you have. Answers a and d are incorrect because the factors are used for authentication, not identification only. Answer b is incorrect because a PIN and ATM are two authentication factors.

30. Which statement describes a property of a logic bomb?

    a. Logic bombs replicate from device to device.

    b. Logic bombs alter their appearance to evade detection.

    c. Logic bombs do not activate until a preset trigger is reached.

    d. Logic bombs leave a backdoor Trojan, like NetBus.

Answer: **c.** After infection, a logic bomb waits until a programmed condition—called a trigger—is met, before activating and beginning its attack. Answer a describes a worm. Answer b describes a polymorphic virus, and answer d describes a Trojan horse.

Chapter 2: Communication Security

1. The protocol within the Wireless Application Protocol (WAP) that performs functions similar to SSL in the TCP/IP protocol is called the _____.

    a. Wireless Session Protocol (WSP)

    b. Wireless Transport Layer Security Protocol (WTLS)

    c. Wireless Transaction Protocol (WTP)

    d. Wireless Application Environment (WAE)

Answer: **b.** The Wireless Transport Layer Security Protocol (WTLS) is similar to SSL, which performs security functions in TCP/IP. The other answers refer to protocols in the WAP protocol stack, but their primary functions are not security.

2. Which IEEE standard uses the Extensible Authentication Protocol to offer authentication and key management for wireless LANs?

    a. 802.15

    b. 802.1x

    c. 802.11g

    d. 802.11a

Answer: **b.** 802.1x ties EAP (EAP [RFC 2284]) to the physical medium (both wired and wireless LAN media) and supports dynamically varying encryption keys. EAP messages are encapsulated in 802.1x messages and referred to as EAPOL, or EAP over LAN. 802.1x also supports multiple authentication methods such as token cards, Kerberos, one-time passwords, certificates, and public key authentication.

Answer a, IEEE 802.15, defines wireless personal area networks (WPANs), such as Bluetooth, in the 2.4–2.5 GHz band. Answer c, IEEE 802.11g, offers wireless transmission over relatively short distances at speeds from 20 Mbps up to 54 Mbps operating in the 2.4 GHz range. Answer d, IEEE 802.11a, specifies high-speed wireless connectivity in the 5 GHz band using Orthogonal Frequency Division Multiplexing with data rates up to 54 Mbps.

3. What protocol adds digital signatures and encryption to Internet Multipurpose Internet Mail Extensions (MIME)?

    a. S/MIME

    b. PGP

    c. SET/MIME

    d. IPSEC

Answer: **a.** S/MIME provides security services such as digital signatures and encryption for MIME-structured e-mail messages. Answer b, Pretty Good Privacy, brings security to e-mail through the use of a symmetric cipher, such as IDEA, to encipher the message, but is not an augmentation of MIME. Answer c is a distractor. Answer d, IPSEC, is not an e-mail protocol but a standard that provides encryption, access control, non-repudiation, and authentication of messages over IP.

4. Which of the following statements is *not* correct about the difference between Layer 2 and Layer 3 tunneling protocols?

    a. Layer 2 tunneling supports multiple payload protocols.

    b. Layer 3 tunneling supports multiple payload protocols.

    c. Layer 3 tunneling protocols typically support only IP networks.

    d. Layer 2 tunneling supports dynamic assignment of client addresses.

Answer: **b.** Layer 2 tunneling supports multiple payload protocols, which makes it easy for tunneling clients to access their corporate networks using IP, IPX, NetBEUI, and so on. In contrast, Layer 3 tunneling protocols, such as IPSec tunnel mode, typically support only target networks that use the IP protocol.

Layer 2 tunneling supports dynamic assignment of client addresses based on the Network Control Protocol (NCP) negotiation mechanism. Generally, Layer 3 tunneling schemes assume that an address has already been assigned prior to initiation of the tunnel.

5. The Wired Equivalency Privacy (WEP) algorithm of the 802.11 Wireless LAN Standard uses which of the following to protect the confidentiality of information being transmitted on the LAN?

   a. A public/private key pair that is shared between a mobile station (for example, a laptop with a wireless Ethernet card) and a base station access point

   b. A digital signature that is sent between a mobile station (for example, a laptop with a wireless Ethernet card) and a base station access point

   c. A secret key that is shared between a mobile station (for example, a laptop with a wireless Ethernet card) and a base station access point

   d. Frequency shift keying (FSK) of the message that is sent between a mobile station (for example, a laptop with a wireless Ethernet card) and a base station access point

Answer: c. Wireless packets are encrypted with a secret key and an Integrity Check (IC) field consisting of a CRC-32 checksum that is attached to the message. WEP uses the RC4 variable key-size stream cipher encryption algorithm. The other answers are distractors.

6. The vulnerability associated with the requirement to change security protocols at a carrier's Wireless Application Protocol (WAP) gateway from the Wireless Transport Layer Security Protocol (WTLS) to SSL or TLS over the wired network is called the _____.

   a. Wired Equivalency Privacy (WEP) gap

   b. Wireless Transaction Protocol (WTP) gap

   c. Wireless Transport Layer Security Protocol (WTLS) gap

   d. Wireless Application Protocol (WAP) gap

Answer: d. The correct answer is d, the WAP gap. The other answers are distractors.

7. Which of the following choices is *not* a Layer 2 tunneling protocol?

   a. PPTP

   b. L2TP

   c. IPSec

   d. L2F

Answer: c. IPSec tunnel mode is an example of a Layer 3 tunneling protocol that encapsulates IP packets in an additional IP header before sending them across an IP internetwork. Point-to-Point Tunneling Protocol (PPTP), Layer 2 Tunneling Protocol (L2TP), and Layer 2 Forwarding (L2F) Protocol all operate at Layer 2.

8. Which statement about Layer 2 tunneling technologies is *not* correct?

    a. Both of the Layer 2 tunnel endpoints must agree to the tunnel and must negotiate configuration variables.

    b. Layer 2 tunnels must be created, maintained, and then terminated.

    c. Layer 2 tunneling technologies generally assume that all of the configuration issues are preconfigured.

    d. Layer 2 tunnels require a tunnel maintenance phase.

Answer: **c.** For Layer 2 tunneling technologies, such as PPTP and L2TP, a tunnel is similar to a session; both of the tunnel endpoints must agree to the tunnel and must negotiate configuration variables, such as address assignment or encryption or compression parameters. In most cases, data transferred across the tunnel is sent using a datagram-based protocol. A tunnel maintenance protocol is used as the mechanism to manage the tunnel.

Layer 3 tunneling technologies generally assume that all of the configuration issues are preconfigured, often by manual processes. For these protocols, there may be no tunnel maintenance phase. For Layer 2 protocols (PPTP and L2TP), however, a tunnel must be created, maintained, and then terminated.

9. Which statement *best* describes PPP?

    a. PPP uses Link Control Protocol (LCP).

    b. PPP was the de facto standard before SLIP.

    c. PPP is a half-duplex protocol.

    d. PPP only uses asynchronous communication.

Answer: **a.** The Point-to-Point Protocol (PPP) uses the Link Control Protocol (LCP) to establish, maintain, and end the physical connection. PPP is a full-duplex protocol and is usually preferred over the earlier de facto standard Serial Line Internet Protocol (SLIP) because it can handle synchronous as well as asynchronous communication.

10. Which of the following statements about CHAP is incorrect?

    a. CHAP sends the password in cleartext.

    b. The password is used to create an MD5 encrypted hash.

    c. CHAP protects against replay attacks.

    d. CHAP protects against remote client impersonation.

Answer: **a.** CHAP is an improvement over PAP because the cleartext password is not sent over the link. Instead, the password is used to create an encrypted hash from the original challenge. CHAP protects against replay attacks by using an arbitrary challenge string for each authentication attempt. CHAP protects against remote client impersonation by unpredictably sending repeated challenges to the remote client throughout the duration of the connection.

11. Which of the following choices is *not* considered a basic VPN requirement?

   a. Multiprotocol support

   b. Data encryption

   c. Clear-text passwords

   d. User authentication

Answer: c. A basic VPN solution should provide user authentication, address management, data encryption, key management, and multiprotocol support. Answer c is a distractor.

12. Which PPP authentication method sends passwords in cleartext?

   a. PAP

   b. CHAP

   c. MS-CHAP

   d. MS-CHAP v2

Answer: a. Password Authentication Protocol (PAP) is a cleartext authentication scheme. When the network access server (NAS) requests the user name and the password, PAP returns them in unencrypted "clear" text. The other three answers all use a hash variation to encrypt the transmitted password.

13. Which statement best describes a replay attack?

   a. A third party takes over an authenticated connection.

   b. An intruder tries many passwords.

   c. The intruder waits until the connection has been authenticated.

   d. An intruder sends captured packets at a later time to create an authenticated connection.

Answer: d. A replay attack occurs when a third party monitors a successful connection and uses captured packets to play back the remote client's response to create an authenticated connection. Answer b describes password guessing, and answers a and c describe elements of remote client impersonation.

14. The algorithm of the 802.11 Wireless LAN Standard that is used to protect transmitted information from disclosure is called the _____.

   a. Wireless Application Environment (WAE)

   b. Wireless Transaction Protocol (WTP)

   c. Wired Equivalency Privacy (WEP)

   d. Wireless Transport Layer Security Protocol (WTLS)

Answer: **c.** WEP is designed to prevent the violation of the confidentiality of data transmitted over the wireless LAN. Another feature of WEP is to prevent unauthorized access to the network.

15. Which statement about a VPN tunnel is *not* correct?

    a. A VPN tunnel can be created by installing software or hardware agents on the client or network.

    b. A VPN tunnel can be created by implementing key and certificate exchange systems.

    c. A tunnel maintenance protocol is used as the mechanism to manage the tunnel.

    d. A VPN tunnel can be created by implementing IPSec devices only.

Answer: **d.** Protocols other than IPSec are commonly used in VPNs, such as PPTP and L2TP. The other three answers are all correct.

16. Which of the following statements describing SSL is *not* true?

    a. SSL uses public key cryptography for secret key exchange

    b. SSL uses a message authentication code (MAC) to verify integrity

    c. SSL uses private key encryption to ensure the confidentiality of transmitted information

    d. SSL provides authentication in one direction only

Answer: **d.** SSL provides for mutual authentication using public key digital signature algorithms such as DSS and RSA.

17. The SSL/TLS protocol comprises two layers. Which choice correctly names these two layers?

    a. Record Protocol and Handshake Protocol

    b. Record Protocol and Authentication Protocol

    c. Exchange Protocol and Authentication Protocol

    d. Exchange Protocol and Handshake Protocol

Answer: **a.** The SSL/TLS Record Protocol is used for encapsulation of higher-level protocols (such as the SSL/TLS Handshake Protocol). The SSL Handshake Protocol is used for client/server mutual authentication, exchange of cryptographic keys, and negotiation of a cryptographic algorithm. Answers b, c, and d are distractors.

18. Which of the following designations on a Web page indicates that HTTP is being used with SSL?

    a. S-HTTP

    b. HTTP/S

    c. SSL/TLS

    d. HTTP/SSL

Answer: **b.** Answer a refers to secure HTTP. S-HTTP is a flexible protocol that is designed to provide secure messaging over HTTP. S-HTTP uses only symmetric key encryption and does not use public key encryption for key exchanges. Answers c and d are distractors.

19. Which of the following statements is *not* true regarding instant messaging (IM)?

    a. It supports the real-time exchange of messages on the Internet.

    b. A user logs on to an instant messaging server and is authenticated by the server.

    c. Communication takes place only between two individuals at a time.

    d. Messages from one user to another are routed through the instant messaging server.

Answer: **d.** The user's client knows the IP address and port number of each of the other users that are logged on to the IM server. Thus, a user can send a message directly to another user without using the IM server as an intermediary. Relative to answer c, real-time messaging among more than two individuals is called a *chat room*.

20. If an Ethernet Network Interface Card (NIC) is programmed to read all messages that it sees on the network, it is said to be operating in what?

    a. Acquisition mode

    b. Broadcast mode

    c. Promiscuous mode

    d. Monitoring mode

Answer: **c.** In promiscuous mode, the NIC acquires all messages, regardless of the 48-bit media access control (MAC) address in the message header. The other answers are distractors.

21. Which choice refers to a standard format whereby Web sites can impart their privacy policies to users through a machine-readable syntax?

   a. Platform for Privacy Preferences
   b. Pretty Good Privacy
   c. Post Office Protocol
   d. Privacy Practices Protocol

Answer: a. The Platform for Privacy Practices (P3P) was developed by the World Wide Web Consortium (W3C). P3P also enables users to specify their privacy preferences through a P3P-enabled browser such as Internet Explorer version 6.0 for comparison to a Web site's privacy practices. Answer b refers to a publicly available encryption algorithm, and answer c refers to an e-mail protocol. The Post Office Protocol version 3 (POP3-RFC 1939) provides a workstation with the capability to dynamically access a maildrop on a server host in order to retrieve mail that the server is holding for it. Answer d is a distractor.

22. Which of the following statements is *not* true regarding JavaScript?

   a. On the client-side, JavaScript is embedded in HTML pages and is interpreted by the browser at runtime.
   b. JavaScript programs running on the server-side are compiled into byte-code executable files.
   c. JavaScript has strong type checking and static typing.
   d. JavaScripts are easier to author than Java programs.

Answer: c. Java has strong type checking and static typing. JavaScript does not.

23. Which of the following statements regarding ActiveX is *not* true?

   a. ActiveX is an environment under which programs are managed and run.
   b. ActiveX programs are downloaded directly to a user's hard drive.
   c. ActiveX does not rely on the digital signing of trusted components.
   d. An ActiveX component carries a security level designation that defines if and when the component can be safely executed.

Answer: c. Because a trusted ActiveX component has full access to the user's hard drive, ActiveX relies on digital signing to verify that trusted components are safe to execute.

24. A component that is used to allow a Java plug-in to access a user's hard drive is called a _____.

  a. Signed applet

  b. Cookie

  c. Buffer

  d. Gateway interface

Answer: **a.** A digitally signed applet can be developed through the use of RSA public key encryption and browser signing tools. Then, an Object Signing Certificate must be obtained from a trusted RSA Certificate Authority. When a signed applet is downloaded, user plug-in software will determine if the CA is valid and trusted. Answer b, a cookie, is a text file that resides on a user's browser and gathers information about the user's Web browsing experiences. Answers c and d are distractors.

25. Which of the following statements regarding the Common Gateway Interface (CGI) is *not* true?

  a. CGI is a standard that defines how HTTP or Web servers interface with client applications.

  b. A CGI program is executable and runs on the server in real time.

  c. CGI does not support the dynamic generation of HTML documents.

  d. A CGI program is invoked when a client requests information from a server.

Answer: **c.** One of the capabilities that CGI programs provide is the generation of dynamic information when a client requests service from a Web server.

26. What is PERL?

  a. A compiled language that is commonly used to write CGI programs

  b. A scripting language that is commonly used to write CGI programs

  c. A compiled language that is suited to text processing

  d. A protocol used to transmit e-mail messages over the Internet

Answer: **b.** PERL is an interpreted language that was originally developed to operate on text files on UNIX platforms. Because of its capabilities, PERL is widely used to develop CGI programs. The other answers are distractors.

27. Which of the following items is *not* a restricted forwarding option provided by the SMTP Relay protocol?

  a. Relay mail for local hosts only

  b. No mail relay

  c. All mail relay

  d. Relay mail for

Answer: **c.** The correct answer is a distractor. Answer a is the SMTP option that limits relay forwarding only to mail hosts on the local server. Answer b applies when all users send and receive e-mail from local hosts running on the SMTP server. Answer d is the option that provides for the specification of a range of IP addresses to which e-mail can be forwarded.

28. Which of the following is *not* a valid step that is performed by SSL/TLS-enabled clients to authenticate a server using digital certificates?

    a. Verifying that the current date and time are within the certificate's validity period

    b. Verifying that the domain name in the server's certificate corresponds to the domain name of the server

    c. Using the CA's private key to validate the CA's digital signature for the server's certificate

    d. Verifying that the issuing CA is on the list of trusted CAs maintained by the client

Answer: **c.** The CA's public key is used to validate the CA's digital signature.

29. Which choice is *not* a component of an LDAP attribute?

    a. A Distinguished Name

    b. A Designated Name

    c. A type

    d. A set of values corresponding to a type

Answer: **b.** The correct answer is b, a distractor.

30. Which of the following items is *not* a characteristic of LDAP?

    a. It is platform-independent.

    b. It supports confidentiality, authentication, and integrity.

    c. Searches are based on an entry's object class and attributes.

    d. It is not suitable for implementation at small, workgroup levels.

Answer: **d.** LDAP can be implemented on large public servers, organizational servers, and workgroup servers.

Chapter 3: Infrastructure Security

1. Which two TCP/UDP ports does FTP use?

    a. 22 and 23

    b. 23 and 25

    c. 20 and 21

    d. 67 and 65

Answer: c. FTP uses two ports, port 21 for authentication and port 20 for the actual data transfer. Port 22 is used by SSH, port 23 is used by TELNET, and port 25 is used by SMTP. Ports 67 and 68 are used by DHCP, server and client, respectively.

2. What is one of the most common drawbacks to using a dual-homed host firewall?

    a. The examination of the packet at the Network layer introduces latency.

    b. The examination of the packet at the Application layer introduces latency.

    c. The ACLs must be manually maintained on the host.

    d. Internal routing may accidentally become enabled.

Answer: d. A dual-homed host uses two NICs to attach to two separate networks, commonly a trusted network and an untrusted network. It's important that the internal routing function of the host be disabled to create an Application-layer chokepoint and filter packets. Many systems come with routing enabled by default, such as IP forwarding, which makes the firewall useless.

3. Which TCP/UDP port range should a security administrator be concerned about intruders scanning?

    a. 1–512

    b. 0–65535

    c. 513–1023

    d. 1025–65535

Answer: b. All TCP/UDP ports up to 65535 are vulnerable to port scanning. Port numbers are divided into three ranges: the Well-Known Ports, the Registered Ports, and the Dynamic and/or Private Ports. The Well-Known Ports are those from 0 through 1023. The Registered Ports are those from 1024 through 49151. The Dynamic and/or Private Ports are those from 49152 through 65535.

4. Which LAN topology listed is least vulnerable to a single point of failure?

   a. Ethernet Bus

   b. PPTP

   c. LDAP

   d. FDDI

Answer: **d.** FDDI employs a second ring that remains dormant until an error condition is detected. The primary ring is then isolated and the secondary ring begins working, thus creating an extremely fault-tolerant network. This fault tolerance is occasionally overridden in certain implementations that use both rings to create more bandwidth.

5. Which choice below is *not* an element of a fiber optic cable?

   a. Core

   b. Medium

   c. Jacket

   d. Cladding

Answer: **b.** Fiber optic cable has three basic physical elements: the core, the cladding, and the jacket. Answer b is a distractor.

6. Which type of cabling is most commonly installed in new LAN infrastructures?

   a. ThickNet

   b. Token Ring

   c. Twinax

   d. Twisted pair

Answer: **d.** Category 5 Unshielded Twisted Pair (UTP) is rated for very high data throughput (100 Mbps) at short distances (up to 100 meters), and is the standard cable type for Ethernet installations.

7. Which protocol is used to resolve a known MAC address to an unknown IP address?

   a. ARP

   b. RARP

   c. ICMP

   d. TFTP

Answer: **c.** The Reverse Address Resolution Protocol (RARP) is commonly used on diskless machines when the MAC is known but not the IP address. It asks a RARP server to provide a valid IP address.

8. Which choice defines an interface to the first commercially successful connection-oriented packet-switching network?

    a. X.25

    b. Frame Relay

    c. SMDS

    d. ATM

Answer: **a.** X.25 defines an interface to the first commercially successful connection-oriented packet-switching network, in which the packets travel over virtual circuits.

9. Which statement below is *not* correct regarding VLANs?

    a. A VLAN restricts flooding to only those ports included in the VLAN.

    b. A VLAN is a network segmented physically, not logically.

    c. A VLAN is more secure when implemented in conjunction with private port switching.

    d. A "closed" VLAN configuration is a very secure configuration.

Answer: **b.** A VLAN is segmented logically, rather than physically. The other three answers are true statements about VLANs.

10. Which protocol below pertains to e-mail?

    a. SMTP

    b. SNMP

    c. CHAP

    d. PPTP

Answer: **a.** The Simple Mail Transfer Protocol (RFCs 821 and 1869) is used by a mail gateway to deliver e-mail over the Internet.

11. Which statement is true about the SOCKS protocol?

    a. It is sometimes referred to as a stateful inspection firewall.

    b. It uses an ESP for authentication and encryption.

    c. It operates in the Data Link layer of the OSI model.

    d. Network applications need to be SOCKS-ified to operate.

Answer: **d.** SOCKS replaces the standard network systems calls with its own calls. These calls open connections to a SOCKS proxy server for client authentication transparently to the user. Common network utilities, such as TELNET or FTP, need to be SOCKS-ified, or have their network calls altered to recognize SOCKS proxy calls.

12. Which level of RAID actually lessens fault tolerance?

    a. RAID 0

    b. RAID 1

    c. RAID 3

    d. RAID 5

Answer: **a.** RAID 0 provides some performance gains by striping the data across multiple drives, but reduces fault tolerance since the failure of any single drive disables the whole volume.

13. Which choice is a link-state hierarchical routing algorithm intended as a successor to RIP?

    a. RIP

    b. OSPF

    c. IGRP

    d. EAP

Answer: **b.** Open Shortest Path First (OSPF) is a link-state hierarchical routing algorithm intended as a successor to RIP. It features least-cost routing, multipath routing, and load balancing.

14. Which category of UTP wiring was originally rated for 16 Mbps Token Ring LANs?

    a. Category 1

    b. Category 3

    c. Category 4

    d. Category 5

Answer: **c.** Category 4 twisted-pair wire was the first UTP rated for 16 Mbps and is used in 4/16 Mbps Token Ring LANs.

15. Which process below operates primarily at the Data Link layer?

    a. Internetwork packet routing

    b. LAN bridging

    c. SMTP Gateway services

    d. Signal regeneration and repeating

Answer: **b.** Bridging is a Data Link layer function.

16. In the DoD reference model, which layer conforms to the OSI Network layer?

   a. Process/Application layer

   b. Host-to-Host layer

   c. Internet layer

   d. Network Access layer

Answer: c. The DoD reference model Internet layer corresponds to the OSI's Network layer.

17. Which IEEE protocol defines wireless connectivity?

   a. IEEE 802.5

   b. IEEE 802.3

   c. IEEE 802.11

   d. IEEE 802.1D

Answer: c. IEEE 802.11 is the IEEE standard that specifies 1 Mbps and 2 Mbps wireless connectivity in the 2.4 MHz ISM (Industrial, Scientific, Medical) band.

18. Which type of routing maintains a copy of every other router's Link State Protocol (LSP) frame?

   a. Static routing

   b. Distance vector routing

   c. Link state routing

   d. Dynamic control protocol routing

Answer: c. Link state routers function like distance vector routers but only use first-hand information when building routing tables by maintaining a copy of every other router's Link State Protocol (LSP) frame. This helps eliminate routing errors and considerably lessens convergence time.

19. Which TCP/IP protocol operates at the OSI Transport layer?

   a. FTP

   b. IP

   c. TCP

   d. Bridging

Answer: c. Both TCP and UDP operate at the OSI Transport layer, which is similar to the TCP/IP Host-to-Host layer.

20. Which statement is true regarding the difference between TCP and UDP?

   a. UDP is considered a connectionless protocol and TCP is connection-oriented.

   b. TCP is considered a connectionless protocol, and UDP is connection-oriented.

   c. UDP acknowledges the receipt of packets, and TCP does not.

   d. TCP is sometimes referred to as an unreliable protocol.

Answer: **a.** As opposed to the Transmission Control Protocol (TCP), the User Datagram Protocol (UDP) is a connectionless protocol. It does not sequence the packets, acknowledge the receipt of packets, and is referred to as an unreliable protocol.

21. Which media control is the least secure method to prevent data remanence on magnetic tapes or floppy disks?

   a. Formatting the media at least seven times

   b. Degaussing the media

   c. Applying a concentration of hydriodic acid (55 percent to 58 percent solution) to the a gamma ferric oxide disk surface

   d. Making sure the disk is re-circulated as quickly as possible to prevent object reuse

Answer: **a.** To purge the media, the DoD requires overwriting with a pattern, then its complement, and finally with another pattern. For example, overwrite first with 0011 0101, followed by 1100 1010, then 1001 0111. Seven times is recommended.

22. Which choice is an example of a personnel control?

   a. Sanitizing the media before disposition

   b. Printing to a printer in a secured room

   c. Physically protecting copies of backup media

   d. Conducting background checks on individuals

Answer: **d.** Answer d is a personnel control. The other three answers are examples of media controls.

23. When should a service pack be installed on a production server?

   a. Immediately when released

   b. After testing on a test server

   c. Only if the service pack addresses a known vulnerability in the system

   d. Never, if the production server is operating properly

Answer: **b.** It is not advisable to apply service packs immediately upon release, unless the service pack addresses an urgent vulnerability that has been identified in the production environment. Install the service pack or hot fix first in a test environment to see its impact on applications, then install on a production server.

24. Which choice *best* describes coaxial cable?

   a. Coax consists of two insulated wires wrapped around each other in a regular spiral pattern.

   b. Coax consists of a hollow outer cylindrical conductor surrounding a single, inner conductor.

   c. Coax does not require the fixed spacing between connections that UTP requires.

   d. Coax carries signals as light waves.

Answer: **b.** Coax consists of a hollow outer cylindrical conductor surrounding a single, inner conductor. The other choices are incorrect.

25. Which firewall type uses a dynamic state table to inspect the content of packets?

   a. A packet filtering firewall

   b. An application-level firewall

   c. A circuit-level firewall

   d. A stateful inspection firewall

Answer: **d.** A stateful inspection firewall intercepts incoming packets at the Network level, and then uses an Inspection Engine to extract state-related information from upper layers. It maintains the information in a dynamic state table and evaluates subsequent connection attempts.

26. Which statement is *not* accurate in describing the difference between 802.11b WLAN ad hoc and infrastructure modes?

   a. Infrastructure mode uses an access point to communicate to the wired network.

   b. Wireless nodes can only communicate peer-to-peer in the infrastructure mode.

   c. Wireless nodes can communicate peer-to-peer in the ad hoc mode.

   d. Access points are a vulnerability to the wired LAN.

Answer: **b.** In infrastructure mode, the wireless nodes communicate to an access point, which operates much like a bridge or router and manages traffic between the wireless network and the wired network. The backdoor that the access point opens into the wired network is a serious security concern.

27. Which statement is *not* accurate about the concept of object reuse?

   a. Object reuse protects against physical attacks on the storage medium.

   b. Object reuse ensures that users do not obtain residual information from system resources.

   c. Object reuse applies to all primary and secondary storage media.

   d. Data remanence vulnerability can result from improperly controlled object reuse.

Answer: **a.** Object reuse does not necessarily protect against physical attacks on the storage medium. Object reuse mechanisms ensure that system resources are allocated and reassigned among authorized users in a way that prevents the leak of sensitive information, and ensure that the authorized user of the system does not obtain residual information from system resources. Object reuse applies to all primary and secondary storage media, such as removable media, fixed media, real and virtual main memory (including registers), and cache memory. Data remanence vulnerability can result from improperly controlled object reuse.

28. Which of the choices is an OSI reference model Presentation layer protocol, standard, or interface?

   a. RPC

   b. MIDI

   c. ASP

   d. SQL

Answer: **b.** The Musical Instrument Digital Interface (MIDI) standard is a Presentation layer standard for digitized music. The other answers are all Session layer protocols or standards.

29. Which IEEE protocol defines wireless transmission in the 2.4 GHz band with data rates up to 54 Mbps?

   a. IEEE 802.11a

   b. IEEE 802.11b

   c. IEEE 802.11g

   d. IEEE 802.15

Answer: **c.** IEEE 802.11g is a new standard that offers wireless transmission over relatively short distances at speeds from 20 Mbps up to 54 Mbps and operates in the 2.4 GHz range (and is therefore expected to be backward-compatible with existing 802.11b-based networks). Answer a, IEEE 802.11a, specifies high-speed wireless connectivity in the 5 GHz band using Orthogonal Frequency Division Multiplexing with data rates up to 54 Mbps. Answer b, IEEE 802.11b, specifies high-speed wireless connectivity in the 2.4 GHz ISM band up to 11 Mbps. Answer d, IEEE 802.15, defines wireless personal area networks (WPANs), such as Bluetooth, in the 2.4–2.5 GHz band.

30. Which choice relates to analog dial-up hacking?

   a. War dialing

   b. War walking

   c. War driving

   d. War chalking

Answer: **a.** War dialing is a method that enables someone to hack into computers by using a software program that automatically calls a large pool of telephone numbers, searching for those that have a modem attached. The other three choices all relate to wireless network scanning.

Chapter 4: Basics of Cryptography

1. Which of the following statements is *not* true regarding the Exclusive Or function?

   a. 1 + 1 = 0

   b. 1 + 0 = 1

   c. 0 + 0 = 0

   d. 1 + 1 = 1

Answer: **d.** The XOR operation results in a 0 if the two input bits are identical and a 1 if one of the bits is a 1 and the other is a 0.

2. The Secure Hash Algorithm–1 (SHA–1) is specified in the _____.

   a. Data Encryption Standard

   b. Digital Signature Standard

   c. Digital Encryption Standard

   d. Advanced Encryption Standard

Answer: **b.** The correct answer is b. Answer a refers to DES, a symmetric encryption algorithm; answer c is a distractor; answer d is the Advanced Encryption Standard, which has replaced DES.

3. The Digital Signature Standard (DSS) uses which digital signature algorithm(s)?

   a. Either the RSA digital signature algorithm or the Digital Signature Algorithm (DSA)

   b. DSA only

   c. RSA only

   d. Either the El Gamal digital signature algorithm or the Digital Signature Algorithm (DSA)

Answer: **a.** The correct answer is a. DSS specifies that either the RSA or DSA algorithms can be used.

4. The RSA digital signature algorithm and the DSA use which of the following hash algorithms?

    a. MD5

    b. MD4

    c. SHA–1

    d. HAVAL

Answer: **c.** The RSA digital signature algorithm and the DSA both use the Secure Hash Algorithm (SHA–1) described in FIPS 180 (National Institute of Standards and Technology, NIST FIPS PUB 180, "Secure Hash Standard," U.S. Department of Commerce, May 1993). SHA–1 sequentially processes blocks of 512 bits and generates a message digest of 160 bits in length when any message less than 2^{64} bits is provided as an input.

5. Elliptic curve algorithms in public key cryptography are based on _____.

    a. Prime factors of very large numbers

    b. The discrete logarithm problem

    c. Modular addition

    d. The Knapsack problem

Answer: **b.** Modular exponentiation that is used in the elliptic curve algorithm is the analog of the modular discrete logarithm problem. Answer a is incorrect because prime factors are involved with RSA public key systems; answer c is incorrect because modular addition in elliptic curves is the analog of modular multiplication; and answer d is incorrect because the Knapsack problem is not an elliptic curve problem.

6. The U.S. Escrowed Encryption Standard employed which of the following symmetric key algorithms?

    a. IDEA

    b. DES

    c. 3 DES

    d. SKIPJACK

Answer: **d.** The SKIPJACK algorithm is specified in the Clipper Chip. Answers a, b, and c are other symmetric key algorithms.

7. Key clustering is _____.

   a. The condition where many keys in use are very similar
   b. When one key encrypts a plaintext message into two different ciphertexts
   c. When two different keys encrypt a plaintext message into the same ciphertext
   d. Escrowing of keys

Answer: **c.** The other answers are distractors.

8. A cipher that breaks a message into fixed length units for encryption is called a _____.

   a. Block cipher
   b. An asymmetric key algorithm
   c. Message digest
   d. Hash function

Answer: **a.** Answer b is incorrect because a block cipher applies to symmetric key algorithms; answer c describes the result of a hashing operation where a variable-length of plaintext is converted into a fixed length message digest. Answer d refers to the hash function that generates the message digest.

9. Digital signatures are created using _____.

   a. Private key cryptography
   b. Public key cryptography
   c. DES
   d. 3 DES

Answer: **b.** Answer a is incorrect because private key cryptography does not create digital signatures; answers c and d are incorrect because DES and 3 DES are private key cryptosystems and, therefore, follow the same logic as in a.

10. Which of the following is *not* an asymmetric key algorithm?

    a. Knapsack
    b. RSA
    c. Diffie-Hellman
    d. Rijndael

Answer: **d.** The correct answer is the Advanced Encryption Standard (AES). The other answers are examples of asymmetric key systems.

11. A hybrid cryptosystem employs which of the following methodologies?

    a. Private key encryption to encrypt and send the secret key that will be used to encrypt and send the message using public key encryption.

    b. Public key encryption to encrypt and send the secret key that will be used to encrypt and send the message using private key encryption.

    c. Public key encryption to encrypt and send the secret key that will be used to encrypt and send the message using public key encryption.

    d. Private key encryption to encrypt and send the secret key that will be used to encrypt and send the message using private key encryption.

Answer: **b.** Public key encryption is slower than private key encryption. In a hybrid system, public key encryption is used to encrypt and send the smaller secret key, while private key encryption uses that secret key to encrypt much larger volumes of data to be securely transmitted.

12. In public key cryptography, which of the following statements is *not* true?

    a. A message encrypted with Bob's public key can only be decrypted with Bob's private key.

    b. A message encrypted with Bob's private key can only be decrypted with Bob's public key.

    c. A message encrypted with Bob's public key can be decrypted with Bob's public key.

    d. Given Bob's public key, it is very difficult or impossible to determine his private key.

Answer: **c.** All the other answers are true.

13. What is the block length of Advanced Encryption Standard (AES)?

    a. 64 bits

    b. 128 bits

    c. Variable

    d. 256 bits

Answer: **b.** The correct answer is b.

14. Which of the following is *not* one of the AES key sizes?

    a. 128 bits

    b. 512 bits

    c. 192 bits

    d. 256 bits

Answer: b. AES is made up of three key sizes, 128-, 192-, and 256-bits, with a fixed block size of 128 bits. Depending on which of the three keys is used, the standard may be referred to as "AES-128," "AES-192," or "AES-256."

15. A polyalphabetic cipher is also known as _____.

    a. One-time pad

    b. Vernam cipher

    c. Steganography

    d. Vigenère cipher

Answer: d. The Vigenère cipher substitutes letters from multiple alphabets instead of a single alphabet, as in monoalphabetic substitution. The use of multiple alphabets thwarts attacks based on the frequency of letters used in a given alphabet. Answer a is incorrect because a one-time pad uses a random key with a length equal to the plaintext message and is used only once. Answer b is incorrect because it applies to stream ciphers that are XORed with a random key string. Answer c is the process of sending a message with no indication that a message even exists.

16. A method that is used to securely transmit secret messages and is based on keeping the existence of the messages unknown is called _____.

    a. Private key encryption

    b. Blind signatures

    c. Steganography

    d. A zero-knowledge proof

Answer: c. Examples of steganography include imbedding data into digital images and shrinking information into microdots.

17. Confusion in block cipher algorithms does which of the following?

    a. Hides the relationship between the plaintext and ciphertext

    b. Spreads the influence of the plaintext over many ciphertext characters

    c. Disguises the fact that a cipher is being used

    d. Hides the relationship between the plaintext and the key

Answer: **a.** Answer b defines diffusion and the other answers are distractors.

18. Which of the following modes is *not* a DES mode?

    a. Cipher Block Chaining

    b. Electronic Code Book

    c. Output Feedback

    d. Electronic Feedback

Answer: **d.** There is no DES Electronic Feedback mode.

19. Which of the following is true?

    a. The work factor of triple DES is the same as for double DES.

    b. The work factor of single DES is the same as for triple DES.

    c. The work factor of double DES is the same as for single DES.

    d. No successful attacks have been reported against double DES.

Answer: **c.** The Meet-in-the-Middle attack has been successfully applied to double DES and the work factor is equivalent to that of single DES. Thus, answer d is incorrect. Answer a is false because the work factor of triple DES is greater than that for double DES. In triple DES, three levels of encryption and/or decryption are applied to the message. The work factor of double DES is equivalent to the work factor of single DES. Answer b is false because the work factor of single DES is less than for triple DES. In triple DES, three levels of encryption and/or decryption are applied to the message in triple DES.

20. Which of the following characteristics does *not* apply to a one-time pad, if it is used properly?

    a. The key is truly random with no repeating sequences or patterns.

    b. It can be used, carefully, more than once.

    c. It is unbreakable.

    d. The key must be of the same length as the message to be encrypted.

Answer: **b.** The one-time pad should be used only once, less the key become compromised. If the one-time-pad is used only once and its corresponding key is truly random and does not have repeating characters, it is unbreakable. The key must be the same length as the message.

21. The key length of the DES key is _____.

    a. 128 bits

    b. 56 bits

    c. 64 bits

    d. 256 bits

Answer: **b.**

22. In generating a digitally signed message using a hash function, _____.

    a. The message is encrypted in the public key of the sender.

    b. The message digest is encrypted in the private key of the sender.

    c. The message digest is encrypted in the public key of the sender.

    d. The message is encrypted in the private key of the sender.

Answer: **b.** The hash function generates a message digest. The message digest is encrypted with the private key of the sender. Thus, if the message digest can be opened with the sender's public key (known to all), the message must have come from the sender. The message is not encrypted with the private key because the message is usually longer than the message digest and would take more computing resources to encrypt and decrypt. Because the message digest uniquely characterizes the message, it can also be used to verify the integrity of the message.

Answers a and c are not correct because a message encrypted in the public key of the sender can only be read by using the sender's private key. Because the sender is the only one who knows this key, no one else can read the message. Answer d is incorrect because the message is not encrypted, but the message digest is encrypted.

23. The difficulty of finding the prime factors of very large numbers is the strong, one-way function used in which of the following public key cryptosystems?

    a. El Gamal

    b. Diffie-Hellman

    c. RSA

    d. Elliptic curve

Answer: **c.** The other answers are based on the difficulty of finding discrete logarithms in a finite field.

24. Elliptic curve cryptosystems _____.

    a. Have a higher strength per bit than an RSA cryptosystem

    b. Have a lower strength per bit than an RSA cryptosystem

    c. Cannot be used to implement digital signatures

    d. Cannot be used to implement encryption

Answer: **a.** It is more difficult to compute elliptic curve discrete logarithms than conventional discrete logarithms or factoring. Smaller key sizes in the elliptic curve implementation can yield higher levels of security. Therefore, answer b is incorrect. Answers c and d are incorrect because elliptic curve cryptosystems can be used for digital signatures and encryption.

25. Digital certification, certification authority, timestamping, Lightweight Directory Access Protocol (LDAP), and non-repudiation support a portion of what services?

    a. Cryptanalysis

    b. Public Key Infrastructure

    c. Steganography

    d. Disaster recovery

Answer: **b.** PKI describes the integration of digital certificates, digital signatures, and other services necessary to support e-commerce. The other answers are distractors.

26. In an X.500 directory, the Directory Server Agents (DSAs) exchange and share information through which of the following mechanisms?

    a. Shadowing

    b. Chaining

    c. Transitioning

    d. Depositing

Answer: **b.**

27. Version 2 of the X.509 certificate is concerned with _____.

    a. The reuse of names

    b. Certificate extensions

    c. Message digests

    d. Revoked certificates

Answer: **a.**

28. Version 3 of the X.509 certificate is concerned with _____.

   a. The reuse of names

   b. Certificate extensions

   c. Message digests

   d. Revoked certificates

Answer: **b.**

29. Which of the following is *not* a type of X.509 certificate?

   a. Rollover certificate

   b. End entity certificate

   c. Confidential certificate

   d. CA certificate

Answer: **c.** It is a distractor. Answer a, rollover certificate, is issued by a CA to transition from an old public key to a new public key; answer b, end entity certificates, are issued to entities that are not CAs. Answer d refers to certificates issued to CAs.

30. A Certificate Revocation List (CRL) that is generated by a CA that covers its entire population is known as what type of CRL?

   a. Critical

   b. Global

   c. Complete

   d. Full

Answer: **d.**

Chapter 5: Operational/Organizational Security

1. Which of the following statements is *true*?

    a. An organizational security policy is a detailed and specific listing of management's requirements and its implementation is mandatory.

    b. An organizational security policy is a general statement of management's intent, and its implementation is in the form of guidelines.

    c. An organizational security policy is a general statement of management's intent, and its implementation is mandatory.

    d. An organizational security policy is a detailed and specific listing of management's requirements, and its implementation is in the form of guidelines.

Answer: c. The organizational security policy is a document outlining management's intent in general terms and its implementation is mandatory. Therefore, the other answers are incorrect. Guidelines, referred to in answers b and d, are non-compulsory, recommended actions that take into account the different types of information systems.

2. Which of the following definitions *best* describes standards?

    a. The compulsory use of specific hardware and software technologies in a uniform manner

    b. Non-mandatory guidelines for the use of specific hardware and software technologies in a uniform manner

    c. Detailed step-by-step actions that must be accomplished

    d. Detailed step-by-step actions that are presented as nonmandatory guidelines

Answer: a. Answer b is incorrect. Answer c defines procedures. Thus, answers c and d are incorrect.

3. The definition "describe how to implement security mechanisms to ensure that security is being accomplished in a uniform manner on the various platforms and operating systems throughout the enterprise" applies to which of the following terms?

    a. Baselines

    b. Guidelines

    c. Procedures

    d. Standard recommendations

Answer: a. Answers b and c are discussed in Questions 1 and 2, respectively. Answer d is a distractor.

4. The statement "The user must take full responsibility for his or her actions in using a computer account and accept all recourses for their actions." is an example of which of the following administrative policies?

   a. Prudent use

   b. Due diligence

   c. Due care

   d. Acceptable use

Answer: **d.** An acceptable or appropriate use policy details the conditions to which a user must agree to use an account on an information system. Answer a is a distractor, and answers b and c refer to the requirement that an individual or organization engage in good business practices relative to the organization's industry. This concept is related to the prudent man rule, which requires senior officials to perform their duties with the care that ordinary, prudent people would exercise under similar circumstances.

5. Privacy is defined as an individual's right to protection from unauthorized disclosure of his personally identifiable information (PII). Which of the following items is *not* one of the fundamental privacy principles?

   a. Notice

   b. Recount

   c. Choice

   d. Security

Answer: **b.** Answer a refers to the privacy principle regarding providing notice of collection, use and disclosure of personally identifiable information (PII). Answer c is the choice to opt out or opt in regarding disclosure of PII to third parties, and answer d is the protection of PII from unauthorized disclosure.

6. The following items are typical components of what type of policy?

   - The type of information collected, such as name, address, credit card number, phone numbers, and so on

   - Information gathered through cookies and Web server logs and how that information is used

   - How information is shared with affiliates and strategic partners

   - Mechanisms to secure information transmissions, such as encryption and digital signatures

a. Fair use

b. Transaction

c. Security

d. Privacy

Answer: **d.** Answers a and b are distractors, and answer c refers to the protection of the confidentiality, integrity, and availability of information.

7. Which of the following areas is *not* addressed in the Health Insurance Portability and Accountability Act (HIPAA), Administrative Simplification Title?

   a. Privacy

   b. Security

   c. Costs

   d. Electronic transactions and code sets

Answer: **c.** It is a distractor.

8. What specification defines how Web sites can express their privacy practices in a standard format that can be retrieved automatically and interpreted easily by user agents?

   a. The Platform for Privacy Preferences (P3P)

   b. Web Privacy Standard (WPS)

   c. Web Privacy Platform (WPP)

   d. European Union (EU) Privacy Principles

Answer: **a.** P3P user agents allow users to be informed of site practices (in both machine- and human-readable formats). Then, privacy decisions can be made and automated based on these practices when appropriate. Answers b and c are distractors. Answer d refers to the European Union (EU) privacy principles that are designed to protect individually identifiable information.

9. What administrative control divides responsibility among a number of different individuals?

   a. Need-to-know

   b. Separation of duties

   c. Least privilege

   d. Least authority

Answer: **b.** Answers a and c refer to providing the minimum information required for an individual to perform his or her assigned tasks. Answer d is a distractor.

10. The overwriting of data media (primarily magnetic) intended to be reused in the same organization or monitored environment is known as what?

    a. Purging

    b. Destruction

    c. Removing

    d. Clearing

Answer: **d.** Answer a, purging, is the degaussing or overwriting of media intended to be removed from a monitored environment, such as during resale (laptops) or donations to charity. Answer b, destruction, refers to completely destroying the media, and therefore the residual data. Answer c is a distractor.

11. The Carnegie Mellon University CERT Coordination Center (CERT/CC) recommends which of the following sets of incident response practices?

    a. Prepare, notify, follow-up

    b. Prepare, handle, follow-up

    c. Notify, handle, follow-up

    d. Prepare, handle, notify

Answer: **b.** The other answers are distractors.

12. Which of the following classifications is best described as "responsible for ensuring that the appropriate security controls are in place, for assigning the initial classification to the data to be protected, for approving access requests from other parts of the organization, and for periodically reviewing the data classifications and access rights?"

    a. Custodian

    b. Security analyst

    c. Owner

    d. User supervisor

Answer: **c.** Answer a, custodian, is responsible for back up, retention, and recovery of data. Security analyst, answer b, determines the strategies for achieving data security. In answer d, the supervisor of the user has the responsibility for user IDs, informing other relevant organizational entities of a change in the user's status, reporting of security incidents, and security awareness training.

13. Which of the following is a potential vulnerability when using single sign-on (SSO)?

   a. The ability to use stronger passwords

   b. Easier administration of changing or deleting passwords

   c. The user can freely roam the network resources without any restrictions

   d. Requires less time to access resources

Answer: c. If a cracker makes it past the authentication process for the single sign-on password, he or she can access numerous network resources and may not be traced.

14. In what type of control can administrators and/or owners of information specify the privileges assigned to a subject to access that information?

   a. Role-based

   b. Discretionary

   c. Mandatory

   d. Supervisory

Answer: b. Discretionary controls are not based on a policy, and are assigned at the discretion of the owner/administrator as opposed to using labels and clearances. In answer a, role-based access control assigns privileges to individuals relative to certain objects, based on the individual's role in the organization. Role-based controls are applicable in organizations that experience frequent personnel changes. Because the access privileges are assigned to a role instead of an individual, there is no need to change access privileges whenever a new person assumes the same role. In answer c, privileges are determined by labels assigned to sensitive material and clearances assigned to subjects seeking access to that material. Answer d is a distractor.

15. The type of evidence that proves or disproves a specific act through oral testimony based on information gathered through the witness's five senses is called what?

   a. Hearsay evidence

   b. Best evidence

   c. Conclusive evidence

   d. Direct evidence

Answer: d. Answer a, hearsay or 3rd party evidence, is evidence that is not based on personal, first-hand knowledge of the witness, but was obtained from another source. Answer b, best evidence, is original or primary evidence rather than a copy or duplicate of the evidence. Conclusive evidence, answer c, is evidence that is incontrovertible; it overrides all other evidence.

16. Which choice describes a control?

- **a.** Competitive advantage, credibility, or good will
- **b.** Events or situations that could cause a financial or operational impact to the organization
- **c.** Personnel compensation and retirement programs
- **d.** Protection devices or procedures in place that reduce the effects of threats

Answer: **d.** Protection devices or procedures are controls that can reduce the effect of a threat, such as a UPS, sprinkler systems, or generators. Answer a describes an asset. Answer b is a definition of a threat. Answer c is a distractor.

17. Which backup method will probably require the backup operator to use the least number of tapes for a complete system restoration, if a different tape is used every night in a five-day rotation?

- **a.** Ad hoc backup method
- **b.** Differential backup method
- **c.** Incremental backup method
- **d.** Reactive backup method

Answer: **b.** The Differential backup method backs up only files that have been created or modified since the last backup was made, like an incremental backup. However, the difference between an incremental backup and a differential backup is that the Archive file attribute is not reset after the differential backup is completed; therefore, the changed file is backed up every time the differential backup is run. The backup set grows in size until the next full backup as these files continue to be backed up during each subsequent differential backup, until the next complete backup occurs. The advantage of this backup method is that the backup operator should only need the full backup and the one differential backup to restore the system.

Answer c. The Incremental backup method backs up only files that have been created or modified since the last backup was made, because the Archive file attribute is reset. The backup operator may thus need several tapes to do a complete restoration, as every tape with changed files as well as the last full backup tape will need to be restored.

Answers a and d are distractors.

18. Which statement is true about security awareness and educational programs?

    a. Awareness and training help users become more accountable for their actions.

    b. Security education assists management in determining who should be promoted.

    c. A security awareness and training program helps prevent the occurrence of natural disasters.

    d. Security awareness is not necessary for high-level senior executives.

Answer: **b.** Making computer system users aware of their security responsibilities and teaching them correct practices helps users change their behavior. It also supports individual accountability because without the knowledge of the necessary security measures and how to use them, users cannot be truly accountable for their actions.

19. Which choice is an example of an inert gas fire suppression agent?

    a. FC-3-1-10

    b. HFC-23

    c. HCFC-22

    d. IG-541

Answer: **d.** IG-541 is an inert gas agent. Inert gas agents can be replacements for Halon 1301 and Halon 1211 in gas-discharge fire extinguishing systems. Common inert gas agents for fire extinguishing systems are IG-01, IG-100, IG-55, and IG-541.

20. Which statement most accurately describes a "wet pipe" sprinkler system?

    a. Wet pipe is the most commonly used sprinkler system.

    b. Wet pipe contains air pressure.

    c. Wet pipe sounds an alarm and delays water release.

    d. Wet pipe may contain carbon dioxide.

Answer: **a.** Wet pipe is the most commonly used sprinkler system, and dry pipe is second. In a wet pipe system, water is standing in the pipe and is released when heat breaks the sprinkler head seal.

Answer b describes a dry pipe. In a dry pipe system, air pressure is maintained until the sprinkler head seal is ruptured. The air then escapes, and the water is brought into the room. Answer c describes a pre-action pipe, which sounds an alarm and delays the water release. This allows computer operations to shut down before the release of water.

21. Which choice is an example of a "dirty" fire-extinguishing agent?

    a. CO_2

    b. IG-55

    c. IG-01

    d. HCFC-22

Answer: **a.** "Clean" agents do not leave a residue on electronic parts after evaporation, whereas "dirty" agents do. CO_2, carbon dioxide, leaves a corrosive residue and is therefore not recommended for computer facility fire suppression systems. Answers b, c, and d, are considered clean agents.

22. Which statement accurately describes smoke exposure to electronic equipment?

    a. Smoke exposure for a relatively short period does little immediate damage.

    b. Continuing power to the smoke-exposed equipment won't increase the damage.

    c. Moisture and oxygen corrosion constitute less main damage to the equipment than smoke exposure.

    d. The primary damage done by smoke exposure is immediate.

Answer: **a.** Immediate, short-term smoke exposure to electronic equipment does little damage; however, power should be immediately disconnected to the affected equipment, as continuing voltage can plate the contaminants into the circuitry permanently.

23. Which choice describes a social engineering technique used to gain physical access to a secure facility?

    a. Asserting authority or pulling rank to intimidate

    b. Using a Trojan horse to create a network back door

    c. Eavesdropping on electronic emanations

    d. Employing the salami accounting fraud

Answer: **a.** Answer a refers to someone who professes to have the authority, perhaps supported with altered identification, to enter a facility. The other three answers are not examples of social engineering.

24. Which choice is an example of an electronic physical access control method?

    a. Deadbolts

    b. Access tokens

    c. Key locks

    d. Pushbutton locks

Answer: **b.** Answers a, c, and d are examples of mechanical locks, whereas choice b is an element of an electronic system. An electronic system can be very sophisticated — perhaps using smart cards, random keypads, auditing features, and time-operation limits.

25. Which statement about disaster recovery plan testing is incorrect?

    a. If no deficiencies were found during the test, the plan is probably perfect.

    b. Testing prepares and trains the personnel to execute their emergency duties.

    c. If no deficiencies were found during the test, the test was probably flawed.

    d. Testing identifies deficiencies in the recovery procedures.

Answer: **a.** Every DRP has weaknesses. After the test, all parties should be advised of the results and the plan updated to reflect the new information. The other three answers are accurate statements about disaster recovery plan testing.

26. Which statement is *not* true regarding company/employee relations during and after a disaster?

    a. The organization has a responsibility to continue salaries or other funding to the employees and/or families affected by the disaster.

    b. The organization's responsibility to the employees' families ends when the disaster stops the business from functioning.

    c. Employees do not have the right to obtain compensatory damages fraudulently if the organization cannot compensate them.

    d. The company must be insured to the extent it can properly compensate its employees and families.

Answer: **b.** The organization has a responsibility to its employees and their families during and after a disaster or other disruptive event.

27. Which choice is considered an appropriate role for senior management in the disaster recovery process?

    a. Continuously reassessing the recovery site's stability

    b. Recovering and constructing all critical data

    c. Remaining visible to employees and stakeholders

    d. Identifying and prioritizing mission-critical applications

Answer: **c.** Senior management has many very important roles in the process of disaster recovery, but it must resist the temptation to participate hands-on in the recovery effort. Information or technology management tasks, as identified in answers a, b, and d, should be delegated.

28. In developing a recovery plan, which choice would be considered a long-term objective?

    a. Priorities for restoration

    b. Acceptable downtime before restoration

    c. Minimum resources needed to accomplish the restoration

    d. The organization's strategic plan

Answer: **d.** The organization's strategic plan is considered a long-term goal. The other three answers are examples of short-term goals and objectives.

29. Which choice is considered an appropriate role for financial management in the business continuity and disaster recovery process?

    a. Providing appropriate retraining

    b. Providing employees and their families with counseling and support

    c. Formally notifying insurers of claims

    d. Monitoring productivity of personnel

Answer: **c.** In addition to formally notifying insurers of claims, the financial area is responsible for tracking recovery costs, reassessing cash flow projections, re-establishing accounting processes, and re-establishing transaction controls. The other three answers are emergency recovery tasks associated with human resources.

30. Which choice is *not* a reason to control the humidity in computer operations areas?

    a. Computer operators do not perform at their peak if the humidity is too high.

    b. Electrostatic discharges can harm electronic equipment.

    c. Electrical connections become inefficient in high humidity.

    d. If the air is too humid, electroplating of conductors may occur.

Answer: **a.** The other three answers are all good reasons to control the humidity in computer operations areas.

✦ ✦ ✦

Glossary of Terms and Acronyms

* property (or star property) A Bell-LaPadula security model rule enabling a subject write access to an object only if the security level of the object dominates the security level of the subject. Also called *confinement property*.

1000BaseT 1000 Mbps (1Gbps) baseband Ethernet using twisted pair wire

100BaseT 100 Mbps baseband Ethernet using twisted pair wire

10Base2 802.3 IEEE Ethernet standard for 10 Mbps Ethernet using coaxial cable (thinnet) rated to 185 meters

10Base5 10 Mbps Ethernet using coaxial cable (thicknet) rated to 500 meters

10BaseF 10 Mbps baseband Ethernet using optical fiber

10BaseT 10 Mbps UTP Ethernet rated to 100 meters

10Broad36 10 Mbps broadband Ethernet rated to 3,600 meters

3DES Triple Data Encryption Standard

802.10 IEEE standard that specifies security and privacy access methods for LANs

802.11 IEEE standard that specifies 1 Mbps and 2 Mbps wireless connectivity. Defines aspects of frequency hopping and direct-sequence spread spectrum (DSSS) systems for use in the 2.4 MHz ISM (industrial, scientific, medical) band. Also refers to the IEEE committee responsible for setting wireless LAN standards.

802.11a Specifies high-speed wireless connectivity in the 5 GHz band using *orthogonal frequency division multiplexing (OFDM)* with data rates up to 54 Mbps

802.11b Specifies high-speed wireless connectivity in the 2.4 GHz ISM band up to 11 Mbps

802.15 Specification for Bluetooth LANs in the 2.4–2.5 GHz band

802.2 Standard that specifies the *LLC (logical link control)*

802.3 Ethernet bus topology using carrier sense medium access control/carrier detect (CSMA/CD) for 10 Mbps wired LANs. Currently, the most popular LAN topology.

802.4 Specifies a token-passing bus access method for LANs

802.5 Specifies a token-passing ring access method for LANs

A

acceptance inspection The final inspection to determine whether or not a facility or system meets the specified technical and performance standards. Note: This inspection is held immediately after facility and software testing and is the basis for commissioning or accepting the information system.

acceptance testing A type of testing used to determine whether the network is acceptable to the actual users

access A specific type of interaction between a subject and an object that results in the flow of information from one to the other

access control The process of limiting access to system resources only to authorized programs, processes, or other systems (on a network). This term is synonymous with *controlled access* and *limited access*.

access control mechanism Hardware or software features, operating procedures, management procedures, and various combinations thereof that are designed to detect and prevent unauthorized access and to permit authorized access in an automated system.

access level The hierarchical portion of the security level that is used to identify the sensitivity of data and the clearance or authorization of users. Note: The access level, in conjunction with the nonhierarchical categories, forms the sensitivity label of an object. See *category*, *security level*, and *sensitivity label*.

access list A list of users, programs, and/or processes, and the specifications of access categories to which each is assigned; a list denoting which users have what privileges to a particular resource

access period A segment of time, generally expressed on a daily or weekly basis, during which access rights prevail

access point (AP) A wireless LAN transceiver interface between the wireless network and a wired network. Access points forward frames between wireless devices and hosts on the LAN

access port A logical or physical identifier that a computer uses to distinguish different terminal input/output data streams

access type The nature of an access right to a particular device, program, or file (for example, read, write, execute, append, modify, delete, or create)

accountability The property that enables activities on a system to be traced to individuals who might then be held responsible for their actions

accreditation A formal declaration by the DAA that the AIS is approved to operate in a particular security mode by using a prescribed set of safeguards. Accreditation is the official management authorization for operation of an AIS and is based on the certification process as well as on other management considerations. The accreditation statement affixes security responsibility with the DAA and shows that due care has been taken for security.

accreditation authority Synonymous with *Designated Approving Authority*

ACK Acknowledgment; a short-return indication of the successful receipt of a message

acknowledged connectionless service A datagram-style service that includes error-control and flow-control mechanisms

ACO Authenticated ciphering offset

adaptive routing A form of network routing whereby the path data packets traverse from a source to a destination node depending upon the current state of the network by calculating the best path through the network

add-on security The retrofitting of protection mechanisms implemented by hardware or software

Address Resolution Protocol (ARP) A TCP/IP protocol that binds logical (IP) addresses to physical addresses

administrative security The management constraints and supplemental controls established to provide an acceptable level of protection for data. Synonymous with *procedural security*.

Advanced Encryption Standard (AES) (Rijndael) A symmetric block cipher with a block size of 128 bits in which the key can be 128, 192, or 256 bits. The Advanced Encryption Standard replaces the Date Encryption Standard (DES) and was announced on November 26, 2001, as Federal Information Processing Standard Publication (FIPS PUB 197).

AIS *Automated Information System*

analog signal An electrical signal with an amplitude that varies continuously

Application layer The top layer of the OSI model, which is concerned with application programs. It provides services such as file transfer and e-mail to the network's end users.

application process An entity, either human or software, that uses the services offered by the Application layer of the OSI reference model

application program interface A software interface provided between a specialized communications program and an end user application

application software Software that accomplishes functions such as database access, electronic mail, and menu prompts

architecture As refers to a computer system, an architecture describes the type of components, interfaces, and protocols the system uses and how they fit together

assurance A measure of confidence that the security features and architecture of an AIS accurately mediate and enforce the security policy. Grounds for confidence that an IT product or system meets its security objectives. See *DITSCAP*.

asymmetric (public) key encryption Cryptographic system that employs two keys, a public key and a private key. The public key is made available to anyone wishing to send an encrypted message to an individual holding the corresponding private key of the public-private key pair. Any message encrypted with one of these keys can be decrypted with the other. The private key is always kept private. It should not be possible to derive the private key from the public key.

Asynchronous Transfer Mode A cell-based connection-oriented data service offering high-speed data communications. ATM integrates circuit and packet switching to handle both constant and burst information at rates up to 2.488 Gbps. Also called *cell relay*.

asynchronous transmission Type of communications data synchronization with no defined time relationship between transmission of data frames. *See synchronous transmission.*

attachment unit interface (AUI) A 15-pin interface between an Ethernet Network Interface Card and a transceiver

attack The act of trying to bypass security controls on a system. An attack can be active, resulting in data modification, or passive, resulting in the release of data. Note: The fact that an attack is made does not necessarily mean that it will succeed. The degree of success depends on the vulnerability of the system or activity and the effectiveness of existing countermeasures.

audit trail A chronological record of system activities that is sufficient to enable the reconstruction, reviewing, and examination of the sequence of environments and activities surrounding or leading to an operation, a procedure, or an event in a transaction from its inception to its final result.

Authenticate (1) To verify the identity of a user, device, or other entity in a computer system, often as a prerequisite to allowing access to system resources. (2) To verify the integrity of data that has been stored, transmitted, or otherwise exposed to possible unauthorized modification.

authentication device A device whose identity has been verified during the lifetime of the current link based on the authentication procedure

authentication Generically, the process of verifying "'who'" is at the other end of a transmission

authenticator The means used to confirm the identity or verify the eligibility of a station, originator, or individual

authorization The granting of access rights to a user, program, or process

automated data processing security Synonymous with *automated information systems security*

automated information system (AIS) An assembly of computer hardware, software, and/or firmware that is configured to collect, create, communicate, compute, disseminate, process, store, and/or control data or information

automated information system security Measures and controls that protect an AIS against Denial of Service (DoS) and unauthorized (accidental or intentional) disclosure, modification, or destruction of AISs and data. AIS security includes consideration of all hardware and/or software functions, characteristics and/or features; operational procedures, accountability procedures, and access controls at the central computer facility, remote computers and terminal facilities; management constraints; physical structures and devices; and personnel and communication controls that are needed to provide an acceptable level of risk for the AIS and for the data and information contained in the AIS. It includes the totality of security safeguards needed to provide an acceptable protection level for an AIS and for data handled by an AIS.

automated security monitoring The use of automated procedures to ensure that security controls are not circumvented

availability of data The condition in which data is in the place needed by the user, at the time the user needs it, and in the form needed by the user

B

backbone network A network that interconnects other networks

back door Synonymous with *trapdoor*

backup plan Synonymous with *contingency plan*

backward chaining In an expert system, the process of beginning with a possible solution and using the knowledge in the knowledge base to justify the solution based on the raw input data. Backward chaining is generally used when a large number of possible solutions exist relative to the number of inputs.

bandwidth Specifies the amount of the frequency spectrum that is usable for data transfer. In other words, bandwidth identifies the maximum data rate a signal can attain on the medium without encountering significant attenuation (loss of power). Also, the amount of information one can send through a connection.

baud rate The number of signal pulses that occurs in one second. Thus, baud rate is the speed at which the digital signal pulses travel. Also, the rate at which data is transferred.

Bell-LaPadula model A formal state transition model of computer security policy that describes a set of access control rules. In this formal model, the entities in a computer system are divided into abstract sets of subjects and objects. The notion of a secure state is defined, and it is proven that each state transition preserves security by moving from secure state to secure state, thereby inductively proving that the system is secure. A system state is defined to be secure if the only permitted access modes of subjects to objects are in accordance with a specific security policy. In order to determine whether or not a specific access mode is allowed, the clearance of a subject is compared to the classification of the object, and a determination is made as to whether the subject is authorized for the specific access mode. See *star property (* property)* and *simple security property*.

benign environment A nonhostile environment that might be protected from external hostile elements by physical, personnel, and procedural security countermeasures

between-the-lines entry Unauthorized access obtained by tapping the temporarily inactive terminal of a legitimate user. See *piggyback*.

beyond A1 A level of trust defined by the *DoD Trusted Computer System Evaluation Criteria (TCSEC)* that is beyond the state-of-the-art technology available at the time the criteria was developed. It includes all of the A1-level features plus additional features that are not required at the A1 level.

binary digit See *bit*

biometrics Access control method in which an individual's physiological or behavioral characteristics are used to determine that individual's access to a particular resource

BIOS *Basic Input/Output System* The BIOS is the first program to run when the computer is turned on. BIOS initializes and tests the computer hardware, loads and runs the operating system, and manages Setup for making changes in the computer.

bit Short for *binary digit*. A single digit number in binary, 0 or 1.

bit rate The transmission rate of binary symbols 0s and 1s. Bit rate is equal to the total number of bits transmitted in one second.

blackboard An expert system reasoning methodology in which a solution is generated by the use of a virtual "blackboard" wherein information or potential solutions are placed on the blackboard by a plurality of individuals or expert knowledge sources. As more information is placed on the blackboard in an iterative process, a solution is generated.

blind signature A form of digital signature where the signer is not privy to the content of the message

block cipher A symmetric key algorithm that operates on a fixed-length block of plaintext and transforms it into a fixed-length block of ciphertext. A block cipher is obtained by segregating plaintext into blocks of *n* characters or bits and applying the identical same encryption algorithm and key to each block.

Bluetooth An open specification for wireless communication of data and voice, based on a low-cost short-range radio link facilitating protected ad hoc connections for stationary and mobile communication environments

bridge A network device that provides internetworking functionality by connecting networks. Bridges can provide segmentation of data frames and can be used to connect LANs by forwarding packets across connections at the media access control (MAC) sublayer of the OSI model's Data Link layer.

broadband A transmission system in which signals are encoded and modulated into different frequencies and then transmitted simultaneously with other signals (that is, having undergone a shift in frequency). A LAN broadband signal is commonly analog.

browsing The act of searching through storage to locate or acquire information without necessarily knowing the existence or the format of the information being sought

BSI ISO/IEC 17799:2000, BS 7799-I: 2000, Information technology — Code of practice for information security management, British Standards Institution, London, UK A standard intended to "provide a comprehensive set of controls comprising best practices in information security." ISO refers to the International Organization for Standardization, and IEC is the International Electrotechnical Commission.

bus topology A type of network topology wherein all nodes are connected to a single length of cabling with a terminator at each end

Business Software Alliance (BSA) An international organization representing leading software and e-commerce developers in 65 countries around the world. BSA efforts include educating computer users about software copyrights; advocating for public policy that fosters innovation and expands trade opportunities; and fighting software piracy.

byte A set of bits, usually eight, that represents a single character

C

call back A procedure for identifying a remote terminal. In a call back, the host system disconnects the caller and then dials the authorized telephone number of the remote terminal in order to re-establish the connection. Synonymous with *dial back*.

capability A protected identifier that both identifies the object and specifies the access rights allowed to the accessor who possesses the capability. In a capability-based system, access to protected objects (such as files) is granted if the would-be accessor possesses a capability for the object.

Capstone A Very Large Scale Integration (VLSI) chip that employs the Escrowed Encryption Standard and incorporates the Skipjack algorithm, similar to the Clipper Chip. As such, it has a Law Enforcement Access Field (LEAF). Capstone also supports public key exchange and digital signatures. At this time, Capstone products have their LEAF function suppressed and a certificate authority provides for key recovery.

Carnivore A device used by the U.S. FBI to monitor ISP traffic (S.P. Smith, et. al., Independent Technical Review of the Carnivore System—Draft report, U.S. Department of Justice Contract # 00-C-328 IITRI, CR-022-216, November 17, 2000)

carrier current LAN A LAN that uses power lines within the facility as a medium for data transport

carrier sense multiple access (CSMA) The technique used to reduce transmission contention by listening for contention before transmitting

carrier sense multiple access/collision detection (CSMA/CD) The most common Ethernet cable access method

category A restrictive label that has been applied to classified or unclassified data as a means of increasing the protection of the data and further restricting its access.

category 1 twisted pair wire Used for early analog telephone communications; not suitable for data

category 2 twisted pair wire Rated for 4 Mbps and used in 802.5 Token Ring networks

category 3 twisted pair wire Rated for 10 Mbps and used in 802.3 10BaseT Ethernet networks

category 4 twisted pair wire Rated for 16 Mbps and used in 802.5 Token Ring networks

category 5 twisted pair wire Rated for 100 Mbps and used in 100BaseT Ethernet networks

CBC Cipher block chaining is an encryption mode of the Data Encryption Standard (DES) that operates on plaintext blocks 64 bits in length.

CC Common Criteria are a standard for specifying and evaluating the features of computer products and systems.

Centronics A de facto standard 36-pin parallel 200 Kbps asynchronous interface for connecting printers and other devices to a computer

CERT Coordination Center (CERT(r)/CC) A unit of the Carnegie Mellon University Software Engineering Institute (SEI). SEI is a federally funded R&D Center. CERT's mission is to alert the Internet community to vulnerabilities and attacks and to conduct research and training in the areas of computer security, including incident response.

certification The comprehensive evaluation of the technical and nontechnical security features of an AIS and other safeguards, made in support of the accreditation process, that establishes the extent to which a particular design and implementation meets a specified set of security requirements.

Chinese Wall model Uses internal rules to "compartmentalize" areas in which individuals may work to prevent disclosure of proprietary information and to avoid conflicts of interest. The Chinese Wall model also incorporates the principle of separation of duty.

cipher A cryptographic transformation that operates on characters or bits

ciphertext or cryptogram An unintelligible encrypted message

circuit-switched The application of a network wherein a dedicated line is used to transmit information; contrast with *packet-switched*

client A computer that accesses a server's resources

client/server architecture A network system design in which a processor or computer designated as a file server or database server provides services to other client processors or computers. Applications are distributed between a host server and a remote client.

closed security environment An environment in which both of the following conditions hold true: 1) Application developers (including maintainers) have sufficient clearances and authorizations to provide an acceptable presumption that they have not introduced malicious logic, and 2) Configuration control provides sufficient assurance that applications and the equipment are protected against the introduction of malicious logic prior to and during the operation of system applications.

closed shop Data processing area using physical access controls to limit access to authorized personnel

Clustering Situation in which a plaintext message generates identical ciphertext messages using the same transformation algorithm, but with different cryptovariables or keys

coaxial cable (coax) Type of transmission cable consisting of a hollow outer cylindrical conductor that surrounds a single inner wire conductor for current flow. Because the shielding reduces the amount of electrical noise interference, coax can extend to much greater lengths than twisted pair wiring.

code division multiple access **(CDMA)** A spread spectrum digital cellular radio system that uses different codes to distinguish users

codes Cryptographic transformation that operates at the level of words or phrases

collision detection The detection of simultaneous transmission on the communications medium

Common Object Model (COM) A model that allows two software components to communicate with each other independent of their platforms' operating systems and languages of implementation. As in the object-oriented paradigm, COM works with encapsulated objects.

Common Object Request Broker Architecture (CORBA) A standard that uses the Object Request Broker (ORB) to implement exchanges among objects in a heterogeneous, distributed environment

Communications Assistance for Law Enforcement Act (CALEA) of 1994 An act that required all communications carriers to make wiretaps possible in ways approved by the FBI

communications security (COMSEC) Measures taken to deny unauthorized persons information derived from telecommunications of the U.S. government concerning national security and to ensure the authenticity of such telecommunications. Communications security includes cryptosecurity, transmission security, emission security, and physical security of communications security material and information.

compartment A class of information that has need-to-know access controls beyond those normally provided for access to confidential, secret, or top secret information

compartmented security mode See *modes of operation*

compensating controls A combination of controls, such as physical and technical or technical and administrative (or all three)

composition model An information security model that investigates the resultant security properties when subsystems are combined

compromise A violation of a system's security policy such that unauthorized disclosure of sensitive information might have occurred

compromising emanations Unintentional data-related or intelligence-bearing signals that, when intercepted and analyzed, disclose the information transmission that is received, handled, or otherwise processed by any information processing equipment. See *TEMPEST*

COMPUSEC Computer security

computer abuse The misuse, alteration, disruption, or destruction of data-processing resources. The key is that computer abuse is intentional and improper.

computer cryptography The use of a crypto-algorithm in a computer, microprocessor, or microcomputer to perform encryption or decryption in order to protect information or to authenticate users, sources, or information.

computer facility The physical structure housing data processing operations

computer forensics Information collection from and about computer systems that is admissible in a court of law

computer fraud Computer-related crimes involving deliberate misrepresentation, alteration, or disclosure of data in order to obtain something of value (usually for monetary gain). A computer system must have been involved in the perpetration or cover-up of the act or series of acts. A computer system might have been involved through improper manipulation of input data, output or results, applications programs, data files, computer operations, communications, or computer hardware, systems software, or firmware.

computer security (COMPUSEC) Synonymous with *automated information systems security*

computer security subsystem A device that is designed to provide limited computer security features in a larger system environment

Computer Security Technical Vulnerability Reporting Program (CSTVRP) A program that focuses on technical vulnerabilities in commercially available hardware, firmware, and software products acquired by DoD. CSTVRP provides for the reporting, cataloging, and discrete dissemination of technical vulnerability and corrective measure information to DoD components on a need-to-know basis.

COMSEC See *communications security*

concealment system A method of achieving confidentiality in which sensitive information is hidden by embedding it inside irrelevant data

confidentiality The concept of holding sensitive data in confidence, limited to an appropriate set of individuals or organizations

configuration control The process of controlling modifications to the system's hardware, firmware, software, and documentation that provides sufficient assurance that the system is protected against the introduction of improper modifications prior to, during, and after system implementation. Compare with *configuration management*

configuration management The management of security features and assurances through control of changes made to a system's hardware, software, firmware, documentation, test, test fixtures, and test documentation throughout the development and operational life of the system. Compare with *configuration control*

confinement The prevention of the leaking of sensitive data from a program

confinement channel Synonymous with *covert channel*

confinement property Synonymous with *star property (* property)*

confusion A method of hiding the relationship between the plaintext and the ciphertext

connection-oriented service Service that establishes a logical connection that provides flow control and error control between two stations who need to exchange data

connectivity A path through which communications signals can flow

connectivity software A software component that provides an interface between the networked appliance and the database or application software located on the network

Construction Cost Model (COCOMO), Basic version Estimates software development effort and cost as a function of the size of the software product in source instructions

containment strategy A strategy for containment (in other words, stopping the spread) of the disaster and the identification of the provisions and processes required to contain the disaster

contamination The intermixing of data at different sensitivity and need-to-know levels. The lower-level data is said to be contaminated by the higher-level data; thus, the contaminating (higher-level) data might not receive the required level of protection.

contingency management Establishing actions to be taken before, during, and after a threatening incident

contingency plan A plan for emergency response, backup operations, and post-disaster recovery maintained by an activity as a part of its security program; this plan ensures the availability of critical resources and facilitates the continuity of operations in an emergency situation. Synonymous with *disaster plan* and *emergency plan*.

continuity of operations Maintenance of essential IP services after a major outage

control zone The space, expressed in feet of radius, surrounding equipment processing sensitive information that is under sufficient physical and technical control to preclude an unauthorized entry or compromise

controlled access See *access control*

controlled sharing The condition that exists when access control is applied to all users and components of a system

Copper Data Distributed Interface (CDDI) A version of FDDI specifying the use of unshielded twisted pair wiring

cost-risk analysis The assessment of the cost of providing data protection for a system versus the cost of losing or compromising the data

countermeasure Any action, device, procedure, technique, or other measure that reduces the vulnerability of or threat to a system

countermeasure/safeguard An entity that mitigates the potential risk to an information system

covert channel A communications channel that enables two cooperating processes to transfer information in a manner that violates the system's security policy. Synonymous with *confinement channel*.

covert storage channel A covert channel that involves the direct or indirect writing of a storage location by one process and the direct or indirect reading of the storage location by another process. Covert storage channels typically involve a finite resource (for example, sectors on a disk) that is shared by two subjects at different security levels.

covert timing channel A covert channel in which one process signals information to another by modulating its own use of system resources (for example, CPU time) in such a way that this manipulation affects the real response time observed by the second process

CPU The central processing unit of a computer

criteria See *DoD Trusted Computer System Evaluation Criteria*

CRL Certificate revocation list

cryptanalysis Refers to the ability to "break" the cipher so that the encrypted message can be read. Cryptanalysis can be accomplished by exploiting weaknesses in the cipher or in some fashion determining the key.

crypto-algorithm A well-defined procedure or sequence of rules or steps used to produce a key stream or ciphertext from plaintext, and vice versa. Step-by-step procedure that is used to encipher plaintext and decipher ciphertext. Also called a *cryptographic algorithm*.

cryptographic algorithm See *crypto-algorithm*

cryptographic application programming interface (CAPI) An interface to a library of software functions that provide security and cryptography services. CAPI is designed for software developers to call functions from the library, which makes it easier to implement security services.

cryptography The principles, means, and methods for rendering information unintelligible and for restoring encrypted information to intelligible form. The word *cryptography* comes from the Greek *kryptos,* meaning "hidden," and *graphein*, "to write."

cryptosecurity The security or protection resulting from the proper use of technically sound cryptosystems

cryptosystem A set of transformations from a message space to a ciphertext space. This system includes all cryptovariables (keys), plaintexts and ciphertexts associated with the transformation algorithm.

cryptovariable See *key*

CSMA/CA Carrier sense multiple access/collision avoidance, commonly used in 802.11 Ethernet and LocalTalk

CSMA/CD Carrier sense multiple access/collision detection, used in 802.3 Ethernet

CSTVRP See *Computer Security Technical Vulnerability Reporting Program*

cyclic redundancy check (CRC) A common error-detection process. A mathematical operation is applied to the data when transmitted. The result is appended to the core packet. Upon receipt, the same mathematical operation is performed and checked against the CRC. A mismatch indicates a very high probability that an error has occurred during transmission.

D

DAA See *designated approving authority*

DAC See *discretionary access control*

data dictionary A database that comprises tools to support the analysis, design, and development of software and support good software engineering practices

Data Encryption Standard (DES) A cryptographic algorithm for the protection of unclassified data, published in Federal Information Processing Standard (FIPS) 46. The DES, which was approved by the National Institute of Standards and Technology (NIST), is intended for public and government use.

data flow control See *information flow control*

data integrity When data meet a prior expectation of quality

Data Link layer The OSI level that performs the assembly and transmission of data packets, including error control

data mart A database that comprises data or relations that have been extracted from the data warehouse. Information in the data mart is usually of interest to a particular group of people.

data mining The process of analyzing large data sets in a data warehouse to find non-obvious patterns

data scrubbing Maintenance of a data warehouse by deleting information that is unreliable or no longer relevant

data security The protection of data from unauthorized (accidental or intentional) modification, destruction, or disclosure

Data service unit/channel service unit (DSU/CSU) A set of network components that reshape data signals into a form that can be effectively transmitted over a digital transmission medium, typically a leased 56 Kbps or T1 line

data warehouse A subject-oriented, integrated, time-variant, non-volatile collection of data in support of management's decision-making process

database A persistent collection of data items that form relations among each other

database shadowing A data redundancy process that uses the live processing of remote journaling but creates even more redundancy by duplicating the database sets to multiple servers.

datagram service A connectionless form of packet switching whereby the source does not need to establish a connection with the destination before sending data packets

DB-15 A standard 15-pin connector commonly used with RS-232 serial interfaces, Ethernet transceivers, and computer monitors

DB-25 A standard 25-pin connector commonly used with RS-232 serial interfaces. The DB-25 connector supports all RS-232 functions.

DB-9 A standard 9-pin connector commonly used with RS-232 serial interfaces on portable computers. The DB-9 connector does not support all RS-232 functions.

de facto standard A standard based on broad usage and support but not directly specified by the IEEE

decipher To unscramble the encipherment process in order to make the message human-readable

declassification of AIS storage media An administrative decision or procedure to remove or reduce the security classification of the subject media

DeCSS A program that bypasses the Content Scrambling System (CSS) software used to prevent the viewing of DVD movie disks on unlicensed platforms

dedicated security mode *See modes of operation.*

default A value or option that is automatically chosen when no other value is specified

default classification A temporary classification reflecting the highest classification being processed in a system. The default classification is included in the caution statement that is affixed to the object.

Defense Information Technology Systems Certification and Accreditation Process (DITSCAP) Establishes for the defense entities, a standard process, set of activities, general task descriptions, and a management structure to certify and accredit IT systems that will maintain the required security posture. The process is designed to certify that the IT system meets the accreditation requirements and that the system will maintain the accredited security posture throughout the system lifecycle. The four phases to the DITSCAP are Definition, Verification, Validation, and Post Accreditation.

degauss The purpose of degaussing magnetic storage media

Degausser Products List (DPL) A list of commercially produced degaussers that meet National Security Agency specifications. This list is included in the NSA Information Systems Security Products and Services Catalogue and is available through the Government Printing Office.

degraded fault tolerance Specifies which capabilities the TOE will still provide after a system failure. Examples of general failures are flooding of the computer room, short-term power interruption, breakdown of a CPU or host, software failure, or buffer overflow. Only functions specified must be available.

***Denial of Service* (DoS)** Any action (or series of actions) that prevents any part of a system from functioning in accordance with its intended purpose. This action includes any action that causes unauthorized destruction, modification, or delay of service. Synonymous with *interdiction*.

DES See *Data Encryption Standard*

Descriptive Top-Level Specification (DTLS) A top-level specification that is written in a natural language (for example, English), an informal design notation, or a combination of the two

designated approving authority The official who has the authority to decide on accepting the security safeguards prescribed for an AIS, or the official who might be responsible for issuing an accreditation statement that records the decision to accept those safeguards

dial back Synonymous with *call back*

dial-up The service whereby a computer terminal can use the telephone to initiate and effect communication with a computer

diffusion A method of obscuring redundancy in plaintext by spreading the effect of the transformation over the ciphertext

Digital Millennium Copyright Act (DMCA) of 1998 In addition to addressing licensing and ownership information, the DMCA prohibits trading, manufacturing, or selling in any way that is intended to bypass copyright protection mechanisms.

Direct-sequence spread spectrum (DSSS) A method used in 802.11b to split the frequency into 14 channels, each with a frequency range, by combining a data signal with a chipping sequence. Data rates of 1, 2, 5.5, and 11 Mbps are obtainable. DSSS spreads its signal continuously over this wide-frequency band.

disaster A sudden, unplanned, calamitous event that produces great damage or loss; any event that creates an inability on the organization's part to provide critical business functions for some undetermined period of time

disaster plan Synonymous with *contingency plan*

disaster recovery plan Procedure for emergency response, extended backup operations, and post-disaster recovery when an organization suffers a loss of computer resources and physical facilities

discovery In the context of legal proceedings and trial practice, a process in which the prosecution presents information it has uncovered to the defense. This information may include potential witnesses, reports resulting from the investigation, evidence, and so on. During an investigation, discovery refers to:

- The process undertaken by the investigators to acquire evidence needed for prosecution of a case
- A step in the computer forensic process

discretionary access control A means of restricting access to objects based on the identity and need-to-know of the user, process, and/or groups to which they belong. The controls are discretionary in the sense that a subject that has certain access permissions is capable of passing that permission (perhaps indirectly) on to any other subject. Compare with *mandatory access control*.

disk image backup Conducting a bit-level copy, sector-by-sector of a disk, which provides the capability to examine slack space, undeleted clusters, and possibly, deleted files

Distributed Component Object Model (DCOM) A distributed object model that is similar to the Common Object Request Broker Architecture (CORBA). DCOM is the distributed version of COM that supports remote objects as if the objects reside in the client's address space. A COM client can access a COM object through the use of a pointer to one of the object's interfaces and then invoke methods through that pointer.

Distributed Queue Dual Bus (DQDB) The IEEE 802.6 standard that provides full-duplex 155 Mbps operation between nodes in a metropolitan area network

distributed routing A form of routing wherein each router on the network periodically identifies neighboring nodes, updates its routing table, and, with this information, sends its routing table to all of its neighbors. Because each node follows the same process, complete network topology information propagates through the network and eventually reaches each node.

DITSCAP See *Defense Information Technology Systems Certification and Accreditation Process*

DoD U.S. Department of Defense

DoD Trusted Computer System Evaluation Criteria (TCSEC) A document published by the National Computer Security Center containing a uniform set of basic requirements and evaluation classes for assessing degrees of assurance in the effectiveness of hardware and software security controls built into systems. These criteria are intended for use in the design and evaluation of systems that process and/or store sensitive or classified data. This document is Government Standard DoD 5200.28-STD and is frequently referred to as "The Criteria" or "The Orange Book."

DoJ U.S. Department of Justice

domain The unique context (for example, access control parameters) in which a program is operating; in effect, the set of objects that a subject has the ability to access. See *process* and *subject*.

dominate Security level S1 is said to *dominate* security level S2 if the hierarchical classification of S1 is greater than or equal to that of S2 and if the nonhierarchical categories of S1 include all those of S2 as a subset.

DoS attack Denial of Service attack

DPL Degausser Products List

DT Data terminal

DTLS Descriptive Top-Level Specification

due care That care which an ordinary prudent person would have exercised under the same or similar circumstances. The terms *due care* and *reasonable care* are used interchangeably.

Dynamic Host Configuration Protocol (DHCP) A protocol that issues IP addresses automatically within a specified range to devices such as PCs when they are first powered on. The device retains the use of the IP address for a specific license period that the system administrator can define.

E

EAP Extensible Authentication Protocol. Cisco proprietary protocol for enhanced user authentication and wireless security management.

EBCDIC Extended Binary-Coded Decimal Interchange Code. An 8-bit character representation developed by IBM in the early 1960s.

ECC Elliptic curve cryptography

ECDSA Elliptic curve digital signature algorithm

Echelon A cooperative, worldwide signal intelligence system that is run by the NSA of the United States, the Government Communications Head Quarters (GCHQ) of England, the Communications Security Establishment (CSE) of Canada, the Australian Defense Security Directorate (DSD), and the General Communications Security Bureau (GCSB) of New Zealand

Electronic Communications Privacy Act (ECPA) of 1986 An act that prohibited eavesdropping or the interception of message contents without distinguishing between private or public systems

Electronic Data Interchange (EDI) A service that provides communications for business transactions. ANSI standard X.12 defines the data format for EDI.

electronic vaulting A term that refers to the transfer of backup data to an off-site location. This process is primarily a batch process of dumping the data through communications lines to a server at an alternate location.

Electronics Industry Association (EIA) A U.S. standards organization that represents a large number of electronics firms

emanations See *compromising emanations*.

embedded system A system that performs or controls a function, either in whole or in part, as an integral element of a larger system or subsystem

emergency plan Synonymous with *contingency plan*

emission security The protection resulting from all measures that are taken to deny unauthorized persons information of value that might be derived from intercept and from an analysis of compromising emanations from systems

encipher To make the message unintelligible to all but the intended recipients

Endorsed Tools List (ETL) The list of formal verification tools endorsed by the NCSC for the development of systems that have high levels of trust

end-to-end encryption Encrypted information sent from the point of origin to the final destination. In symmetric key encryption, this process requires the sender and receiver to have the identical key for the session.

Enhanced Hierarchical Development Methodology An integrated set of tools designed to aid in creating, analyzing, modifying, managing, and documenting program specifications and proofs. This methodology includes a specification parser and typechecker, a theorem prover, and a multilevel security checker. Note: This methodology is not based upon the Hierarchical Development Methodology.

entrapment The deliberate planting of apparent flaws in a system for the purpose of detecting attempted penetrations

environment The aggregate of external procedures, conditions, and objects that affect the development, operation, and maintenance of a system

EPL Evaluated Products List

erasure A process by which a signal recorded on magnetic media is removed. Erasure is accomplished in two ways: 1) by alternating current erasure, by which the information is destroyed when an alternating high and low magnetic field is applied to the media; or 2) by direct current erasure, in which the media is saturated by applying a unidirectional magnetic field.

Ethernet An industry-standard local area network media access method that uses a bus topology and CSMA/CD. IEEE 802.3 is a standard that specifies Ethernet.

Ethernet repeater A component that provides Ethernet connections among multiple stations sharing a common collision domain. Also referred to as a *shared Ethernet hub*.

Ethernet switch More intelligent than a hub, with the capability to connect the sending station directly to the receiving station

ETL Endorsed Tools List

ETSI European Telecommunications Standards Institute

Evaluated Products List (EPL) A list of equipment, hardware, software, and/or firmware that have been evaluated against, and found to be technically compliant, at a particular level of trust with the DoD TCSEC by the NCSC. The EPL is included in the National Security Agency Information Systems Security Products and Services Catalogue, which is available through the Government Printing Office (GPO).

Evaluation Assessment of an IT product or system against defined security functional and assurance criteria performed by a combination of testing and analytic techniques

Evaluation Assurance Level (EAL) In the Common Criteria, the degree of examination of the product to be tested. EALs range from EA1 (functional testing) to EA7 (detailed testing and formal design verification). Each numbered package represents a point on the CCs predefined assurance scale. An EAL can be considered a level of confidence in the security functions of an IT product or system.

executive state One of several states in which a system can operate and the only one in which certain privileged instructions can be executed. Such instructions cannot be executed when the system is operating in other (for example, user) states. Synonymous with *supervisor state*.

exigent circumstances doctrine Specifies that a warrantless search and seizure of evidence can be conducted if there is probable cause to suspect criminal activity or destruction of evidence

expert system shell An off-the-shelf software package that implements an inference engine, a mechanism for entering knowledge, a user interface and a system to provide explanations of the reasoning used to generate a solution. It provides the fundamental building blocks of an expert system and supports the entering of domain knowledge.

exploitable channel Any information channel that is usable or detectable by subjects that are external to the trusted computing base whose purpose is to violate the security policy of the system. See *covert channel*.

exposure An instance of being exposed to losses from a threat

F

fail over automatically switching over to a backup system when one system/application fails

fail safe A term that refers to the automatic protection of programs and/or processing systems to maintain safety when a hardware or software failure is detected in a system

fail secure A term that refers to a system that preserves a secure state during and after identified failures occur

fail soft A term that refers to the selective termination of affected nonessential processing when a hardware or software failure is detected in a system

failure access An unauthorized and usually inadvertent access to data resulting from a hardware or software failure in the system

failure control The methodology that is used to detect and provide fail-safe or fail-soft recovery from hardware and software failures in a system

fault A condition that causes a device or system component to fail to perform in a required manner

fault-resilient systems Systems designed without redundancy; in the event of failure, they result in a slightly longer down time.

FCC Federal Communications Commission

FDMA Frequency division multiple access. A spectrum-sharing technique whereby the available spectrum is divided into a number of individual radio channels.

FDX Full-duplex

Federal Intelligence Surveillance Act (FISA) of 1978 An act that limited wiretapping for national security purposes as a result of the Nixon Administration's history of using illegal wiretaps.

fetch protection A system-provided restriction to prevent a program from accessing data in another user's segment of storage

Fiber-Distributed Data Interface (FDDI) An ANSI standard for token-passing networks. FDDI uses optical fiber and operates at 100 Mbps in dual, counter-rotating rings.

Fiestel cipher An iterated block cipher that encrypts by breaking a plaintext block into two halves and, with a subkey, applying a "round" transformation to one of the halves. The output of this transformation is then XOR'd with the remaining half. The round is completed by swapping the two halves.

FIFO Acronym for "first in, first out."

file server A computer that provides network stations with controlled access to sharable resources. The network operating system (NOS) is loaded on the file server, and most sharable devices, including disk subsystems and printers, are attached to it.

file protection The aggregate of all processes and procedures in a system designed to inhibit unauthorized access, contamination, or elimination of a file

file security The means by which access to computer files is limited to authorized users only

File Transfer Protocol (FTP) A TCP/IP protocol for file transfer

FIPS Federal Information Processing Standard

firewall A network device that shields the trusted network from unauthorized users in the untrusted network by blocking certain specific types of traffic. Many type of firewalls exist, including packet filtering and stateful inspection.

firmware Executable programs stored in nonvolatile memory

flaw hypothesis methodology A systems analysis and penetration technique in which specifications and documentation for the system are analyzed and then hypotheses made regarding flaws in the system. The list of hypothesized flaws is prioritized on the basis of the estimated probability that a flaw exists, and — assuming that a flaw does exist — on the ease of exploiting it and on the extent of control or compromise that it would provide. The prioritized list is used to direct a penetration attack against the system.

flow control See *information flow control*.

frequency modulation (FM) A method of transmitting information over a radio wave by changing frequencies

formal access approval Documented approval by a data owner to allow access to a particular category of information

Formal Development Methodology A collection of languages and tools that enforces a rigorous method of verification. This methodology uses the Ina Jo specification language for successive stages of system development, including identification and modeling of requirements, high-level design, and program design.

formal proof A complete and convincing mathematical argument presenting the full logical justification for each proof step for the truth of a theorem or set of theorems

formal security policy model A mathematically precise statement of a security policy. To be adequately precise, such a model must represent the initial state of a system, the way in which the system progresses from one state to another, and a definition of a secure state of the system. To be acceptable as a basis for a TCB, the model must be supported by a formal proof that if the initial state of the system satisfies the definition of a secure state and if all assumptions required by the model hold, then all future states of the system will be secure. Some formal modeling techniques include state transition models, denotational semantics models, and algebraic specification models. *See Bell-LaPadula model.*

Formal Top-Level Specification (FTLS) A top-level specification that is written in a formal mathematical language to enable theorems showing the correspondence of the system specification to its formal requirements to be hypothesized and formally proven

formal verification The process of using formal proofs to demonstrate the consistency between a formal specification of a system and a formal security policy model (design verification) or between the formal specification and its high-level program implementation (implementation verification)

forward chaining The reasoning approach that can be used when a small number of solutions exist relative to the number of inputs. The input data is used to reason "forward" to prove that one of the possible solutions in a small solution set is correct.

fractional T-1 A 64 Kbps increment of a T1 frame

frame relay A packet-switching interface that operates at data rates of 56 Kbps to 2 Mbps. Frame relay is minus the error control overhead of X.25, and assumes that a higher-layer protocol will check for transmission errors.

frequency division multiple access (FDMA) A digital radio technology that divides the available spectrum into separate radio channels. Generally used in conjunction with time division multiple access (TDMA) or code division multiple access (CDMA).

frequency hopping multiple access (FHMA) A system using frequency hopping spread spectrum (FHSS) to permit multiple, simultaneous conversations or data sessions by assigning different hopping patterns to each.

frequency hopping spread spectrum (FHSS) A method used to share the available bandwidth in 802.11b WLANs. FHSS takes the data signal and modulates it with a carrier signal that hops from frequency to frequency on a cyclical basis over a wide band of frequencies. FHSS in the 2.4 GHz frequency band will hop between 2.4 GHz and 2.483 GHz. The receiver must be set to the same hopping code.

frequency shift keying (FSK) A modulation scheme for data communications using a limited number of discrete frequencies to convey binary information

front-end security filter A security filter that could be implemented in hardware or software that is logically separated from the remainder of the system in order to protect the system's integrity

FTLS Formal Top-Level Specification

functional programming A programming method that uses only mathematical functions to perform computations and solve problems

functional testing The segment of security testing in which the advertised security mechanisms of the system are tested, under operational conditions, for correct operation

G

gateway A network component that provides interconnectivity at higher network layers

genetic algorithms Part of the general class known as *evolutionary computing*, which uses the Darwinian principles of survival of the fittest, mutation, and the adaptation of successive generations of populations to their environment. The genetic algorithm implements this process through iteration of generations of a constant-size population of items or individuals.

Gigabyte (GB, GByte) A unit of measure for memory or disk storage capacity; 1,073,741,824 bytes

Gigahertz (GHz) A measure of frequency; one billion hertz

Global System for Mobile (GSM) communications The wireless analog of the ISDN landline system

Gramm-Leach-Bliley (GLB) Act of November 1999 An act that removes Depression-era restrictions on banks that limited certain business activities, mergers, and affiliations. It repeals the restrictions on banks affiliating with securities firms contained in sections 20 and 32 of the Glass-Steagall Act. GLB became effective on November 13, 2001. GLB also requires health plans and insurers to protect member and subscriber data in electronic and other formats. These health plans and insurers will fall under new state laws and regulations that are being passed to implement GLB, since GLB explicitly assigns enforcement of the health plan and insurer regulations to state insurance authorities (15 U.S.C. §6805). Some of the privacy and security requirements of Gramm-Leach-Bliley are similar to those of HIPAA.

granularity An expression of the relative size of a data object; for example, protection at the file level is considered coarse granularity, whereas protection at field level is considered to be of a finer granularity.

guard A processor that provides a filter between two disparate systems operating at different security levels or between a user terminal and a database in order to filter out data that the user is not authorized to access

Gypsy Verification Environment An integrated set of tools for specifying, coding, and verifying programs written in the Gypsy language — a language similar to Pascal that has both specification and programming features. This methodology includes an editor, a specification processor, a verification condition generator, a user-directed theorem prover, and an information flow tool.

H

handshaking procedure A dialogue between two entities (for example, a user and a computer, a computer and another computer, or a program and another program) for the purpose of identifying and authenticating the entities to one another

HDX Half duplex

Hertz (Hz) A unit of frequency measurement; one cycle of a periodic event per second. Used to measure frequency.

Hierarchical Development Methodology A methodology for specifying and verifying the design programs written in the Special specification language. The tools for this methodology include the Special specification processor, the Boyer-Moore theorem prover, and the Feiertag information flow tool.

high-level data link control An ISO protocol for link synchronization and error control

HIPAA See *Kennedy-Kassebaum Act of 1996*.

host to front-end protocol A set of conventions governing the format and control of data that is passed from a host to a front-end machine

host A time-sharing computer accessed via terminals or terminal emulation; a computer to which an expansion device attaches

HTTP Hypertext Transfer Protocol

Hypertext Markup Language (HTML) A standard used on the Internet for defining hypertext links between documents

I

I&A Identification and authentication

IAC Inquiry access code; used in inquiry procedures. The IAC can be one of two types: a dedicated IAC for specific devices or a generic IAC for all devices.

IAW Acronym for "in accordance with"

ICV Integrity check value. In WEP encryption, the frame is run through an integrity algorithm, and the ICV generated is placed at the end of the encrypted data in the frame. Then the receiving station runs the data through its integrity algorithm and compares it to the ICV received in the frame. If it matches, the unencrypted frame is passed to the higher layers. If it does not match, the frame is discarded.

ID Common abbreviation for "identifier" or "identity"

identification The process that enables a system to recognize an entity, generally by the use of unique machine-readable user names

IDS Intrusion detection system

IETF Internet Engineering Task Force

IKE Internet key exchange

impersonating Synonymous with *spoofing*

incomplete parameter checking A system design flaw that results when all parameters have not been fully anticipated for accuracy and consistency, thus making the system vulnerable to penetration

individual accountability The ability to positively associate the identity of a user with the time, method, and degree of access to a system

industrial, scientific, and medicine (ISM) bands Radio frequency bands authorized by the Federal Communications Commission (FCC) for wireless LANs. The ISM bands are located at 902 MHz, 2.400 GHz, and 5.7 GHz. The transmitted power is commonly less than 600mw, therefore, but no FCC license is required.

inference engine A component of an artificial intelligence system that takes inputs and uses a knowledge base to infer new facts and solve a problem

information flow control A procedure undertaken to ensure that information transfers within a system are not made from a higher security level object to an object of a lower security level. See *covert channel*, *simple security property*, and *star property (* property)*. Synonymous with *data flow control* and *flow control*.

information flow model Information security model in which information is categorized into classes, and rules define how information can flow between the classes

Information System Security Officer (ISSO) The person who is responsible to the DAA for ensuring that security is provided for and implemented throughout the life cycle of an AIS, from the beginning of the concept development plan through its design, development, operation, maintenance, and secure disposal

Information Systems Security Products and Services Catalogue A catalogue issued quarterly by the National Security Agency that incorporates the DPL, EPL, ETL, PPL, and other security product and service lists. This catalogue is available through the U.S. Government Printing Office, Washington, D.C., 20402

infrared (IR) light Light waves having wavelengths ranging from about 0.75 to 1,000 microns — this is lower in frequency than the spectral colors, but higher in frequency than radio waves

inheritance (in object-oriented programming) When all the methods of one class, called a *superclass*, are inherited by a subclass. Thus, all messages understood by the superclass are understood by the subclass.

Institute of Electrical and Electronic Engineers (IEEE) A U.S.–based standards organization participating in the development of standards for data transmission systems. The IEEE has made significant progress in the establishment of standards for LANs, namely the IEEE 802 series.

Integrated Services Digital Network (ISDN) A collection of CCITT standards specifying WAN digital transmission services. The overall goal of ISDN is to provide a single physical network outlet and transport mechanism for the transmission of all types of information, including data, video, and voice.

integration testing Testing process used to verify the interface between network components as the components are installed. The installation crew should integrate components into the network one-by-one and perform integration testing when necessary to ensure proper gradual integration of components.

integrity A term that refers to a sound, unimpaired, or perfect condition

interdiction See *Denial of Service*.

Interface Definition Language (IDL) A standard interface language that is used by clients to request services from objects

internal security controls Hardware, firmware, and software features within a system that restrict access to resources (hardware, software, and data) to authorized subjects only (persons, programs, or devices)

International Standards Organization (ISO) A non-treaty standards organization active in the development of international standards, such as the Open System Interconnection (OSI) network architecture

International Telecommunications Union (ITU) An intergovernmental agency of the United States responsible for making recommendations and standardization regarding telephone and data communications systems for public and private telecommunication organizations and for providing coordination for the development of international standards

International Telegraph and Telephone Consultative Committee (CCITT) An international standards organization that is part of the ITU and dedicated to establishing effective and compatible telecommunications among members of the United Nations. CCITT develops the widely used V-series and X-series standards and protocols.

Internet Protocol (IP) The Internet standard protocol that defines the Internet datagram as the information unit passed across the Internet. IP provides the basis of a best-effort packet delivery service. The Internet protocol suite is often referred to as TCP/IP because IP is one of the two fundamental protocols, the other being the Transfer Control Protocol.

Internet The largest network in the world. Successor to ARPANET, the Internet includes other large internetworks. The Internet uses the TCP/IP protocol suite and connects universities, government agencies, and individuals around the world.

Internetwork Packet Exchange (IPX) NetWare protocol for the exchange of message packets on an internetwork. IPX passes application requests for network services to the network drives and then to other workstations, servers, or devices on the internetwork.

IPSec Secure Internet Protocol

Isochronous transmission Type of synchronization whereby information frames are sent at specific times

isolation The containment of subjects and objects in a system in such a way that they are separated from one another as well as from the protection controls of the operating system

ISP Internet service provider

ISSO Information System Security Officer

ITA Industrial Telecommunications Association

IV Initialization vector; for WEP encryption

J
joint application design (JAD) A parallel team design process simultaneously defining requirements composed of users, sales people, marketing staff, project managers, analysts, and engineers. Members of this team are used to simultaneously define requirements.

K

Kennedy-Kassebaum Health Insurance Portability and Accountability Act (HIPAA) of 1996 A set of regulations that mandate the use of standards in health care record keeping and electronic transactions. The act requires that health care plans, providers, insurers, and clearinghouses do the following:

- Provide for restricted access by the patient to personal healthcare information
- Implement administrative simplification standards
- Enable the portability of health insurance
- Establish strong penalties for healthcare fraud

Kerberos A trusted, third party authentication protocol that was developed under Project Athena at MIT. In Greek mythology, Kerberos is a three-headed dog that guards the entrance to the underworld. Using symmetric key cryptography, Kerberos authenticates clients to other entities on a network of which a client requires services.

key clustering A situation in which a plaintext message generates identical ciphertext messages by using the same transformation algorithm but with different cryptovariables

key Information or sequence that controls the enciphering and deciphering of messages. Also known as a *cryptovariable*. Used with a particular algorithm to encipher or decipher the plaintext message.

key schedule A set of subkeys derived from a secret key

Kilobyte (KB, Kbyte) A unit of measurement, of memory or disk storage capacity; a data unit of 2^{10} (1,024) bytes

Kilohertz (kHz) A unit of frequency measurement equivalent to 1,000 Hertz

knowledge acquisition system The means of identifying and acquiring the knowledge to be entered into an expert system's knowledge base

knowledge base Refers to the rules and facts of the particular problem domain in an expert system

L

least privilege The principle that requires each subject to be granted the most restrictive set of privileges needed for the performance of authorized tasks. The application of this principle limits the damage that can result from accident, error, or unauthorized use.

Light-emitting diode (LED) Used in conjunction with optical fiber, an LED emits incoherent light when current is passed through it. Its advantages include low cost and long lifetime, and are capable of operating in the Mbps range.

limited access Synonymous with *access control*

limited fault tolerance Specifies against what type of failures the Target of Evaluation (TOE) must be resistant. Examples of general failures are flooding of the computer room, short-term power interruption, breakdown of a CPU or host, software failure, or buffer overflow. Requires all functions to be available if specified failure occurs.

Link Access Procedure An ITU error correction protocol derived from the HDLC standard

link encryption Each entity has keys in common with its two neighboring nodes in the chain of transmission. Thus, a node receives the encrypted message from its predecessor neighboring node, decrypts it, and re-encrypts it with another key that is common to the successor node. Then, the encrypted message is sent on to the successor node, where the process is repeated until the final destination is reached. Obviously, this mode provides no protection if the nodes along the transmission path are subject to compromise.

list-oriented A computer protection system in which each protected object has a list of all subjects that are authorized to access it. Compare *ticket-oriented*.

LLC Logical Link Control; the IEEE layer 2 protocol

local area network (LAN) A network that interconnects devices in the same office, floor, or building, or close buildings

lock-and-key protection system A protection system that involves matching a key or password with a specific access requirement

logic bomb A resident computer program that triggers the perpetration of an unauthorized act when particular states of the system are realized

Logical Link Control layer The highest layer of the IEEE 802 reference model; provides similar functions to those of a traditional data link control protocol

loophole An error of omission or oversight in software or hardware that permits circumventing the system security policy

LSB Least-significant bit

M

MAC Mandatory Access Control if used in the context of a type of access control; MAC also refers to the Media Access Control address assigned to a network interface card on an Ethernet network.

magnetic remanence A measure of the magnetic flux density that remains after removal of the applied magnetic force. Refers to any data remaining on magnetic storage media after removal of the power.

Mail gateway A type of gateway that interconnects dissimilar e-mail systems

maintenance hook Special instructions in software to enable easy maintenance and additional feature development. These instructions are not clearly defined during access for design specification. Hooks frequently enable entry into the code at unusual points or without the usual checks, so they are a serious security risk if they are not removed prior to live implementation. Maintenance hooks are special types of trap doors.

malicious logic Hardware, software, or firmware that is intentionally included in a system for an unauthorized purpose (for example, a Trojan horse)

MAN Metropolitan area network

management information base (MIB) A collection of managed objects residing in a virtual information store

mandatory access control (MAC) A means of restricting access to objects based on the sensitivity (as represented by a label) of the information contained in the objects and the formal authorization (in other words, clearance) of subjects to access information of such sensitivity. Compare *discretionary access control*.

MAPI Microsoft's mail application programming interface

masquerading See *spoofing*

Media access control (MAC) An IEEE 802 standards sublayer used to control access to a network medium, such as a wireless LAN. Also deals with collision detection. Each computer has its own unique MAC address.

Medium access The Data Link layer function that controls how devices access a shared medium. IEEE 802.11 uses either CSMA/CA or contention-free access modes. Also, a data link function that controls the use of a common network medium.

Megabits per second (Mbps) One million bits per second

Megabyte (MB, Mbyte) A unit of measurement for memory or disk storage capacity. 220 (usually 1,048,576) bytes; sometimes interpreted as 1 million bytes.

Megahertz (MHz) A measure of frequency equivalent to one million cycles per second

Middleware An intermediate software component located on the wired network between the wireless appliance and the application or data residing on the wired network. Middleware provides appropriate interfaces between the appliance and the host application or server database.

mimicking See *spoofing*

Mobile IP A protocol developed by the IETF that enables users to roam to parts of the network associated with a different IP address than the one loaded in the user's appliance. Also refers to any mobile device that contains the IEEE 802.11 MAC and physical layers.

modes of operation A description of the conditions under which an AIS functions, based on the sensitivity of data processed and the clearance levels and authorizations of the users. Four modes of operation are authorized:

1. Dedicated mode—An AIS is operating in the dedicated mode when each user who has direct or indirect individual access to the AIS, its peripherals, remote terminals, or remote hosts has all of the following:

    a. A valid personnel clearance for all information on the system

    b. Formal access approval; furthermore, the user has signed nondisclosure agreements for all the information stored and/or processed (including all compartments, subcompartments, and/or special access programs)

    c. A valid need-to-know for all information contained within the system

2. System-high mode—An AIS is operating in the system-high mode when each user who has direct or indirect access to the AIS, its peripherals, remote terminals, or remote hosts has all of the following:

    a. A valid personnel clearance for all information on the AIS

    b. Formal access approval, and signed nondisclosure agreements, for all the information stored and/or processed (including all compartments, subcompartments, and/or special access programs)

    c. A valid need-to-know for some of the information contained within the AIS

3. Compartmented mode—An AIS is operating in the compartmented mode when each user who has direct or indirect access to the AIS, its peripherals, remote terminals, or remote hosts has all of the following:

    a. A valid personnel clearance for the most restricted information processed in the AIS

    b. Formal access approval, and signed nondisclosure agreements, for that information which he or she will be able to access

    c. A valid need-to-know for that information which he or she will be able to access

4. Multilevel mode — An AIS is operating in the multilevel mode when all of the following statements are satisfied concerning the users who have direct or indirect access to the AIS, its peripherals, remote terminals, or remote hosts:

   a. Some do not have a valid personnel clearance for all the information processed in the AIS.

   b. All have the proper clearance and the appropriate formal access approval for that information to which they are to have access.

   c. All have a valid need-to-know for that information to which they are to have access.

Modulation The process of translating the baseband digital signal to a suitable analog form. Any of several techniques for combining user information with a transmitter's carrier signal.

MSB Most significant bit

multilevel device A device that is used in a manner that permits it to simultaneously process data of two or more security levels without risk of compromise. To accomplish this, sensitivity labels are normally stored on the same physical medium and in the same form (for example, machine-readable or human-readable) as the data being processed.

multilevel secure A class of system containing information with different sensitivities that simultaneously permits access by users with different security clearances and needs-to-know but that prevents users from obtaining access to information for which they lack authorization.

multilevel security mode See *modes of operation*.

Multipath The signal variation caused when radio signals take multiple paths from transmitter to receiver

Multipath fading A type of fading caused by signals taking different paths from the transmitter to the receiver and consequently interfering with each other

multiple access rights terminal A terminal that can be used by more than one class of users; for example, users who have different access rights to data

multiple inheritance In object-oriented programming, a situation where a subclass inherits the behavior of multiple superclasses

multiplexer A network component that combines multiple signals into one composite signal in a form suitable for transmission over a long-haul connection, such as leased 56 Kbps or T1 circuits

Multi-station access unit (MAU) A multiport wiring hub for Token Ring networks

multiuser mode of operation A mode of operation designed for systems that process sensitive, unclassified information in which users might not have a need-to-know for all information processed in the system. This mode is also used for microcomputers processing sensitive unclassified information that cannot meet the requirements of the stand-alone mode of operation.

Musical Instrument Digital Interface (MIDI) A standard protocol for the interchange of musical information between musical instruments and computers

mutually suspicious A state that exists between interacting processes (subsystems or programs) in which neither process can expect the other process to function securely with respect to some property

MUX Multiplexing sublayer; a sublayer of the L2CAP layer

N

NACK or NAK Negative acknowledgement. This can be a deliberate signal that the message was received in error or can be inferred by a time out.

National Computer Security Assessment Program A program designed to evaluate the interrelationship of empirical data of computer security infractions and critical systems profiles while comprehensively incorporating information from the CSTVRP. The assessment builds threat and vulnerability scenarios that are based on a collection of facts from relevant reported cases. Such scenarios are a powerful, dramatic, and concise form of representing the value of loss experience analysis.

National Computer Security Center (NCSC) Originally named the *DoD Computer Security Center,* the NCSC is responsible for encouraging the widespread availability of trusted computer systems throughout the federal government. It is a branch of the National Security Agency (NSA) that also initiates research and develops and publishes standards and criteria for trusted information systems.

National Information Assurance Certification and Accreditation Process (NIACAP) Provides a standard set of activities, general tasks, and a management structure to certify and accredit systems that will maintain the information assurance and security posture of a system or site. The NIACAP is designed to certify that the information system meets documented accreditation requirements and continues to maintain the accredited security posture throughout the system life cycle.

National Security Decision Directive 145 (NSDD 145) Signed by President Ronald Reagan on September 17, 1984, this directive is entitled "National Policy on Telecommunications and Automated Information Systems Security." It provides initial objectives, policies, and an organizational structure to guide the conduct of national activities toward safeguarding systems that process, store, or communicate sensitive information; establishes a mechanism for policy development; and assigns implementation responsibilities.

National Telecommunications and Information System Security Directives (NTISSD) NTISS directives establish national-level decisions relating to NTISS policies, plans, programs, systems, or organizational delegations of authority. NTISSDs are promulgated by the executive agent of the government for telecommunications and information systems security or by the chairman of the NTISSC when so delegated by the executive agent. NTISSDs are binding upon all federal departments and agencies.

National Telecommunications and Information Systems Security Advisory Memoranda/Instructions (NTISSAM, NTISSI) NTISS Advisory Memoranda and Instructions provide advice, assistance, or information on telecommunications and systems security that is of general interest to applicable federal departments and agencies. NTISSAMs/NTISSIs are promulgated by the National Manager for Telecommunications and Automated Information Systems Security and are recommendatory.

NCSC National Computer Security Center

need-to-know The necessity for access to, knowledge of, or possession of specific information that is required to carry out official duties

Network Basic Input/Output System (NetBIOS) A standard interface between networks and PCs that enables applications on different computers to communicate within a LAN. NetBIOS was created by IBM for its early PC network, was adopted by Microsoft, and has since become a de facto industry standard. It is not routable across a WAN.

network file system (NFS) A distributed file system enabling a set of dissimilar computers to access each other's files in a transparent manner

network front end A device that implements the necessary network protocols, including security-related protocols, to enable a computer system to be attached to a network

Network Interface Card (NIC) A network adapter inserted into a computer that enables the computer to be connected to a network

Network monitoring A form of operational support enabling network management to view the network's inner workings. Most network monitoring equipment is nonobtrusive and can be used to determine the network's utilization and to locate faults.

Network re-engineering A structured process that can help an organization proactively control the evolution of its network. Network re-engineering consists of continually identifying factors influencing network changes, analyzing network modification feasibility, and performing network modifications as necessary.

network service access point (NSAP) A point in the network where OSI network services are available to a transport entity

NIST National Institute of Standards and Technology

node Any network-addressable device on the network, such as a router or Network Interface Card. Any network station.

non-interference model The information security model that addresses a situation wherein one group is not affected by another group using specific commands

NSA National Security Agency

NSDD 145 See *National Security Decision Directive 145*.

NTISSC National Telecommunications and Information Systems Security

Number Field Sieve (NFS) A general-purpose factoring algorithm that can be used to factor large numbers

O

object A passive entity that contains or receives information. Access to an object potentially implies access to the information that it contains. Examples of objects include records, blocks, pages, segments, files, directories, directory trees, and programs, as well as bits, bytes, words, fields, processors, video displays, keyboards, clocks, printers, and network nodes.

Object Request Broker (ORB) The fundamental building block of the Object Request Architecture (ORA), which manages the communications between the ORA entities. The purpose of the ORB is to support the interaction of objects in heterogeneous, distributed environments. The objects may be on different types of computing platforms.

object reuse The reassignment and reuse of a storage medium (for example, page frame, disk sector, and magnetic tape) that once contained one or more objects. To be securely reused and assigned to a new subject, storage media must contain no residual data (data remanence) from the object(s) that were previously contained in the media.

object services Services that support the ORB in creating and tracking objects as well as performing access control functions

OFDM Orthogonal frequency division multiplexing; a set of frequency-hopping codes that never use the same frequency at the same time. Used in IEEE 802.11a for high-speed data transfer.

One-time pad Encipherment operation performed using each component ki of the key, K, only once to encipher a single character of the plaintext. Therefore, the key has the same length as the message. The popular interpretation of one-time pad is that the key is used only once and never used again. Ideally, the components of the key are truly random and have no periodicity or predictability, making the ciphertext unbreakable.

Open Database Connectivity (ODBC) A standard database interface enabling interoperability between application software and multivendor ODBC-compliant databases

Open Data-Link Interface (ODI) Novell's specification for Network Interface Card device drivers, allowing simultaneous operation of multiple protocol stacks

open security environment An environment that includes those systems in which at least one of the following conditions holds true: 1) application developers (including maintainers) do not have sufficient clearance or authorization to provide an acceptable presumption that they have not introduced malicious logic, and 2) configuration control does not provide sufficient assurance that applications are protected against the introduction of malicious logic prior to and during the operation of system applications.

Open Shortest Path First (OSPF) A TCP/IP routing protocol that bases routing decisions on the least number of hops from source to destination.

open system authentication The IEEE 802.11 default authentication method, which is a very simple, two-step process: first, the station that wants to authenticate with another station sends an authentication management frame containing the sending station's identity. The receiving station then sends back a frame alerting whether it recognizes the identity of the authenticating station.

Open System Interconnection (OSI) An ISO standard specifying an open system capable of enabling the communications between diverse systems. OSI has the following seven layers of distinction: Physical, Data Link, Network, Transport, Session, Presentation, and Application. These layers provide the functions that enable standardized communications between two application processes.

operations security Controls over hardware and media and operators who have access, protects against asset threats, baseline, or selective mechanisms.

Operations Security (OPSEC) An analytical process by which the U.S. government and its supporting contractors can deny to potential adversaries information about capabilities and intentions by identifying, controlling, and protecting evidence of the planning and execution of sensitive activities and operations.

operator An individual who supports system operations from the operator's console: monitors execution of the system, controls the flow of jobs, and mounts input/output volumes (be alert for shoulder surfing)

OPSEC See *Operations Security*.

Orange Book Alternate name for *DoD Trusted Computer Security Evaluation Criteria*

original equipment manufacturer (OEM) A manufacturer of products for integration in other products or systems

OS Commonly used abbreviation for "operating system"

overt channel A path within a computer system or network that is designed for the authorized transfer of data. Compare with *covert channel*.

overwrite procedure A stimulation to change the state of a bit followed by a known pattern. See *magnetic remanence*.

P

packet A basic message unit for communication across a network. A packet usually includes routing information, data, and (sometimes) error-detection information.

packet-switched A network that routes data packets based on an address contained in the data packet is said to be a *packet-switched network*. Multiple data packets can share the same network resources. A communications network that uses shared facilities to route data packets from and to different users. Unlike a circuit-switched network, a packet-switched network does not set up dedicated circuits for each session.

PAD Acronym for *packet assembly/disassembly*

partitioned security mode A mode of operation wherein all personnel have the clearance but not necessarily formal access approval and need-to-know for all information contained in the system. Not to be confused with *compartmented security mode*.

password A protected/private character string that is used to authenticate an identity

PCMCIA Personal Computer Memory Card International Association. The industry group that defines standards for PC cards (and the name applied to the cards themselves). These roughly credit card-sized adapters for memory and modem cards come in three thicknesses: 3.3, 5, and 10.5 mm.

PDN Public data network

PED Personal electronic device

Peer-to-peer network A network in which a group of devices can communicate between a group of equal devices. A peer-to-peer LAN does not depend upon a dedicated server, but allows any node to be installed as a non-dedicated server and share its files and peripherals across the network.

pen register A device that records all the numbers dialed from a specific telephone line.

penetration The successful act of bypassing a system's security mechanisms

penetration signature The characteristics or identifying marks that might be produced by a penetration

penetration study A study to determine the feasibility and methods for defeating the controls of a system

penetration testing The portion of security testing in which the evaluators attempt to circumvent the security features of a system. The evaluators might be assumed to use all system design and implementation documentation, which can include listings of system source code, manuals, and circuit diagrams. The evaluators work under the same constraints that are applied to ordinary users.

performance modeling The use of simulation software to predict network behavior, allowing developers to perform capacity planning. Simulation makes it possible to model the network and impose varying levels of utilization to observe the effects.

performance monitoring Activity that tracks network performance during normal operations. Performance monitoring includes real-time monitoring, during which metrics are collected and compared against thresholds; recent-past monitoring, in which metrics are collected and analyzed for trends that may lead to performance problems; and historical data analysis, in which metrics are collected and stored for later analysis.

periods processing The processing of various levels of sensitive information at distinctly different times. Under periods processing, the system must be purged of all information from one processing period before transitioning to the next, when there are different users who have differing authorizations.

permissions A description of the type of authorized interactions that a subject can have with an object. Examples of permissions types include read, write, execute, add, modify, and delete.

permutation A method of encrypting a message, also known as transposition; operates by rearranging the letters of the plaint

personnel security The procedures that are established to ensure that all personnel who have access to sensitive information possess the required authority as well as appropriate clearances. Procedures to ensure a person's background; provides assurance of necessary trustworthiness.

PGP Pretty Good Privacy; a form of encryption

Physical layer (PHY) The layer of the OSI model that provides the transmission of bits through a communication channel by defining electrical, mechanical, and procedural specifications, and establishes protocols for voltage and data transmission timing and rules for "handshaking."

physical security The application of physical barriers and control procedures as preventive measures or countermeasures against threats to resources and sensitive information

piconet A collection of devices connected via Bluetooth technology in an ad hoc fashion. A piconet starts with two connected devices, such as a portable PC and cellular phone, and can grow to eight connected devices.

piggyback Gaining unauthorized access to a system via another user's legitimate connection. See *between-the-lines entry*.

pipelining In computer architecture, a design in which the decode and execution cycles of one instruction are overlapped in time with the fetch cycle of the next instruction

PKI Public key infrastructure

plain old telephone system (POTS) The original common analog telephone system, which is still in widespread use today

plaintext Message text in cleartext, human-readable form

Platform for Privacy Preferences (P3P) Proposed standards developed by the World Wide Web Consortium (W3C) to implement privacy practices on Web sites

Point-to-Point Protocol (PPP) A protocol that provides router-to-router and host-to-network connections over both synchronous and asynchronous circuits. PPP is the successor to SLIP.

portability Defines network connectivity that can be easily established, used, and then dismantled

PPL Preferred Products List

PRBS Pseudorandom bit sequence

Preferred Products List (PPL) A list of commercially produced equipment that meets TEMPEST and other requirements prescribed by the National Security Agency. This list is included in the NSA Information Systems Security Products and Services Catalogue, issued quarterly and available through the Government Printing Office.

Presentation layer The layer of the OSI model that negotiates data transfer syntax for the Application layer and performs translations between different data types, if necessary

print suppression Eliminating the displaying of characters in order to preserve their secrecy; for example, not displaying a password as it is keyed at the input terminal

private key encryption See *symmetric key encryption*.

privileged instructions A set of instructions (for example, interrupt handling or special computer instructions) to control features (such as storage protection features) that are generally executable only when the automated system is operating in the executive state

PRNG Pseudorandom number generator

procedural language Implies sequential execution of instructions based on the von Neumann architecture of a CPU, memory, and input/output device. Variables are part of the sets of instructions used to solve a particular problem, and therefore, the data is not separate from the statements.

procedural security Synonymous with *administrative security*

process A program in execution. See *domain* and *subject*.

Protected Health Information (PHI) Individually identifiable health information that is:

- Transmitted by electronic media
- Maintained in any medium described in the definition of electronic media (under HIPAA)
- Transmitted or maintained in any other form or medium

protection philosophy An informal description of the overall design of a system that delineates each of the protection mechanisms employed. A combination, appropriate to the evaluation class, of formal and informal techniques is used to show that the mechanisms are adequate to enforce the security policy.

Protection Profile (PP) In the Common Criteria, an implementation-independent specification of the security requirements and protections of a product that could be built

protection ring One of a hierarchy of privileged modes of a system that gives certain access rights to user programs and processes authorized to operate in a given mode

protection-critical portions of the TCB Those portions of the TCB whose normal function is to deal with access control between subjects and objects. Their correct operation is essential to the protection of the data on the system.

protocols A set of rules and formats, semantic and syntactic, that permits entities to exchange information

Prototyping A method of determining or verifying requirements and design specifications. The prototype normally consists of network hardware and software that support a proposed solution. The approach to prototyping is typically a trial-and-error experimental process.

pseudoflaw An apparent loophole deliberately implanted in an operating system program as a trap for intruders

PSTN Public-switched telephone network; the general phone network

public key cryptography See *asymmetric key encryption*.

Public Key Cryptography Standards (PKCS) A set of public key cryptography standards that support algorithms such as Diffie-Hellman and RSA, as well as algorithm-independent standards

Public Law 100-235 (P.L. 100-235) Also known as the *Computer Security Act of 1987*, this law creates a means for establishing minimum acceptable security practices for improving the security and privacy of sensitive information in federal computer systems. This law assigns to the National Institute of Standards and Technology responsibility for developing standards and guidelines for federal computer systems processing unclassified data. The law also requires establishment of security plans by all operators of federal computer systems that contain sensitive information.

pump In a multilevel security system, or MLS, a one-way information flow device or data diode. In an analog to a pump operation, it permits information flow in one direction only, from a lower level of security classification or sensitivity to a higher level. The pump is a convenient approach to multilevel security in that it can be used to put together systems with different security levels.

purge The removal of sensitive data from an AIS, AIS storage device, or peripheral device with storage capacity at the end of a processing period. This action is performed in such a way that there is assurance proportional to the sensitivity of the data that the data cannot be reconstructed. An AIS must be disconnected from any external network before a purge. After a purge, the medium can be declassified by observing the review procedures of the respective agency.

R
RADIUS Remote Authentication Dial-In User Service

RC4 RSA cipher algorithm 4

read A fundamental operation that results only in the flow of information from an object to a subject

read access Permission to read information

recovery planning The advance planning and preparations that are necessary to minimize loss and to ensure the availability of the critical information systems of an organization

recovery procedures The actions that are necessary to restore a system's computational capability and data files after a system failure or outage/disruption

Red Book A document of the United States *National Security Agency* (NSA) defining criteria for secure networks

Reduced Instruction Set Computer (RISC) A computer architecture designed to reduce the number of cycles required to execute an instruction. A RISC architecture uses simpler instructions but makes use of other features, such as optimizing compilers, to reduce the number of instructions required, large numbers of general-purpose registers in the processor, and data caches.

reference monitor concept An access-control concept that refers to an abstract machine that mediates all accesses to objects by subjects

reference validation mechanism An implementation of the reference monitor concept. A security kernel is a type of reference-validation mechanism.

reliability The probability of a given system performing its mission adequately for a specified period of time under expected operating conditions

remote bridge A bridge connecting networks separated by longer distances. Organizations use leased 56 Kbps circuits, T1 digital circuits, and radio waves to provide long-distance connections between remote bridges.

remote journaling Refers to the parallel processing of transactions to an alternate site, as opposed to a batch dump process such as electronic vaulting. A communications line is used to transmit live data as it occurs, which enables the alternate site to be fully operational at all times and introduces a very high level of fault tolerance.

repeater A network component that provides internetworking functionality at the Physical layer of a network's architecture. A repeater amplifies network signals, extending the distance they can travel.

residual risk The portion of risk that remains after security measures have been applied

residue Data left in storage after processing operations are complete but before degaussing or rewriting has taken place

resource encapsulation The process of ensuring that a resource not be directly accessible by a subject but that it be protected so that the reference monitor can properly mediate access to it

restricted area Any area to which access is subject to special restrictions or controls for reasons of security or safeguarding of property or material

RFC Acronym for request for comment

RFP Acronym for request for proposal

ring topology A topology in which a set of nodes are joined in a closed loop

risk The probability that a particular threat will exploit a particular vulnerability of the system

risk analysis The process of identifying security risks, determining their magnitude, and identifying areas needing safeguards. Risk analysis is a part of risk management. Synonymous with *risk assessment*.

risk assessment See *risk analysis*

risk index The disparity between the minimum clearance or authorization of system users and the maximum sensitivity (for example, classification and categories) of data processed by a system. See CSC-STD-003-85 and CSC-STD-004-85 for a complete explanation of this term.

risk management The total process of identifying, controlling, and eliminating or minimizing uncertain events that might affect system resources. It includes risk analysis, a cost-benefit analysis, selection, implementation and tests, a security evaluation of safeguards, and an overall security review.

ROM Read-only memory

router A network component that provides internetworking at the Network layer of a network's architecture by allowing individual networks to become part of a WAN. A router works by using logical and physical addresses to connect two or more separate networks. It determines the best path by which to send a packet of information.

Routing Information Protocol (RIP) A common type of routing protocol. RIP bases its routing path on the distance (number of hops) to the destination. RIP maintains optimum routing paths by sending out routing update messages if the network topology changes.

RS-232 A serial communications interface. Serial communication standards are defined by the Electronic Industries Association (EIA). The ARS-232n EIA standard that specifies up to 20 Kbps, 50 foot, serial transmission between computers and peripheral devices.

RS-422 An EIA standard specifying electrical characteristics for balanced circuits (in other words, both transmit and return wires are at the same voltage above ground). RS-422 is used in conjunction with RS-449.

RS-423 An EIA standard specifying electrical characteristics for unbalanced circuits (in other words, the return wire is tied to the ground). RS-423 is used in conjunction with RS-449.

RS-449 An EIA standard specifying a 37-pin connector for high-speed transmission

RS-485 An EIA standard for multipoint communications lines

S

S/MIME A protocol that adds digital signatures and encryption to Internet MIME (Multipurpose Internet Mail Extensions)

safeguards See security safeguards.

SAISS Subcommittee on Automated Information Systems Security of NTISSC

sandbox An access control–based protection mechanism. It is commonly applied to restrict the access rights of mobile code that is downloaded from a Web site as an applet. The code is set up to run in a "sandbox" that blocks its access to the local workstation's hard disk, thus preventing the code from malicious activity. The sandbox is usually interpreted by a virtual machine such as the Java Virtual Machine (JVM).

SBU Abbreviation for *sensitive but unclassified*; an information designation

scalar processor A processor that executes one instruction at a time

scavenging Searching through object residue to acquire unauthorized data

SDLC Synchronous data link control

secure configuration management The set of procedures that are appropriate for controlling changes to a system's hardware and software structure for the purpose of ensuring that changes will not lead to violations of the system's security policy.

secure state A condition in which no subject can access any object in an unauthorized manner

secure subsystem A subsystem that contains its own implementation of the reference monitor concept for those resources it controls. The secure subsystem, however, must depend on other controls and the base operating system for the control of subjects and the more primitive system objects.

security critical mechanisms Those security mechanisms whose correct operation is necessary to ensure that the security policy is enforced

security evaluation An evaluation that is performed to assess the degree of trust that can be placed in systems for the secure handling of sensitive information. One type, a product evaluation, is an evaluation performed on the hardware and software features and assurances of a computer product from a perspective that excludes the application environment. The other type, a system evaluation, is made for the purpose of assessing a system's security safeguards with respect to a specific operational mission; it is a major step in the certification and accreditation process.

security fault analysis A security analysis, usually performed on hardware at the gate level, to determine the security properties of a device when a hardware fault is encountered

security features The security-relevant functions, mechanisms, and characteristics of system hardware and software. Security features are a subset of system security safeguards.

security filter A trusted subsystem that enforces a security policy on the data that pass through it

security flaw An error of commission or omission in a system that might enable protection mechanisms to be bypassed

security flow analysis A security analysis performed on a formal system specification that locates the potential flows of information within the system

Security functional requirements Requirements, preferably from the Common Criteria, Part 2, that when taken together specify the security behavior of an IT product or system

security kernel The hardware, firmware, and software elements of a Trusted Computer Base (TCB) that implement the reference monitor concept. The security kernel must mediate all accesses, be protected from modification, and be verifiable as correct.

security label A piece of information that represents the security level of an object

security level The combination of a hierarchical classification and a set of nonhierarchical categories that represents the sensitivity of information

security measures Elements of software, firmware, hardware, or procedures that are included in a system for the satisfaction of security specifications

security objective A statement of intent to counter specified threats and/or satisfy specified organizational security policies and assumptions

security perimeter The boundary where security controls are in effect to protect assets

security policy The set of laws, rules, and practices that regulates how an organization manages, protects, and distributes sensitive information

security policy model A formal presentation of the security policy enforced by the system. It must identify the set of rules and practices that regulate how a system manages, protects, and distributes sensitive information. See *Bell-LaPadula model* and *formal security policy model*.

security range The highest and lowest security levels that are permitted in or on a system, system component, subsystem, or network

security requirements The types and levels of protection that are necessary for equipment, data, information, applications, and facilities to meet security policy

security requirements baseline A description of minimum requirements necessary for a system to maintain an acceptable level of security

security safeguards The protective measures and controls that are prescribed to meet the security requirements specified for a system. Those safeguards can include (but are not necessarily limited to) the following: hardware and software security features, operating procedures, accountability procedures, access and distribution controls, management constraints, personnel security, and physical structures, areas, and devices. Also called *safeguards*.

security specifications A detailed description of the safeguards required to protect a system

Security Target (ST) In the Common Criteria, a listing of the security claims for a particular IT security product. A set of security functional and assurance requirements and specifications to be used as the basis for evaluating an identified product or system.

security test and evaluation An examination and analysis of the security safeguards of a system as they have been applied in an operational environment to determine the security posture of the system

security testing A process that is used to determine that the security features of a system are implemented as designed. This process includes hands-on functional testing, penetration testing, and verification.

sensitive information Information that, if lost, misused, modified, or accessed by unauthorized individuals, could affect the national interest or the conduct of federal programs or the privacy to which individuals are entitled under Section 552a of Title 5, U.S. Code, but that has not been specifically authorized under criteria established by an executive order or an act of Congress to be kept classified in the interest of national defense or foreign policy.

sensitivity label A piece of information that represents the security level of an object. Sensitivity labels are used by the TCB as the basis for mandatory access control decisions.

serial interface An interface to provide serial communications service

Serial Line Internet Protocol (SLIP) An Internet protocol used to run IP over serial lines and dial-up connections

Session layer One of the seven OSI model layers. Establishes, manages, and terminates sessions between applications.

shared key authentication A type of authentication that assumes each station has received a secret shared key through a secure channel, independent from an 802.11 network. Stations authenticate through shared knowledge of the secret key. Use of shared key authentication requires implementation of the 802.11 Wireless Equivalent Privacy (WEP) algorithm.

Simple Mail Transfer Protocol (SMTP) The Internet e-mail protocol

Simple Network Management Protocol (SNMP) The network management protocol of choice for TCP/IP-based Internets. Widely implemented with 10BaseT Ethernet. A network management protocol that defines information transfer between management information bases (MIBs).

simple security condition See *simple security property*.

simple security property A Bell-LaPadula security model rule enabling a subject read access to an object only if the security level of the subject dominates the security level of the object. Synonymous with *simple security condition*.

single user mode OS loaded without Security Front End

single-level device An automated information systems device that is used to process data of a single security level at any one time

SMS Short (or small) message service

SNR Signal-to-noise ratio

software development methodologies Methodologies for specifying and verifying design programs for system development. Each methodology is written for a specific computer language. See *Enhanced Hierarchical Development Methodology, Formal Development Methodology, Gypsy Verification Environment*, and *Hierarchical Development Methodology*.

software engineering The science and art of specifying, designing, implementing and evolving programs, documentation and operating procedures whereby computers can be made useful to man

software process A set of activities, methods, and practices that are used to develop and maintain software and associated products

software process capability Describes the range of expected results that can be achieved by following a software process

software process maturity The extent to which a software process is defined, managed, measured, controlled, and effective

software process performance The result achieved by following a software process

software security General-purpose (executive, utility, or software development tools) and applications programs or routines that protect data that are handled by a system

software system test and evaluation process A process that plans, develops, and documents the quantitative demonstration of the fulfillment of all baseline functional performance and operational and interface requirements

spoofing An attempt to gain access to a system by posing as an authorized user. Synonymous with *impersonating, masquerading,* or *mimicking*.

SSL Secure Sockets Layer

SSO System Security Officer

Subcommittee on Automated Information Systems Security The SAISS is composed of one voting member from each organization that is represented on the NTISSC.

ST connector An optical fiber connector that uses a bayonet plug and socket

standalone (shared system) A system that is physically and electrically isolated from all other systems and is intended to be used by more than one person, either simultaneously (for example, a system that has multiple terminals) or serially, with data belonging to one user remaining available to the system while another user uses the system (for example, a personal computer that has nonremovable storage media, such as a hard disk).

standalone (single-user system) A system that is physically and electrically isolated from all other systems and is intended to be used by one person at a time, with no data belonging to other users remaining in the system (for example, a personal computer that has removable storage media, such as a floppy disk).

star property See * *property*.

Star topology A topology wherein each node is connected to a common central switch or hub

State Delta Verification System A system that is designed to give high confidence regarding microcode performance by using formulae that represent isolated states of a computation to check proofs concerning the course of that computation

state variable A variable that represents either the state of the system or the state of some system resource

storage object An object that supports both read and write access

Structured Query Language (SQL) An international standard for defining and accessing relational databases

STS Subcommittee on Telecommunications Security of NTISSC

Subcommittee on Telecommunications Security (STS) NSDD-145 authorizes and directs the establishment, under the NTISSC, of a permanent subcommittee on Telecommunications Security. The STS is composed of one voting member from each organization that is represented on the NTISSC.

subject An active entity, generally in the form of a person, process, or device, that causes information to flow among objects or that changes the system state. Technically, a process/domain pair.

subject security level A subject's security level is equal to the security level of the objects to which it has both read and write access. A subject's security level must always be dominated by the clearance of the user with which the subject is associated.

superscalar processor A processor that allows concurrent execution of instructions in the same pipelined stage. The term *superscalar* denotes multiple, concurrent operations performed on scalar values, as opposed to vectors or arrays that are used as objects of computation in array processors.

supervisor state See *executive state*.

Switched Multimegabit Digital Service (SMDS) A packet-switching connectionless data service for WANs

symmetric (private) key encryption Cryptographic system in which the sender and receiver both know a secret key that is used to encrypt and decrypt the message

Synchronous Optical NETwork (SONET) A fiber optic transmission system for high-speed digital traffic. SONET is part of the B-ISDN standard.

Synchronous transmission Type of communications data synchronization whereby frames are sent within defined time periods. It uses a clock to control the timing of bits being sent. See *asynchronous transmission*.

system Data processing facility

System Development Methodologies Methodologies developed through software engineering to manage the complexity of system development. Development methodologies include software engineering aids and high-level design analysis tools.

system high security mode System and all peripherals *protected in accordance with* (IAW) requirements for highest security level of material in system; personnel with access have security clearance but not need-to-know. See *modes of operation*.

system integrity A characteristic of a system when it performs its intended function in an unimpaired manner, free from deliberate or inadvertent unauthorized manipulation of the system.

system low The lowest security level supported by a system at a particular time or in a particular environment

System Security Officer (SSO) See *Information System Security Officer*.

System testing Type of testing that verifies the installation of the entire network. Testers normally complete system testing in a simulated production environment, simulating actual users in order to ensure the network meets all stated requirements.

Systems Network Architecture (SNA) IBM's proprietary network architecture

Systems Security Steering Group The senior government body established by NSDD-145 to provide top-level review and policy guidance for the telecommunications security and automated information systems security activities of the United States government. This group is chaired by the assistant to the President for National Security Affairs and consists of the Secretary of State, Secretary of Treasury, Secretary of Defense, Attorney General, Director of the Office of Management and Budget, and Director of Central Intelligence.

T

T1 A standard specifying a time division multiplexing scheme for point-to-point transmission of digital signals at 1.544 Mbps

tampering An unauthorized modification that alters the proper functioning of an equipment or system in a manner that degrades the security or functionality that it provides

Target of Evaluation (TOE) In the Common Criteria, TOE refers to the product to be tested.

TCB See *Trusted Computing Base*.

TCSEC See *DoD Trusted Computer System Evaluation Criteria*.

technical attack An attack that can be perpetrated by circumventing or nullifying hardware and software protection mechanisms, rather than by subverting system personnel or other users

technical vulnerability A hardware, firmware, communication, or software flaw that leaves a computer processing system open for potential exploitation, either externally or internally — thereby resulting in a risk to the owner, user, or manager of the system

TELNET A virtual terminal protocol used in the Internet, enabling users to log in to a remote host. A terminal emulation defined as part of the TCP/IP protocol suite.

TEMPEST The study and control of spurious electronic signals emitted by electrical equipment

terminal identification The means used to uniquely identify a terminal to a system

test case An executable test with a specific set of input values and a corresponding expected result

threat Any circumstance or event that can cause harm to a system in the form of destruction, disclosure, modification of data, and/or denial of service

threat agent A method that is used to exploit a vulnerability in a system, operation, or facility

threat analysis The examination of all actions and events that might adversely affect a system or operation

threat monitoring The analysis, assessment, and review of audit trails and other data that are collected for the purpose of searching for system events that might constitute violations or attempted violations of system security

ticket-oriented A computer protection system in which each subject maintains a list of unforgeable bit patterns, called *tickets*, one for each object the subject is authorized to access. Compare with *list-oriented*.

time-dependent password A password that is valid only at a certain time of day or during a specified interval of time

Time-domain reflectometer (TDR) Mechanism used to test the effectiveness of network cabling

TLA Top-level architecture

TLS Transport layer security

Token bus A network that uses a logical token-passing access method. Unlike a token passing ring, permission to transmit is usually based on the node address rather than the position in the network. A token bus network uses a common cable set with all signals broadcast across the entire LAN.

Token Ring A local area network (LAN) standard developed by IBM that uses tokens to control access to the communication medium. A medium access method that provides multiple access to a ring-type network through the use of a token. FDDI and IEEE 802.5 are Token Ring standards.

top-level specification A nonprocedural description of system behavior at the most abstract level; typically, a functional specification that omits all implementation details

Topology A description of the network's geographical layout of nodes and links

tranquility A security model rule stating that an object's security level cannot change while the object is being processed by an AIS

transceiver A device for transmitting and receiving packets between the computer and the medium

Transmission Control Protocol (TCP) A commonly used protocol in wide use for establishing and maintaining communications between applications on different computers. TCP provides full-duplex, acknowledged, and flow-controlled service to upper-layer protocols and applications.

Transmission Control Protocol/Internet Protocol (TCP/IP) A de facto, industry-standard protocol for interconnecting disparate networks. Standard protocols that define both the reliable full-duplex transport level and the connectionless, "best effort" unit of information passed across an Internet.

Transport layer OSI model layer that provides mechanisms for the establishment, maintenance, and orderly termination of virtual circuits while shielding the higher layers from the network implementation details

trap door A hidden software or hardware mechanism that can be triggered to permit system protection mechanisms to be circumvented. It is activated in a manner that appears innocent—for example, a special "random" key sequence at a terminal. Software developers often introduce trap doors in their code to enable them to re-enter the system and perform certain functions. Synonymous with *back door*.

Trojan horse A computer program that has an apparently or actually useful function that contains additional (hidden) functions that surreptitiously exploit the legitimate authorizations of the invoking process to the detriment of security or integrity

trusted computer system A system that employs sufficient hardware and software assurance measures to enable its use for simultaneous processing of a range of sensitive or classified information

Trusted Computing Base (TCB) The totality of protection mechanisms within a computer system, including hardware, firmware, and software, the combination of which is responsible for enforcing a security policy. A TCB consists of one or more components that together enforce a unified security policy over a product or system. The ability of a TCB to correctly enforce a unified security policy depends solely on the mechanisms within the TCB and on the correct input of parameters by system administrative personnel (for example, a user's clearance level) related to the security policy.

trusted distribution A trusted method for distributing the TCB hardware, software, and firmware components, both originals and updates, that provides methods for protecting the TCB from modification during distribution and for the detection of any changes to the TCB that might occur.

trusted identification forwarding An identification method used in networks whereby the sending host can verify that an authorized user on its system is attempting a connection to another host. The sending host transmits the required user authentication information to the receiving host. The receiving host can then verify that the user is validated for access to its system. This operation might be transparent to the user.

trusted path A mechanism by which a person at a terminal can communicate directly with the TCB. This mechanism can only be activated by the person or by the TCB and cannot be imitated by untrusted software.

trusted process A process whose incorrect or malicious execution is capable of violating system security policy

trusted software The software portion of the TCB

Twisted-pair wire Type of medium using metallic-type conductors twisted together to provide a path for current flow. The wire in this medium is twisted in pairs to minimize the electromagnetic interference between one pair and another.

U
U.S. Federal Computer Incident Response Center (FedCIRC) FedCIRC provides assistance and guidance in incident response and provides a centralized approach to incident handling across U.S. government agency boundaries.

U.S. Patriot Act of October 26, 2001 A law that permits the following:

- Subpoena of electronic records
- Monitoring of Internet communications
- Search and seizure of information on live systems (including routers and servers), backups, and archives
- Reporting of cash and wire transfers of $10,000 or more

Under the Patriot Act, the government has new powers to subpoena electronic records and to monitor Internet traffic. In monitoring information, the government can require the assistance of ISPs and network operators. This monitoring can even extend into individual organizations.

U.S. Uniform Computer Information Transactions Act (UCITA) of 1999 A model act that is intended to apply uniform legislation to software licensing

UART Universal asynchronous receiver transmitter. A device that converts parallel data into serial data for transmission, or converts serial data into parallel data for receiving data

untrusted process A process that has not been evaluated or examined for adherence to the security policy. It might include incorrect or malicious code that attempts to circumvent the security mechanisms.

user A person or process that is accessing an AIS either by direct connections (for example, via terminals), or by indirect connections (in other words, prepare input data or receive output that is not reviewed for content or classification by a responsible individual)

User datagram protocol UDP uses the underlying Internet protocol (IP) to transport a message. This is an unreliable, connectionless delivery scheme. It does not use acknowledgments to ensure that messages arrive and does not provide feedback to control the rate of information flow. UDP messages can be lost, duplicated, or arrive out of order.

user ID A unique symbol or character string that is used by a system to identify a specific user

user profile Patterns of a user's activity that can be used to detect changes in normal routines

V

V.21 An ITU standard for asynchronous 0-300 bps full-duplex modems

V.21FAX An ITU standard for facsimile operations at 300 bps

V.34 An ITU standard for 28,800 bps modems

validation (in software engineering) To establish the fitness or worth of a software product for its operational mission

vaulting Running mirrored data centers in separate locations

verification The process of comparing two levels of system specification for proper correspondence (for example, a security policy model with top-level specification, top-level specification with source code, or source code with object code). This process might or might not be automated.

very-long-instruction word (VLIW) processor A processor in which multiple, concurrent operations are performed in a single instruction. The number of instructions is reduced relative to those in a scalar processor. However, for this approach to be feasible, the operations in each VLIW instruction must be independent of each other.

VIM Lotus' vendor-independent messaging system

virus A self-propagating Trojan horse composed of a mission component, a trigger component, and a self-propagating component

vulnerability A weakness in system security procedures, system design, implementation, internal controls, and so on that could be exploited to violate system security policy

vulnerability analysis The systematic examination of systems in order to determine the adequacy of security measures, identify security deficiencies, and provide data from which to predict the effectiveness of proposed security measures

vulnerability assessment A measurement of vulnerability that includes the susceptibility of a particular system to a specific attack and the opportunities that are available to a threat agent to mount that attack

W

WAP Wireless Application Protocol. A standard commonly used for the development of applications for wireless Internet devices.

wide area network (WAN) A network that interconnects users over a wide area, usually encompassing different metropolitan areas

Wired Equivalency Privacy (WEP) The algorithm of the 802.11 wireless LAN standard that is used to protect transmitted information from disclosure. WEP is designed to prevent the violation of the confidentiality of data transmitted over the wireless LAN. WEP generates secret shared encryption keys that both source and destination stations use to alter frame bits to avoid disclosure to eavesdroppers.

wireless Describes any computing device that can access a network without a wired connection

wireless metropolitan area network (wireless MAN) Provides communications links between buildings, avoiding the costly installation of cabling or leasing fees and the downtime associated with system failures

WLAN Wireless local area network

Work breakdown structure (WBS) A diagram of the way a team will accomplish the project at hand by listing all tasks the team must perform and the products they must deliver

work factor An estimate of the effort or time needed by a potential intruder who has specified expertise and resources to overcome a protective measure

work function (factor) The difficulty in recovering the plaintext from the ciphertext, as measured by cost and/or time. The security of the system is directly proportional to the value of the work function. The work function need only be large enough to suffice for the intended application. If the message to be protected loses its value after a short period of time, the work function need only be large enough to ensure that the decryption would be highly infeasible in that period of time.

write A fundamental operation that results only in the flow of information from a subject to an object

write access Permission to write to an object

X

X.12 An ITU standard for EDI

X.121 An ITU standard for international address numbering

X.21 An ITU standard for a circuit-switching network

X.25 An ITU standard for an interface between a terminal and a packet-switching network. X.25 was the first public packet-switching technology, developed by the CCITT and offered as a service during the 1970s and still available today. X.25 offers connection-oriented (virtual circuit) service; it operates at 64 Kbps, which is too slow for some high-speed applications.

X.400 An ITU standard for OSI messaging

X.500 An ITU standard for OSI directory services

X.75 An ITU standard for packet switching between public networks

✦   ✦   ✦

APPENDIX C

Common Internet Vulnerabilities

By Ken Brandt, President of Griffin Global Systems, a system security consulting firm (kb@ggsys.com) and Stu Green, an Associate Professor of Computer Science at the McCombs Business School, University of Texas (stugreen@cos-internet.com).

Ken Brandt and Stu Green are formerly of Tiger Testing, a firm that specialized in ethical hacking and external penetration vulnerability testing. This document is an attempt to index and compile the various types of vulnerabilities they encountered over the years.

There are tens of thousands of common Internet security vulnerabilities and exposures, encompassing a wide variety of areas, such as the following:

- Network protocols such as TCP, ICMP, IGMP, NetBIOS, and LDAP
- Network devices such as routers, load balancers, and switches
- Security devices, Intrusion Detection Systems (IDS), and firewalls
- Servers, servicing mail, File Transfer Protocol (FTP), database, and proxy services
- Web applications such as ASP, CGI, Cold Fusion, Java, and Perl
- Operating systems, including NT, UNIX, and Novell

These vulnerabilities and exposures cover a wide range of complexity to exploit, from those that can be identified with simple scans to those that require thorough analysis, cross correlation, vulnerability linking, and multiple steps.

We've grouped these common Internet vulnerabilities and exposures into 15 categories. These categories include documented vulnerabilities, new vulnerabilities, CERT alerts, SANS/FBI "Top Twenty" vulnerabilities, and the Mitre.org Common Vulnerabilities and Exposures (CVE). Obviously, many of these vulnerabilities can be placed in more than one group. We've placed them where they seemed to make the most sense. At the end of each description is a listing of Mitre's CVE entry.

1. Address Spoofing and Source Concealment

Address spoofing and source concealment is the act of disguising the originating address of packets so that the packet appears to be from a recognized system to gain unauthorized entry to a target system. For spoofing to succeed, the target system must believe that the spoofed packets are legitimate packets from a system that it recognizes. If the target system recognizes the spoofed packets, it will process them.

Spoofing involves protocol-level packet alteration, and is used to attack Internet-connected systems that provide TCP/IP services. Spoofing can be performed at the Transmission Control Protocol (TCP) level, or at the TCP component level (for example, compromising the identification query functions of the User Datagram Protocol (UDP)). Spoofing at the Internet Protocol (IP) level is known as IP spoofing. The Internet Protocol uses both the Internet Control Message Protocol (ICMP) and the Internet Group Message Protocol (IGMP), each of which has address spoofing and source concealment vulnerabilities.

Vulnerability examples include CVE-2000-0289 and CAN-2002-0400.

ICMP Spoofing

The ICMP protocol is sometimes referred to as a network management protocol, because ICMP messages are used to pass network status information and error messages between any two points on a network. The most recognized of ICMP messages is the echo request, or Packet INternet Groper (PING). A package (full message) may be composed of more than one packet. ICMP messages report error conditions at the user datagram level, but also contain routing and network information. If an intruder manipulates the message's content and/or directives, he would be able to bypass certain packet logging software, IP accounting software, and firewalls.

Because ICMP lacks authentication and "manages" network problems, ICMP address spoofing can take on the form of a Denial of Service (DoS). For example, forged ICMP packets could indicate that valid destinations are unreachable or erroneously indicate that protocol timers (TTL) have been exceeded.

A standard function of ICMP is to redirect messages when one host mistakenly believes that another host is outside the local network (that is, when a netmask is improperly set). Rather than place the manipulated information directly in either the target system's router or the target system's routing table, an attacker could place the ICMP change in a temporary file. As a result, messages sent by the target system would be temporarily routed to a system selected by the attacker, rather than to their intended destination. This redirection would remain in effect until the transfer of the next package is completed.

Vulnerability examples include CVE-1999-0214, CVE-1999-0265, and CVE-1999-0875.

IGMP Spoofing

IGMP is also referred to as a network management protocol because IGMP messages are used to identify the participants in multicast datagrams that span multiple networks (for example, to identify the IP addresses of multicast group members on another network). Members of a multicast group respond to queries by sending IGMP replies noting the multicast group to which they belong. Multicast routers forward multicast datagrams from one multicast group to all other networks that have members in the same group.

An intruder could exploit this capability by issuing an IGMP join message to the multicast group to gain membership, then congest the network by flooding it with malformed or gibberish UDP packets, causing resolution and redirection errors. This would result in a Denial of Service (DoS), the inability of anyone to use or access the machines in the multicast group.

Vulnerability examples include CVE-1999-0918.

TCP Spoofing

The Transmission Control Protocol (TCP) is used to carry connection-oriented traffic. Connection orientation involves explicit session control that requires a three-way handshake to establish and tear down a connection. TCP traffic is often associated with specific services and ports, such as HTTP (TCP port 80 for Web activities), TELNET (TCP port 23), SMTP (TCP port 25 for e-mail), RPC (various ports for remote procedure calls), and FTP (TCP port 21 for file transfer). By disguising and introducing itself as a legitimate system, an attacking system could exploit the services it targets.

> **Note**
> Other types of TCP exploits that may also utilize some level of disguise are described in (6) Fragmented or Abnormal Packets and (14) TCP/IP Sequence and Port Attacks.

Vulnerability examples include CVE-2000-0315.

2. Domain Name System and Berkeley Internet Name Domain

The Domain Name System (DNS) protocols provide the standards used to build and maintain the distributed Internet directory service, consisting of data, servers, and conventions for fetching and delivering data. DNS enables the translation of domain names to IP addresses, and vice versa. Berkeley Internet Name Domain (BIND) is an implementation of the DNS protocols. Most of the name servers deployed on the Internet use BIND. Alternatives to BIND include MS DNS and djbdns.

Vulnerability examples include the following:

- SRV bug
- ZXFR bug
- SANS/FBI "Top Twenty" number U9 (BIND/DNS)
- CVE-1999-0010
- CVE-1999-0011
- CVE-1999-0274
- CVE-1999-0835
- CVE-1999-0848
- CVE-1999-0849
- CVE-1999-0851
- CVE-2000-0335
- CAN-2002-0400

DNS Buffer Overflow

Attackers can cause DNS buffer overflows by issuing commands containing unexpected or overly long arguments. The buffer overflow would enable an attacker to execute commands at the DNS server's privilege level.

Vulnerability examples include CVE-1999-0009 and CVE-1999-0833.

DNS Cache Attack

DNS can be vulnerable to a cache attack (also known as cache poisoning). A cache attack involves accessing the target system DNS's temporary memory to make it appear as though the user is from a "trusted system" and has the correct domain identification and Internet address to launch an unauthorized remote service. Also, the DNS cache could become corrupted, resulting in a crash of the target system's Domain Name Server, creating a Denial of Service (the inability of anyone to send information to or receive information from the target machines).

Vulnerability examples include CVE-1999-0024.

DNS Flood Attack

In a flooding attack, an attacker causes a Denial of Service (DoS) by sending a large uninterrupted stream of DNS request packets to a target DNS's service port 53.

Vulnerability examples include CVE-1999-0275 and CVE 2000-0020.

3. File Transfer Protocol

The File Transfer Protocol (FTP) is one of the original protocols defined at the inception of the Internet. It is an application protocol, part of the TCP/IP protocol stack, used for transferring files between network nodes or systems. One of the common uses of FTP is to provide files (such as drivers and patches) to the general public.

Vulnerability examples include the following:

- FTP Bounce
- SANS/FBI "Top Twenty" number U5 (File Transfer Protocol [FTP])
- CVE-1999-0075
- CVE-1999-0185
- CVE-1999-0202
- CVE-1999-0362
- CVE-1999-0432
- CVE-2000-0514
- CVE-2000-0636
- CVE-2000-0717
- CVE-2000-0761
- CAN-2000-0856

FTP Buffer Overflow

FTP servers are vulnerable to induced error conditions. An induced error occurs when an FTP server executes a command designed to force a buffer overflow. A basic buffer overflow attack occurs when a process receives much more data than expected. If the process does not have an error handling routine to deal with this excessive amount of data, it acts in a way that the intruder can exploit. If the buffer overflow results in a Denial of Service, no one can use the server, and the system may lose all logging functions. If the buffer overflow allows the intruder to gain the privilege level of the server, the intruder could execute arbitrary code.

Other examples of induced errors include the use of logon names or passwords over 256 characters in length and the improper use of the HELP command. The induced error exposure is exacerbated if the target FTP server permits anonymous logons, as mentioned below in "FTP File Protection."

Vulnerability examples include the following:

- AIX ftpd overflow
- CVE-1999-0256
- CVE-1999-0349
- CVE-1999-0368
- CVE-1999-0789
- CVE-1999-0838
- CVE-1999-0878
- CVE-1999-0879
- CVE-1999-0950
- CVE-2000-0573
- CVE-2000-0574
- CVE-2001-0053

FTP File Protection

Configuration of FTP servers includes defining which groups of users can access and transfer which files. If the configuration is set too permissively, more files will be accessible to more people (including intruders) than desired. In addition, even if the permissions are set correctly, some FTP implementations allow access to files beyond the scope defined in the server configuration. These issues can be compounded when FTP servers are configured to facilitate the distribution of files to the general public (that is, allow "anonymous" access, where a person would use the word `anonymous`, `guest`, or `ftp` as their ID and their e-mail address as their password).

This type of vulnerability could allow an intruder to access, alter, or distribute the system configuration files themselves, password files, and/or other data on the server. Other common ways to exploit these openings are by using the FTP server to distribute the intruder's files, and uploading so much data that all of the FTP server's disk space is filled (a form of DoS).

Vulnerability examples include the following:

- Pizza Thief
- CVE-1999-0080
- CVE-1999-0081
- CVE-1999-0082
- CVE-1999-0083
- CVE-1999-0201
- CVE-1999-0202
- CVE-1999-0777
- CVE-2000-0577
- CVE-2000-0640
- CVE-2001-0054

4. Finger Information Requests

The Finger command is used to share user information. After originating on UNIX, it was ported to other operating systems. Finger is supported by UNIX, other operating systems, and TCP/IP implementations. Remote access to Finger's daemon process can provide an attacker with information about the target system's operating system and users, including user names, contact information, activities, and logon times. This information could be used by an attacker as a knowledge base or foundation for follow-up attacks.

Vulnerability examples include the following:

- CVE-1999-0150
- CVE-1999-0152
- CVE-1999-0612
- CVE-1999-0797
- CVE-2000-0128
- CVE-2000-0915

5. Flooding, Spraying, and Broadcasting

Flooding, spraying, and broadcasting are ways to send a large quantity of request packets to a targeted system. The large quantity of request packets prevents the target system from doing anything other than responding to the requests, resulting in a Denial of Service (DoS). Smurf and Fraggle attacks are versions of flooding, spraying, and broadcasting, except that one target company's systems are used as the platform to launch a Denial of Service attack against a second target company's systems. A Distributed Denial of Service (DDoS) attack is similar to a DoS except that multiple machines participate in the attack. The participating machines could be multiple attackers' machines or they could be Zombies, machines on which (unbeknownst to their owners) the attackers have planted flooding, spraying, or broadcasting programs.

Types of Attacks

Flooding, spraying, and broadcasting attacks can be used as individual attacks or they can be combined with each other for more impact. The three can be differentiated as follows:

- **Flooding**—An attacker sends multiple request packets to a single target port
- **Spraying**—An attacker sends multiple request packets to many target ports
- **Broadcasting**—An attacker sends the same request packet to all devices residing on a single network or subnetwork of the target system

Vulnerability examples include the following:

- Stream.c attacks
- CVE-1999-0103
- CVE-2000-0314
- CVE-2000-0522
- CVE-2000-0669
- CVE-2000-0914
- CVE 2000-1182

Smurf and Fraggle Attacks

A Smurf attack uses a combination of IP spoofing and ICMP messages to saturate a target network with traffic, thereby causing a Denial of Service (DoS). It consists of three elements: the attacker's site, the bounce site, and the target site. The attacker (the source site) sends a spoofed PING packet to the broadcast address of a large network (the bounce site). This modified packet contains the address of the target site. This causes the bounce site to broadcast the misinformation to all of the devices on its local network. All of these devices now respond with a reply to the target system, which becomes saturated with those replies. A Fraggle attack is similar, but occurs at the UDP, rather than the ICMP level.

Vulnerability examples include CVE-1999-0513 (Smurf) and CVE-1999-0514 (Fraggle).

6. Fragmented or Abnormal Packets

Internet messages are automatically divided into packets. This applies to all packet transmissions using protocols in the TCP/IP suite, such as TCP, UDP, ICMP, and ARP. The packet size is adjustable up to the Maximum Transfer Unit (MTU), allowing an attacker to create various size packets. For Ethernet, the MTU is defined as 1,516 bytes. Intel-based PCs often have the MTU set to 512 bytes for better compatibility with their buffers. The first packet of a multipacket message contains fragmentation information in its header, which includes the source address and fragment offset. While subsequent packets also carry fragmentation information in their headers, it is the first packet's information that is processed to establish and maintain the session. When splitting TCP data over multiple packets, the TCP segments are assigned sequence numbers. When the packets reach their destination, the message is reassembled from the TCP sequence numbers and fragment offsets. If left unchecked, the reassembly process could be exploited. In addition, some firewalls process subsequent packets that contain extraneous TCP data, even if the source address information in the subsequent packets does not match the source address information contained in the first packet's segment header.

Abnormal Packet Size and Tiny Fragment Attacks

Because their abnormal size requires additional interpretation, these packets use up the targeted system's resources. Responding to these abnormal packets fully occupies the target system's resources; therefore, it can't handle normal functions and services (such as providing user access and forwarding and receiving messages) in a timely manner.

In addition, similar to the zero-offset attack described below, when a very small packet fragment is sent, some of the packet's TCP segment header information may be forced into the next packet fragment or packet. If minimum packet size filtering is not in place, the next packet fragment or packet could bypass or crash content examining firewalls, load balancers, and routers. Zero length packet attacks are a form of tiny fragment attacks.

Vulnerability examples include the following:

- Ping of Death
- CVE-1999-0052
- CVE-2000-0305
- CVE-2000-0310
- CVE-2000-0394
- CVE-2000-0463
- CVE-2000-0482
- CVE-2000-0896

Zero-Offset IP Fragmentation Attacks

Zero-offset IP fragmentation attacks use varied IP datagram fragmentation to disguise the attacker's TCP packets from the target's IP filtering devices.

Teardrop attacks consist of modifying the length and fragmentation offset fields in sequential IP packets. The target system becomes confused and crashes after it receives contradictory instructions as to how the fragments are offset on these packets.

In an overlapping fragment attack, a subsequent packet overwrites the destination address information of an initial packet and the subsequent packet passes through the target's filtering devices. This can happen if the target's filtering devices do not enforce a minimum fragment offset for fragments with non-zero offsets.

Vulnerability examples include Bonk attacks, Nestea attacks, and CVE-1999-0157.

7. E-mail

E-mail uses several different protocols and services, such as Internet Mail Access Protocol (IMAP), Multipurpose Internet Mail Extension (MIME), Post Office Protocol (POP), Sendmail, and Simple Mail Transfer Protocol (SMTP). Sendmail is the most widely used Mail Transfer Agent (MTA), a program that sends, receives, and forwards most electronic mail. SMTP is a common mechanism for transporting electronic mail among different hosts. MIME is a standard for encoding and decoding nontextual (or plain ASCII) data. POP and IMAP are protocols used by client e-mail applications to retrieve e-mail from a mail server. POP3 (version 3 of POP) can, in certain circumstances, be used without SMTP. An example of a vulnerability that can involve either buffer overflow or command manipulation is SANS/FBI "Top Twenty" number U8 (Sendmail).

Buffer Overflows

The fields within an SMTP packet are of specific defined sizes. If one of the fields contains much more data than it can handle, a temporary error condition occurs in the target system's buffer (communication message storage space). This error ends up giving the sender of the packet (attacker) SMTP server-level privileges.

A MIME conversion buffer overflow attack is similar to the above, except that the goal is a Denial of Service (DoS) rather than the attainment of SMTP server-level privileges.

Vulnerability examples include the following:

- Malformed MIME header
- CVE-1999-0047
- CVE-1999-0206
- CVE-1999-0940
- CVE-2000-0196
- CVE-2000-0425
- CVE-2000-0472

Sendmail Command Manipulation

By manipulating commands such as EXPN or VRFY, the attacker can cause a range of problems, from gathering information on users and accounts to overwhelming Sendmail, which would destabilize other communication programs and crash the target system. These service-level attacks take advantage of Sendmail's privileges by allowing unauthorized access to information under the guise of administrative modifications. This type of attack is aimed at the acquisition of configuration files or the capability to write to any file on the targeted system.

Vulnerability examples include the following:

- CVE-1999-0057
- CVE-1999-0203
- CVE-1999-0204
- CVE-2000-0348
- CVE-2001-0653

Mail Flood Attacks

In a mail flood attack, the attacker sends so much mail to the target system that the target system's Mail Transfer Agent (MTA) program is overwhelmed. This destabilizes other communication programs and crashes the target system, creating a DoS. Flooding a system with e-mail is a crude, but effective, means of bringing down a mail server. A less crude mail flood attack involves creating endless feedback loops between two e-mail systems' auto-response functions.

Vulnerability examples include Message Redirection attacks and CAN-2001-0504.

8. Password Attacks

Password attacks are the process of gaining system entry by obtaining and then using a legitimate user password and login ID. This can be accomplished by trying common user names/passwords, capturing individual user name/password combinations, or capturing an entire user name/password file. Passwords are often encrypted, so password attacks often include decryption.

Brute Force Attack

In a brute force attack, the attacker uses a database and program to test a large number of common logon names and passwords. Brute force logon attacks are faster and more powerful than password guessing, which uses manual entry or simple scripts to guess common passwords.

Common passwords include default passwords, null (no) passwords, and widely used passwords. Default passwords are also known as manufacturers' backdoors: unchanged user or system name/password combinations that were originally set up by hardware manufacturers or software vendors.

Vulnerability examples include the following:

- ✦ One-time (s/key) password authentication
- ✦ SANS/FBI "Top Twenty" number W5 (Anonymous logon — Null sessions)
- ✦ W6 (LAN manager authentication — Weak LM hashing)
- ✦ W7 (General Windows authentication — Accounts with no passwords or weak passwords)
- ✦ U10 (General UNIX authentication — Accounts with no passwords or weak passwords)
- ✦ CVE-1999-0291
- ✦ CVE-1999-0421

- CVE-1999-0407
- CAN-1999-0502
- CVE-1999-0889
- CVE-2000-0159
- CVE-1999-0916
- CVE-2000-0222
- CVE-2000-0485
- CVE-2000-0808
- CVE-2000-0937
- CVE-2001-0056
- CVE-2000-1200

Password Cracking

An attacker employing password cracking uses programs to decrypt encrypted passwords. Prior to starting the decryption process, an attacker must locate and retrieve the password or password file.

Vulnerability examples include the following:

- CVE-1999-0458
- CVE-1999-0470
- CVE-1999-0701
- CVE-1999-0884
- CVE-1999-0953
- CVE-1999-0994
- CVE-2000-0981

Password Sniffing

An attacker may be able to capture passwords by planting a "sniffer" on the appropriate port. These passwords may be plaintext (unencrypted) or they may be encrypted. Although sniffers are a passive listening tool, the listening process itself may slow down the network traffic to and from the target port. Common target ports include HTTPD, POP3, RSH, SMB, and TELNET.

Vulnerability examples include CAN-1999-0619 and CAN-1999-0651.

9. Program Insertion

An attacker can plant (or insert) destructive programs (malware) on targeted systems. These destructive programs vary in the speed with which they work, the systems they can be planted on, and the damage they can do. Attackers plant programs that provide them with information (such as every keystroke made by a targeted user, user IDs, or passwords) or that give them the ability to destroy targeted files. If the inserted program replaces a legitimate program and does the legitimate program's tasks (as well as the attacker's tasks), it is known as a Trojan horse. If the inserted program becomes active at a time or date predetermined by the attacker, it is known as a *time bomb*. If the inserted program is placed on a system to participate in a DDoS attack against another system, it is known as a *zombie*.

Vulnerability examples include the following:

- BackOrifice
- Code Red
- I LOVE YOU
- Netbus
- Nimda
- QAZ Trojan
- R00tkits
- SubSeven
- Trin00 (or Trinoo)
- SANS/FBI "Top Twenty" number W10 (Windows Scripting Host)
- CVE-2000-0650
- CVE-2000-0663
- CVE-2000-0854
- CVE-2000-1073
- CVE-2000-1074
- CVE-2001-0149
- CVE-2001-0289
- CAN-2001-1325

10. Proxy Servers

Proxy servers improve system response time by distributing request processing among multiple hosts. In order to perform this function, proxy servers have a trusted relationship with the multiple hosts with which they are associated. If the connections between the proxy server and its associated hosts are not secured by both authentication and encryption, a breach of the proxy servers' security would facilitate privileged access to the associated hosts.

Vulnerability examples include the following:

- CVE-1999-0168
- CVE-1999-0290
- CVE-2000-0582
- CVE-2000-1182
- CVE-2001-0142

11. Trusted Host

To facilitate the exchange of information and the sharing of services or resources, two or more hosts are configured to allow transparent cooperative processing across associated systems. This is known as a *trusting*, or *trusted, relationship*. R-Commands require trust on the operating system level, while SNMP, SSH, and SSL require trust on the network level.

Also, although they are not technically considered Remote Command and Trusted Host vulnerabilities, the vulnerabilities associated with SANS/FBI "Top Twenty" number W9 (Remote Registry Access) are somewhat similar (see also CAN-1999-0562 and CAN-2002-0642).

Remote Command Processing

Remote Command Processing (Remote Procedure Calls — RPC, UNIX remote execution commands, or r-commands) is used to communicate between systems that recognize, trust, and allow access to each other. They are widely used to access network services to obtain system information and run programs. R-commands use a list of trusted hosts as their only authentication mechanism. If the target system believes that an intruder's R-commands are coming from a system that it recognizes and trusts, it processes them with the same level of privilege as the recognized and trusted system (allowing the same level of access to systems and data). However, the most common R-command exploit is a comparatively simple DoS. Once an intruder has established an RPC connection, a deliberately malformed command could cause a buffer overflow, which would crash the service associated with the connection (TCP port and TCP session), creating a DoS for that particular service.

Vulnerability examples include the following:

- Named pipes over RPC
- SANS/FBI "Top Twenty" number U1 (Remote Procedure Calls (RPC) and U6 (R-Services — Trust relationships)
- CVE-1999-0003
- CVE-1999-0019
- CVE-1999-0046
- CVE-1999-0113
- CVE-1999-0180
- CVE-1999-0687
- CAN-2002-0391

Line Printer Daemon

Although Line Printer Daemons (LPDs) are not R-commands, they do involve local or remote printer connections, which can allow attackers to gain root access. Vulnerability examples include SANS/FBI "Top Twenty" number U7, Line Printer Daemon (LPD) and CAN-2001-0671.

SNMP

Simple Network Management Protocol (SNMP) is used to monitor and administer all types of network-connected devices ranging from routers to printers to computers. The fields within SNMP packets are specifically defined sizes. If one of the packet's fields contains much more data than it was designed to hold, a temporary error condition could occur in the target system's buffer. This error could result in the sender of the packet (the attacker) dropping out of the buffer and into a shell with administrative privileges. Administrative privileges allow access to all system commands and files.

Vulnerability examples include the following:

- CVE-1999-0294
- CVE-2000-0379
- CVE-2000-0515
- CVE-2000-1058
- CVE-2000-0379

SSH/SSL

In some versions of SSHD (Secured Shell service Daemon) only the public encryption key is used for authentication. An intruder could use the public encryption key to create and insert forged packets. The targeted system would assume that the SSH user (the sender of the forged packets) has legitimate system access.

In some versions of SSH, plaintext inserted into the SSH stream can crash the service, which moves the session from the Secured Shell to the more vulnerable Remote Shell protocol and ports.

Secure Socket Layer (SSL) is a protocol that provides cryptographic functionality to applications such as secure Web servers. SSH uses SSL for transport and encryption.

Vulnerability examples include the following:

- Plaintext attack
- SANS/FBI "Top Twenty" number U3 (Secure Shell [SSH])
- CVE-1999-0013
- CVE-1999-0248
- CVE-1999-0310
- CVE-1999-0787
- CVE-1999-1010
- CVE-2000-0217
- CVE-2000-0525
- CVE-2000-0992
- CVE-2001-0080
- CVE-2001-0144
- CAN-2002-0640

12. Remote File Systems

Remote file systems are files that are distributed across a network but appear to be, and can be accessed as, local files. Network File System (NFS) is the most common remote file system in the UNIX operating system world. Server Message Block (SMB) is the most common remote file system in the Microsoft Windows operating system world. When improperly configured, NFS and SMB can give file system access to a hostile party connected to the network. If an intruder gains read/write access to a file that is then exported to the target system, the intruder has a platform on the target system from which to attempt further access. Remote File System vulnerabilities span privileged file access and DoS.

Vulnerability examples include RFPoison packet attack and CAN-2000-1200.

NFS

On the operating system level, NFS uses the Portmapper service to establish and authenticate connections. The Portmapper may be used by an attacker to redirect service requests. These requests would appear to be coming from the local host, bypassing the target's authentication processes. For example, NFS file systems could be mounted through the Portmapper despite export restrictions. Once a connection to the targeted NFS file system is accomplished, the intruder might be able to change directories (cd) and access directories and files that have not been explicitly exported.

Vulnerability examples include the following:

- CVE-1999-0002
- CVE-1999-0166
- CVE-1999-0167
- CVE-1999-0168
- CAN-1999-0554
- CVE-1999-0832

SMB

SMB's functions (including its security functions, such as authentication) are available to members of the workgroup. By initiating a fake SMB session, an attacker can bypass SMB's authentication and access internal network information, such as lists of user accounts, shared resources, or other computer names and addresses. An attacker could take advantage of this information and the sharing nature of the SMB protocol to gain full or partial access to shared data and other system resources. Unprotected network shares contributed to the rapid spread of the Nimda worm and the Sircam virus.

Vulnerability examples include the following:

- Share level password
- SANS/FBI "Top Twenty" number W4 (NETBIOS — Unprotected Windows networking shares)
- CVE-1999-0225
- CVE-2000-1003
- CAN-2000-1079

13. Shotgun Access Attempts

Shotgun access attempts are random attempts made by an attacker or eavesdropper to gain access to a system through its unprotected ports.

Port Scanning, Probing, and Polling

Scanning, probing, and polling investigate a port's state and readiness for contact. By continually scanning and polling a target system's ports, an attacker can learn the functional and defensive aspects of their opening and responding, including whether or not they are programmatically protected by a firewall.

Attackers use these techniques to develop a road map of the target network, including information on which services are available on which targets. This information can be analyzed and used as the basis for planting sniffers (see "Password Sniffing") and other deeper attacks.

Vulnerability examples include the following:

- UDP bomb (or UDP packet storm)
- CAN-1999-0524
- CVE-2000-0289
- CVE-2000-0804
- CAN-2000-1201
- CVE-2001-0414
- CAN-2001-0554

SNMP

Simple Network Management Protocol (SNMP) is a protocol that facilitates the exchange of management information between network devices. SNMP requests can be used to acquire a lot of information about SNMP-enabled devices. This information includes user account names, active services, and operating system versions, all of which can be useful for formulating further attacks. In addition, SNMP uses an unencrypted "community string" as its only authentication mechanism. Attackers can use this vulnerability to remotely reconfigure or shut down targeted devices.

Vulnerability examples include the following:

- SANS/FBI "Top Twenty" number U4 (Simple Network Management Protocol (SNMP))
- CVE-1999-0472
- CAN-2000-0955
- CAN-2002-0796

14. TCP/IP Sequence and Port Attacks

The TCP/IP sequence and port attacks category contains two different, yet related attack techniques. First, TCP/IP sequence attacks exploit predictable patterns in the TCP protocol that an attacker can use to bypass controls and intrude into a system. The SSH and SSL services can be undermined if an attacker knows the TCP sequence. Second, port attacks are various attacks against a target system's ports and the services associated with these ports.

Vulnerability examples include the following:

- CVE-1999-0074
- CVE-1999-0077
- CVE-1999-0416
- CVE-2000-0453
- CVE-2001-0144

Packet Interception

Packet interception entails binding an "active listener" program to the target's remote port to intercept and/or redirect all (or specific types) of packets. These packets could then be redirected to an unauthorized system and read. Also, after the eavesdropper has read them, the packets could either be routed back to the target unchanged (creating a loss of confidentiality), not routed back (creating a loss of confidentiality and availability), or routed back with changes (creating a loss of confidentiality and integrity).

Vulnerability examples include the following:

- Man-in-the-middle
- CVE-2000-0613
- CVE-2000-0394
- CVE-2001-0183

Predictable IP IDs

Internet Protocol (IP) IDs are packet identifiers contained within packet headers. Some messages are divided into packets for transmission and then reassembled upon receipt. IP IDs are used to reassemble packets into messages. If they are not randomized, it is possible to predict the subsequent value of a system's IP IDs. This makes it possible for an attacker to know if a machine is responding, even if it is not responding to the attacker's queries. The subsequent IP ID values could be used to determine if the target is responding to other queries and aids in targeting and refining the port scanning process.

Vulnerability examples include CAN-1999-0454.

SYN Flood

A SYN flood attack occurs when an attacker exploits buffer space used during the TCP session initialization handshake. The attacker floods the target system's small "in-process" queue with connection requests, but does not respond when the target system replies to those requests. This causes the target system to "time out" while waiting for the proper response, which destabilizes or crashes the target system.

Vulnerability examples include the following:

- CVE-1999-0116
- CVE-2000-0692
- CVE-2001-0055
- CVE-2001-0486

TCP/IP Sequence Number Attacks

When one system requests a session with another system, the two systems exchange TCP synchronization numbers as part of their first two messages (the SYN/ACK handshake). Each system should generate random Initial Sequence Numbers (ISNs) and subsequent synchronization numbers. If the generation of these numbers is not sufficiently randomized, an attacker will be able to predict them, and both systems will become potential TCP address spoofing and source concealment targets. Armed with the stolen sequence, an attack system can be disguised as one or both of the target systems, enabling an attacker to bypass packet-filtering firewalls. Armed with both the stolen sequence and the target system's responding ACK, an attacker would be able to highjack the connection and perform a man-in-the-middle attack.

Vulnerability examples include the following:

- CVE-2000-0178
- CVE-2000-0328
- CAN-2000-0916
- CAN-2001-0328

15. Web and Web Applications

The HyperText Transfer Protocol (HTTP) is a protocol for transmitting Web pages and other data across the Internet. HTTP provides a mechanism that allows users to go from one Web server to another by following Universal Resource Links (URLs) on Web pages, forming the World Wide Web. The HyperText Transfer Protocol Daemon (HTTPD), or Web server, is a program that manages Web page content and connections with Web client software (for example, Netscape Navigator and Microsoft Explorer). Apache (open source) and Microsoft Internet Information Server (IIS) are commonly used Web servers. Examples of vulnerabilities that cross several of the subareas below are as follows:

- SANS/FBI "Top Twenty" number W1 (Internet Information Services)
- W8 (Internet Explorer)
- W3 (Microsoft SQL Server)
- U2 (Apache Web Server)
- CAN-2002-0859
- CAN-2002-0982

HTTPD Buffer Overflow

An intruder can induce a buffer overflow at port 80 (HTTPD) by issuing excessively long server requests. The buffer overflow could give the intruder access to HTTPD files. With access to the HTTPD configuration files, an intruder could make a variety of changes, including modifications to the appearance and content of Web pages.

Vulnerability examples include the following:

- Link View Server-Side Component
- Unicode directory traversal (exploited by the Code Blue worm)
- CVE-1999-0071
- CVE-1999-0267
- CVE-2000-0023
- CVE-2000-0065
- CVE-2000-0359
- CVE-2000-0484
- CVE-2000-0561
- CVE-2001-0151

IIS Remote Data Services

Microsoft Internet Information Server's (IIS's) Remote Data Services (RDS) can be used to run remote commands with administrator privileges.

Vulnerability examples include the following:

- Code Red
- Rain Forest Puppy Attack

- SANS/FBI "Top Twenty" number W2 (Microsoft Data Access Components [MDAC] — Remote Data Services)
- CVE-1999-1011
- CAN-2000-0071
- CVE-2000-0630
- CVE-2000-0884
- CVE-2000-0951
- CVE-2001-0333
- CAN-2001-0500

Web Applications

Application vulnerabilities are exploited by automated as well as manual means. Manual exploitation is often an extensive process. Vulnerabilities include the following:

- Web application environments (ASP, CGI, CFM, Java, JSP, Perl, and so on)
- Cross scripting
- Application business logic
- URL vulnerability exposures
- Directory traversal exposures
- Code vulnerabilities
- Account enumeration
- Session management
- Highjacking vulnerabilities
- Exploitation of POST, GET, PUT, and so on
- SQL piggybacking vulnerabilities

Manual exploitation emphasizes the process of drilling into application functionality, source shifting, application design, input validation, and impersonation. Also note that many ISAPI extensions (including the ASP, HTR, IDQ, PRINTER, and SSI extensions) are vulnerable to buffer overflows.

Vulnerability examples include the following:

- Cookie poisoning
- Source fragment disclosure
- CVE-1999-0236
- CVE-1999-0237

- CVE-1999-0269
- CVE-1999-0278
- CVE-1999-0449
- CVE-1999-0947
- CVE-2000-0097
- CVE-2000-0149
- CVE-2000-0272
- CVE-2000-0630
- CVE-2000-0900
- CVE-2000-0942
- CAN-2002-0079
- CAN-2002-0071
- CAN-2002-0193

URL Flood or Corruption

An attacker can crash a Web site by forcing repeated, rapid reload requests to port 80 (HTTP), absorbing all of the Web server's resources. This type of DoS is known as a *URL flood*. A variation on this allows the attacker to create a DoS by using overly long or corrupted URLs.

Vulnerability examples include the following:

- Malformed Extension Data in URL
- Myriad Escaped Characters
- CVE-1999-0281
- CVE-1999-0686
- CVE-2000-0023
- CVE-2000-0064
- CVE-2000-0146
- CVE-2000-0169
- CVE-2000-0209
- CVE-2000-0238
- CVE-2000-0257
- CVE-2000-0538

APPENDIX D

NMap Log

Results of NMapWin Port Scan

Below are the results of the NMap Port scan on the subject network, as described in Chapter 1.

```
# nmap (V. 3.00) scan initiated Fri Aug 30
14:39:01 2002 as: nmap -sW -PT -PI -T 5 -oN
C:\WINDOWS2\Desktop\08-30-2002-1a.log
192.168.123.0/24
All 1601 scanned ports on (192.168.123.101)
are: closed
All 1601 scanned ports on RDVGROUP_NT1
(192.168.123.253) are: closed
Interesting ports on (192.168.123.254):
Port       State       Service
1/tcp      open        tcpmux
2/tcp      open        compressnet
3/tcp      open        compressnet
4/tcp      open        unknown
5/tcp      open        rje
6/tcp      open        unknown
7/tcp      open        echo
8/tcp      open        unknown
9/tcp      open        discard
10/tcp     open        unknown
11/tcp     open        systat
12/tcp     open        unknown
13/tcp     open        daytime
14/tcp     open        unknown
15/tcp     open        netstat
16/tcp     open        unknown
17/tcp     open        qotd
18/tcp     open        msp
19/tcp     open        chargen
20/tcp     open        ftp-data
21/tcp     open        ftp
22/tcp     open        ssh
23/tcp     open        telnet
24/tcp     open        priv-mail
25/tcp     open        smtp
26/tcp     open        unknown
27/tcp     open        nsw-fe
28/tcp     open        unknown
29/tcp     open        msg-icp
```

```
30/tcp      open        unknown
31/tcp      open        msg-auth
32/tcp      open        unknown
33/tcp      open        dsp
34/tcp      open        unknown
35/tcp      open        priv-print
36/tcp      open        unknown
37/tcp      open        time
38/tcp      open        rap
39/tcp      open        rlp
40/tcp      open        unknown
41/tcp      open        graphics
42/tcp      open        nameserver
43/tcp      open        whois
44/tcp      open        mpm-flags
45/tcp      open        mpm
46/tcp      open        mpm-snd
47/tcp      open        ni-ftp
48/tcp      open        auditd
49/tcp      open        tacacs
50/tcp      open        re-mail-ck
51/tcp      open        la-maint
52/tcp      open        xns-time
53/tcp      open        domain
54/tcp      open        xns-ch
55/tcp      open        isi-gl
56/tcp      open        xns-auth
57/tcp      open        priv-term
58/tcp      open        xns-mail
59/tcp      open        priv-file
60/tcp      open        unknown
61/tcp      open        ni-mail
62/tcp      open        acas
63/tcp      open        via-ftp
64/tcp      open        covia
65/tcp      open        tacacs-ds
66/tcp      open        sql*net
67/tcp      open        dhcpserver
68/tcp      open        dhcpclient
69/tcp      open        tftp
70/tcp      open        gopher
71/tcp      open        netrjs-1
72/tcp      open        netrjs-2
73/tcp      open        netrjs-3
74/tcp      open        netrjs-4
75/tcp      open        priv-dial
76/tcp      open        deos
77/tcp      open        priv-rje
78/tcp      open        vettcp
79/tcp      open        finger
80/tcp      open        http
```

81/tcp	open	hosts2-ns
82/tcp	open	xfer
83/tcp	open	mit-ml-dev
84/tcp	open	ctf
85/tcp	open	mit-ml-dev
86/tcp	open	mfcobol
87/tcp	open	priv-term-l
88/tcp	open	kerberos-sec
89/tcp	open	su-mit-tg
90/tcp	open	dnsix
91/tcp	open	mit-dov
92/tcp	open	npp
93/tcp	open	dcp
94/tcp	open	objcall
95/tcp	open	supdup
96/tcp	open	dixie
97/tcp	open	swift-rvf
98/tcp	open	linuxconf
99/tcp	open	metagram
100/tcp	open	newacct
101/tcp	open	hostname
102/tcp	open	iso-tsap
103/tcp	open	gppitnp
104/tcp	open	acr-nema
105/tcp	open	csnet-ns
106/tcp	open	pop3pw
107/tcp	open	rtelnet
108/tcp	open	snagas
109/tcp	open	pop-2
110/tcp	open	pop-3
111/tcp	open	sunrpc
112/tcp	open	mcidas
113/tcp	open	auth
114/tcp	open	audionews
115/tcp	open	sftp
116/tcp	open	ansanotify
117/tcp	open	uucp-path
118/tcp	open	sqlserv
119/tcp	open	nntp
120/tcp	open	cfdptkt
121/tcp	open	erpc
122/tcp	open	smakynet
123/tcp	open	ntp
124/tcp	open	ansatrader
125/tcp	open	locus-map
126/tcp	open	unitary
127/tcp	open	locus-con
128/tcp	open	gss-xlicen
129/tcp	open	pwdgen
130/tcp	open	cisco-fna
131/tcp	open	cisco-tna

```
132/tcp     open     cisco-sys
133/tcp     open     statsrv
134/tcp     open     ingres-net
135/tcp     open     loc-srv
136/tcp     open     profile
137/tcp     open     netbios-ns
138/tcp     open     netbios-dgm
139/tcp     open     netbios-ssn
140/tcp     open     emfis-data
141/tcp     open     emfis-cntl
142/tcp     open     bl-idm
143/tcp     open     imap2
144/tcp     open     news
145/tcp     open     uaac
146/tcp     open     iso-tp0
147/tcp     open     iso-ip
148/tcp     open     cronus
149/tcp     open     aed-512
150/tcp     open     sql-net
151/tcp     open     hems
152/tcp     open     bftp
153/tcp     open     sgmp
154/tcp     open     netsc-prod
155/tcp     open     netsc-dev
156/tcp     open     sqlsrv
157/tcp     open     knet-cmp
158/tcp     open     pcmail-srv
159/tcp     open     nss-routing
160/tcp     open     sgmp-traps
161/tcp     open     snmp
162/tcp     open     snmptrap
163/tcp     open     cmip-man
164/tcp     open     cmip-agent
165/tcp     open     xns-courier
166/tcp     open     s-net
167/tcp     open     namp
168/tcp     open     rsvd
169/tcp     open     send
170/tcp     open     print-srv
171/tcp     open     multiplex
172/tcp     open     cl-1
173/tcp     open     xyplex-mux
174/tcp     open     mailq
175/tcp     open     vmnet
176/tcp     open     genrad-mux
177/tcp     open     xdmcp
178/tcp     open     nextstep
179/tcp     open     bgp
180/tcp     open     ris
181/tcp     open     unify
182/tcp     open     audit
```

```
183/tcp     open        ocbinder
184/tcp     open        ocserver
185/tcp     open        remote-kis
186/tcp     open        kis
187/tcp     open        aci
188/tcp     open        mumps
189/tcp     open        qft
190/tcp     open        gacp
191/tcp     open        prospero
192/tcp     open        osu-nms
193/tcp     open        srmp
194/tcp     open        irc
195/tcp     open        dn6-nlm-aud
196/tcp     open        dn6-smm-red
197/tcp     open        dls
198/tcp     open        dls-mon
199/tcp     open        smux
200/tcp     open        src
201/tcp     open        at-rtmp
202/tcp     open        at-nbp
203/tcp     open        at-3
204/tcp     open        at-echo
205/tcp     open        at-5
206/tcp     open        at-zis
207/tcp     open        at-7
208/tcp     open        at-8
209/tcp     open        tam
210/tcp     open        z39.50
211/tcp     open        914c-g
212/tcp     open        anet
213/tcp     open        ipx
214/tcp     open        vmpwscs
215/tcp     open        softpc
216/tcp     open        atls
217/tcp     open        dbase
218/tcp     open        mpp
219/tcp     open        uarps
220/tcp     open        imap3
221/tcp     open        fln-spx
222/tcp     open        rsh-spx
223/tcp     open        cdc
224/tcp     open        unknown
225/tcp     open        unknown
226/tcp     open        unknown
227/tcp     open        unknown
228/tcp     open        unknown
229/tcp     open        unknown
230/tcp     open        unknown
231/tcp     open        unknown
232/tcp     open        unknown
233/tcp     open        unknown
```

```
234/tcp     open        unknown
235/tcp     open        unknown
236/tcp     open        unknown
237/tcp     open        unknown
238/tcp     open        unknown
239/tcp     open        unknown
240/tcp     open        unknown
241/tcp     open        unknown
242/tcp     open        direct
243/tcp     open        sur-meas
244/tcp     open        dayna
245/tcp     open        link
246/tcp     open        dsp3270
247/tcp     open        subntbcst_tftp
248/tcp     open        bhfhs
249/tcp     open        unknown
250/tcp     open        unknown
251/tcp     open        unknown
252/tcp     open        unknown
253/tcp     open        unknown
254/tcp     open        unknown
255/tcp     open        unknown
256/tcp     open        FW1-secureremote
257/tcp     open        FW1-mc-fwmodule
258/tcp     open        Fw1-mc-gui
259/tcp     open        esro-gen
260/tcp     open        openport
261/tcp     open        nsiiops
262/tcp     open        arcisdms
263/tcp     open        hdap
264/tcp     open        bgmp
265/tcp     open        maybeFW1
266/tcp     open        unknown
267/tcp     open        unknown
268/tcp     open        unknown
269/tcp     open        unknown
270/tcp     open        unknown
271/tcp     open        unknown
272/tcp     open        unknown
273/tcp     open        unknown
274/tcp     open        unknown
275/tcp     open        unknown
276/tcp     open        unknown
277/tcp     open        unknown
278/tcp     open        unknown
279/tcp     open        unknown
280/tcp     open        http-mgmt
281/tcp     open        personal-link
282/tcp     open        cableport-ax
283/tcp     open        unknown
284/tcp     open        unknown
```

```
285/tcp     open        unknown
286/tcp     open        unknown
287/tcp     open        unknown
288/tcp     open        unknown
289/tcp     open        unknown
290/tcp     open        unknown
291/tcp     open        unknown
292/tcp     open        unknown
293/tcp     open        unknown
294/tcp     open        unknown
295/tcp     open        unknown
296/tcp     open        unknown
297/tcp     open        unknown
298/tcp     open        unknown
299/tcp     open        unknown
300/tcp     open        unknown
301/tcp     open        unknown
302/tcp     open        unknown
303/tcp     open        unknown
304/tcp     open        unknown
305/tcp     open        unknown
306/tcp     open        unknown
307/tcp     open        unknown
308/tcp     open        novastorbakcup
309/tcp     open        entrusttime
310/tcp     open        bhmds
311/tcp     open        asip-webadmin
312/tcp     open        vslmp
313/tcp     open        magenta-logic
314/tcp     open        opalis-robot
315/tcp     open        dpsi
316/tcp     open        decauth
317/tcp     open        zannet
318/tcp     open        unknown
319/tcp     open        unknown
320/tcp     open        unknown
321/tcp     open        pip
322/tcp     open        unknown
323/tcp     open        unknown
324/tcp     open        unknown
325/tcp     open        unknown
326/tcp     open        unknown
327/tcp     open        unknown
328/tcp     open        unknown
329/tcp     open        unknown
330/tcp     open        unknown
331/tcp     open        unknown
332/tcp     open        unknown
333/tcp     open        unknown
334/tcp     open        unknown
335/tcp     open        unknown
```

```
336/tcp     open        unknown
337/tcp     open        unknown
338/tcp     open        unknown
339/tcp     open        unknown
340/tcp     open        unknown
341/tcp     open        unknown
342/tcp     open        unknown
343/tcp     open        unknown
344/tcp     open        pdap
345/tcp     open        pawserv
346/tcp     open        zserv
347/tcp     open        fatserv
348/tcp     open        csi-sgwp
349/tcp     open        mftp
350/tcp     open        matip-type-a
351/tcp     open        matip-type-b
352/tcp     open        dtag-ste-sb
353/tcp     open        ndsauth
354/tcp     open        bh611
355/tcp     open        datex-asn
356/tcp     open        cloanto-net-1
357/tcp     open        bhevent
358/tcp     open        shrinkwrap
359/tcp     open        tenebris_nts
360/tcp     open        scoi2odialog
361/tcp     open        semantix
362/tcp     open        srssend
363/tcp     open        rsvp_tunnel
364/tcp     open        aurora-cmgr
365/tcp     open        dtk
366/tcp     open        odmr
367/tcp     open        mortgageware
368/tcp     open        qbikgdp
369/tcp     open        rpc2portmap
370/tcp     open        codaauth2
371/tcp     open        clearcase
372/tcp     open        ulistserv
373/tcp     open        legent-1
374/tcp     open        legent-2
375/tcp     open        hassle
376/tcp     open        nip
377/tcp     open        tnETOS
378/tcp     open        dsETOS
379/tcp     open        is99c
380/tcp     open        is99s
381/tcp     open        hp-collector
382/tcp     open        hp-managed-node
383/tcp     open        hp-alarm-mgr
384/tcp     open        arns
385/tcp     open        ibm-app
386/tcp     open        asa
```

```
387/tcp    open    aurp
388/tcp    open    unidata-ldm
389/tcp    open    ldap
390/tcp    open    uis
391/tcp    open    synotics-relay
392/tcp    open    synotics-broker
393/tcp    open    dis
394/tcp    open    embl-ndt
395/tcp    open    netcp
396/tcp    open    netware-ip
397/tcp    open    mptn
398/tcp    open    kryptolan
399/tcp    open    iso-tsap-c2
400/tcp    open    work-sol
401/tcp    open    ups
402/tcp    open    genie
403/tcp    open    decap
404/tcp    open    nced
405/tcp    open    ncld
406/tcp    open    imsp
407/tcp    open    timbuktu
408/tcp    open    prm-sm
409/tcp    open    prm-nm
410/tcp    open    decladebug
411/tcp    open    rmt
412/tcp    open    synoptics-trap
413/tcp    open    smsp
414/tcp    open    infoseek
415/tcp    open    bnet
416/tcp    open    silverplatter
417/tcp    open    onmux
418/tcp    open    hyper-g
419/tcp    open    ariel1
420/tcp    open    smpte
421/tcp    open    ariel2
422/tcp    open    ariel3
423/tcp    open    opc-job-start
424/tcp    open    opc-job-track
425/tcp    open    icad-el
426/tcp    open    smartsdp
427/tcp    open    svrloc
428/tcp    open    ocs_cmu
429/tcp    open    ocs_amu
430/tcp    open    utmpsd
431/tcp    open    utmpcd
432/tcp    open    iasd
433/tcp    open    nnsp
434/tcp    open    mobileip-agent
435/tcp    open    mobilip-mn
436/tcp    open    dna-cml
437/tcp    open    comscm
```

```
438/tcp    open    dsfgw
439/tcp    open    dasp
440/tcp    open    sgcp
441/tcp    open    decvms-sysmgt
442/tcp    open    cvc_hostd
443/tcp    open    https
444/tcp    open    snpp
445/tcp    open    microsoft-ds
446/tcp    open    ddm-rdb
447/tcp    open    ddm-dfm
448/tcp    open    ddm-ssl
449/tcp    open    as-servermap
450/tcp    open    tserver
451/tcp    open    sfs-smp-net
452/tcp    open    sfs-config
453/tcp    open    creativeserver
454/tcp    open    contentserver
455/tcp    open    creativepartnr
456/tcp    open    macon-tcp
457/tcp    open    scohelp
458/tcp    open    appleqtc
459/tcp    open    ampr-rcmd
460/tcp    open    skronk
461/tcp    open    datasurfsrv
462/tcp    open    datasurfsrvsec
463/tcp    open    alpes
464/tcp    open    kpasswd5
465/tcp    open    smtps
466/tcp    open    digital-vrc
467/tcp    open    mylex-mapd
468/tcp    open    photuris
469/tcp    open    rcp
470/tcp    open    scx-proxy
471/tcp    open    mondex
472/tcp    open    ljk-login
473/tcp    open    hybrid-pop
474/tcp    open    tn-tl-w1
475/tcp    open    tcpnethaspsrv
476/tcp    open    tn-tl-fd1
477/tcp    open    ss7ns
478/tcp    open    spsc
479/tcp    open    iafserver
480/tcp    open    loadsrv
481/tcp    open    dvs
482/tcp    open    bgs-nsi
483/tcp    open    ulpnet
484/tcp    open    integra-sme
485/tcp    open    powerburst
486/tcp    open    sstats
487/tcp    open    saft
488/tcp    open    gss-http
```

```
489/tcp    open    nest-protocol
490/tcp    open    micom-pfs
491/tcp    open    go-login
492/tcp    open    ticf-1
493/tcp    open    ticf-2
494/tcp    open    pov-ray
495/tcp    open    intecourier
496/tcp    open    pim-rp-disc
497/tcp    open    dantz
498/tcp    open    siam
499/tcp    open    iso-ill
500/tcp    open    isakmp
501/tcp    open    stmf
502/tcp    open    asa-appl-proto
503/tcp    open    intrinsa
504/tcp    open    citadel
505/tcp    open    mailbox-lm
506/tcp    open    ohimsrv
507/tcp    open    crs
508/tcp    open    xvttp
509/tcp    open    snare
510/tcp    open    fcp
511/tcp    open    passgo
512/tcp    open    exec
513/tcp    open    login
514/tcp    open    shell
515/tcp    open    printer
516/tcp    open    videotex
517/tcp    open    talk
518/tcp    open    ntalk
519/tcp    open    utime
520/tcp    open    efs
521/tcp    open    ripng
522/tcp    open    ulp
523/tcp    open    ibm-db2
524/tcp    open    ncp
525/tcp    open    timed
526/tcp    open    tempo
527/tcp    open    stx
528/tcp    open    custix
529/tcp    open    irc-serv
530/tcp    open    courier
531/tcp    open    conference
532/tcp    open    netnews
533/tcp    open    netwall
534/tcp    open    mm-admin
535/tcp    open    iiop
536/tcp    open    opalis-rdv
537/tcp    open    nmsp
538/tcp    open    gdomap
539/tcp    open    apertus-ldp
```

```
540/tcp    open    uucp
541/tcp    open    uucp-rlogin
542/tcp    open    commerce
543/tcp    open    klogin
544/tcp    open    kshell
545/tcp    open    ekshell
546/tcp    open    dhcpv6-client
547/tcp    open    dhcpv6-server
548/tcp    open    afpovertcp
549/tcp    open    idfp
550/tcp    open    new-rwho
551/tcp    open    cybercash
552/tcp    open    deviceshare
553/tcp    open    pirp
554/tcp    open    rtsp
555/tcp    open    dsf
556/tcp    open    remotefs
557/tcp    open    openvms-sysipc
558/tcp    open    sdnskmp
559/tcp    open    teedtap
560/tcp    open    rmonitor
561/tcp    open    monitor
562/tcp    open    chshell
563/tcp    open    snews
564/tcp    open    9pfs
565/tcp    open    whoami
566/tcp    open    streettalk
567/tcp    open    banyan-rpc
568/tcp    open    ms-shuttle
569/tcp    open    ms-rome
570/tcp    open    meter
571/tcp    open    umeter
572/tcp    open    sonar
573/tcp    open    banyan-vip
574/tcp    open    ftp-agent
575/tcp    open    vemmi
576/tcp    open    ipcd
577/tcp    open    vnas
578/tcp    open    ipdd
579/tcp    open    decbsrv
580/tcp    open    sntp-heartbeat
581/tcp    open    bdp
582/tcp    open    scc-security
583/tcp    open    philips-vc
584/tcp    open    keyserver
585/tcp    open    imap4-ssl
586/tcp    open    password-chg
587/tcp    open    submission
588/tcp    open    cal
589/tcp    open    eyelink
590/tcp    open    tns-cml
```

```
591/tcp    open    http-alt
592/tcp    open    eudora-set
593/tcp    open    http-rpc-epmap
594/tcp    open    tpip
595/tcp    open    cab-protocol
596/tcp    open    smsd
597/tcp    open    ptcnameservice
598/tcp    open    sco-websrvrmg3
599/tcp    open    acp
600/tcp    open    ipcserver
601/tcp    open    unknown
602/tcp    open    unknown
603/tcp    open    unknown
604/tcp    open    unknown
605/tcp    open    unknown
606/tcp    open    urm
607/tcp    open    nqs
608/tcp    open    sift-uft
609/tcp    open    npmp-trap
610/tcp    open    npmp-local
611/tcp    open    npmp-gui
612/tcp    open    unknown
613/tcp    open    unknown
614/tcp    open    unknown
615/tcp    open    unknown
616/tcp    open    unknown
617/tcp    open    unknown
618/tcp    open    unknown
619/tcp    open    unknown
620/tcp    open    unknown
621/tcp    open    unknown
622/tcp    open    unknown
623/tcp    open    unknown
624/tcp    open    unknown
625/tcp    open    unknown
626/tcp    open    unknown
627/tcp    open    unknown
628/tcp    open    qmqp
629/tcp    open    unknown
630/tcp    open    unknown
631/tcp    open    ipp
632/tcp    open    unknown
633/tcp    open    unknown
634/tcp    open    ginad
635/tcp    open    unknown
636/tcp    open    ldapssl
637/tcp    open    lanserver
638/tcp    open    unknown
639/tcp    open    unknown
640/tcp    open    unknown
641/tcp    open    unknown
```

```
642/tcp    open    unknown
643/tcp    open    unknown
644/tcp    open    unknown
645/tcp    open    unknown
646/tcp    open    unknown
647/tcp    open    unknown
648/tcp    open    unknown
649/tcp    open    unknown
650/tcp    open    unknown
651/tcp    open    unknown
652/tcp    open    unknown
653/tcp    open    unknown
654/tcp    open    unknown
655/tcp    open    unknown
656/tcp    open    unknown
657/tcp    open    unknown
658/tcp    open    unknown
659/tcp    open    unknown
660/tcp    open    mac-srvr-admin
661/tcp    open    unknown
662/tcp    open    unknown
663/tcp    open    unknown
664/tcp    open    unknown
665/tcp    open    unknown
666/tcp    open    doom
667/tcp    open    unknown
668/tcp    open    unknown
669/tcp    open    unknown
670/tcp    open    unknown
671/tcp    open    unknown
672/tcp    open    unknown
673/tcp    open    unknown
674/tcp    open    unknown
675/tcp    open    unknown
676/tcp    open    unknown
677/tcp    open    unknown
678/tcp    open    unknown
679/tcp    open    unknown
680/tcp    open    unknown
681/tcp    open    unknown
682/tcp    open    unknown
683/tcp    open    unknown
684/tcp    open    unknown
685/tcp    open    unknown
686/tcp    open    unknown
687/tcp    open    unknown
688/tcp    open    unknown
689/tcp    open    unknown
690/tcp    open    unknown
691/tcp    open    resvc
692/tcp    open    unknown
```

```
693/tcp    open    unknown
694/tcp    open    unknown
695/tcp    open    unknown
696/tcp    open    unknown
697/tcp    open    unknown
698/tcp    open    unknown
699/tcp    open    unknown
700/tcp    open    unknown
701/tcp    open    unknown
702/tcp    open    unknown
703/tcp    open    unknown
704/tcp    open    elcsd
705/tcp    open    unknown
706/tcp    open    silc
707/tcp    open    unknown
708/tcp    open    unknown
709/tcp    open    entrustmanager
710/tcp    open    unknown
711/tcp    open    unknown
712/tcp    open    unknown
713/tcp    open    unknown
714/tcp    open    unknown
715/tcp    open    unknown
716/tcp    open    unknown
717/tcp    open    unknown
718/tcp    open    unknown
719/tcp    open    unknown
720/tcp    open    unknown
721/tcp    open    unknown
722/tcp    open    unknown
723/tcp    open    unknown
724/tcp    open    unknown
725/tcp    open    unknown
726/tcp    open    unknown
727/tcp    open    unknown
728/tcp    open    unknown
729/tcp    open    netviewdm1
730/tcp    open    netviewdm2
731/tcp    open    netviewdm3
732/tcp    open    unknown
733/tcp    open    unknown
734/tcp    open    unknown
735/tcp    open    unknown
736/tcp    open    unknown
737/tcp    open    unknown
738/tcp    open    unknown
739/tcp    open    unknown
740/tcp    open    netcp
741/tcp    open    netgw
742/tcp    open    netrcs
743/tcp    open    unknown
```

744/tcp	open	flexlm
745/tcp	open	unknown
746/tcp	open	unknown
747/tcp	open	fujitsu-dev
748/tcp	open	ris-cm
749/tcp	open	kerberos-adm
750/tcp	open	kerberos
751/tcp	open	kerberos_master
752/tcp	open	qrh
753/tcp	open	rrh
754/tcp	open	krb_prop
755/tcp	open	unknown
756/tcp	open	unknown
757/tcp	open	unknown
758/tcp	open	nlogin
759/tcp	open	con
760/tcp	open	krbupdate
761/tcp	open	kpasswd
762/tcp	open	quotad
763/tcp	open	cycleserv
764/tcp	open	omserv
765/tcp	open	webster
766/tcp	open	unknown
767/tcp	open	phonebook
768/tcp	open	unknown
769/tcp	open	vid
770/tcp	open	cadlock
771/tcp	open	rtip
772/tcp	open	cycleserv2
773/tcp	open	submit
774/tcp	open	rpasswd
775/tcp	open	entomb
776/tcp	open	wpages
777/tcp	open	unknown
778/tcp	open	unknown
779/tcp	open	unknown
780/tcp	open	wpgs
781/tcp	open	hp-collector
782/tcp	open	hp-managed-node
783/tcp	open	hp-alarm-mgr
784/tcp	open	unknown
785/tcp	open	unknown
786/tcp	open	concert
787/tcp	open	unknown
788/tcp	open	unknown
789/tcp	open	unknown
790/tcp	open	unknown
791/tcp	open	unknown
792/tcp	open	unknown
793/tcp	open	unknown
794/tcp	open	unknown

```
795/tcp     open        unknown
796/tcp     open        unknown
797/tcp     open        unknown
798/tcp     open        unknown
799/tcp     open        controlit
800/tcp     open        mdbs_daemon
801/tcp     open        device
802/tcp     open        unknown
803/tcp     open        unknown
804/tcp     open        unknown
805/tcp     open        unknown
806/tcp     open        unknown
807/tcp     open        unknown
808/tcp     open        unknown
809/tcp     open        unknown
810/tcp     open        unknown
811/tcp     open        unknown
812/tcp     open        unknown
813/tcp     open        unknown
814/tcp     open        unknown
815/tcp     open        unknown
816/tcp     open        unknown
817/tcp     open        unknown
818/tcp     open        unknown
819/tcp     open        unknown
820/tcp     open        unknown
821/tcp     open        unknown
822/tcp     open        unknown
823/tcp     open        unknown
824/tcp     open        unknown
825/tcp     open        unknown
826/tcp     open        unknown
827/tcp     open        unknown
828/tcp     open        unknown
829/tcp     open        unknown
830/tcp     open        unknown
831/tcp     open        unknown
832/tcp     open        unknown
833/tcp     open        unknown
834/tcp     open        unknown
835/tcp     open        unknown
836/tcp     open        unknown
837/tcp     open        unknown
838/tcp     open        unknown
839/tcp     open        unknown
840/tcp     open        unknown
841/tcp     open        unknown
842/tcp     open        unknown
843/tcp     open        unknown
844/tcp     open        unknown
845/tcp     open        unknown
```

```
846/tcp     open        unknown
847/tcp     open        unknown
848/tcp     open        unknown
849/tcp     open        unknown
850/tcp     open        unknown
851/tcp     open        unknown
852/tcp     open        unknown
853/tcp     open        unknown
854/tcp     open        unknown
855/tcp     open        unknown
856/tcp     open        unknown
857/tcp     open        unknown
858/tcp     open        unknown
859/tcp     open        unknown
860/tcp     open        unknown
861/tcp     open        unknown
862/tcp     open        unknown
863/tcp     open        unknown
864/tcp     open        unknown
865/tcp     open        unknown
866/tcp     open        unknown
867/tcp     open        unknown
868/tcp     open        unknown
869/tcp     open        unknown
870/tcp     open        unknown
871/tcp     open        supfilesrv
872/tcp     open        unknown
873/tcp     open        rsync
874/tcp     open        unknown
875/tcp     open        unknown
876/tcp     open        unknown
877/tcp     open        unknown
878/tcp     open        unknown
879/tcp     open        unknown
880/tcp     open        unknown
881/tcp     open        unknown
882/tcp     open        unknown
883/tcp     open        unknown
884/tcp     open        unknown
885/tcp     open        unknown
886/tcp     open        unknown
887/tcp     open        unknown
888/tcp     open        accessbuilder
889/tcp     open        unknown
890/tcp     open        unknown
891/tcp     open        unknown
892/tcp     open        unknown
893/tcp     open        unknown
894/tcp     open        unknown
895/tcp     open        unknown
896/tcp     open        unknown
```

```
897/tcp      open         unknown
898/tcp      open         unknown
899/tcp      open         unknown
900/tcp      open         unknown
901/tcp      open         samba-swat
902/tcp      open         unknown
903/tcp      open         unknown
904/tcp      open         unknown
905/tcp      open         unknown
906/tcp      open         unknown
907/tcp      open         unknown
908/tcp      open         unknown
909/tcp      open         unknown
910/tcp      open         unknown
911/tcp      open         unknown
912/tcp      open         unknown
913/tcp      open         unknown
914/tcp      open         unknown
915/tcp      open         unknown
916/tcp      open         unknown
917/tcp      open         unknown
918/tcp      open         unknown
919/tcp      open         unknown
920/tcp      open         unknown
921/tcp      open         unknown
922/tcp      open         unknown
923/tcp      open         unknown
924/tcp      open         unknown
925/tcp      open         unknown
926/tcp      open         unknown
927/tcp      open         unknown
928/tcp      open         unknown
929/tcp      open         unknown
930/tcp      open         unknown
931/tcp      open         unknown
932/tcp      open         unknown
933/tcp      open         unknown
934/tcp      open         unknown
935/tcp      open         unknown
936/tcp      open         unknown
937/tcp      open         unknown
938/tcp      open         unknown
939/tcp      open         unknown
940/tcp      open         unknown
941/tcp      open         unknown
942/tcp      open         unknown
943/tcp      open         unknown
944/tcp      open         unknown
945/tcp      open         unknown
946/tcp      open         unknown
947/tcp      open         unknown
```

```
948/tcp    open    unknown
949/tcp    open    unknown
950/tcp    open    oftep-rpc
951/tcp    open    unknown
952/tcp    open    unknown
953/tcp    open    rndc
954/tcp    open    unknown
955/tcp    open    unknown
956/tcp    open    unknown
957/tcp    open    unknown
958/tcp    open    unknown
959/tcp    open    unknown
960/tcp    open    unknown
961/tcp    open    unknown
962/tcp    open    unknown
963/tcp    open    unknown
964/tcp    open    unknown
965/tcp    open    unknown
966/tcp    open    unknown
967/tcp    open    unknown
968/tcp    open    unknown
969/tcp    open    unknown
970/tcp    open    unknown
971/tcp    open    unknown
972/tcp    open    unknown
973/tcp    open    unknown
974/tcp    open    unknown
975/tcp    open    securenetpro-sensor
976/tcp    open    unknown
977/tcp    open    unknown
978/tcp    open    unknown
979/tcp    open    unknown
980/tcp    open    unknown
981/tcp    open    unknown
982/tcp    open    unknown
983/tcp    open    unknown
984/tcp    open    unknown
985/tcp    open    unknown
986/tcp    open    unknown
987/tcp    open    unknown
988/tcp    open    unknown
989/tcp    open    ftps-data
990/tcp    open    ftps
991/tcp    open    unknown
992/tcp    open    telnets
993/tcp    open    imaps
994/tcp    open    ircs
995/tcp    open    pop3s
996/tcp    open    xtreelic
997/tcp    open    maitrd
998/tcp    open    busboy
```

Port	State	Service
999/tcp	open	garcon
1000/tcp	open	cadlock
1001/tcp	open	unknown
1002/tcp	open	unknown
1003/tcp	open	unknown
1004/tcp	open	unknown
1005/tcp	open	unknown
1006/tcp	open	unknown
1007/tcp	open	unknown
1008/tcp	open	ufsd
1009/tcp	open	unknown
1010/tcp	open	unknown
1011/tcp	open	unknown
1012/tcp	open	unknown
1013/tcp	open	unknown
1014/tcp	open	unknown
1015/tcp	open	unknown
1016/tcp	open	unknown
1017/tcp	open	unknown
1018/tcp	open	unknown
1019/tcp	open	unknown
1020/tcp	open	unknown
1021/tcp	open	unknown
1022/tcp	open	unknown
1023/tcp	open	unknown
1024/tcp	open	kdm
1025/tcp	open	NFS-or-IIS
1026/tcp	open	LSA-or-nterm
1027/tcp	open	IIS
1029/tcp	open	ms-lsa
1030/tcp	open	iad1
1031/tcp	open	iad2
1032/tcp	open	iad3
1033/tcp	open	netinfo
1050/tcp	open	java-or-OTGfileshare
1058/tcp	open	nim
1059/tcp	open	nimreg
1067/tcp	open	instl_boots
1068/tcp	open	instl_bootc
1080/tcp	open	socks
1083/tcp	open	ansoft-lm-1
1084/tcp	open	ansoft-lm-2
1103/tcp	open	xaudio
1109/tcp	open	kpop
1110/tcp	open	nfsd-status
1112/tcp	open	msql
1127/tcp	open	supfiledbg
1139/tcp	open	cce3x
1155/tcp	open	nfa
1178/tcp	open	skkserv
1212/tcp	open	lupa

```
1222/tcp     open        nerv
1234/tcp     open        hotline
1241/tcp     open        msg
1248/tcp     open        hermes
1346/tcp     open        alta-ana-lm
1347/tcp     open        bbn-mmc
1348/tcp     open        bbn-mmx
1349/tcp     open        sbook
1350/tcp     open        editbench
1351/tcp     open        equationbuilder
1352/tcp     open        lotusnotes
1353/tcp     open        relief
1354/tcp     open        rightbrain
1355/tcp     open        intuitive-edge
1356/tcp     open        cuillamartin
1357/tcp     open        pegboard
1358/tcp     open        connlcli
1359/tcp     open        ftsrv
1360/tcp     open        mimer
1361/tcp     open        linx
1362/tcp     open        timeflies
1363/tcp     open        ndm-requester
1364/tcp     open        ndm-server
1365/tcp     open        adapt-sna
1366/tcp     open        netware-csp
1367/tcp     open        dcs
1368/tcp     open        screencast
1369/tcp     open        gv-us
1370/tcp     open        us-gv
1371/tcp     open        fc-cli
1372/tcp     open        fc-ser
1373/tcp     open        chromagrafx
1374/tcp     open        molly
1375/tcp     open        bytex
1376/tcp     open        ibm-pps
1377/tcp     open        cichlid
1378/tcp     open        elan
1379/tcp     open        dbreporter
1380/tcp     open        telesis-licman
1381/tcp     open        apple-licman
1383/tcp     open        gwha
1384/tcp     open        os-licman
1385/tcp     open        atex_elmd
1386/tcp     open        checksum
1387/tcp     open        cadsi-lm
1388/tcp     open        objective-dbc
1389/tcp     open        iclpv-dm
1390/tcp     open        iclpv-sc
1391/tcp     open        iclpv-sas
1392/tcp     open        iclpv-pm
1393/tcp     open        iclpv-nls
```

```
1394/tcp    open        iclpv-nlc
1395/tcp    open        iclpv-wsm
1396/tcp    open        dvl-activemail
1397/tcp    open        audio-activmail
1398/tcp    open        video-activmail
1399/tcp    open        cadkey-licman
1400/tcp    open        cadkey-tablet
1401/tcp    open        goldleaf-licman
1402/tcp    open        prm-sm-np
1403/tcp    open        prm-nm-np
1404/tcp    open        igi-lm
1405/tcp    open        ibm-res
1406/tcp    open        netlabs-lm
1407/tcp    open        dbsa-lm
1408/tcp    open        sophia-lm
1409/tcp    open        here-lm
1410/tcp    open        hiq
1411/tcp    open        af
1412/tcp    open        innosys
1413/tcp    open        innosys-acl
1414/tcp    open        ibm-mqseries
1415/tcp    open        dbstar
1416/tcp    open        novell-lu6.2
1417/tcp    open        timbuktu-srv1
1418/tcp    open        timbuktu-srv2
1419/tcp    open        timbuktu-srv3
1420/tcp    open        timbuktu-srv4
1421/tcp    open        gandalf-lm
1422/tcp    open        autodesk-lm
1423/tcp    open        essbase
1424/tcp    open        hybrid
1425/tcp    open        zion-lm
1426/tcp    open        sas-1
1427/tcp    open        mloadd
1428/tcp    open        informatik-lm
1429/tcp    open        nms
1430/tcp    open        tpdu
1431/tcp    open        rgtp
1432/tcp    open        blueberry-lm
1433/tcp    open        ms-sql-s
1434/tcp    open        ms-sql-m
1435/tcp    open        ibm-cics
1436/tcp    open        sas-2
1437/tcp    open        tabula
1438/tcp    open        eicon-server
1439/tcp    open        eicon-x25
1440/tcp    open        eicon-slp
1441/tcp    open        cadis-1
1442/tcp    open        cadis-2
1443/tcp    open        ies-lm
1444/tcp    open        marcam-lm
```

1445/tcp	open	proxima-lm
1446/tcp	open	ora-lm
1447/tcp	open	apri-lm
1448/tcp	open	oc-lm
1449/tcp	open	peport
1450/tcp	open	dwf
1451/tcp	open	infoman
1452/tcp	open	gtegsc-lm
1453/tcp	open	genie-lm
1454/tcp	open	interhdl_elmd
1455/tcp	open	esl-lm
1456/tcp	open	dca
1457/tcp	open	valisys-lm
1458/tcp	open	nrcabq-lm
1459/tcp	open	proshare1
1460/tcp	open	proshare2
1461/tcp	open	ibm_wrless_lan
1462/tcp	open	world-lm
1463/tcp	open	nucleus
1464/tcp	open	msl_lmd
1465/tcp	open	pipes
1466/tcp	open	oceansoft-lm
1467/tcp	open	csdmbase
1468/tcp	open	csdm
1469/tcp	open	aal-lm
1470/tcp	open	uaiact
1471/tcp	open	csdmbase
1472/tcp	open	csdm
1473/tcp	open	openmath
1474/tcp	open	telefinder
1475/tcp	open	taligent-lm
1476/tcp	open	clvm-cfg
1477/tcp	open	ms-sna-server
1478/tcp	open	ms-sna-base
1479/tcp	open	dberegister
1480/tcp	open	pacerforum
1481/tcp	open	airs
1482/tcp	open	miteksys-lm
1483/tcp	open	afs
1484/tcp	open	confluent
1485/tcp	open	lansource
1486/tcp	open	nms_topo_serv
1487/tcp	open	localinfosrvr
1488/tcp	open	docstor
1489/tcp	open	dmdocbroker
1490/tcp	open	insitu-conf
1491/tcp	open	anynetgateway
1492/tcp	open	stone-design-1
1493/tcp	open	netmap_lm
1494/tcp	open	citrix-ica
1495/tcp	open	cvc

```
1496/tcp    open        liberty-lm
1497/tcp    open        rfx-lm
1498/tcp    open        watcom-sql
1499/tcp    open        fhc
1500/tcp    open        vlsi-lm
1501/tcp    open        sas-3
1502/tcp    open        shivadiscovery
1503/tcp    open        imtc-mcs
1504/tcp    open        evb-elm
1505/tcp    open        funkproxy
1506/tcp    open        utcd
1507/tcp    open        symplex
1508/tcp    open        diagmond
1509/tcp    open        robcad-lm
1510/tcp    open        mvx-lm
1511/tcp    open        3l-l1
1512/tcp    open        wins
1513/tcp    open        fujitsu-dtc
1514/tcp    open        fujitsu-dtcns
1515/tcp    open        ifor-protocol
1516/tcp    open        vpad
1517/tcp    open        vpac
1518/tcp    open        vpvd
1519/tcp    open        vpvc
1520/tcp    open        atm-zip-office
1521/tcp    open        oracle
1522/tcp    open        rna-lm
1523/tcp    open        cichild-lm
1524/tcp    open        ingreslock
1525/tcp    open        orasrv
1526/tcp    open        pdap-np
1527/tcp    open        tlisrv
1528/tcp    open        mciautoreg
1529/tcp    open        support
1530/tcp    open        rap-service
1531/tcp    open        rap-listen
1532/tcp    open        miroconnect
1533/tcp    open        virtual-places
1534/tcp    open        micromuse-lm
1535/tcp    open        ampr-info
1536/tcp    open        ampr-inter
1537/tcp    open        sdsc-lm
1538/tcp    open        3ds-lm
1539/tcp    open        intellistor-lm
1540/tcp    open        rds
1541/tcp    open        rds2
1542/tcp    open        gridgen-elmd
1543/tcp    open        simba-cs
1544/tcp    open        aspeclmd
1545/tcp    open        vistium-share
1546/tcp    open        abbaccuray
```

```
1547/tcp    open    laplink
1548/tcp    open    axon-lm
1549/tcp    open    shivahose
1550/tcp    open    3m-image-lm
1551/tcp    open    hecmtl-db
1552/tcp    open    pciarray
1600/tcp    open    issd
1650/tcp    open    nkd
1651/tcp    open    shiva_confsrvr
1652/tcp    open    xnmp
1661/tcp    open    netview-aix-1
1662/tcp    open    netview-aix-2
1663/tcp    open    netview-aix-3
1664/tcp    open    netview-aix-4
1665/tcp    open    netview-aix-5
1666/tcp    open    netview-aix-6
1667/tcp    open    netview-aix-7
1668/tcp    open    netview-aix-8
1669/tcp    open    netview-aix-9
1670/tcp    open    netview-aix-10
1671/tcp    open    netview-aix-11
1672/tcp    open    netview-aix-12
1680/tcp    open    CarbonCopy
1720/tcp    open    H.323/Q.931
1723/tcp    open    pptp
1827/tcp    open    pcm
1900/tcp    open    UPnP
1986/tcp    open    licensedaemon
1987/tcp    open    tr-rsrb-p1
1988/tcp    open    tr-rsrb-p2
1989/tcp    open    tr-rsrb-p3
1990/tcp    open    stun-p1
1991/tcp    open    stun-p2
1992/tcp    open    stun-p3
1993/tcp    open    snmp-tcp-port
1994/tcp    open    stun-port
1995/tcp    open    perf-port
1996/tcp    open    tr-rsrb-port
1997/tcp    open    gdp-port
1998/tcp    open    x25-svc-port
1999/tcp    open    tcp-id-port
2000/tcp    open    callbook
2001/tcp    open    dc
2002/tcp    open    globe
2003/tcp    open    cfingerd
2004/tcp    open    mailbox
2005/tcp    open    deslogin
2006/tcp    open    invokator
2007/tcp    open    dectalk
2008/tcp    open    conf
2009/tcp    open    news
```

```
2010/tcp    open    search
2011/tcp    open    raid-cc
2012/tcp    open    ttyinfo
2013/tcp    open    raid-am
2014/tcp    open    troff
2015/tcp    open    cypress
2016/tcp    open    bootserver
2017/tcp    open    cypress-stat
2018/tcp    open    terminaldb
2019/tcp    open    whosockami
2020/tcp    open    xinupageserver
2021/tcp    open    servexec
2022/tcp    open    down
2023/tcp    open    xinuexpansion3
2024/tcp    open    xinuexpansion4
2025/tcp    open    ellpack
2026/tcp    open    scrabble
2027/tcp    open    shadowserver
2028/tcp    open    submitserver
2030/tcp    open    device2
2032/tcp    open    blackboard
2033/tcp    open    glogger
2034/tcp    open    scoremgr
2035/tcp    open    imsldoc
2038/tcp    open    objectmanager
2040/tcp    open    lam
2041/tcp    open    interbase
2042/tcp    open    isis
2043/tcp    open    isis-bcast
2044/tcp    open    rimsl
2045/tcp    open    cdfunc
2046/tcp    open    sdfunc
2047/tcp    open    dls
2048/tcp    open    dls-monitor
2049/tcp    open    nfs
2053/tcp    open    knetd
2064/tcp    open    distrib-net-losers
2065/tcp    open    dlsrpn
2067/tcp    open    dlswpn
2105/tcp    open    eklogin
2106/tcp    open    ekshell
2108/tcp    open    rkinit
2111/tcp    open    kx
2112/tcp    open    kip
2120/tcp    open    kauth
2201/tcp    open    ats
2232/tcp    open    ivs-video
2241/tcp    open    ivsd
2301/tcp    open    compaqdiag
2307/tcp    open    pehelp
2401/tcp    open    cvspserver
```

2430/tcp	open	venus
2431/tcp	open	venus-se
2432/tcp	open	codasrv
2433/tcp	open	codasrv-se
2500/tcp	open	rtsserv
2501/tcp	open	rtsclient
2564/tcp	open	hp-3000-telnet
2600/tcp	open	zebrasrv
2601/tcp	open	zebra
2602/tcp	open	ripd
2603/tcp	open	ripngd
2604/tcp	open	ospfd
2605/tcp	open	bgpd
2627/tcp	open	webster
2638/tcp	open	sybase
2766/tcp	open	listen
2784/tcp	open	www-dev
2998/tcp	open	iss-realsec
3000/tcp	open	ppp
3001/tcp	open	nessusd
3005/tcp	open	deslogin
3006/tcp	open	deslogind
3049/tcp	open	cfs
3052/tcp	open	PowerChute
3064/tcp	open	distrib-net-proxy
3086/tcp	open	sj3
3128/tcp	open	squid-http
3141/tcp	open	vmodem
3264/tcp	open	ccmail
3268/tcp	open	globalcatLDAP
3269/tcp	open	globalcatLDAPssl
3306/tcp	open	mysql
3333/tcp	open	dec-notes
3372/tcp	open	msdtc
3389/tcp	open	ms-term-serv
3421/tcp	open	bmap
3455/tcp	open	prsvp
3456/tcp	open	vat
3457/tcp	open	vat-control
3462/tcp	open	track
3900/tcp	open	udt_os
3984/tcp	open	mapper-nodemgr
3985/tcp	open	mapper-mapethd
3986/tcp	open	mapper-ws_ethd
3999/tcp	open	remoteanything
4000/tcp	open	remoteanything
4008/tcp	open	netcheque
4045/tcp	open	lockd
4132/tcp	open	nuts_dem
4133/tcp	open	nuts_bootp
4144/tcp	open	wincim

4321/tcp	open	rwhois
4333/tcp	open	msql
4343/tcp	open	unicall
4444/tcp	open	krb524
4480/tcp	open	proxy-plus
4500/tcp	open	sae-urn
4557/tcp	open	fax
4559/tcp	open	hylafax
4672/tcp	open	rfa
4987/tcp	open	maybeveritas
4998/tcp	open	maybeveritas
5000/tcp	open	UPnP
5001/tcp	open	commplex-link
5002/tcp	open	rfe
5010/tcp	open	telelpathstart
5011/tcp	open	telelpathattack
5050/tcp	open	mmcc
5145/tcp	open	rmonitor_secure
5190/tcp	open	aol
5191/tcp	open	aol-1
5192/tcp	open	aol-2
5193/tcp	open	aol-3
5232/tcp	open	sgi-dgl
5236/tcp	open	padl2sim
5300/tcp	open	hacl-hb
5301/tcp	open	hacl-gs
5302/tcp	open	hacl-cfg
5303/tcp	open	hacl-probe
5304/tcp	open	hacl-local
5305/tcp	open	hacl-test
5308/tcp	open	cfengine
5400/tcp	open	pcduo-old
5405/tcp	open	pcduo
5432/tcp	open	postgres
5510/tcp	open	secureidprop
5520/tcp	open	sdlog
5530/tcp	open	sdserv
5540/tcp	open	sdreport
5550/tcp	open	sdadmind
5555/tcp	open	freeciv
5631/tcp	open	pcanywheredata
5632/tcp	open	pcanywherestat
5680/tcp	open	canna
5713/tcp	open	proshareaudio
5714/tcp	open	prosharevideo
5715/tcp	open	prosharedata
5716/tcp	open	prosharerequest
5717/tcp	open	prosharenotify
5800/tcp	open	vnc-http
5801/tcp	open	vnc-http-1
5802/tcp	open	vnc-http-2

```
5803/tcp    open    vnc-http-3
5900/tcp    open    vnc
5901/tcp    open    vnc-1
5902/tcp    open    vnc-2
5903/tcp    open    vnc-3
5977/tcp    open    ncd-pref-tcp
5978/tcp    open    ncd-diag-tcp
5979/tcp    open    ncd-conf-tcp
5997/tcp    open    ncd-pref
5998/tcp    open    ncd-diag
5999/tcp    open    ncd-conf
6000/tcp    open    X11
6001/tcp    open    X11:1
6002/tcp    open    X11:2
6003/tcp    open    X11:3
6004/tcp    open    X11:4
6005/tcp    open    X11:5
6006/tcp    open    X11:6
6007/tcp    open    X11:7
6008/tcp    open    X11:8
6009/tcp    open    X11:9
6050/tcp    open    arcserve
6101/tcp    open    VeritasBackupExec
6103/tcp    open    RETS-or-BackupExec
6105/tcp    open    isdninfo
6106/tcp    open    isdninfo
6110/tcp    open    softcm
6111/tcp    open    spc
6112/tcp    open    dtspc
6141/tcp    open    meta-corp
6142/tcp    open    aspentec-lm
6143/tcp    open    watershed-lm
6144/tcp    open    statsci1-lm
6145/tcp    open    statsci2-lm
6146/tcp    open    lonewolf-lm
6147/tcp    open    montage-lm
6148/tcp    open    ricardo-lm
6346/tcp    open    gnutella
6502/tcp    open    netop-rc
6547/tcp    open    PowerChutePLUS
6548/tcp    open    PowerChutePLUS
6558/tcp    open    xdsxdm
6588/tcp    open    analogx
6666/tcp    open    irc-serv
6667/tcp    open    irc
6668/tcp    open    irc
6699/tcp    open    napster
6969/tcp    open    acmsoda
7000/tcp    open    afs3-fileserver
7001/tcp    open    afs3-callback
7002/tcp    open    afs3-prserver
```

```
7003/tcp    open    afs3-vlserver
7004/tcp    open    afs3-kaserver
7005/tcp    open    afs3-volser
7006/tcp    open    afs3-errors
7007/tcp    open    afs3-bos
7008/tcp    open    afs3-update
7009/tcp    open    afs3-rmtsys
7010/tcp    open    ups-onlinet
7070/tcp    open    realserver
7100/tcp    open    font-service
7200/tcp    open    fodms
7201/tcp    open    dlip
7326/tcp    open    icb
7597/tcp    open    qaz
8007/tcp    open    ajp12
8009/tcp    open    ajp13
8080/tcp    open    http-proxy
8081/tcp    open    blackice-icecap
8082/tcp    open    blackice-alerts
8888/tcp    open    sun-answerbook
8892/tcp    open    seosload
9090/tcp    open    zeus-admin
9100/tcp    open    jetdirect
9111/tcp    open    DragonIDSConsole
9152/tcp    open    ms-sql2000
9535/tcp    open    man
9876/tcp    open    sd
9991/tcp    open    issa
9992/tcp    open    issc
10000/tcp   open    snet-sensor-mgmt
10005/tcp   open    stel
10082/tcp   open    amandaidx
10083/tcp   open    amidxtape
11371/tcp   open    pksd
12000/tcp   open    cce4x
12345/tcp   open    NetBus
12346/tcp   open    NetBus
13701/tcp   open    VeritasNetbackup
13702/tcp   open    VeritasNetbackup
13705/tcp   open    VeritasNetbackup
13706/tcp   open    VeritasNetbackup
13708/tcp   open    VeritasNetbackup
13709/tcp   open    VeritasNetbackup
13710/tcp   open    VeritasNetbackup
13711/tcp   open    VeritasNetbackup
13712/tcp   open    VeritasNetbackup
13713/tcp   open    VeritasNetbackup
13714/tcp   open    VeritasNetbackup
13715/tcp   open    VeritasNetbackup
13716/tcp   open    VeritasNetbackup
13717/tcp   open    VeritasNetbackup
```

```
13718/tcp   open        VeritasNetbackup
13720/tcp   open        VeritasNetbackup
13721/tcp   open        VeritasNetbackup
13722/tcp   open        VeritasNetbackup
13782/tcp   open        VeritasNetbackup
13783/tcp   open        VeritasNetbackup
16959/tcp   open        subseven
17007/tcp   open        isode-dua
18000/tcp   open        biimenu
20005/tcp   open        btx
22273/tcp   open        wnn6
22289/tcp   open        wnn6_Cn
22305/tcp   open        wnn6_Kr
22321/tcp   open        wnn6_Tw
22370/tcp   open        hpnpd
26208/tcp   open        wnn6_DS
27374/tcp   open        subseven
27665/tcp   open        Trinoo_Master
31337/tcp   open        Elite
32770/tcp   open        sometimes-rpc3
32771/tcp   open        sometimes-rpc5
32772/tcp   open        sometimes-rpc7
32773/tcp   open        sometimes-rpc9
32774/tcp   open        sometimes-rpc11
32775/tcp   open        sometimes-rpc13
32776/tcp   open        sometimes-rpc15
32777/tcp   open        sometimes-rpc17
32778/tcp   open        sometimes-rpc19
32779/tcp   open        sometimes-rpc21
32780/tcp   open        sometimes-rpc23
32786/tcp   open        sometimes-rpc25
32787/tcp   open        sometimes-rpc27
43188/tcp   open        reachout
44442/tcp   open        coldfusion-auth
44443/tcp   open        coldfusion-auth
47557/tcp   open        dbbrowse
49400/tcp   open        compaqdiag
54320/tcp   open        bo2k
61439/tcp   open        netprowler-manager
61440/tcp   open        netprowler-manager2
61441/tcp   open        netprowler-sensor
65301/tcp   open        pcanywhere
# Nmap run completed at Fri Aug 30 14:42:31 2002 -- 256 IP
addresses (3 hosts up) scanned in 210 seconds
```

◆   ◆   ◆

What's on the CD-ROM?

APPENDIX E

This appendix provides you with information on the contents of the CD that accompanies this book. For the latest and greatest information, please refer to the ReadMe file located at the root of the CD. Here is what you will find:

- System requirements
- Using the CD with Windows
- What's on the CD
- Troubleshooting

System Requirements

Make sure your computer meets the minimum system requirements listed in this section. If your computer doesn't match up to most of them, you may have a problem using the contents of the CD.

For Windows 9*x*, Windows 2000, Windows NT4 (with SP 4 or later), Windows Me, or Windows XP:

- PC with a Pentium processor running at 120 MHz or faster
- At least 32MB of total RAM installed on your computer; for best performance, we recommend at least 64MB
- Ethernet network interface card (NIC) or modem with a speed of at least 28,800 bps
- A CD-ROM drive

Using the CD with Windows

To install the items from the CD to your hard drive, follow these steps:

1. Insert the CD into your computer's CD-ROM drive.
2. A window appears with the following options: Install, Explore, and Exit.

   Install: Gives you the option to install the supplied software and/or the author-created samples on the CD-ROM.

   Explore: Allows you to view the contents of the CD-ROM in its directory structure.

   Exit: Closes the autorun window.

If you do not have autorun enabled or if the autorun window does not appear, follow these steps to access the CD:

1. Click Start ➪ Run.
2. In the dialog box that appears, type ***d*:\setup.exe**, where *d* is the letter of your CD-ROM drive. This brings up the autorun window described above.
3. Choose the Install, Explore, or Exit option from the menu. (See Step 2 in the preceding list for a description of these options.)

What's on the CD

The CD-ROM includes a testing engine that is powered by Boson Software. This program enables you to practice test-taking while continuing to learn from the questions and answers provided from the book's examples.

When installed and run, the test engine presents you with a multiple-choice, question-and-answer format. Each question deals directly with exam-related material. The categories or content areas can be selected and focused on if certain job content domains need to be emphasized. Right and wrong answers are recorded and tracked for analysis of strengths and weaknesses after each quiz.

After you select what you believe to be the correct answer for each question, the test engine not only notes whether you are correct or not, but also provides information as to why the right answer is right and the wrong answers wrong, providing you with valuable information for further review. Thus, the test engine gives not only valuable simulated exam experience but useful tutorial direction as well.

Troubleshooting

If you have difficulty installing or using any of the materials on the companion CD, try the following solutions:

- **Turn off any antivirus software that may be running.** Installers sometimes mimic virus activity and can make your computer incorrectly believe that it is being infected by a virus. (Be sure to turn the antivirus software back on later.)
- **Close all running programs.** The more programs you run, the less memory you make available to other programs. Installers also typically update files and programs; if you keep other programs running, installation may not work properly.
- **Reference the ReadMe file.** Please refer to the ReadMe file located at the root of the CD-ROM for the latest product information at the time of publication.

If you still have trouble with the CD, please call the Customer Care phone number: (800) 762-2974. Outside the United States, call 1 (317) 572-3994. You can also contact Customer Service by e-mail at techsupdum@wiley.com. Wiley Publishing, Inc. will provide technical support only for installation and other general quality control items; for technical support on the applications themselves, consult the program's vendor or author.

✦ ✦ ✦

Index

Symbols and Numerics
@stake, L0pht Crack software, 25–26
4th Amendment, computer crime considerations, 256–257
The 1973 U.S. Code of Fair Information Practices, 239
The 2001 U.S. Patriot Act, 240
8.3 naming conventions, vulnerability issues, 67–68
801.11b standard, 83
801.11g standard, 83–84
802.11 standards, 81–85
802.113 standard, 84
802.11a standard, 83
802.16 standard, 84
802.1x standard, 84–85
802.WBA standard, 84

A
abnormal packets, vulnerability, 389–390
acceptability, biometrics evaluation factor, 17
acceptable use policy, 237–238
access attempts, 399
access control lists (ACLs), 4–5, 123
access controls, 4–8, 89
access point (AP), mobile devices, 135
accountability, access control element, 4
accounts, 166–167
acoustical-seismic motion detector, 219
activation, virus lifecycle phase, 28
ActiveX, Web-based system vulnerabilities, 72
ad hoc mode, wireless networks, 134–135
Addleman, L. M. (RSA algorithm), 194
Address Resolution Protocol (ARP), 121–122
address spoofing, 382–383
Advanced Encryption Standard (AES), 188–189
Advances in Cryptology-AUSCRYPT '92 Proceedings (Springer-Verlag), 181
AH. *See* authentication header
AIM. *See* America Online's Instant Messenger
AirMagnet, wireless communications tool, 100–104
AiroPeek, wireless communications tool, 106–110
AirSnort, wireless VPN attacks, 57
AIX operating system, software exploitation vulnerabilities, 26
alarm systems, physical security, 219
ALE. *See* annual loss expectancy
algorithms
    asymmetric, 190–203
    birthday attacks, 24

Data Encryption Standard (DES), 62, 184–187
Exclusive OR (XOR) function, 179
FIPS approved, 57
hash function, 24, 179–181
HVAL, 181
International Data Encryption Algorithm (IDEA), 189
keyed hash, 181
linear (flat key space), 22
mathematical attack vulnerability, 23
Message Digest 5 (MD5), 181
modern symmetric key encryption, 184–190
nonlinear key space, 22
number field sieve (NFS), 23
Public Key Infrastructure (PKI), 197–203
RC2, 62
Rijndael Block Cipher, 188–189
RSA, 23, 194
S/MIME, 62
Secure Hash Algorithm-1 (SHA-1), 180–181
Skipjack symmetric key, 204
Spanning Tree Algorithm (STA), 130
symmetric, 181–184
Triple-DES, 62
weak key attacks, 22
Wireless Transport Layer Security Protocol (WTLS), 88–89
alternate sites, disaster recovery plan (DRP), 229–230
America Online's Instant Messenger (AIM), 66
annual loss expectancy (ALE), 261
annual rate of occurrence (ARO), 261
anonymizer server, avoiding cookies, 73
ANSI X9.52 standard, triple DES encryption, 187–188
answers, 275–322
anti-virus management, software exploitation vulnerabilities, 27
AP. *See* access point
applets, JavaScript, 70–72
Application Layer (Layer 7), 86, 118–119, 124
Application Programming Interfaces (APIs), JDK element, 73
application-layer gateway, firewalls, 124
application-level firewalls, 124
application/operational threat, 262
architectures, firewalls, 125–128
ARO (annual rate of occurrence), 261
ARP (Address Resolution Protocol), 121–122
AS. *See* authentication server

asset identification, methods, 260–261
assets, 258, 261
asymmetric algorithms, 190–203
asymmetric digital subscriber line (ASDL), Point-to-Point Protocol, 55
asynchronous dynamic passwords, token type, 14
asynchronous external connections, back door attack vulnerability, 20
AT&T's Privacy Bird software, PCP implementation, 70
ATM cards, token authentication method, 14
attachments, 28, 60
attack evidence removal, system scanning element, 32
attacks
    back doors, 20
    birthday, 24, 180, 205–206
    brute force, 25, 206
    buffer overflow, 20
    chosen ciphertext, 206
    chosen plaintext, 206
    ciphertext only, 206
    Denial-of-Service (DoS), 18–20, 95
    dictionary attacks, 25
    differential cryptanalysis, 206
    differential linear cryptanalysis, 206
    Distributed Denial-of-Service (DDoS), 19–20
    dumpster diving, 23–24
    factoring attack, 206
    fragmentation, 22
    insertion, 96
    IP spoofing, 20–21
    known plaintext, 206
    linear cryptanalysis, 206
    man-in-the-middle, 15, 21, 206
    mathematical, 23
    meet-in-the-middle, 188, 206
    overlapping fragment attack, 22
    password guessing, 24–26
    Ping of Death, 20
    replay, 21
    rogue access points, 96–97
    smurf attack, 20
    social engineering, 23
    software exploitation, 26–27
    spoofing, 20–21
    statistical attack, 206
    SYN attack, 20
    system scanning, 31–41
    TCP/hijacking, 22
    teardrop attack, 20
    tiny fragment attack, 22
    types, 388
    war driving/war walking, 99
    weak keys, 22
attributes, LDAP element, 79
auditing, 168, 251–252
auditing access, physical security, 219
authentication
    biometrics, 16–17
    Callback, 12
    certificates, 12–13
    Challenge Handshake Authentication Protocol (CHAP), 11–12
    defined, 2
    digital certificates, 76–79
    dynamic passwords, 13
    INFOSEC element, 2
    Kerberos, 8–11
    LanMan, 167
    multi-factor, 14–15
    mutual, 15
    one-time passwords, 13
    passphrase, 13
    passwords, 13
    PPP methods, 55
    S/MIME, 61–62
    static passwords, 13
    tokens, 13–14
    two-factor, 14–15
    user names, 13
    WEP methods, 92–93
authentication header (AH), IPSec, 54
authentication server (AS), 9, 250
authorization, Bell-LaPadula model, 6
auxiliary station alarm system, physical security, 219
Axiom Three, Biba Integrity model, 7

B

back door attacks, 20
backdoors, removing attack traces, 32
background checks, administrative control, 4
BackOrifice, Trojan horse type, 29
backup media protection, disaster recovery, 231–232
backup tapes, storage/destruction/reuse issues, 147–150
backups, disaster recovery, 230–231
Barricade Plus Cable/DSL Broadband Router, 136–137
baseband, coaxial cable transmission method, 144
baselines, organizational security policy hierarchy, 237
bastion host, 127, 168
BCP. *See* business continuity plan
behavior-based detection, IDS approach, 160
behavior-based ID systems, 161
Belkin Components, 137–138
Bell-LaPadula, access control model, 6–7
Berkeley Internet Name Domain (BIND), 384
Biba Integrity, access control model, 7

biometric devices, facility access devices, 218
biometrics, 16–17
birthday attack, 24, 180, 205–206
BlackBerry device, 142
BLOWFISH, symmetric key algorithm, 190
boot partition, server hardening, 166
Bootstrap Protocol (BOOTP), 169
Boson Software, testing engine, 438
bounce attack (TCP FTP proxy) scanning, 35
Brave, Ken (President, Griffin Global Systems), 381
bridges, described, 128–129
broadband, coaxial cable transmission method, 144
broadcast domains, 153
broadcast storm, 129–130
broadcasting attacks, 388–389
brute force attacks, 25, 206, 392–393
buffer overflow, 20, 72–73, 391
business continuity plan (BCP), 226, 232–236
business impact assessment (BIA), 233

C

The Cable Communications Policy Act, 239
cable modems, 12
cable runs, physical control, 4
cables, 143–146
Callback, authentication method, 12
callback systems, access privilege management, 250–251
campus area network (CAN), 153
capstone cryptosystem, computer communications, 204
Cascade, macro virus, 28
CBC. *See* Cipher Block Chaining
CCK. *See* complementary code keying
CDI. *See* constrained data item
CDMA. *See* code division multiple access
CDR, destruction methods, 150
CD-ROM
    contents, 437–438
    destruction methods, 150
CDRW, destruction methods, 150
cell phones, Internet-enabled, 140–142
central station system, physical security, 219
centralized privilege management, methods, 250–251
CER. *See* Crossover Error Rate
certificate authorities (CAs), 13, 76–79, 200
certificate revocation list (CRL), 13, 101
certificates, 12–13, 199–200
Certified Information Systems Security Professionals (CISSPs), 246–247
CGI. *See* Common Gateway Interface
chain of evidence, computer forensics element, 254
chaining mechanism, Directory Server Agents (DSAs), 198
Challenge Handshake Authentication Protocol (CHAP), 11–12, 55–56, 251

challenge-response token, 14
change controls, documentation, 265–266
chat rooms, Instant Messaging (IM) similarities, 66
Children's Online Privacy Protection Act (COPPA), 239
chosen ciphertext attack, 206
chosen plaintext attack, 206
Cipher Block Chaining (CBC) mode, 185, 187
Cipher Feedback (CFB), DES mode, 185–186
ciphers, versus code, 178
ciphertext, 177
ciphertext only attack, 206
circuit-level firewalls, 124
Cisco Systems, 802.1x standard implementation, 85
CISSPs. *See* Certified Information Systems Security Professionals
classifications, mandatory access control (MAC) element, 4
clearances, mandatory access control (MAC) element, 4
clearing, 148, 244
clipper chip, telephone communications, 204
clipper cryptosystem, telephone communications, 204
closed-circuit television, physical security, 218
coaxial cables, 143–144
code, versus ciphers, 178
code division multiple access (CDMA), Internet-enabled cell phones, 140
code of ethics policy, 245–247
collisions, message digest (MD), 180
columnar transposition cipher, symmetric algorithm, 183
combustible classes, fire detection, 221–222
commands, Finger, 387
Common Gateway Interface (CGI), Web-based systems, 74–75
communications
    capstone cryptosystem, 204
    clipper cryptosystem, 204
    directory/CA recognition, 76–79
    e-mail, 60–62
    File Transfer Protocol (FTP), 79–81
    Instant Messaging (IM), 65–70
    intranet access VPNs, 52
    network-to-network VPNs, 51
    RADIUS, 58–60
    remote access methods, 49–60
    remote access VPN, 50–51
    TACACS, 58–60
    virtual private networks (VPNs), 49–58
    VPN tunneling, 52–53
    Web-based systems, 62–76
    wireless security, 81–110
    wireless VPNs, 57–58
complementary code keying (CCK), 83

components, ActiveX element, 72
computer communications, capstone cryptosystem, 204
Computer Ethics Institute's Ten Commandments of Computer Ethics, 246
computer forensics, 253–257
Computer Incident Response Team (CIRT), responsibilities, 162–163
computer infrastructure threat, 262
Computer Oracle and Password System (COPS), system scanning tool, 37
computer room fire safety, physical security, 224–225
Concept, macro virus, 28
confidentiality, 1
confidentiality loss, PDA issues, 140
confusion concept, DES, 184–185
consistency, internal versus external, 1–2
constrained data item (CDI), Clark-Wilson Integrity model, 7
contamination and damage, fire, 223–224
content-dependent access controls, 6–7
context-dependent access controls, 7
contingency plan (CP), 226
continuity and recovery definitions, 226
continuity of operations plans (COOP), 226
controls
    ActiveX element, 72
    administrative, 4
    backup media viability, 232
    corrective, 3
    detective, 3
    media storage/destruction/reuse, 147–140
    physical, 4
    preventive, 3
    technical, 4
cookies, Web-based system vulnerability, 73
COPPA. *See* Children's Online Privacy Protection Act
COPS. *See* Computer Oracle and Password System
corpus, biometrics image database, 17
corrective controls, 3
countermeasure, 258
counters, logic bomb trigger, 30
CP. *See* contingency plan
criminal threat, 262
CRL. *See* certificate revocation list
Crossover Error Rate (CER), biometrics performance measure, 16
cryptanalysis, 178
cryptography. *See also* encryption
    algorithms, 178–203
    asymmetric algorithms, 190–203
    birthday attack, 205–206
    brute force attack, 206
    capstone cryptosystem, 204
    chosen ciphertext attack, 206
    chosen plaintext attack, 206
    ciphers versus code, 178
    ciphertext only attack, 206
    clipper chip, 204
    clipper cryptosystem, 204
    defined, 177–178
    differential cryptanalysis attack, 206
    differential linear cryptanalysis attack, 206
    end-to-end encryption, 178
    equations, 178
    escrowed encryption, 204
    Exclusive OR (XOR) function, 179
    factoring attack, 206
    hash algorithms, 179–181
    hybrid systems, 204–205
    known plaintext attack, 206
    linear cryptanalysis attack, 206
    link encryption, 178
    man-in-the-middle attack, 206
    meet-in-the-middle attack, 206
    Public Key Infrastructure (PKI), 197–203
    statistical attack, 206
    superincreasing, 196
    symmetric algorithms, 181–184
    symmetric key, 8
    symmetric key encryption algorithms, 184–190
    transposition ciphers, 182–183
    work factor, 178
cryptology, 178
cryptosystem, 178
crypto-variables (keys), encrypting/decrypting plaintext messages, 177
custodians, 3, 250
Customer Proprietary Network Information Rules, 239

D

DACs. *See* discretionary access controls
Daemen, Dr. Joan (Rijndael Block Cipher), 188–189
DAP. *See* Directory Access Protocol
data backup tapes, storage/destruction/reuse issues, 147–150
data classification threat, 262
Data Encryption Algorithm (DEA), 184
Data Encryption Standard (DES), 22, 184–187
Data Link Layer (Layer 2), 54, 119, 128–131
data remanence, 148–149, 244
database shadowing, 234
databases, corpus, 17
DDoS. *See* Distributed Denial of Service

de Vigenére, Blaise (polyalphabetic cipher developer), 182
decentralized privilege management, methods, 250–251
deciphering (decrypting), plaintext messages, 177
decryption, WEP, 90–91
default account exploitation, system access method, 32
degaussing, magnetic media, 149
delayed processing threat, 262
demilitarized zone (DMZ), 125, 127–128
Denial-of-Service (DoS) attacks, 18–20, 95, 382–383
DES. *See* Data Encryption Standard
DES algorithm, S/MIME, 62
DES-CBC algorithms, WTLS support, 89
destruction
    data erasure method, 148
    defined, 244
    media types, 150
detective controls, 3
DHCP. *See* Dynamic Host Configuration Protocol
dial-up modems, back door attack vulnerability, 20
dictionary attacks, 25
differential cryptanalysis attack, 206
differential linear cryptanalysis attack, 206
Diffie-Hellman algorithms, WTLS support, 89
diffusion concept, DES, 185
digital certificates, 77, 197–198
digital envelope, S/MIME, 62
Digital Equipment Corporation, Spanning Tree Protocol (STP), 130
digital signature standard (DSS), asymmetric algorithms, 193
digital signatures, asymmetric algorithms, 192–193
digitally-encoded cards, facility access devices, 218
directories, 13, 198
Directory Access Protocol (DAP), X.500, 198
Directory Information Shadowing Protocol (DISP), X.500, 198
Directory Server Agents (DSAs), X.500, 198
Directory Service Protocol (DSP), X.500, 198
Directory User Agents (DUAs), X.500, 198
direct-sequence spread spectrum (DSSS), 133–134
disaster recovery, 230–232
disaster recovery plan (DRP), 226–230
discovery scanning, 33
discretionary access controls (DACs), 5, 253
Discretionary Security Property, 6
disk space triggers, logic bombs, 30
DISP. *See* Directory Information Shadowing Protocol
disposal/destruction policy, 244
distance vector routing, 132
Distinguished Name (DN), LDAP attributes, 79
Distributed Denial of Service (DDoS), 19–20, 388

DMZ. *See* demilitarized zone
DNS buffer overflow, vulnerability, 384
DNS cache attack, 384–385
DNS flood attack, 385
documentation, 265–267
dogs, physical security, 216–217
Domain Name System (DNS), internet security, 384
domain names, network reconnaissance target, 31
door locks, physical control, 4
DoS. *See* Denial-of-Service
double DES, meet-in-the-middle attack vulnerability, 188
DRP. *See* disaster recovery plan
DSAs. *See* Directory Server Agents
DSP. *See* Directory Service Protocol
DSS. *See* digital signature standard
DSSS. *See* direct-sequence spread spectrum
dual-homed host firewalls, 126
DUAs. *See* Directory User Agents
due care policy, 238
dumpster diving attacks, 23–24
Dynamic Host Configuration Protocol (DHCP), 169–170
dynamic packet filtering firewalls, 125
dynamic passwords, security advantages, 13

E

EAP. *See* Extensible Authentication Protocol
EAP Transport Level Security (EAP-TLS), VPN support, 57
eavesdropping, wireless communications, 99
education, security awareness, 263–265
EEPROMS, key destruction, 203
EF. *See* exposure factor
electrical power, physical security, 220–221
electromagnetic interference (EMI), 146, 220
Electronic Code Book (ECB), DES mode, 185
The Electronic Communications Privacy Act, 239
electronic vaulting, 233
elliptic curve, asymmetric algorithm, 195–196
e-mail
    hoaxes, 61
    Internet Message Access Protocol (IMAP), 61
    macro-enabled file viruses, 28
    Post Office Protocol 3 (POP3), 61
    Pretty Good Privacy (PGP), 62
    Secure Multipurpose Internet Mail Extensions (S/MIME), 61–62
    Simple Mail Transport Protocol (SMTP), 61
    social engineering attack vulnerability, 23
    spam, 61
    Trojan horse vulnerability, 29
    virus concerns, 60
    vulnerability, 390–392

EMI. *See* electromagnetic interference
encapsulated tunnel, virtual private networks (VPNs), 50
Encapsulating Security Payload (ESP), IPSec, 54
enciphering (encrypting), plaintext messages, 177
encryption. *See also* cryptography
    end-to-end, 178
    escrowed, 204
    Exclusive OR (XOR) function, 179
    hybrid systems, 204–205
    link, 178
    packet sniffing prevention, 68
    Pretty Good Privacy (PGP), 62
    private key, 181–184
    technical control, 4
    WEP, 90
end entity certificates, X.509, 200
end users, 3, 237–238
end-to-end encryption, 178
enrollment time, biometrics evaluation factor, 17
entry, LDAP element, 79
environmental threat, 262
EPOC devices, 139
EPROM, key destruction, 203
equipment locks, physical control, 4
ESP. *See* Encapsulating Security Payload
ethical hacking, 381
European Union (EU), privacy principles, 240
events, audit log types, 252
evidence life cycles, computer forensics, 254–255
evidence types, computer forensics, 256
Exclusive OR (XOR) function, encryption method, 179
executing, disaster recovery plan (DRP), 228–229
Exigent Circumstances Doctrine, computer crimes, 257
exposure, 258
exposure factor (EF), 261
Extensible Authentication Protocol, VPN support, 57
external consistency, 2
extinguishing systems, fires, 222–223
extranets, 154

F

facial scans, biometrics method, 17
facility access cards, 151
facility access devices, physical security, 218
factoring attack, 206
False Acceptance Rate (FAR), biometrics performance measure, 16
false negatives, 41
false positives, 40
False Rejection Rate (FRR), biometrics performance measure, 16

fast-packet keying, WEP, 94
FEAL, symmetric key algorithm, 190
Federal Information Processing Standards (FIPS), wireless VPNs, 58
fences, physical security, 217
FHSS. *See* frequency-hopping spread spectrum
fiber optic cables, 145
field-powered devices, system-sensing cards, 151
File Transfer Protocol (FTP), 63, 79–81, 385–387
The Financial Services Modernization Act, 239
finger information requests, vulnerability, 387
finger scans, biometrics method, 17
fingerprint systems, biometrics method, 17
fire detection and suppression, 221–225
fire detectors, 222
fire-resistant, 225
firewalls, 32, 79, 123–128
flame-actuated devices, 222
flat key space (linear), algorithms, 22
flooding attacks, 388–389
Forest Green book, 149
Form, macro virus, 28
Fraggle attacks, 388–389
fragmentation attacks, 22
fragmented packets, vulnerability, 389–390
frequency-hopping spread spectrum (FHSS), 133–134
FRR. *See* False Rejection Rate
FTP buffer overflow, vulnerability, 386
FTP downloads, Trojan horse vulnerability, 29
FTP file protection, vulnerability, 386–387
FTP servers, OS type determination method, 36
full access components, ActiveX element, 72
functional policies, organizational security policy hierarchy, 237
functions, 179–181, 196–197

G

Gamal (cryptographer), 194–195
Generic Routing Encapsulation (GRE), PPTP support, 53
global system for mobile communication (GSM), 140–141
GOST, symmetric key algorithm, 190
Green, Stu (Assoc. Professor of Computer Science University of Texas), 381
Griffin Global Systems, security consulting firm, 381
groups, privilege management responsibilities, 249
guards, 4, 216
guidelines, organizational security policy hierarchy, 237

H

hackers, war driving (war walking), 99
hand geometry, biometrics method, 17
Handheld Device Markup Language (HDML), 86
handwritten signature dynamics, biometrics method, 17
hash function algorithm, 24, 279–280
HAVAL-A One-Way Hashing Algorithm, 181
header condition signatures, network-based ID systems, 160
The Health Insurance Portability and Accountability Act (HIPAA), 240
heat-actuated devices, 222
heavy traffic, vulnerability scanning concerns, 40
Hellman, M. (Merkle-Hellman Knapsack one-way function), 196–197
heuristic analysis, long-term infection detection, 31
hidden messages, steganography, 207
High Speed Data Link Control (HDLC), PPP packet encapsulation, 55
hoaxes, e-mail issues, 61
honey pots, 161–162
host-based ID systems, 158–159
Host-to-Host layer, TCP/IP model, 120
HPing, system scanning tool, 37
HTTP/S, Web-based systems, 65
hubs, 128
human resources policy, 244–245
humidity and static, electrical power, 221
HVAL, hash algorithm, 181
HyperText Transfer Protocol (HTTP), 63, 65, 401
HyperText Transfer Protocol Daemon (HTTPD), 402

I

I Love You, macro virus, 28
IAB. *See* Internet Activities Board
IANA. *See* Internet Assigned Numbers Authority
IC. *See* Integrated Circuit
ICMP. *See* Internet Control Message Protocol
ICQ, instant messaging, 66
IDEA. *See* International Data Encryption Algorithm
IDEA algorithms, WTLS support, 89
iDEN phones, 141–142
identification, biometrics element, 16
identity-based DAC, 5
IEEE. *See* Institute of Electrical and Electronics Engineers
IGMP join message, 383
IGMP spoofing, 383
IIS. *See* Microsoft Internet Information Server
IM. *See* Instant Messaging
images, corpus database, 17

IMAP. *See* Internet Message Access Protocol
i-mode phones, 141
incident response policy, 247–249
information security (INFOSEC), 1
information warfare, 262
Infrared Data Association (IrDA), 142–143
infrastructure
　broadcast domains, 153
　campus area network (CAN), 153
　extranets, 154
　firewalls, 123–128
　Internet, 153
　intranet, 153–154
　Intrusion Detection and Response systems, 158–164
　local area networks (LANs), 152–153
　media types, 143–151
　metropolitan area network (MAN), 153
　Network Address Translation (NAT), 155–156
　network devices, 123–143
　network reconnaissance target, 32
　Open Systems Interconnect (OSI) model, 117–119
　protocol models, 117–123
　TCP/IP model, 119–120
　TCP/IP protocols, 120–122
　topologies, 152–158
　Virtual LANs (VLANs), 154
　VPN tunneling, 156–158
　wide area networks (WANs), 153
　wireless devices, 133–143
　workstation hardening, 165
infrastructure mode, wireless networks, 133–136
insertion attacks, 96
Instant Messaging (IM), 65–68
Institute of Electrical and Electronics Engineers (IEEE), 81–85
Integrated Circuit (IC) chip, facility access cards, 151
integrated services digital network (ISDN), 12, 55
integrity, 1
integrity verification procedure (IVP), Clark-Wilson Integrity model, 7
intelligent agents, host-based ID systems, 158–159
interference, cabling vulnerabilities, 145–146
interlock protocol, mutual authentication, 15
internal consistency, 1–2
International Data Encryption Algorithm (IDEA), 189
Internet, described, 153
Internet Activities Board (IAB), ethics and the Internet, 247
Internet Assigned Numbers Authority (IANA), IP address assignment, 155

Internet Control Message Protocol (ICMP), 35, 20, 121, 382–383
Internet Engineering Task Force (IETF), 66
Internet layer, TCP/IP model, 120
Internet Message Access Protocol (IMAP), e-mail support, 61
Internet Protocol (IP), 20–21, 31, 35
Internet Protocol (IP) IDs, security threat, 400
Internet Protocol Security (IPSec), 54, 157
Internet Service Provider (ISP), 50–51, 54
Internet vulnerabilities
    abnormal packet size attacks, 389–390
    abnormal packets, 389–390
    address spoofing/source concealment, 382–383
    attack types, 388
    Berkeley Internet Name Domain (BIND), 384
    broadcasting attacks, 388–389
    DNS buffer overflow, 384
    DNS cache attack, 384–385
    DNS flood attack, 385
    Domain Name System (DNS), 384
    e-mail, 390–392
    File Transfer Protocol (FTP), 385–387
    finger information requests, 387
    flooding attacks, 388–389
    Fraggle attacks, 388–389
    fragmented packets, 389–390
    FTP buffer overflow, 386
    FTP file protection, 386–387
    password attacks, 392
    port attacks, 400–401
    program insertion, 394
    proxy servers, 395
    remote file systems, 397–398
    shotgun access attempts, 399
    Smurf attacks, 388–389
    spraying, 388–389
    TCP/OP sequence, 400–401
    tiny fragment attacks, 388–389
    trusted host, 395–397
    URL flood or corruption, 404
    Web, 401–404
    Web applications, 403–404
    zero-offset IP fragmentation attack, 390
Internet-enabled cell phones, 140–142
intranet, 153–154
intranet access VPNs, 52
intrusion detection and response systems, 158–164, 218–219
IP. *See* Internet Protocol
IP blocks, network reconnaissance target, 31
IP fragments, TDP/UDP scan type, 35

IPSec. *See* Internet Protocol Security
IPSec-compatible devices, 157–158
IrDA. *See* Infrared Data Association
iris scans, biometrics method, 17
ISDN. *See* integrated services digital network
ISP. *See* Internet Service Provider
ISS, RealSecure software, 159
items, Kerberos symbols, 9–10
IVP. *See* integrity verification procedure

J

Java, 72–74
Java Archive (JAR) files, 73
Java Development Kit (JDK), Application Programming Interfaces (APIs), 73
JavaScript, 70–72
Jerusalem, macro virus, 28
junk mail, spam, 61

K

Kerberos, 8–11, 250–251
key destruction, PKI, 203
Key Distribution Center (KDC), 9, 250
key distribution, PKI, 202
key encryption key, PKI, 202
key escrow, key recovery method, 202
key management, distributed versus centralized, 203
key mappings table, 94
key recovery, PKI, 202
key renewal, PKI, 203
key revocation, PKI, 202
key rings, 12
keyed hash algorithms, 181
keys (crypto-variables), 177, 191–192, 202–203
kill files, SMTP, 76
knowledge-based ID systems, 160
known plaintext attack, 206
Koblitz, Neal (elliptic curve algorithm), 195–196
KryptoKnight, Single Sign-On (SSO) support, 250

L

L0pht Crack, password cracking software, 25–26
Lai, Xuejia (IDEA algorithm development role), 189
LanMan authentication, disabling, 167
LANs, campus area network (CAN), 153
lattice-based access controls, 6
Layer 2 Forwarding Protocol (L2F), VPN support, 54
Layer 2 Tunneling Protocol (L2TP), VPN support, 54, 157
Layer 3 switches, 133
lease periods, DHCP, 169
least privilege, 242

Legion, system scanning tool, 37
legislation, privacy-related, 239–241
liability, computer forensics, 257
life cycles, 28, 254–255
lighting, physical security, 217
Lightweight Directory Access Protocol (LDAP), 77–79, 198–199
Line Printer Daemon (LPDs), Trusted Host vulnerabilities, 396
linear (flat key space), algorithms, 22
linear cryptanalysis attack, 206
link encryption, 178
Link State Protocol (LSP), link state routers, 132–133
link state routers, 132–133
local alarm system, physical security, 219
local area networks (LANs), 152–153
locks, 4, 217
logs, event auditing types, 252
LOK, symmetric key algorithm, 190
long-term infection detection, virus detection method, 31
LPDs. *See* Line Printer Daemons

M

MAC. *See* media access control
MAC address, WEP authentication, 93
macro viruses, types, 28
magnetic media, 147–151
magnetic stripe cards (smart cards), 150–151
mail flood attacks, 392
maintenance, disaster recovery plan (DRP), 228
maintenance hooks, failure to disable vulnerability, 19
malicious code, 27–31
MAN. *See* metropolitan area network
mandatory access controls (MACs), 4–5, 252–253
man-in-the-middle attack, 15, 21, 206
man-made disasters, 225
mantrap, 217
Massey, James (IDEA algorithm development role), 189
mathematical attacks, 23
Mauborgne, Major Joseph (one-time pad developer), 184
MD. *See* message digest
MD5 Message Digest Algorithm, 181
media access control (MAC) address, packet sniffing, 68–69
media librarian, job description, 232
media types, 143–151, 244
medical information, social engineering attack vulnerability, 23
meet-in-the-middle attack, 188, 206
Melissa, macro virus, 28

Merkle, R. C. (Merkle-Hellman Knapsack one-way function), 196–197
message digest (MD), 179–181
Message Digest 5 (MD5), hash algorithm, 181
metropolitan area network (MAN), 153
Micali, Sylvio (key escrow system), 204
Microsoft Challenge Handshake Authentication Protocol (MS-CHAP), 55–56
Microsoft Excel, macro virus vulnerability, 28
Microsoft Internet Explorer 6 (IE6), P3P support, 70
Microsoft Internet Information Server (IIS), 403–404
Microsoft New Technology File System (NTFS), 8.3 naming conventions, 67–68
Microsoft Pocket PC 2002 OS, personal digital assistants (PDAs), 139
Microsoft Windows 2000, 57
Microsoft Word, macro virus vulnerability, 28
modems, back door attack vulnerability, 20
monoalphabetic substitution cipher, symmetric algorithm, 182
motion detectors, physical security, 218–219
Motorola, iDEN phones, 141–142
MS Internet Information Server (IIS) Remote Data services (RDS), 402–403
MS-CHAP. *See* Microsoft Challenge Handshake Authentication Protocol
MS-CHAP v2, VPN support, 56–57
multi-factor authentication, factor types, 14–15
multiple keys, PKI, 203
mutual authentication, 15

N

NAS. *See* network access server
NAT. *See* Network Address Translation
National Fire Protection Association (NFPA), 224
National Institute of Standards and Technology (NIST), 193, 204
natural disasters, 225
need-to-know policy, 242
Nessus, system scanning tool, 37
NetBus, Trojan horse type, 29
NetSP, Single Sign-On (SSO) support, 250
NetStumbler, wireless communications tool, 105–106
Network Access layer, TCP/IP model, 120
network access server (NAS), 55–57
Network Address Translation (NAT), 155–156
network devices, 123–143
Network Layer (Layer 3), 54, 118, 123, 130–133
network reconnaissance, system scanning element, 31–32
network-based ID systems, 159–160
network-to-network VPNs, 51

NFPA. *See* National Fire Protection Association
NFS. *See* number field sieve
NIST. *See* National Institute of Standards and Technology
NMap, system scanning tool, 37–39
NMAP log, 405–436
noise interference, electrical power, 220–221
nonce, replay attack prevention, 21
non-discretionary access controls, 6
non-essential services, 18–19
non-IPSec-compatible devices, 157–158
nonlinear key space, algorithms, 22
non-repudiation, 2
Novel Web Server, software exploitation vulnerabilities, 26
NT file system (NTFS), 166
NTFS. *See* Microsoft New Technology File System
NTT DoCoMo, i-mode phones, 141
number field sieve (NFS) algorithm, 23, 194

O

object reuse, media controls, 147–148
objectives, disaster recovery plan (DRP), 226–227
objects, 2, 5
OECD. *See* Organization for Economic Cooperation and Development
OFB. *See* Output Feedback
OFDM. *See* orthogonal frequency-division multiplexing
one-time pad, symmetric algorithm, 183–184
one-time passwords, security advantages, 13
one-to-many identification search, biometrics, 16
one-to-one search, biometrics authentication, 16
one-way function, 191, 196
open system authentication, WEP, 92
Open Systems Interconnect (OSI) model, 117–119
OPENSSH program, 80
operational/application threat, 262
Organization for Economic Cooperation and Development (OECD), 240–241
organizational security policy, hierarchy, 236–237
orthogonal frequency-division multiplexing (OFDM), 83
OS type determination, system scanning, 36
Output Feedback (OFB), DES mode, 185–186
output message digest (MD), birthday attack vulnerability, 24
overlapping fragment attacks, 22
owners, 2, 238, 249

P

P3P. *See* Platform for Privacy Preferences
P3P1.0. *See* Platform for Privacy Preferences 1.0
packet filtering firewalls, 123
packet filtering routers, firewall uses, 125
packet interception attack, 400
Packet INternet Groper (PING) utility, ICMP message use, 121, 382
packet sniffers, wireless communications, 100–110
packet sniffing, Web-based systems, 68
Palm OS, personal digital assistants (PDAs), 139
palm scans, biometrics method, 17
PalmPilot devices, 139
passive devices, system-sensing cards, 151
passphrase, 13
password attacks, 392–393
Password Authentication Protocol (PAP), 12, 55
password cracking, 32, 393
password guessing attacks, 24–26
password management policy, 242–243
password sniffing attack, 393
passwords, 13–14, 23–26, 167
pattern-matching, IDS approach, 160
performance, IDS issues, 164
perimeter devices, network reconnaissance target, 32
perimeter intrusion detectors, physical security, 218
perimeter network, screened subnet firewalls, 127
PERL. *See* Practical Extraction and Report Language
permissions, 166–167
permutation cipher, symmetric algorithm, 182
personal background checks, administrative control, 4
personal digital assistants (PDAs), 138–140
personal electronic devices (PEDs), 137–142
Personal Identification Number (PIN), smart cards, 150
personally identifiable information (PII), privacy policies, 238–241
personnel threat, 262
PGP. *See* Pretty Good Privacy
photo image cards, facility access devices, 218
photometric motion detectors, 218
physical access control, 216–219
physical contact, system access method, 32
Physical Layer (Layer 1), 119, 128–129
physical loss, PDA issues, 140
physical security, 215–225
piggybacking, invasion method, 217
PII. *See* personally identifiable information
PIN. *See* Personal Identification Number
Ping of Death attack, buffer overflow cause, 20
PING. *See* Packet INternet Groper utility
ping-sweep (ICMP scanning), TDP/UDP scan type, 35
PKI. *See* Public Key Infrastructure
plaintext messages, encrypting/decrypting, 177
Platform for Privacy Preferences (P3P), 241
Platform for Privacy Preferences 1.0 (P3P1.0), Web-based systems, 69–70
platforms, network reconnaissance target, 31

Point-to-Point Protocol (PPP), 54–55
Point-to-Point Tunneling Protocol (PPTP), 53–54, 156
policies
    acceptable use, 237–238
    administrative control, 4
    baselines, 237
    code of ethics, 245–247
    disposal/destruction, 244
    due care, 238
    FTP service, 80
    functional, 237
    guidelines, 237
    human resources, 244–245
    incident response, 247–249
    least privilege, 242
    need-to-know, 242
    organizational security, 236–237
    password management, 242–243
    privacy, 238–241
    procedures, 237
    separation of duties, 241–242
    service level agreements (SLAs), 243
    standards, 237
polyalphabetic substitution cipher, symmetric algorithm, 182
polymorphic viruses, 28–29
POP3. *See* Post Office Protocol
Port 7 (Echo service), Denial-of-Service (DoS) attack vulnerability, 18
port attacks, vulnerability, 400–401
port probing, 399
port scanning, 33–36, 399
port signatures, network-based ID systems, 160
port trolling, 399
ports
    7 (Echo service), 18
    closing unneeded, 168
    commonly attacked, 40
    non-essential, 18–19
    TCP connect() scan attack, 34
    TCP FIN scan attack, 35
    TCP FTP proxy (bounce attack) scan, 35
    TCP SYN (half-open) scan attack, 34
    TCP SYN/ACK scan attack, 35
    Trojan horse vulnerability, 29–30
    UDP, 169–170
    unregistered numbers, 41
Post Office Protocol 3 (POP3), e-mail support, 61
power fluctuations, physical security, 221
PPP. *See* Point-to-Point Protocol
PPTP. *See* Point-to-Point Tunneling Protocol
Practical Extraction and Report Language (PERL), Web-based systems, 75

Presentation Layer (Layer 6), OSI model, 118
Pretty Good Privacy (PGP), 62, 205
preventive controls, 3
privacy
    European Union (EU) principles, 240
    S/MIME, 61–62
    Web-based systems, 69–70
    WEP, 89–90
privacy policy, 238–241
private key encryption, symmetric algorithms, 181–184
private keys, asymmetric algorithms, 191–192
privilege management, 249–253
privileges, access control list (ACL) element, 5
probes, port scanning, 33
procedures, 4, 237
program insertion, vulnerability, 394
promiscuous mode, packet sniffing, 68
Proprietary alarm system, physical security, 219
protocol models, 117–122
protocols, 18–19, 31, 61, 167
proximity motion detector, 219
proxy firewalls, 124
proxy servers, 124, 395
prudent man rule, 238, 257
Psion Series 7 devices, 139
public key certificates, authentication method, 13
public key cryptography, 191–192, 196–197
Public Key Cryptography Standards (PKCS), S/MIME, 62
Public Key Infrastructure (PKI), 197–203
public keys, 21, 191–192, 194
purging
    data erasure method, 148
    defined, 244
    DoD requirements, 150

Q

qualitative risk analysis, 261
quantitative risk analysis, 260–261

R

Radio frequency interference (RFI), physical security, 220
RADIUS. *See* Remote Authentication Dial-In User Server
RAID. *See* Redundant Array of Inexpensive Disks
rail fence transposition cipher, symmetric algorithm, 182–183
RAPS. *See* Remote Access Perimeter Scanner
RARP. *See* Reverse Address Resolution Protocol
RBAC. *See* role-based access control
RC2, S/MIME, 62

RC4 encryption engine, 91, 190
RC5, symmetric key algorithm, 190
RC5-CBC algorithms, WTLS support, 89
RDS. *See* Remote Data Services
RealSecure, host-based intrusion detection software, 159
records, retention guidelines, 266–267
recovery time frame classification, disaster recovery plan (DRP), 230
Redundant Array of Inexpensive Disks (RAID), 235–236
redundant communications lines, 234
reference monitor, 5
remote access, 49–60
Remote Access Perimeter Scanner (RAPS), 37
remote access servers, CHAP, 12
remote access VPN, 50–51
Remote Authentication Dial-In User Server (RADIUS), 54, 58–60, 250
Remote command processing, Trusted Host vulnerabilities, 395–396
Remote Data Services (RDS), vulnerability, 402–403
remote file system vulnerabilities, 397–398
remote journaling, 233
remote users, Callback authentication, 12
removable media, 146–151
repair technicians, social engineering attack issues, 23
repeaters, 128–129
replay attacks, 21
replication, 28, 30
Research In Motion Limited (RIM), BlackBerry device, 142
retina scans, biometrics method, 17
Reverse Address Resolution Protocol (RARP), 121
Rijmen, Dr. Vincent (Rijndael Block Cipher), 188–189
Rijndael Block Cipher, symmetric key encryption algorithm, 188–189
risk acceptance, 258
risk analysis (RA), 259–261
risk assessment, risk identification element, 259–260
risk identification, 259–263
risk reduction, 258
risk transference, 258
risks, defined, 3
Rivest, Ron L.
    Message Digest 5 (MD5) developer, 181
    RSA algorithm, 194
rogue access points, wireless communication attacks, 96–97
role-based access control (RBAC), 5–6, 253
roles, privilege management responsibilities, 249
rollover certificates, X.509, 200
rootkit tools, system file replacement, 32
routers, 125, 131–133
Routing Information Protocol (RIP), distance vector routing, 132
RSA algorithms, 23, 89
rule-based access controls, MAC type, 4

S

S/MIME. *See* Secure Multipurpose Internet Mail Extensions
S/MIME Certificate Handling, 62
S/MIME Message Specification, 62
safe software storage, software exploitation vulnerabilities, 27
safeguard, defined, 258
SAFER, symmetric key algorithm, 190
SAINT. *See* Security Administrator's Integrated Network Tool
sandbox, JavaScript protection method, 70
sandbox components, ActiveX element, 72
SATAN. *See* System Administrator Tool for Analyzing Networks
scanners, wireless communications, 100–110
scanning 33–34, 99
schemas, LDAP server, 79
screened host firewalls, 125–126
screened subnet firewalls, 127
scripts, 74–75
SEAL, symmetric key algorithm, 190
secret keys, Kerberos, 9
secure encrypted tunnel, VPNs, 156
Secure File Transfer Protocol (SFTP), 80
Secure Hash Algorithm-1 (SHA-1), birthday attack resistance, 180–181
Secure HTTP (S-HTTP), Web-based systems, 65
Secure Multipurpose Internet Mail Extensions (S/MIME), e-mail, 61–62
Secure Shell (SSH), 80
Secure Shell-2 (SSH-2), 80
Secure Sockets Layer (SSL) Protocol, Web-based systems, 63–65
Secure Shell Service/Secure Socket Layer (SSH/SSL), 397
Security Administrator's Integrated Network Tool (SAINT), 37
security awareness, education, 263–265
security kernel, 5
Security Layer, Wireless Application Protocol (WAP), 87
security logs, editing/clearing to eliminate attack traces, 32
security perimeter, Trusted Computing Base (TCB) boundary, 4–5
segregation of duties, policies and procedures, 242
self-issued certificates, X.509, 200

sendmail command manipulation, e-mail attack, 391
sensitivity, mandatory access control (MAC) element, 4
separation of duties policy, 241–242
Serial Line Internet Protocol (SLIP), 54
server clustering, 234, 235
server redundancy, 234
server scanning, 33
servers, hardening practices, 165–168
service level agreements (SLAs), 243
service packs, maintaining, 168
service set identifier (SSID), 98–99
services, 18–19, 31, 167
SESAME, Single Sign-On (SSO) support, 250
session hijacking, system access method, 32
Session Layer (Layer 5), 86–87, 118
SFTP. *See* Secure File Transfer Protocol
SHA-1. *See* Secure Hash Algorithm-1
Shamir, A. (RSA algorithm), 194
Shannon, Claude, confusion/diffusion concepts, 184–185
shared key authentication, WEP, 92–93
shielded twisted pair (STP) cables, 144
short-term infection detection, virus detection method, 31
shotgun access attempts, 399
S-HTTP. *See* Secure HTTP
signed applets, Web-based system vulnerability, 73–74
Simple Integrity Axiom, Biba Integrity model, 7
Simple Mail Transport Protocol (SMTP), 61, 75–76
Simple Network Management Protocol (SNMP), 396, 399
Simple Security Property (SS Property), 6
single loss expectancy (SLE), 261
single sign-on (SSO), 8, 250
Skipjack symmetric key algorithm, clipper chip, 204
SLAs. *See* service level agreements
SLE. *See* single loss expectancy
SLIP. *See* Serial Line Internet Protocol
smart cards, 4, 13–14, 150–151, 202
smarter cards, 150–151
SMC Networks, Barricade Plus Cable/DSL Broadband Router, 136–137
smoke detectors, 222
smoke-actuated devices, 222
SMTP. *See* Simple Mail Transport Protocol
smurf attack, 20, 388–389
sniffer attacks, AirSnort, 57
sniffing, system access method, 32
SNMP. *See* Simple Network Management Protocol
social engineering, 23, 32, 219
Socket Security (SOCKS), firewall protection, 127
software exploitation attacks, 26–27

software testing, exploitation vulnerabilities, 27
software utilities, exploitation vulnerabilities, 27
source concealment, 382–383
spam, e-mail issues, 61
Spanning Tree Algorithm (STA), broadcast storm prevention, 130
Spanning Tree Protocol (STP), broadcast storm prevention, 130
Spartan syctale, symmetric algorithm, 183
spectral analysis, long-term infection detection, 31
spoofed scans, 34
spoofing, attack type, 20–21
spraying attacks, 388–389
spread spectrum technologies, wireless devices, 133–134
SSH. *See* Secure Shell
SSH/SSH-2 protocols, 80–81
SSH/SSL (Secure Shell Service/Secure Socket Layer), 397
SSH-2. *See* Secure Shell-2
SSL. *See* Secure Sockets Layer Protocol
SSL Handshake Protocol, 63
SSL Record Protocol, 63
SSL/TLS-enabled clients, digital certificate user, 77
STA. *See* Spanning Tree Algorithm
standards, organizational security policy hierarchy, 237
Star (*) Integrity Axiom, Biba Integrity model, 7
Star (*) Security Property, Bell-LaPadula model, 6
stateful inspection firewalls, 124
static passwords, 13–14
static routing, 132
statistical anomaly detection, IDS approach, 160
statistical attack, 206
stealth scans, 34
stealth viruses, 29
steganography, 207
storage, record retention guidelines, 266–267
STP. *See* shielded twisted pair cables
STP. *See* Spanning Tree Protocol
string signatures, network-based ID systems, 160
subjects, 2, 5
SubSeven, Trojan horse type, 29
substitution cipher, symmetric algorithm, 182
superincreasing, 196
supervision, administrative control, 4
suppression medium, fires, 223
switches, 130–131, 163–164
Symbian OS, Internet-enabled cell phones, 140
symbols, Kerberos, 9–10
symmetric algorithms, 181–184
symmetric key algorithms, Skipjack, 204
symmetric key cryptography, Kerberos, 8

symmetric key encryption algorithms, 185–190
SYN attacks, DoS attack type, 20
SYN flood attack, 401
synchronous dynamic passwords, token type, 14
Syslog server, compromising to eliminate attack traces, 32
system access, system scanning element, 32
System Administrator Tool for Analyzing Networks (SATAN), 37
system crash, vulnerability scanning concerns, 41
system files, replacing to eliminate attack traces, 32
system requirements, CD, 438
system scanning, 31–41
system-sensing wireless proximity readers, 151

T

tables, key mappings, 94
TACACS. *See* Terminal Access Controller Access Control System
TACACS+. *See* Terminal Access Controller Access Control System+
task-based access controls, 5
TCB. *See* Trusted Computing Base
TCP. *See* Transmission Control Protocol
TCP connect(), TDP/UDP scan type, 34
TCP FIN, TDP/UDP scan type, 35
TCP FTP proxy (bounce attack), TDP/UDP scan type, 35
TCP SYN (half-open), TDP/UDP scan type, 34
TCP SYN/ACK, TDP/UDP scan type, 35
TCP (Transmission Control Protocol) spoofing, 383
TCP, versus UDP, 121
TCP/hijacking attacks, 22
TCP/IP stack fingerprinting, OS type determination method, 36
TCP/IP. *See* Transmission Control Protocol/Internet Protocol
TCP/OP sequence, vulnerability, 400–401
TCP/UDP scanning types, 34–35
Tcpview, system scanning tool, 37
TDMA. *See* time division multiple access
teardrop attacks, DoS attack type, 20
telephone communications, clipper cryptosystem, 204
Telephone Consumer Protection Act, 239
TELNET, SSL/TLS support, 63
TELNET banners, OS type determination method, 36
Terminal Access Controller Access Control System (TACACS), 54, 58–60, 251
Terminal Access Controller Access Control System+ (TACACS+), 58–59
terms, 323–380

testing and adjusting, disaster recovery plan (DRP), 227
testing engine, CD, 438
testing types, disaster recovery plan (DRP), 227–228
TFTP. *See* Trivial File Transfer Protocol
thicknet, coaxial cable type, 144
thinnet, coaxial cable type, 144
threat agent, 258
threats, 3, 250, 262
throughput rate, biometrics evaluation factor, 17
Ticket Granting Service (TGS), Kerberos, 9–11
tickets, Kerberos, 9
time division multiple access (TDMA), 140–141
Time To Live (TTL) values, OS type determination, 36
timestamps, replay attack prevention, 21
tiny fragment attacks, 22, 388–389
TLS. *See* Transport Layer Security
TLS Record Protocol, Web-based systems, 64–65
tokens, 13–14
topologies, 143, 152–158
training, 4, 263–265
Transaction Layer, Wireless Application Protocol (WAP), 87
transformation procedure (TP), Clark-Wilson Integrity model, 7
Transmission Control Protocol (TCP), 20, 120
Transmission Control Protocol/Internet Protocol (TCP/IP) model, 119–120
transponders, system-sensing cards, 151
Transport Layer (Layer 4), 87–88, 118, 127
Transport Layer Security (TLS), Web-based systems, 63–65
transposition ciphers, symmetric algorithm, 182–183
trap doors, failure to disable vulnerability, 19
trash cans, dumpster diving attack vulnerability, 23–24
triggers, logic bombs, 30
Trino, Trojan horse type, 29
triple DES, 62, 187–188
Trivial File Transfer Protocol (TFTP), 81
troubleshooting, CD, 439
trunking, VLAN process, 154
trusted components, ActiveX element, 72
trusted computer system, 5
Trusted Computing Base (TCB), 4–5
Trusted Host vulnerabilities, 395–397
trusted paths, Trusted Computing Base (TCB) element, 5
tunnels, 50
twisted pair cables, 144
two-factor authentication, 14–15
TWOFISH, symmetric key algorithm, 190

U

UDP ports, Dynamic Host Configuration Protocol (DHCP) uses, 169–170
unconstrained data item (UDI), 7
unneeded ports, closing, 168
unneeded protocols, disabling, 167
unneeded services, removing, 167
unregistered port numbers, vulnerability scanning concerns, 41
unshielded twisted pair (UTP) cables, categories, 144
URL flood or corruption, vulnerability, 404
U.S. Escrowed Encryption Standard, 204
U.S. Federal Sentencing Guidelines, computer crimes, 256–257
User Datagram Protocol (UDP), 120–121
user names, authentication method, 13
user supervisors, privilege management responsibilities, 250
user-activated wireless proximity readers, 151
user-directed DAC, 5
users, 3, 237–238, 249–250

V

Vector Sum Excited Linear Prediction (VSELP), 142
Vernam cipher, one-time pad, 184
viability controls, backup media, 232
video mode triggers, logic bombs, 30
Virtual LANs (VLANs), 154
virtual private networks (VPNs), 49–60, 156–158
virus detection, malicious code prevention, 31
virus prevention, malicious code prevention, 31
virus scanners, malicious code prevention, 30
viruses, 27–29, 60–61
VLAN Trunking Protocol (VTP), 154
voice, biometrics method, 17
VPN tunneling, 52–53, 156–158
VPNs. *See* virtual private networks
VSELP. *See* Vector Sum Excited Linear Prediction
VTP. *See* VLAN Trunking Protocol
vulnerability, 3, 258
vulnerability assessment matrix, 263
vulnerability scanning, 32–33, 40–41

W

W3C. *See* World Wide Web Consortium
WAE. *See* wireless application environment
WAP. *See* Wireless Application Protocol
WAP GAP, wireless communications, 95–96
WAP-enabled phones, 141
war driving, wireless hackers, 99
war walking, wireless hackers, 99
wave motion detectors, 218
WDP. *See* Wireless Datagram Protocol
weak key attacks, 22
Web applications, vulnerability, 403–404
Web-based systems
    8.3 naming convention vulnerabilities, 67–68
    ActiveX, 72
    buffer overflow, 72–73
    Common Gateway Interface (CGI), 74–75
    cookies, 73
    HTTP/S, 65
    Instant Messaging (IM), 65–70
    JavaScript, 70–72
    packet sniffing, 68
    Platform for Privacy Preferences 1.0 (P3P1.0), 69–70
    Practical Extraction and Report Language (PERL), 75
    privacy issues, 69–70
    Secure HTTP (S-HTTP), 65
    Secure Sockets Layer (SSL) Protocol, 63–65
    signed applets, 73–74
    Simple Mail Transfer Protocol (SMTP), 75–76
    TLS Record Protocol, 64–65
    Transport Layer Security (TLS), 63–65
    vulnerabilities, 70–76, 401–404
Web sites
    802.1x standard information, 85
    AirMagnet, 100
    AiroPeek, 106
    Belkin Components, 137
    Hedy Lamar's spread spectrum involvement, 133
    ICQ, 66
    IrDA information, 142
    NetStumbler, 105
    policy editors, 69
    RealSecure, 159
    SMC Networks, 136
    WEP attack investigations, 97–98
    WEP crack activity, 94
    Wireless Ethernet Compatibility Alliance (WECA), 82
WEP. *See* Wired Equivalent Privacy
wide area networks (WANs), 153
Wi-Fi, defined, 82
Windows, using with CD, 438
Windows 9x, software exploitation vulnerabilities, 26
Windows CE, personal digital assistants (PDAs), 139
Windows handhelds, 139–140
Windows NT, software exploitation vulnerabilities, 27

Wired Equivalent Privacy (WEP)
    access control, 89
    authentication methods, 92–93
    decryption, 90–91
    encryption, 90
    encryption workarounds, 98
    fast-packet keying, 94
    key management, 94
    key mappings table, 94
    Media Access Control authentication, 93
    open system authentication, 92
    privacy, 89–90
    RC4 encryption engine, 91
    shared key authentication, 92–93
    version2 patches, 94
    weaknesses, 97–98
    wireless communications, 89–94
wireless application environment (WAE), 86
Wireless Application Protocol (WAP), 85–88, 140–141
wireless communications
    802.11 standards, 81–88
    AirMagnet, 100–105
    AiroPeek, 106–110
    Denial-of-Service (DoS) attacks, 95
    eavesdropping concerns, 99
    insertion attacks, 96
    NetStumbler, 105–106
    packet sniffers, 100–110
    rogue access points, 96–97
    scanners, 100–110
    scanning concerns, 99
    service set identifier (SSID) issues, 98–99
    vulnerabilities, 95–110
    WAP, 85–88
    WAP GAP, 95–100
    war driving/war walking, 99
    WEP, 89–95
    WEP encryption workarounds, 98
    WEP weaknesses, 97–98
    WTLS, 88–89

Wireless Datagram Protocol (WDP), 87–88
wireless devices, 133–134
Wireless Markup Language (WML), 86
wireless proximity readers, 151, 218
Wireless Session Protocol (WSP), 86
wireless telephony APIs (WTAs), 86
Wireless Transactional Protocol (WTP), 87
Wireless Transport Layer Security, 87–89
Wireless Transport Layer Security Protocol
    (WTLS), 88–89
wireless VPNs, 57–58
WLAN devices, 136–137
WLAN operational modes, network devices, 134–136
work factor, 178
workstation scanning, 33
workstations, hardening principles, 165
World Wide Web Consortium (W3C), 69–70, 241
WSP. *See* Wireless Session Protocol
WTAs. *See* wireless telephony APIs
WTLS. *See* Wireless Transport Layer Security
WTP. *See* Wireless Transactional Protocol

X

X.500 directory, 13, 198
X.509 certificate standard, 13, 62, 198–200
X9.52 standard, triple DES encryption, 187–188
xDSL, CHAP, 12
XOR (Exclusive OR) function, encryption method, 179

Y

Yahoo Instant Messenger, 66

Z

zero-offset IP fragmentation attack, 390
Zimmerman, Philip R.
    The Official PGP User's Guide, 62
    Pretty Good Privacy (PGP) e-mail encryption, 189